ACT®

Strategies, Practice, and Review

2014 Edition

Kaplan offers resources and options to help you prepare for the PSAT, SAT, ACT, AP exams, and other high-stakes exams. Go to www.kaptest.com or scan this code below with your phone (you will need to download a QR code reader) for free events and promotions.

snap.vu/m87n

Related Titles for College-Bound Students

AP Biology

AP Calculus AB & BC

AP Chemistry

AP English Language & Composition

AP English Literature & Composition

AP Environmental Science

AP European History

AP Human Geography

AP Macroeconomics/Microeconomics

AP Physics B & C

AP Psychology

AP Statistics

AP U.S. Government & Politics

AP U.S. History

AP World History

ACT Strategies, Practice, and Review

ACT Premier

ACT English and Reading Workbook

ACT Math and Science Workbook

ACT Strategies for Super Busy Students

SAT Strategies, Practice, and Review

SAT Premier

12 Practice Tests for the SAT

SAT 2400

SAT Critical Reading Workbook

SAT Math Workbook

SAT Writing Workbook

SAT Comprehensive Vocabulary

SAT Strategies for Super Busy Students

Frankenstein: A Kaplan SAT Score-Raising Classic

The Tales of Edgar Allan Poe: A Kaplan SAT Score-Raising Classic

Dr. Jekyll and Mr. Hyde: A Kaplan SAT Score-Raising Classic

The Scarlet Letter: A Kaplan SAT Score-Raising Classic

The War of the Worlds: A Kaplan SAT Score-Raising Classic

Wuthering Heights: A Kaplan SAT Score-Raising Classic

SAT Score-Raising Dictionary

SAT Subject Test: Biology E/M

SAT Subject Test: Chemistry

SAT Subject Test: Literature

SAT Subject Test: Mathematics Level 1

SAT Subject Test: Mathematics Level 2

SAT Subject Test: Physics

SAT Subject Test: Spanish

SAT Subject Test: U.S. History

SAT Subject Test: World History

ACT®

Strategies, Practice, and Review

2014

KAPLAN

PUBLISHING

New York

Published by Kaplan Publishing, a division of Kaplan, Inc.
395 Hudson St., 4th Floor
New York, NY 10014

Printed in the United States of America

10 9 8 7 6 5 4 3 2 1

ISBN-13: 978-1-61865-058-0

Contents WITHDRAWN

Welcome to *Kaplan ACT: Strategies, Practice, and Review* ix

PART ONE: ACT Basics

CHAPTER 1: Introduction to the ACT 3

    Four Keys to ACT Success 4

    What Is the ACT? 8

    Overview of the ACT 9

    ACT FAQs 10

    ACT Registration Overview 14

    Taking the PLAN Exam 16

CHAPTER 2: The Subject Tests: A Preview 17

    English 17

    Math 22

    Reading 25

    Science 30

    Writing 34

CHAPTER 3: Taking Control: The Top Ten Strategies 39

    The ACT Mind-Set 40

    Ten Strategies for Mastering the ACT 42

    Take Control 55

    Basic Strategy Reference Sheet 56

PART TWO: Skill-Building Workouts

> **CHAPTER 4: English Workout 1: When in Doubt, Take It Out** 61
>
> > Economy Questions 62
> >
> > The Kaplan Method for ACT English 68
>
> **CHAPTER 5: English Workout 2: Make It Make Sense** 75
>
> > Grammar Rules and Sense Questions 82
> >
> > Nonstandard-Format Questions 92
>
> **CHAPTER 6: English Workout 3: Look and Listen** 95
>
> > Listen to the Choices 95
> >
> > Grammar Rules to Know 99
>
> **CHAPTER 7: Math Workout 1: The End Justifies the Means** 109
>
> > The ACT Math Mind-Set 110
> >
> > The Kaplan Method for ACT Math 115
> >
> > Kaplan's Two-Pass Plan for ACT Math 124
> >
> > To Calculate or Not to Calculate 127
>
> **CHAPTER 8: Math Workout 2: Shake It Up!** 133
>
> > Ten Textbook Algebra and Coordinate Geometry Questions 134
> >
> > Three Ways to Shake It Up 135
> >
> > Typical Story Problems 142
> >
> > What to Do Next 146
>
> **CHAPTER 9: Math Workout 3: Figuring It Out** 149
>
> > Ten Textbook Geometry Questions 149
> >
> > Tackling More Complex Geometry Questions 156
>
> **CHAPTER 10: Reading Workout 1: Know Where You're Going** 165
>
> > The Key to Active ACT Reading 165
> >
> > The Kaplan Method for ACT Reading 169
>
> **CHAPTER 11: Reading Workout 2: Look It Up!** 179
>
> > The Kaplan Method (Again) 180
> >
> > Important Question Types 181
> >
> > Find and Paraphrase…and Other Tips 188

CHAPTER 12: Reading Workout 3: Subject Matters 191

The Prose Fiction Passage 192

The Natural Sciences Passage 199

Emergency Strategy for Test Day 204

CHAPTER 13: Science Workout 1: Look for Patterns 207

The Kaplan Method for ACT Science 209

Reading Tables and Graphs 213

The Real Thing: Practice Passage 219

CHAPTER 14: Science Workout 2: Think Like a Scientist 225

How Scientists Think 225

How Experiments Work 227

Handling Experiment Questions 229

The Real Thing: Practice Passage 235

CHAPTER 15: Science Workout 3: Keep Your Viewpoints Straight 241

Prereading the Conflicting Viewpoints Passage 242

The Real Thing: Practice Passage 243

The Deep End: Facing Tough Science Passages 250

CHAPTER 16: Writing Workout: Write What Counts 257

Just the Facts 257

The Kaplan Method for the ACT Essay 259

Know the Score: Sample Essays 268

Preparing for the Essay 276

Practice Essay 278

PART THREE: Ready, Set, Go

CHAPTER 17: Strategic Summaries 287

English Test 287

Math Test 290

Reading Test 293

Science Test 297

Writing Test 300

CHAPTER 18: Last-Minute Tips 303

Three Days before the Test 303

Two Days before the Test. 304

The Day before the Test 304

The Morning of the Test. 305

During the Test 306

After the Test 306

PART FOUR: Practice Test and Explanations

Practice Test 311

Answer Key. 384

Answers and Explanations 385

Compute Your Score 415

100 Key Math Concepts for the ACT 417

Welcome to *Kaplan ACT: Strategies, Practice, and Review*

Are you ready to conquer the ACT?

Kaplan knows the ACT exam is important to you. A great score on the ACT can help you stand out from the crowd when applying to colleges and can also help you get scholarships and financial aid to pay for it all.

Kaplan has more than 75 years of experience getting students ready for exams. We've spent decades building a powerful arsenal of test-taking tools designed with *you* in mind, and the book you now hold in your hands contains everything you need to score higher on the ACT.

The name of this book says it all: The 2014 edition of *Kaplan ACT: Strategies, Practice, and Review* includes proven ACT strategies, realistic test practice, and in-depth review of all tested material. Kaplan's exclusive ACT tools work. Use them to your advantage, and get ready to score higher on the ACT!

LET'S GET STARTED!

Kaplan ACT: Strategies, Practice, and Review has everything you need to get ready for test day, but how you use it is *your* choice. Kaplan realizes that no one knows your test-prep needs better than you, so we've designed this book to put you in control of the variety and amount of study that best suits your needs.

This book is designed to allow you to determine the path your test prep takes. Use it front to back or jump around and focus on the test sections that you need the most help with—it's your call.

On top of all the great test prep inside the book, we've put a diagnostic test online to help you determine your test strengths and weaknesses and focus your study plan. This is a great place to get started.

TAKE THE ONLINE DIAGNOSTIC QUIZ

Taking the online diagnostic quiz is a great way to figure out where your ACT skills stand and how to structure your study time between now and test day. Take the test and see what test sections are your strongest and which may require the most prep.

Here's how to access your ACT diagnostic quiz online:

1. Go to kaptest.com/booksonline.
2. Follow the on-screen instructions. Please have a copy of your book available.

BUILD YOUR ACT STUDY PLAN

Okay, so you've taken the diagnostic quiz. Now what? Well, now that you have a good idea which test sections are your strongest and which need the most attention, you are ready to make the most of this book and build your study plan.

YOUR ACT STUDY PLAN—5 STEPS TO SUCCESS

1. Carefully go through the lessons in this book, paying close attention to the ones that focus on the test sections you were weakest in on your diagnostic quiz.

2. Take the end-of-chapter practice sets to see how well you're progressing. Be sure to read the answer explanations carefully—they'll help you figure out where you might have gone wrong during your problem solving.

3. Don't be afraid to review challenging lessons and concepts more than once. Isn't doing well on the ACT worth the extra study time?

4. Take time to practice your writing skills for the ACT essay. Use the strategies provided in this book to wow the essay graders on test day!

5. Once you're comfortable with the various ACT question types and test material, dive into the full-length practice test at the back of the book. Test yourself under realistic test-day conditions and chart your progress. If your strengths and weaknesses change, adjust your study plan.

KAPLAN'S GOT YOU COVERED!

In addition to all the proven test-prep material in this book, based on decades of experience preparing students for the ACT, we've asked some of Kaplan's premier test experts to provide you with exclusive advice, tips, and strategies for scoring higher on the ACT.

Whenever you see these icons:

we recommend you read the quote carefully and follow the advice given as you get ready for test day.

These helpful hints come from the following sources:

Kaplan Expert Tutor Tips

One of Kaplan's expert ACT tutors provides valuable insight on how you can make the most of your ACT prep and score higher.

Kaplan Perfect Score Tips

Did you know that in any given year, less than .0001 percent of test takers get a perfect ACT score? It's a pretty rare and impressive feat and one which a Kaplan student recently achieved! Our very own perfect score whiz gives you the secret to her ACT success!

Good luck on test day!

PART ONE

ACT Basics

CHAPTER 1

Introduction to the ACT

Before you plunge into studying for the ACT, let's take a step back and look at the big picture. What's the ACT all about? How can you prepare for it? How is it scored? This chapter will answer these questions and more.

The ACT is an opportunity, not a barrier. In fact, you should be grateful that you have to take it. Really. A strong ACT score is one credential that doesn't depend on things you can't control. It doesn't depend on how good your high school is. It doesn't depend on how many academic luminaries you know, or how rich and famous your family is, or whether any of your teachers are gullible enough to swear in a letter of recommendation that you're the greatest scientific mind since Isaac Newton. No, your ACT score depends on only you.

> **EXPERT TUTOR TIP**
> If you have two weeks or fewer to prep for the ACT, don't panic. The first thing you should do is become familiar with the test. This chapter is the place to start.

Granted, the ACT is a tough exam, but you should be grateful for that, too. Really. If the ACT were easy, everyone would do well. A good score wouldn't mean much. However, because it is so challenging, the ACT can be your single best opportunity to show what you can do and prove to colleges that you are the candidate of choice—for admission, for advanced placement, for scholarships.

It's important, though, that you take the test in the right spirit. Don't be timid in the face of the ACT or let it bully you. You've got to take control of the test. Our mission in this book is to show you exactly how to do that.

It helps to think of the ACT challenge as a contest—not only between you and the test, but also between you and that other person trying to get your spot in college. The ACT, after all, is meant to provide a way for all college applicants to compete on an even playing field. How do you compete successfully in a fair academic fight?

You train—harder and smarter than the next person. First, you learn whatever knowledge and skills you need to know. Also, just as importantly, you learn how to show what you know, in ways that the test is designed to reward. You learn how to be a savvy test taker.

> ✓ **PERFECT SCORE TIP**
> The best thing you can do for yourself is really get to know the test. The ACT is a very predictable test, and being familiar with it will help you with both time and nerves on test day.

FOUR KEYS TO ACT SUCCESS

There are four basic keys to achieving ACT success. Following any of these by itself will improve your score. Following all four together will make you nothing less than awesome.

1. Learn the Test

The ACT is very predictable. You'd think the test makers would get bored after a while, but they don't. The same kinds of questions, testing the same skills and concepts, appear every time the ACT is given.

Because the test specifications rarely change, you can learn in advance what to expect on every section. Just a little familiarity can make an enormous difference on the ACT. Here are a few ways in which learning the test will boost your score:

- **You'll learn the directions.** Why waste valuable time reading directions when you can have them down pat beforehand? You need every second during the test to answer questions and get points.

- **You'll learn the difficulty range of questions.** The typical ACT test taker only gets about half the questions right. Knowing this will stop you from panicking when you hit an impossible science passage or trigonometry question. Relax! You can skip many tough questions on the ACT and still get a great score! Also, once you know that the questions aren't arranged in order of difficulty, you'll know that just beyond that awful question will be one, two, or even three easy questions that you can get right with no sweat at all.

- **You'll learn how to get extra points by guessing.** Unlike other standardized tests, the ACT has no wrong-answer penalty. Knowing that simple fact can boost your score significantly. If you can't answer a question, guess.

- **You'll learn what makes a high-scoring essay.** If you are taking the optional Writing test, learning how it is scored will help you craft a good essay.

We'll help you get a better understanding of the ACT in the next chapter, entitled "The Subject Tests: A Preview."

> ✓ **PERFECT SCORE TIP**
> The ACT will not penalize you for a wrong answer. So answer every question, and don't lose possible points by leaving questions blank.

2. Learn the Kaplan Methods and Strategies

The ACT isn't a normal exam. Most normal exams test your memory. Instead the ACT tests problem-solving skills in a standardized-test format. Therefore, arming yourself with the Kaplan Methods and Strategies will earn you points!

Most students miss a lot of ACT questions for no good reason. They see a tough-looking question, say to themselves, "Uh-oh, I don't remember how to do that," and start to gnaw on their No. 2 pencils.

However, many ACT questions can be answered without perfect knowledge of the material being tested. Often, all you need to do to succeed on the ACT is to think strategically and creatively. We call this kind of strategic, creative frame of mind the ACT Mind-Set.

How do you put yourself into the ACT Mind-Set? You continually ask yourself questions such as: "What does this mean? How can I put this into a form I can understand and use? How can I do this faster?" Once you develop some savvy test-taking skills, you'll find yourself capable of working out problems that, at first reading, might have scared you half to death! In fact, we'll show you how you can sometimes get right answers when you don't even understand the question or the passage.

> ✓ **PERFECT SCORE TIP**
> Don't let tough questions scare you. The Kaplan Methods and Strategies will help teach you how to tackle them. And remember: You don't need to know every question to do well.

There are many, many specific strategies you can use to boost your score. For instance, here are just a few things you'll learn:

- **You'll learn the peculiarities of the ACT format.** Except for the Writing test, the ACT is a multiple-choice test. The correct answer is **always** right there in front of you. We'll show you how to develop specific tactics for each question type to maximize your chances of selecting the correct answer. The wrong answers often take predictable forms. For example, in the English section the shortest answer is the correct answer surprisingly often. Knowing statistical information like this can give you an important edge.

- **You'll learn a plan of attack for each subject test.** We'll show you some really useful ways of attacking each subject test. You'll learn how to do "question triage"—deciding which questions to do now and which to save for later. You'll learn the Kaplan Method—designed to get you points quickly and systematically—for each ACT subject test. You'll learn gridding techniques to avoid any answer sheet disasters.

- **You'll learn "unofficial" ways of getting right answers fast.** On the ACT, nobody cares how you decide which choice to select. The only thing that matters is picking the right answer. That's different from the way it works on most high school tests, where you get credit for showing that you've done the questions the "right" way (that is, the way you were taught to do them by your high school teacher). We'll show you how to find creative shortcuts to the correct answers—"unofficial" methods that will save you precious time and net you extra points.

> ✓ **PERFECT SCORE TIP**
> Test-taking tips can only take you so far if you don't know the material. Figure out which topics you need the most help on, and make sure to focus time on learning or refreshing those topics.

The basic test-smart techniques and strategies for the whole test are covered in the chapter called "Taking Control: The Top Ten Strategies." The Kaplan Methods and Strategies for each subject test, plus specific hints, techniques, and strategies for individual question types, are found in the Skill-Building Workouts. These are then summarized in the Strategic Summaries.

3. Learn the Material Tested

The ACT is designed to test skills and concepts learned in high school and needed for college. Familiarity with the test, coupled with smart test-taking strategies, will take you only so far. For your best score, you need to sharpen up the skills and content-related knowledge that the ACT tests.

The good news is that most of the content on the ACT is pretty basic. You've probably already learned most of what the ACT expects you to know, but you may need help remembering. That's partly what this book is for—to remind you of the knowledge you already have and to build and refine the specific skills you've developed in high school. Here are just a few of the things we'll remind you of:

- **You'll learn how to read graphs and tables.** Many Science questions rely on your ability to use data presented in the form of graphs and tables. (We'll teach you how to read graphs and tables in Science Workout 1.)

- **Have you met any FANBOYS lately?** Don't know? Well, this is the acronym for the conjunctions used with a comma to connect two independent clauses in a sentence. We know you want to know more about this, so here's a sneak preview: FANBOYS help you remember **F**or, **A**nd, **N**or, **B**ut, **O**r, **Y**et, **S**o. For more grammar rules, check out English Workout 3.

- **If your math "engine" is rusty when it comes to triangles, probabilities, algebraic expressions**, and more, we'll get you up and running. The three Math Workout chapters and the 100 Key Math Concepts for the ACT will have that engine purring again in no time.

- **You'll learn how to do trigonometry problems.** Do you remember exactly what a cotangent is? A cosine? We didn't think so. But there are four trig problems on every ACT. (You can learn about trigonometry problems in 100 Key Math Concepts for the ACT, items 96–100.)

- **You'll learn the difference between *lie* and *lay*.** Is it "I lay down on the couch" or "I lie down on the couch"? You may want to lie down yourself if you encounter such issues on the ACT, but don't fret. We'll remind you of the common grammar traps the test lays for you. (For a discussion of this tested issue, see Classic Grammar Rule #9 in English Workout 3.)

4. Practice, Practice, Practice

Practice creates confidence. On test day, you need to have all the Kaplan Methods and Strategies and the tested concepts in your brain and to be relaxed and ready to go. Reading and understanding the contents of this book are key, but there's one more step. For the Kaplan Methods to be most effective on test day, you need to make them part of your everyday routine. The best way to do that is to practice as much as possible.

Test day often becomes THE DAY. You're in a room full of people, all in a state of anticipation and nervousness—the anxiety is contagious! Don't let the moment take over and make you forget what you know about doing well. Your best ally is the confidence that practice gives you.

Note: If you don't have time to practice with all of the sections, you can (and should!) practice in the areas you feel weakest.

These specifics we've discussed comprise what we call the ACT knowledge base. The components of this knowledge base are reviewed along the way throughout this book. The resources in this book and online summarize this information for the two sections of the ACT that explicitly test knowledge: English and Math.

In sum, then, follow these four keys to ACT success:

1. **Learn the test.**
2. **Learn the strategies.**
3. **Learn the material tested.**
4. **Practice, practice, practice.**

If you do, you'll find yourself just where you should be: in full command of your ACT test-taking experience. Count on it.

> ✔ **PERFECT SCORE TIP**
> Don't be tricked into thinking the ACT is a test based solely on intelligence. Anyone can do well on this test if he or she really studies for it.

WHAT IS THE ACT?

As you know, the ACT is a standardized test. That means it tests predefined concepts in predictable ways. For example, the ACT English section always includes ten questions that test punctuation. The ACT Math section always includes four questions that test trigonometry. The format of the ACT is also predictable. For example, the Reading section always includes four passages, each with ten questions. The Science section always includes seven passages; one of those will always present conflicting viewpoints and will feature seven questions. You'll learn more about the tested concepts and the predictability of the ACT as you work with this book. For now, though, you should understand one thing—the more you know about how the test is written and structured, the more in control you'll feel on test day. Sure, you can work only on the Math section when the proctor announces, "You have the next 60 minutes to work on Section 2." However, you don't necessarily need to work on the questions in their exact order. In fact, you shouldn't. The methods and strategies you'll learn in this book are designed to put you in control of your test-taking experience and earn you the most points possible in each section. Your success begins with knowing exactly what to expect on the ACT.

So, before anything, take some time and get to know this test. Let's start with the basics. The ACT is a three-hour exam (three and a half hours if you take the optional Writing test) taken by high school juniors and seniors for admission to college. It is not an IQ test; it's a test of problem-solving skills—which means that you can improve your performance by preparing for it.

But let's be realistic about ACT scores. It's a neat and easy way of comparing all students numerically, no matter what their academic backgrounds and no matter how much grade inflation exists at their high schools. You know the admissions people are going to take a serious look at your test scores.

The ACT consists of four subject tests: English, Math, Reading, and Science, as well as the optional Writing test. All the subject tests are primarily designed to test skills rather than knowledge, though some knowledge is required—particularly in English, for which a familiarity with grammar and usage is important. In Math, you will need to know the basic math concepts taught in a regular high school curriculum. The Writing section tests your ability to clearly communicate your position on an issue.

▶ OVERVIEW OF THE ACT

- **The ACT is about three hours long (three and a half with the Writing test).**
- **There will be a short break between the Math and Reading subtests.**
- **The ACT consists of a total of 215 scored multiple-choice questions and one optional essay.**
- **The exam is comprised of four subject tests and an optional Writing test:**
  - **English (45 minutes, 75 questions)**
  - **Math (60 minutes, 60 questions)**
  - **Reading (35 minutes, 40 questions)**
  - **Science (35 minutes, 40 questions)**
  - **Writing (30 minutes, 1 essay question)**

ACT FAQS

Here are some quick answers to the questions students ask most frequently about the ACT.

How Is the ACT Scored?

The ACT is scored differently from most tests you take at school. Your ACT score on a test section is not reported as the total number of questions you answered correctly, nor does your ACT score indicate the percentage of questions you answered correctly. Instead, the test makers add up all of your correct answers in a section to get what's called your raw score for that section. They then use a conversion chart, or scale, that matches up a particular raw score with what's called a scaled score. The scaled score is the number that gets reported as your score for that ACT subtest. For each version of the ACT administered, the test maker uses a unique conversion chart that equates a particular raw score with a particular scaled score.

> **EXPERT TUTOR TIP**
> Most ACT test takers score between 17 and 23. A score below 17 will seriously limit your choice of colleges. Any score above 23 will be an asset in your quest for admission to a competitive college.

ACT scaled scores range from 1 to 36. Nearly half of all test takers score within a much narrower range: 17–23. Tests at different dates vary slightly, but the following data is based on a recent administration of the test and can be considered typical.

ACT Approximate Percentile Rank*	Scaled (or Composite) Score	Percentage of Questions Correct
99%	31	90%
90%	26	75%
76%	23	63%
54%	20	53%
28%	17	43%

*Percentage of ACT takers scoring at or below given score

Notice that to earn a score of 20 (the national average), you need to answer only about 53 percent of the questions correctly. On most tests, getting only a bit more than half the questions right would be terrible. Not so on the ACT. A score of 20 puts you in the middle range of test takers.

EXPERT TUTOR TIP
Just a few questions right or wrong on the ACT can make a big difference. Answering only five extra questions correctly on each subject test can move you from the bottom of the applicant pool into the middle or from the middle up to the top.

The score table includes two very strong scores: 26 and 31. Either score would impress almost any college admissions officer. A 26 would put you in the top 10 percent of the students who take the exam, and a 31 would put you in the top 1 percent. Even a 31 requires getting only about 90 percent of the questions right! The best student in your high school will probably get at least a dozen questions wrong. The ACT includes questions that even your smartest teachers might get wrong.

If you earn a score of 23, you'll be in about the 76th percentile. That means that 76 percent of the test takers did as well as, or worse than, you did—in other words, that only 24 percent did better than you. It means you're in the top quarter of the people who take the ACT. That's a good score, but notice that to earn this score, you need only about 63 percent of the questions correct. On most tests, a score of 63 is probably a D or an F. But on the ACT, it's about a B+.

How Many ACT Scores Will You Get?

The ACT scaled score we've talked about so far is technically called the composite score. While it's really important, you actually receive 12 different scores when you take the ACT: the composite score, 4 (or 5) subject scores, and 7 subscores. Though the subject scores can play a role in decisions at some schools, the subscores usually aren't important for most people, so feel free to ignore the following chart if you don't feel like looking at it.

Here's the full battery of ACT scores (1–36) you'll receive. Few people (except your parents, maybe) will care about anything except your composite score for college admissions, though some schools use subscores for course placement.

English Score (1–36)	Usage/Mechanics subscore (1–18); Rhetorical Skills subscore (1–18)
Math Score (1–36)	Pre-Algebra/Elementary Algebra subscore (1–18); Algebra/Coordinate Geometry subscore (1–18); Plane Geometry/Trigonometry subscore (1–18)
Reading Score (1–36)	Social Sciences/Sciences subscore (1–18); Arts/Literature subscore (1–18)
Science Score (1–36)	There are no subscores in Science.
(Optional) Writing Score (2–12)	There are no subscores in Writing.
(Optional) Combined English-Writing Score (1–36)	There are no subscores for the Combined English-Writing score. This score does not count toward your composite score, but colleges will see it.

How Do Colleges Use Your ACT Score?

The most important score is typically the composite score (which is an average of the four major subject scores). This is the score used by most colleges and universities in the admissions process. The subject scores and subscores may be used for advanced placement or occasionally for scholarships, but they are primarily used by college advisors to help students select majors and first-year courses.

Although many schools deny that they use benchmark scores as cutoffs, we're not sure we really believe them. Big Ten universities and colleges with similarly competitive admissions generally decline to accept students with composite scores below 22 or 23. For less competitive schools, the benchmark score may be lower than that; for some very selective schools, the cutoff may be higher.

To be fair, no school uses the ACT as an absolute bar to admission; for most applicants, though, a low ACT score is decisive. As a rule, only students whose backgrounds are extremely unusual or who have overcome enormous disadvantages are accepted if their ACT scores are below the benchmark.

> ✓ **PERFECT SCORE TIP**
> Many people are scared of taking the Writing test because they compare it to the SAT Writing section. The two tests are very different—so be sure to read chapter 16 before making your choice.

Should You Take the Optional Writing Test?

You should decide whether to take the ACT Writing test based on the admissions policies of your target schools and on the advice of your high school guidance counselors. A list of colleges requiring the test is maintained on the ACT website, www.act.org/aap/writing. If you are unsure about what schools you will apply to, you should plan to take the Writing test. However, testing will be available later if you decide not to take the Writing test and discover later that you need it.

> ✓ **PERFECT SCORE TIP**
> Many schools prefer that you take the ACT Writing test. If you don't know yet where you will be applying, consider taking this optional test to reduce the chances you will have to take the ACT again.

How Do Schools Use the Optional Writing Test?

The ACT Writing test may be used for either admissions or course placement purposes or sometimes both. Students who take the Writing test will receive an English score, a Writing subscore, and a combined English-Writing score on a 1–36 scale. (The combined English-Writing score is not averaged into the composite score.) Copies of the essay (with the graders' comments) will also be available online for downloading. Schools that do not require the Writing test will also receive the Combined English-Writing score for students who have taken the Writing test, unless the school specifically asks *not* to receive those results.

Should You Guess on the ACT?

The short answer? Yes! The long answer? Yes, of course!

As we saw, ACT scores are only based on the number of correct answers. Questions that you leave blank and questions you answer incorrectly simply don't count. Unlike some other standardized tests, the ACT has no wrong answer penalty. That's why you should **always** guess on every ACT question you can't answer, even if you don't have time to read it. Though the questions vary enormously in difficulty, harder questions are worth exactly the same as easier ones, so it pays to guess on the really hard questions and spend your time breezing through the really easy ones.

Can You Retake the Test?

You can take the ACT as many times as you like. You can then select whichever test score you prefer to be sent to colleges when you apply. However, you cannot take advantage of this option if, at the time you register for the test, you designate certain colleges to receive your scores. Thus, it is crucial that you not designate any colleges when you register for the test. You can (for a small additional fee) have ACT scores sent to colleges at any time after the scores are reported.

> **EXPERT TUTOR TIP**
> When you sign up for the ACT, you can choose colleges to receive your score. Unless time is of the essence, don't do it, even though the first four score reports are sent for free. Wait until you get your score, then send it out (for a small additional fee) if you're happy. If you hate your score, you can take the test again and send only the new, improved score.

Unless you don't have enough money for that small extra fee, or you're taking the ACT under the wire and you need your scores to reach your target schools ASAP, give yourself the freedom to retake the test. What this means, of course, is that even if you blow the ACT once, you can give yourself another chance without the schools of your choice knowing about it. The ACT is one of the few areas of your academic life in which you get a second chance.

> **PERFECT SCORE TIP**
> The ACT is offered many times per year, so think hard about which test date will give you the most time to prepare. For example, I took it in September because I knew during the school year I would not have enough time to give my studying the attention it deserved.

ACT REGISTRATION OVERVIEW

- **To get a registration packet, see your guidance counselor, or contact:**

    ACT Registration
    301 ACT Drive
    P.O. Box 414
    Iowa City, IA 52243-0414
    Phone: (319) 337-1270
    Web: www.act.org

- **You can also register online at www.actstudent.org.**

- **Students with disabilities or with other special circumstances can call (319) 337-1332.**

GO ONLINE

Visit the test maker's website at www.act.org for the latest information on test registration, fees, and content.

- **The basic fee at press time for the ACT is $35 without the W**
  $50.50 with the Writing test in the United States. (For student
  the 50 United States, the fee is $65, $80.50 for the ACT with V
  (319) 337-1448 for more information on taking the test outside tl

  This price includes reports for you, your high school, and up
  choices. There are additional fees for late registration, standby t
  test centers or test dates, and additional services and products.

- **In the United States, the ACT is administered in Septe**
  December, February, April, and June. (The February date is no
  state of New York.) In selected states, the ACT is also offered in
  Register early to secure the time you want at the test center of your choice and
  to avoid late registration fees.

- **You may take the ACT as often as you wish.** Many students take it twice, once
  as a junior and again as a senior. There are no limitations on how many times you
  can take the ACT, but there are some restrictions on how often you can test. For
  example, you can test only once per national test date.

- **Be sure you take your test center admission ticket and acceptable identification with you to the test center.** Acceptable forms of identification are a photo
  ID or a recently published photo with your full name printed. Unacceptable forms
  of identification are a birth certificate, Social Security card, or any other ID without
  photo. You will not be admitted without acceptable identification.

- **Check with ACT, Inc., for all the latest information on the test.** Every effort
  is made to keep the information in this book up-to-date, but changes may occur
  after the book is published.

- **Go online (act.org) to make sure you know ALL the ACT regulations for test
  day.** For example, all electronic devices (including cell phones) must be turned
  off from the time you're admitted to the test until you're dismissed after testing
  concludes.

Note: Violations of these rules, such as an alarm going off or a phone ringing in the
test room, may result in your dismissal from the room and the nonscoring of your
answer sheet.

- **You might be considering whether to take the ACT, the SAT, or both.** For more information on the SAT, go to the College Board's website at www.collegeboard.com.

> ✓ **PERFECT SCORE TIP**
> The ACT and SAT are very different tests. Many people have an affinity for one over the other. Try some sample questions from each, and decide which one works best for you.

TAKING THE PLAN EXAM

Students should also be aware of the PLAN® exam, which offers a preview of the format and content of the material found on the ACT. A student's success on this exam is often an accurate predictor of success on the ACT. The PLAN exam helps students decide which courses to take in their junior and senior years of high school; it also helps them consider certain career paths prior to college, based on their strengths or weaknesses as indicated by their scores. The PLAN is generally offered to students in the fall of their sophomore year. To learn more, visit PLAN's website for student information at www.actstudent.org/plan.

▶ IF YOU LEARNED ONLY FIVE THINGS IN THIS CHAPTER...

1. The ACT consists of four required subject tests (English, Math, Reading, and Science), plus an optional Writing test.

2. Total testing time is about three hours, plus half an hour for Writing.

3. All questions are multiple-choice except on the Writing test (one essay question).

4. There is no penalty for a wrong answer, so you should guess.

5. ACT composite scores range from 1–36.

CHAPTER 2

The Subject Tests: A Preview

Okay, you've seen how the ACT is set up. But to really do well, you've got to know something about the ACT subject tests.

As we'll see, the questions in every subject test vary widely in difficulty. Some are so easy that most elementary school students could answer them. Others would give even Einstein a little trouble. Recall: **The questions are not arranged in order of difficulty.** That's different from some other tests, in which easier questions come first. Skipping past hard questions is very important, since otherwise you may **never** reach easy ones toward the end of the exam.

Here's a preview of the types of questions you'll see on the subject tests. We'll keep them toward the easy end of the difficulty scale here, but later, in the Skill-Building Workouts, we'll challenge you with tougher questions.

After we look at the four required subject tests, we'll give you a preview of the optional Writing test.

> ✔ **PERFECT SCORE TIP**
> The structure of the ACT is very predictable. Know the order, number of questions, and time for each section cold by the time you get to test day.

ENGLISH

The English test lasts 45 minutes and includes 75 questions. That works out to about 30 seconds per question. When it comes down to it, though, you should spend less time on easier questions and more on harder questions. The test is divided into five passages, each with about 15 questions.

Note: You're not tested on spelling or vocabulary here. Rather, the ACT is designed to test your understanding of the conventions of English—punctuation, grammar, sentence structure—and of rhetorical skills. Rhetorical skills are more strategic things like organizing the text and making sure it's consistently styled and concise.

Students nearly **always** get more questions correct in English than in any other section. That tends to make them think that English is a lot easier than the rest of the ACT. Alas, it's not that simple. Because most students do well, the test makers have much higher expectations for English than for other parts of the test. They know that it's generally easier to get English questions right than, say, Science questions. That's why, to earn an average English subscore (a 20, say), you have to get almost two-thirds of the questions right, while on the rest of the test you need to get only about half of them right.

The Format

More than half of the English questions follow a standard format. A word, phrase, or sentence in a passage is underlined. You're given four options: to leave the underlined portion alone (NO CHANGE, which is **always** the first choice) or to replace it with one of three alternatives.

Example

...Pike's Peak in Southwest Colorado is named before Zebulon Pike, an early explorer. He traveled through the area, exploring...

37. A. NO CHANGE
    B. before Zebulon Pike became an explorer, and he
    C. after Zebulon Pike, when he
    D. after Zebulon Pike. He

The right answer for number 37 is choice D. The other choices all have various problems: grammatical, stylistic, logical. Only choice D makes the sentence sensible and correct.

Notice that a single question can test several kinds of writing errors. We find that about a third of the English questions test your ability to write concisely (we call them Economy questions), about another third test for logic and sense (Sense questions), and only the remaining third test hard-and-fast rules of grammar (Technicality questions). There's a lot of overlap between these question types, so don't worry too much about categories. We provide them simply to give you an idea of the kinds of errors you'll be expected to correct.

✔ **PERFECT SCORE TIP**
In English passages, always read the options in context, pretending you are saying them out loud. Often, the mistake will become clear to you when you say it to yourself.

TO OMIT OR NOT TO OMIT

Some English questions offer, as one of the alternatives, the chance to completely omit the underlined portion, usually as the last of the four choices.

Example

Later, Pike fell while valiantly defending

America in the War of 1812. It goes
                          ‾‾‾‾‾‾‾
                           40

without saying that this took place after
‾‾
                   40

he discovered Pike's Peak. He actually
‾‾‾‾‾‾‾‾‾‾‾‾‾‾‾‾‾‾‾‾‾‾‾‾‾
          40

died near York (now called Toronto)…

40. F. NO CHANGE

 G. Clearly, this must have occurred
     subsequent to his discovering
     Pike's Peak.

 H. This was after he found Pike's
     Peak.

 J. OMIT the underlined portion

In this case, choice J is correct. The idea really does "go without saying." For that reason, it shouldn't be stated. On recent ACTs, when OMIT has appeared as an answer choice, it's been correct more than half of the time. Before choosing OMIT, however, read the passage text *without* the underlined portion to ensure the passage is clear and correct when it is left out. When offered as a choice, OMIT is often correct, but not always.

> ✔ **PERFECT SCORE TIP**
> Answer A or F in many English questions is NO CHANGE. Remember that this is sometimes the answer. If you are sure the sentence is completely correct, select this answer instead of making up nonexistent grammar problems.

The Directions

The directions on the English test illustrate why there's an advantage to knowing them beforehand. The directions are long and complicated. Here's what they'll look like, but take our advice—don't bother reading them. We'll show you what you'll need to do. Then, while everyone else is reading the directions on test day, you'll be racking up points.

> ✔ **PERFECT SCORE TIP**
> OMIT is often the correct answer, so don't be scared to think of part of the passage as unnecessary. There will be more tips about this in the first English Workout.

Directions: In the five passages that follow, certain words and phrases are underlined and numbered. In the right-hand column, you will find alternatives for the underlined parts. In most cases, you are to choose the one that best expresses the idea, makes the statement appropriate for standard written English, or is worded most consistently with the style and tone of the passage as a whole. If you think the original version is best, choose NO CHANGE. In some cases, you will find in the right-hand column a question about the underlined part. You are to choose the best answer to the question.

You will also find questions about a section of the passage or about the passage as a whole. These questions do not refer to an underlined portion of the passage, but rather are identified by a number or numbers in a box.

> ✓ **PERFECT SCORE TIP**
> Don't waste valuable time reading the directions on test day, or miss valuable points by not following them. Most directions are not that complicated—so make sure you know them cold before test day.

For each question, choose the alternative you consider best and fill in the corresponding oval on your answer grid. Read each passage through once before you answer the questions that accompany it. For many questions, you must read several sentences beyond the underlined portion to determine the answer. Be sure that you have read enough ahead each time you answer a question.

Nonstandard-Format Questions

Some ACT English questions—about 20 per test—don't follow the more typical format of presenting you with an underlined portion and three possible revisions. A Nonstandard-Format question might appear with an underlined part of the passage and ask you to determine which choice is the LEAST acceptable alternative to the underlined part. Another nonstandard-format question might ask you which of the offered choices best accomplishes a specific goal. You might also be asked whether you should add or delete material, and then choose the appropriate reason for adding or deleting it. For questions like these, it's important to read very carefully! Here's an example of how question 40, which you saw earlier, could be presented as a Nonstandard-Format question.

Example

…Later, Pike fell while valiantly defending America in the War of 1812. 40 He actually died near York (now called Toronto)…

40. Suppose the author considered adding the following sentence at this point: "It goes without saying that this occurred after he discovered Pike's Peak." Given the overall purpose of the passage, would this sentence be appropriate?

F. No, because the sentence adds nothing to the meaning of the passage.

G. No, because the passage is not concerned with Pike's achievements.

H. Yes, because otherwise the sequence of events would be unclear.

J. Yes. Though the sentence is not needed, the author recognizes this fact by using the phrase "it goes without saying."

The correct answer for this question is choice F. Though choice G correctly states that the sentence doesn't belong in the passage, it offers a pretty inappropriate reason. The passage *is* concerned with Pike's achievements. Choices H and J are wrong because they recommend including a sentence that is clearly redundant.

Many of the nonstandard questions occur at the end of a passage. Some ask about the meaning, purpose, or tone of individual paragraphs or of the passage as a whole. Others ask you to evaluate the passage. And still others ask you to determine the proper order of words, sentences, or paragraphs that have been scrambled in the passage.

We think you'll like the English subject test. It can actually be fun. We'll cover strategies for the English question types in the English Workouts.

MATH

The Math test is 60 minutes long and includes 60 questions. That works out to one minute per question, but you'll want to spend less time on easy questions and more on the tough ones.

The Format

All of the Math questions have the same basic multiple-choice format. They ask a question and offer five possible choices (unlike questions on the other subject tests, which have only four choices each).

> ✓ **PERFECT SCORE TIP**
> While studying, if you come across any questions for which you do not know or remember the material, review it! Especially in math, tricks can only get you so far if you don't remember the math behind them.

The questions cover a full range of math topics, from pre-algebra and elementary algebra to plane geometry and even a little bit of trigonometry. If you have specific weaknesses in any of these areas, the 100 Key Math Concepts for the ACT section at the end of this book will help.

Although the Math questions aren't ordered in terms of difficulty, questions drawn from elementary school or junior high tend to come earlier in the section, while those from high school math curricula tend to come later. But this doesn't mean that the easy questions come first and the hardest ones come later. We've found that high school subjects tend to be fresher in most students' minds than things they were taught years ago, so you may actually find the later questions easier. (Do *you* remember the math you learned in seventh grade?)

The Directions

Here's what the Math directions will look like:

Directions: Solve each problem, choose the correct answer, and then fill in the corresponding oval on your answer document.

Do not linger over problems that take too much time. Solve as many as you can, then return to the others in the time you have left for this test.

You are permitted to use a calculator on this test. You may use your calculator for any problems you choose, but some of the problems may best be done without using a calculator.

Note: Unless otherwise noted, all of the following should be assumed:

1. Illustrative figures are NOT necessarily drawn to scale.

2. Geometric figures lie in a plane.

3. The word *line* indicates a straight line.

4. The word *average* indicates arithmetic mean.

Again, when it comes to directions on the ACT, the golden rule is: **Don't read them on test day!** You'll already know what they say by the time you take the test.

The Math directions don't really tell you much anyway. Of the four special notes at the end of the Math directions, #2, #3, and #4 almost go without saying. Note #1—that figures are *not* necessarily drawn to scale—seems pretty scary, but in fact, the vast majority of ACT figures *are* drawn to scale. As we'll see, this has significant implications for how to guess on geometry questions.

> ✓ **PERFECT SCORE TIP**
> The use of a calculator is discussed later. You should be familiar with your calculator, and learn when using it is really necessary for you.

READING AND DRAWING DIAGRAMS

We find that about a third of the Math questions either give you a diagram or describe a situation that should be diagrammed. For these questions, the diagrams are crucial.

Example

1. The figure below contains five congruent triangles. The longest side of each triangle is 4 meters long. What is the area of the whole figure?

A. 12.5 square meters

B. 15 square meters

C. 20 square meters

D. 30 square meters

E. Cannot be determined from the given information.

> **EXPERT TUTOR TIP**
> In ACT Math questions, the answer choice "cannot be determined" is rare. When it does appear, it's usually wrong. "Cannot be determined" is **almost always** wrong in a question that comes with a diagram or for which you can draw one.

The key to this question is to let the diagram tell you what you need to know: Each triangle represents one-quarter of the area of the square and the sides of the *square* are 4 meters (you can figure this out because the top side of the square is the hypotenuse—or longest side—of the triangle that makes the "roof"). Since the area of a square can be found by squaring its side, the area of the square is 16 square meters. Thus, each triangle has an area one-fourth as much—4 square meters. Since the whole figure consists of *five* triangles, each with area 4, the total area is 5 × 4 = 20. The answer is C.

HOW TO APPROACH A STORY PROBLEM

We find that about another third of the Math questions are story problems like the following:

Example

2. Evan drove halfway home at 20 miles per hour, then sped up and drove the rest of the way at 30 miles per hour. What was his average speed for the entire trip?

    F.   20 miles per hour
    G.   22 miles per hour
    H.   24 miles per hour
    J.   25 miles per hour
    K.   28 miles per hour

A good way to comprehend—and resolve—a story problem like this is to think of a real situation just like the one in the story. For example, what if Evan had 120 miles to drive? (You should pick a distance that's easily divisible by both rates.) He would go 60 miles at 30 mph, then 60 miles at 20 mph. How long would it take? Well, 60 miles at 30 mph is two hours; 60 miles at 20 mph is three hours. That's a total of 120 miles in five hours; 120 divided by 5 gives an average speed of 24 mph. The correct answer is thus choice H. (Note: We'll show you alternative ways to answer questions like this later on.)

> **PERFECT SCORE TIP**
> Don't let variables or abstract stories confuse you. When you see them, calm down and make them simpler by putting real numbers in for the variables. You'll learn more about this Picking Numbers Strategy in Math Workout 1.

GETTING THE CONCEPT

Finally, we find that about a third of the questions directly ask you to demonstrate your knowledge of specific math concepts.

Example

3. If angles A and B are supplementary, and the measure of angle A is 57°, what is the measure, in degrees, of angle B?

   A. 33
   B. 43
   C. 47
   D. 123
   E. 147

This question simply requires that you know the concept of supplementary angles. Two angles are *supplementary* when they form a straight line—in other words, when they add up to 180°. Thus, question 3 boils down to this: What number, added to 57, makes 180? The answer is choice D, 123.

These three types of Math questions, of course, will be discussed more fully in the Math Workouts.

READING

The Reading test is 35 minutes long and includes 40 questions. It contains four passages, each followed by ten questions. You should allow three minutes (or less) to read and mark up the passage. You will then have about 30 seconds per question.

The Format

There are four categories of reading passages: Prose Fiction, Social Science, Humanities, and Natural Science. You'll get one passage in each category. The passages are about 1,000 words long and are written at about the same difficulty level as college textbooks and readings. After each passage, you'll find ten questions.

The Social Science, Humanities, and Natural Science passages are usually well-organized essays. Each has a very specific purpose. Questions expect you to recognize this purpose, to comprehend specific facts contained in the passage, and to understand the structure of the essay. Prose Fiction passages require you to understand the thoughts, feelings, and motivations of fictional characters, even when these are not explicitly stated in the passage (we'll have a special section on Prose Fiction passages in Reading Workout 3).

There are really only three different categories of Reading questions:

1. Specific Detail questions (What does the author say?)
2. Inference questions (Why is this included? What conclusions can you make?)
3. Big Picture questions (What's the overall topic?)

> ☑ **PERFECT SCORE TIP**
> Unlike reading on the SAT, ACT Reading will always have the same format. You will always have four passages, and they will always appear in this order: Prose, Social Science, History, Natural Science.

The Directions

The Reading directions are general:

Directions: There are four passages in this test. Each passage is followed by several questions. After reading a passage, choose the best answer to each question and fill in the corresponding oval on your answer document. You may refer to the passages as often as necessary.

There's nothing stupefying here, but nothing very substantive either. We'll be a little more specific and strategic than the test makers when we suggest a plan of attack in the three Reading Workouts.

> ☑ **PERFECT SCORE TIP**
> You do not have to do the readings in order. For example, if you always have trouble with Prose but are very good at Natural Science, do Natural Science first to make sure you don't run out of time to get those easy points. Develop a personal order that works for you, especially if you have trouble with time.

NAILING DOWN THE DETAILS

Specific Detail questions ask about things stated explicitly in the passage. Your challenge is the following:

- Find the exact place in the passage where the answer can be found. If the question doesn't give line references to help, you will be glad you marked up the passage.

- Remember the ABCs: **A**bbreviate margin notes, **B**racket key sentences, and **C**ircle key words and phrases.

- Match the detail from the text in the passage with the correct answer (by locating either similar words or paraphrasings).

Note: Many wrong choices will be designed to trip you up by including details from other parts of the passage or by using the same wording as the passage while distorting the meaning. Questions in the ACT Reading section are written to have three wrong answers and *only* one right answer. Some answer choices may appear to be half-right, half-wrong; remember, if an answer choice has *anything* wrong with it, then it cannot be the correct answer! Look for the one choice that is flawless.

Two important points to keep in mind:

1. There is one right answer, but there will be other tempting answers.

2. "Refer to the passage" in the Reading directions means that it's a good idea to look at the text before you try to answer the question. Predict before you peek! That is, predict in your own words, or by pointing to a specific phrase in the passage, what you think the answer will be before you look at the choices provided.

Example

When we say "Bach," we almost always refer to Johann Sebastian Bach (1685–1750), but in fact the name "Bach" belongs to a whole family of Baroque German musicians…

(7 paragraphs and 950 words omitted)

The works of Johann Christian Bach, J. S. Bach's son, clearly prefigure the rich musical developments that followed the Baroque period. Thus, it is both surprising and unfortunate that the rest of J. S. Bach's family isn't more well known.

6. According to the author, J. S. Bach is the best-known:

   F. German Baroque musician.

   G. member of a musical family.

   H. organist in German history.

   J. composer of Lutheran hymns.

7. Johann Christian Bach was:

   A. born earlier than Johann Sebastian Bach.

   B. a composer of the "Romantic" school of music.

   C. a composer whose works are transitional in style.

   D. well known during his own lifetime.

 PERFECT SCORE TIP
Always make sure you read the entire question and answer. The incorrect answers are made to look tempting on purpose, so avoid picking them based on key words.

The answer for question 6 is G. Both the first and last sentences in the passage refer to J. S. Bach as the most famous member of a whole family of musicians. You might think J. S. Bach is the best-known German Baroque musician (choice F), but that's not what the passage says, so it's wrong.

The answer for question 7 is choice C. At the end of the passage, the author says that Johann Christian's work "prefigure[d]" the music that followed the Baroque. Thus, it must have had some Baroque characteristics and some new aspects. In other words, it was transitional.

> ☑ **PERFECT SCORE TIP**
> Remember, the scorers do not care about your opinions or ideas about the passage. Base all your answer choices on what is explicitly written in the passage—not your own knowledge of the material.

MAKING AN INFERENCE

Most Reading passages also include a large number of Inference questions, which require you to make an inference from the passage (to "read between the lines"). They differ somewhat from Specific Detail questions. For one thing, students usually consider them harder. An example of each follows.

Example

…though schizophrenia and multiple personality disorder (MPD) may be related, and are often confused by laymen, the two terms have radically different meanings…

32. Which of the following best expresses the relationship between schizophrenia and multiple personality disorder?

   F. They are two terms that describe essentially the same phenomenon.

   G. The two disorders have nothing in common.

   H. Though the two have some similarities, they are fundamentally different.

   J. The two are not exactly alike, but are very close.

33. Suppose that a patient has been diagnosed with schizophrenia. Based on the passage, which of the following is LEAST likely?

   A. The patient's doctors immediately assume that the patient also suffers from MPD.

   B. The patient is a layman.

   C. The patient denies that he has MPD.

   D. The patient is related to someone with MPD.

> ✓ **PERFECT SCORE TIP**
> Note trick words such as *except* or *least likely*. Circle them when you read them in questions so you don't mistakenly answer the opposite question.

Note the differences between Specific Detail and Inference questions: 32, a Specific Detail question, requires that you understand the explicitly stated idea that schizophrenia and MPD have some connection but are not the same. That's what choice H says. Question 33, on the other hand, requires you to apply the idea that the two disorders are different. If they are, it's highly unlikely that doctors would simply assume that a patient suffering from one disorder must suffer from the other. Therefore, choice A is least likely—and therefore correct. The other choices may or may not be true, and nothing in the passage leads us to think one way or the other about them. Question 33 is what we'd call a garden-variety Inference question.

> ✓ **PERFECT SCORE TIP**
> Even when the test asks you to infer an answer, the answer will be based on the passage and what the author says. Do not make unsubstantiated judgments on the reading.

GETTING THE BIG PICTURE

Although the majority of Reading questions are Specific Detail and Inference questions, the Reading subtest also includes another type of question that we call Big Picture questions. Some Big Picture questions ask about the passage as a whole, requiring you to find the purpose, tone, or structure of the passage. Others ask you to evaluate the writing. Here's a typical Big Picture question that might have appeared with the Bach family passage we talked about earlier.

Example

9. The author's main point in the passage is to:

    A. show that many of the lesser-known members of the Bach family also influenced music history.
    B. argue that J. C. Bach was actually a greater composer than his father, J. S. Bach.
    C. demonstrate that musical talent **always** runs in families.
    D. dispute the claim that the Bach family was the best-known family of German Baroque musicians.

In order to answer this kind of question, you've got to have a good sense of the Big Picture—the shape and flow of the whole passage. Of course, we printed only a few selected lines from the passage, but that should have been enough to lead you to choice A as the answer. The first line definitely indicates that the subject of the passage is going to be the entire Bach family, with a focus on the ones who aren't as well known as the famous J. S. Bach.

SCIENCE

The Science test is 35 minutes long and includes 40 questions. It has seven passages, each with five to seven questions. This breaks down to approximately five minutes per passage.

No, you don't have to be a scientist to succeed on the ACT Science test. You don't have to know the atomic number of cadmium or the preferred mating habits of the monarch butterfly. All that's required is common sense (though a knowledge of standard scientific processes and procedures sure does help). You'll be given passages containing various kinds of scientific information—drawn from the fields of biology, chemistry, physics, geology, astronomy, and meteorology—which you'll have to understand and use as a basis for inferences.

The Format

On the Science section of the test, the seven passages are broken down as follows:

- Three passages (each with five questions) about tables and graphs
- Three passages (each with six questions) about experiments
- One passage (with seven questions) that presents opposing viewpoints on the same issue

The Directions

Here's what the Science directions will look like:

Directions: There are seven passages in this test. Each passage is followed by several questions. After reading a passage, choose the best answer to each question and fill in the corresponding oval on your answer document. You may refer to the passages as often as necessary. You are NOT permitted to use a calculator on this test.

> ✔️ **PERFECT SCORE TIP**
> The biggest ACT myth is about the Science section: this section is NOT based on scientific knowledge, but scientific skills like analyzing experiments and graphs. You do not need to memorize the periodic table to do very well.

Notice the similarity between these directions for Science and those for Reading. The ACT Science and Reading subtests actually test similar skills and require a similar approach—first read the passage quickly to get the big picture, then refer back to the passage to research the relevant information as you answer each question.

ANALYZING DATA

About two-thirds of the questions on the Science subtest require you to read data from graphs or tables. In easier questions, you need only report the information. In harder questions, you may need to draw inferences or note patterns in the data.

> **EXPERT TUTOR TIP**
> We'll show you the best strategic way to attack this subject test in the three Science Workouts.

Example

Percent of Questions Correct

1. A test taker who scores in approximately the 40th percentile has correctly answered about what fraction of the questions?

   A. $\dfrac{9}{10}$

   B. $\dfrac{2}{3}$

   C. $\dfrac{1}{2}$

   D. $\dfrac{1}{5}$

2. Which of the following best describes the relationship between percentile rank and percent of questions correct?

   F. As percentile rank increases, percent of correct questions also increases.

   G. Percentile rank is inversely proportional to the percent of correct questions.

   H. As percentile rank increases, the percent of correct questions decreases.

   J. As percentile rank decreases, percent of correct questions usually, but not always, also decreases.

The correct answer to question 1 is choice C. The point for the 40th percentile is slightly above the 50 percent point on the horizontal axis (percent or questions correct). Fifty percent is the same as $\dfrac{1}{2}$. Note that this question involves a little simple arithmetic (translating a percent into a fraction)—not uncommon for Science questions.

In question 2, the correct answer is choice F. The points that are higher on the graph (higher percentile) are always farther to the right (higher percentage of correct questions). Note that choices G and H say essentially the same thing (we'll discuss direct and inverse proportionality in Science Workout 1), and thus are wrong for the same reason: they get the relationship backwards. Choice J is wrong because it says that the percent of correct questions does not **always** decrease as percentile rank decreases.

CONDUCTING EXPERIMENTS

Other Science questions require that you understand the way experiments are designed and what they prove. For example, part of a passage might describe an experiment as follows:

Example

EXPERIMENT 1

A scientist adds one drop of nitric acid to Beakers A, B, and C. Each beaker contains water from a different stream. The water in Beaker A came from Stream A, that in Beaker B came from Stream B, and that in Beaker C came from Stream C. Precipitates form in Beakers B and C, but not in Beaker A.

12. Which of the following could properly be inferred on the basis of Experiment 1?

    F. Stream A is more polluted than Streams B and C.

    G. Streams B and C are more polluted than A.

    H. Stream A contains material that neutralizes nitric acid.

    J. Streams B and C contain some substance that reacts in the presence of nitric acid.

The correct answer is choice J. Since a precipitate forms when nitric acid is added to Beakers B and C, which contain water from Streams B and C, something in these streams must be involved. However, we don't know that it is pollution, so choice F and G are unwarranted. We don't know exactly *why* no precipitate formed in Beaker A, so choice H is also an unwarranted conclusion. Scientists *hate* unwarranted conclusions.

THE PRINCIPLE OF THE THING

The remaining Science questions require you either to logically apply a principle or to identify ways of defending or attacking a principle. Often, the question will involve two scientists stating opposing views on the same subject, but this is not **always** the case. A passage might describe a theory that most V-shaped valleys are typically formed by water erosion through soft rock and ask these two Principle questions:

Example

16. Which of the following is most likely to be a V-shaped valley?

    F. A valley formed by glaciers
    G. A river valley which is cut into very hard basalt
    H. A valley formed by wind erosion
    J. A river valley in a region of soft shale rocks

17. Which of the following discoveries would most weaken the theory of V-shaped valley formation given in the passage?

    A. Certain parts of many valleys formed by water that are U-shaped
    B. A group of V-shaped valleys almost certainly formed by wind erosion
    C. A group of U-shaped valleys formed by water erosion in hard rock
    D. A group of valleys on Mars that appear to be V-shaped but that are not near any running water

In question 16, the correct answer is choice J, since this is consistent with the passage as described. The correct answer in question 17 is choice B. Finding V-shaped valleys not formed by water erosion would tend to weaken the theory that they are formed this way. The other answers do not offer evidence about V-shaped valleys on Earth, and thus are irrelevant to a theory about them.

We'll be showing you strategies for each kind of Science question in the three Science Workouts.

WRITING

The Writing test is 30 minutes long and includes one essay. You'll be given a topic or issue on which you must take a position, supporting your point of view with examples and evidence.

You don't have to be a great creative writer to succeed on the ACT Writing test. Instead, you have to show that you can focus on an issue and argue your point of view in a coherent, direct way with concrete examples. Furthermore, the essay graders are not primarily concerned with your grammar and punctuation skills. In terms of writing, clarity is what they are looking for. You are being tested on your ability to communicate in writing.

> ☑ **PERFECT SCORE TIP**
> Organization is the key to success on the Writing section. Get used to reading a question and immediately developing three body paragraphs and a thesis. This will not only make for a better essay, but will also let you finish it in the allowed time.

One of the biggest challenges of the Writing test is the time frame. With only 30 minutes to read about the issue, plan your response, draft the essay, and proofread it, you have to work quickly and efficiently. Coming up with a plan and sticking to it are key to succeeding on the Writing test.

The Format

The Writing test consists of one prompt that lays out the issue and gives directions for your response. There are no choices of topic; you have to respond to the topic that's there. Don't worry too much about not knowing anything about the issue you have to write about. Test makers try to craft topics that will be relevant to high school students and about which they can be expected to have a point of view.

> ☑ **PERFECT SCORE TIP**
> ACT essay topics always deal with "high school situations," so don't worry about not understanding the topics. Read the entire prompt and feel free to use the background info it gives you.

The Directions

Here's what the Writing test directions will look like:

This is a test of your writing skills. You will have thirty (30) minutes to write an essay in English. Before you begin planning and writing your essay, read the writing prompt carefully to understand exactly what you are being asked to do. Your essay will be evaluated on the evidence it provides of your ability to express judgments by taking a position on the issue in the writing prompt; to maintain a focus on the topic throughout the essay; to develop a position by using logical reasoning and by supporting your ideas; to organize ideas in a logical way; and to use language clearly and effectively according to the conventions of standard written English.

You may use the unlined pages in this test booklet to plan your essay. These pages will not be scored. *You must write your essay in pencil on the lined pages in the answer folder.* Your writing on those lined pages will be scored. You may not need all the lined pages, but to ensure you have enough room to finish, do NOT skip lines. You may write corrections or additions neatly between the lines of your essay, but do NOT write in the margins of the lined pages. *Illegible essays cannot be scored, so you must write (or print) clearly.*

If you finish before time is called, you may review your work. Lay your pencil down immediately when time called.

DO NOT OPEN THIS BOOKLET UNTIL TOLD TO DO SO.

☑ **PERFECT SCORE TIP**
The questions will always ask you to take a position. Don't try to argue both opinions or feel tied to the one you agree with. For example, in my essay, I argued a stance I do not agree with personally, but I found it an easier topic for an organized and complete essay.

Writing Test Skills

The graders realize you're writing under time pressure, and they expect you to make some mistakes. **The content of your essay is not relevant; readers are not checking your facts, nor will they judge you on your opinions. They only want to see how well you can communicate a relevant, coherent point of view.**

The test makers identify the following as the skills tested on the Writing test:

- **Stating a clear perspective on an issue.** This means answering the question in the prompt.

- **Providing supporting evidence and logical reasoning.** This means offering relevant support for your opinion and building an argument based on concrete details and examples.

- **Maintaining focus and organizing ideas logically.** You've got to be organized, avoid digressions, and tie all your ideas together in a sensible way.

- **Writing clearly.** This is the only skill addressing your ability to write directly, and it's limited to clarity.

📶 **GO ONLINE**
Try writing an ACT-style essay using one of the sample prompts and model essays in the online companion.

The Writing test is not principally a test of your grammar and punctuation (which are tested in the English section)—colleges want to see your reasoning and communication skills. To learn more about how to plan and draft a high-scoring essay, review the Writing Workout.

▶ IF YOU LEARNED ONLY FIVE THINGS IN THIS CHAPTER...

1. The ACT English test includes 75 questions to be answered in 45 minutes. It tests your knowledge of grammar and usage. You'll be asked to fix errors in passages and sometimes to comment on the passage as a whole.

2. The ACT Math test consists of 60 questions to be answered in 60 minutes. Topics include pre-algebra, elementary and intermediate algebra, coordinate and plane geometry, and trigonometry. Questions are not given in order of difficulty.

3. The ACT Reading test includes 40 questions to be answered in 35 minutes. The questions refer to four passages: Prose Fiction, Social Sciences, Humanities, and Natural Sciences.

4. The ACT Science test is comprised of 40 questions to be answered in 35 minutes. There are seven passages with related questions that ask you to analyze and interpret experiments, figures, and scientists' viewpoints. There will be only one to three questions that call on you to use your existing science knowledge.

5. The ACT Writing test consists of one essay prompt that asks you to take a stand on an issue. You have 30 minutes to write a clear and persuasive essay, supported with evidence from your experience, reading, current events, or other sources.

CHAPTER 3

Taking Control: The Top Ten Strategies

Now that you've got some idea of the kind of challenges you face on the ACT, it's time to start developing strategies for managing them. In other words, you've got to start developing your ACT Mind-Set.

EXPERT TUTOR TIP
This chapter will help you to take control of the ACT. You should read this chapter even if you have less than two weeks to prep.

The ACT, as we've just seen, isn't a normal test, which requires you to rely almost exclusively on your memory. On a normal test, you'd see questions like this:

> The "golden spike," which joined the Union Pacific and Central Pacific Railroads, was driven in Ogden, Utah, in May 1869. Who was president of the United States at the time?

To answer this question, you have to resort to memory dredging. Either you know the answer is Ulysses S. Grant or else you don't. No matter how hard you think, you'll **never** be able to answer this question if you can't remember your history.

But the ACT doesn't test your long-term memory. The answer to every ACT question can be found on the test. Theoretically, if you read carefully and understand the words and concepts the test uses, you can get almost any ACT question right.

✓ PERFECT SCORE TIP
Never let hard questions scare you. You can control your own test taking experience, and this next chapter will show you how to manage these hard questions.

Notice the difference between the regular-test question on the previous page and the ACT-type question below:

Example

1. What is the product of n and m^2, where n is an odd number and m is an even number?

   A. An odd number
   B. A multiple of 4
   C. A noninteger
   D. An irrational number
   E. The square of an integer

Aside from the obvious distinction (this question has answer choices, while the other one does not), there's another difference: the ACT question mostly tests your ability to understand a situation rather than your ability to passively remember a fact. Nobody expects you to know off the top of your head what the product of an odd number and the square of an even number is. But the ACT test makers do expect you to be able to roll up your sleeves and figure it out (as we'll do below).

THE ACT MIND-SET

Most students take the ACT with the same mind-set that they use for normal tests. With their brains on "memory mode," students often panic and give up because they can't seem to remember enough. **But you don't need to remember a ton of picky little rules for the ACT. Don't give up on an ACT question just because your memory fails.**

> **EXPERT TUTOR TIP**
> The mind-set for the ACT is creative problem-solving mode. Don't rely too heavily on your memory. Instead, use your brain's creative thinking cells. The ACT Mind-Set isn't too different from the one you'd use to play chess, work a crossword, or do a sudoku puzzle.

On the ACT, if you understand what a question is really asking, you can almost always answer it. For instance, take the previous math problem. You might have been thrown by the way it was phrased. "How can I solve this problem?" you may have asked yourself. "It doesn't even have numbers in it!"

The key here, as in all ACT questions, is taking control. Take the question and wrestle it into a form you can understand. Ask yourself: What's really being asked here? What does it mean when they say something like "the product of n and m^2"?

Well, you might start by putting it into words. You might say something like this: "I've got to take one number times another. One of the numbers is odd, and the other is an even number squared. Then I've got to see what kind of number I get as an answer." Once you put the question in your own terms like this, it becomes much less intimidating—and much easier to get right. You'll realize that you don't have to do complex algebraic computations with variables. All you have to do is substitute numbers.

So do it! Try picking some easy-to-use numbers. Say that n is 3 (an odd number) and m is 2 (an even number). Then m^2 would be 4, because 2^2 is 4. And $n \times m$ would be 3×4, which is 12—a multiple of 4, but not odd, not a noninteger, not an irrational number, and not a perfect square. The only answer that can be right, then, is B.

See what we mean about figuring out the answer creatively rather than passively remembering it? True, there are some things you had to remember here—what even and odd numbers are, how variables and exponents work, and maybe what integers and irrational numbers are. But these are very basic concepts. Most of what you're expected to know on the ACT is like that: basic.

> **EXPERT TUTOR TIP**
> ACT questions are puzzles to solve. Don't think: "Can I remember?" Think: "Let me figure this thing out!"

Of course, basic doesn't always mean easy. Many ACT questions are built on basic concepts but are tough nonetheless. The previous problem, for instance, is difficult because it requires some thought to figure out what's being asked. This isn't only true in Math—it's the same for every part of the ACT.

The creative, take-control kind of thinking we call the ACT Mind-Set is something you want to bring to virtually every ACT question you encounter. As we'll see, being in the ACT Mind-Set means reshaping the test-taking experience so that you are in the driver's seat.

It means:

- Answering questions **if** you want to (by guessing on the impossible questions rather than wasting time on them).

- Answering questions **when** you want to (by skipping tough but doable questions and coming back to them after you've gotten all of the easy questions done).

- Answering questions **how** you want to (by using "unofficial" ways of getting correct answers fast).

That's really what the ACT Mind-Set boils down to: taking control, being creative, and solving specific problems to get points as quickly and easily as you can.

What follows are the top ten strategies you need to do just that.

 GO ONLINE
With two full-length Practice Tests and eight section-length Practice Tests online, you'll get plenty of opportunities to practice the strategies in this chapter.

TEN STRATEGIES FOR MASTERING THE ACT

1. Do Question Triage

In a hospital emergency room, the triage nurse is the person who evaluates each patient and decides which ones get attention first and which ones should be treated later. You should do the same thing on the ACT.

Practicing triage is one of the most important ways of controlling your test-taking experience. There are some questions on the ACT that most students could **never** answer correctly, no matter how much time or effort they spent on them.

Example

57. If $\sec^2 x = 4$, which of the following could be $\sin x$?

    A. 1.73205
    B. 3.14159
    C. $\sqrt{3}$
    D. $\dfrac{\sqrt{3}}{2}$
    E. Cannot be determined from the given information.

Clearly, even if you could manage to come up with an answer to this question, it would take some time (if you insist on doing so, refer to the following explanation). But would it be worth the time? We think not.

This question clearly illustrates our point: do question triage on the ACT. The first time you look at a question, make a quick decision about how hard and time-consuming it looks. Then decide whether to answer it now or skip it and do it later.

• If the question looks comprehensible and reasonably doable, do it right away.

- If the question looks tough and time-consuming, but ultimately doable, skip it, circle the question number in your test booklet, and come back to it later.

- If the question looks impossible, forget about it. Guess and move on, **never** to return.

This triage method will ensure you spend the time needed to do all the easy questions before getting bogged down with a tough problem. Remember, every question on a subject test is worth the same number of points. It's pointless to spend three minutes struggling on a hard question that you might not even get right when you could move on to two or more easier questions that you could answer correctly instead!

> **EXPERT TUTOR TIP**
> The key to question triage is to evaluate questions quickly. If you linger over these decisions, you will lose valuable time on test day.

Answering easier questions first has another benefit: it gives you confidence to answer harder ones later. Doing problems in the order you choose rather than in the order imposed by the test makers gives you control over the test. Most students don't have time to do all of the problems, so you've got to make sure you do all of the ones you can easily score on!

DO YOU KNOW YOUR TRIG?

Okay, since you're reading this, it's obvious that you want to know the answer to the trig question we just looked at. The answer is choice D. Here's how we got it:

$\sec^2 x = 4$	given
$\sec x = 2 \text{ or } -2$	square root both sides
$\cos x = \dfrac{1}{2} \text{ or } -\dfrac{1}{2}$	$\cos x = \dfrac{1}{\sec x}$
$\cos^2 x = \dfrac{1}{4}$	square both sides
$\sin^2 x = 1 - \dfrac{1}{4}$	$\sin^2 x + \cos^2 x = 1$
$\sin^2 x = \dfrac{3}{4}$	$\sin^2 x = 1 - \cos^2 x$
$\sin x = \sqrt{\dfrac{3}{4}} \text{ or } -\sqrt{\dfrac{3}{4}}$	square root both sides
$\sin x = \dfrac{\sqrt{3}}{2} \text{ or } -\dfrac{\sqrt{3}}{2}$	$\sqrt{4} = 2$

So answer choice D is correct. But if you got it right, don't congratulate yourself quite yet. How long did it take you to get it right? So long that you could have gotten the answers to two easy questions in the same amount of time?

> **EXPERT TUTOR TIP**
> Let's say you took three minutes to get a tough question right. That might feel good, but you would actually be better off if you had skipped the tough question and, in the same amount of time, answered two or three easier questions correctly.

DEVELOP A PLAN OF ATTACK

For the English, Reading, and Science sections, the best plan of attack is to do each passage as a block. Make a longish first pass through the questions (call it the "triage pass"), doing the easy ones, guessing on the impossible ones, and skipping any that look like they might cause trouble. Then make a second pass (call it the "cleanup pass"), and do those questions you think you can solve with some elbow grease.

> **PERFECT SCORE TIP**
> In Reading and Science, try to finish each passage before moving on, as you will waste time rereading the passage if you skip between readings.

For Math, you use the same two-pass strategy, except that you move through the whole subject test twice. Work through the doable questions first. Most, but not all, of these will probably be toward the beginning. Then come back and attack the questions that look possible but tough or time-consuming.

No matter what subject test you're working on, **you should take pains to grid your answers in the right place.** It's easy to misgrid when you're skipping around, so be careful. And of course: *Make sure you have an answer gridded for every question by the time the subject test is over!*

2. Put the Material into a Form You Can Understand and Use

ACT questions are rarely presented in the simplest, most helpful way. In fact, your main job for many questions is to figure out what the question means so you can solve it.

Since the material is presented in such an intimidating way, one of your best strategies for taking control is to recast (reword) the material into a form you can handle better. This is what we did in the math problem about "the product of n and m^2." We took the question and reworded it in a way we could understand.

MARK UP YOUR TEST BOOKLET

This strategy should be employed on all four subject tests. For example, in Reading, many students find the passages overwhelming: 85 to 90 lines of dense verbiage for each one! The secret is to put the passages into a form you can understand and use. Circle or underline the main idea, for one thing. Make yourself a road map of the passage, labeling each paragraph so you understand how the ideas all fit together. That way, you'll also know—later, when you're doing the questions—where in the passage to find certain types of information you need.

> **EXPERT TUTOR TIP**
> Write all over your test booklet. Crossing out wrong answers eliminates confusion and helps you to see clearly which answer is correct. Underlining key points when reading passages helps you to determine the main idea.

REWORD THE QUESTIONS

You'll find that you also need to do some recasting of the *questions*. For instance, take this question from a Science passage:

Example

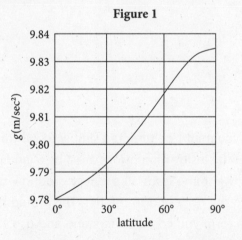

Figure 1

15. According to Figure 1, at approximately what latitude would calculations using an estimated value at sea level of $g = 9.80$ m/sec² produce the least error?

   A.   0°

   B.   20°

   C.   40°

   D.   80°

At what latitude would the calculations using a value of $g = 9.80$ m/sec² produce the least error? Yikes! What does that mean?

Take a deep breath. Ask yourself: where would an estimate for g of 9.80 m/sec² produce the least error? In a latitude where 9.80 m/sec² is the real value of g. If you find that latitude, then using 9.80 m/sec² as an estimate there would produce no error at all!

So, in other words, what this question is asking is: at what latitude does $g = 9.80$ m/sec²? Now that's a form of the question you can understand. In that form, you can answer it easily: choice C, which you can get just by reading the chart.

DRAW DIAGRAMS

Sometimes putting the material into usable form involves drawing with your pencil. For instance, take a look at the following math problem.

Example

2. Jason bought a painting with a frame 1 inch wide. If the dimensions of the outside of the frame are 5 inches by 7 inches, which of the following could be the length of one of the sides of the painting inside the frame?

    F. 3 inches

    G. 4 inches

    H. $5\frac{1}{2}$ inches

    J. $6\frac{1}{2}$ inches

    K. 7 inches

Just looking at the question the first time, you might be tempted simply to subtract 1 from the outside dimensions and think that the inside dimensions are 4 by 6 (and pick choice G). Why isn't this correct? Because the frame goes all the way around—both above and below the painting, and both to the right and to the left. This would have been clear if you had put the problem in a form you could understand and use.

For instance, you might have visualized the situation by actually sketching out the painting frame:

When you draw the picture frame like this, you realize that if the outside dimensions are 5 by 7, the inside dimensions must be 3 by 5. Thus, the correct answer is choice F.

So remember: on the ACT, you've got to put everything into a form that you can understand and use.

3. Ignore Irrelevant Issues

It's easy to waste time on ACT questions by considering irrelevant issues. Just because an issue looks interesting, or you're worried about something, doesn't make it important.

Example

...China was certainly one of the cradles of civilization. <u>It's obvious that, China has a long history.</u> As is the case with
   14
other ancient cultures, the early history of China is lost in mythology...

14. F. NO CHANGE
    G. It's obvious that China has a long history.
    H. Obviously; China has a long history.
    J. OMIT the underlined portion.

In this question, the test makers are counting on you to waste time worrying about punctuation. Does that comma belong? Can you use a semicolon here? These issues might be worrisome, but there's a bigger issue here—namely, does the sentence belong in the passage at all? No, it doesn't. If China has an ancient culture and was a cradle of civilization, it must have a long history, so the sentence really is obvious. Redundancy is the relevant issue here, not punctuation. Choice J is correct.

Remember, you've got limited time, so don't get caught up in issues that won't get you a point.

> ✔ **PERFECT SCORE TIP**
> In English, identify the tested issue. Don't get distracted by other mistakes.

4. Check Back

Remember, the ACT is not a test of your memory, so don't make it one. All of the information you need is in the test itself. Don't be afraid to refer to it. Much of the information is too complex to accurately remember anyway.

In Reading and Science, always refer to the place in the passage where the answer to a question can be found. The question stem will often contain a line reference or a reference to a specific table, graph, or experiment to help you out. Your chosen answer should match the passage—not in exact vocabulary or units of measurement, perhaps, but in meaning.

> **EXPERT TUTOR TIP**
> If there's no line reference in a Reading question, you'll need to use your notes to help you know where to look for help with the answer.

Example

Isaac Newton was born in 1642 in the hamlet of Woolsthorpe in Lincolnshire, England. But he is more famous as a man of Cambridge, where he studied and taught…

7. Which of the following does the author imply is a fact about Newton's birth?

A. It occurred in Lincoln, a small hamlet in England.

B. It took place in a part of England known for raising sheep.

C. It did not occur in a large metropolitan setting.

D. It caused Newton to seek his education at Cambridge.

You might expect the right answer to be that Newton was born in a hamlet, or in Woolsthorpe, or in Lincolnshire. But none of those are offered as choices. Choice A is tempting but wrong. Newton was born in Lincolnshire, *not* Lincoln. Choice B is actually true, but it's wrong here. As its name suggests, Woolsthorpe was once known for its wool—which comes from sheep, but the question asks for something implied in the passage.

The correct answer here is choice C because a hamlet is a small village. That's not a large metropolitan setting.

> **PERFECT SCORE TIP**
> Even if you have the best memory in the world, don't waste points by trusting your memory of the passage. Always refer to where each answer is found in the passage.

Checking back is especially important in Reading and Science because the passages leave many people feeling adrift in a sea of details. Often, the wrong answers will be misplaced details taken from different parts of the passage. They are things that don't answer the question properly but that might sound good to you if you aren't careful. By checking back in the passage, you can avoid choosing such tempting wrong choices.

There's another important lesson here: **don't pick a choice just because it contains key words you remember from the passage.** Many wrong choices, like D in the previous question, are distortions—they use the right words but say the wrong things. Look for answer choices that contain the same ideas you find in the passage.

> **EXPERT TUTOR TIP**
> Researching Reading questions is important because the correct answer directly relates to the passage. Incorrect answers, **even if true**, don't relate well to either the passage OR the question.

One of the best ways to avoid choosing misplaced details and distortions is to refer to the passage.

5. Answer the Right Question

This strategy is a natural extension of the last. As we said, **the ACT test makers often include among the wrong choices for a question the correct answer to a different question.** Under time pressure, it's easy to fall for one of these red herrings, thinking that you know what's being asked for when really you don't.

> **PERFECT SCORE TIP**
> If you do not understand a question, take time and read it again. The extra five seconds is better than trying to answer a question that was not asked and getting an incorrect answer.

Example

7. What is the value of $3x$ if $9x = 5y + 2$ and $y + 4 = 2y - 10$?

   A. 5
   B. 8
   C. 14
   D. 24
   E. 72

To solve this problem, we need to find y first, even though the question asks about x (because x here is given only in terms of y). You could solve the second equation like this:

$$y + 4 = 2y - 10 \qquad \text{given}$$
$$4 = y - 10 \qquad \text{by subtracting } y \text{ from both sides}$$
$$14 = y \qquad \text{by adding 10 to both sides}$$

But choice C, 14, isn't the right answer here because the question doesn't ask for the value of y—it asks about x. We can use the value of y to find x, however, by plugging the calculated value of y into the first equation:

$$9x = 5y + 2 \qquad \text{given}$$
$$9x = 5(14) + 2 \qquad \text{because } y = 14$$
$$9x = 70 + 2$$
$$9x = 72$$

But E, 72, isn't the answer either because the question doesn't ask for $9x$. It doesn't ask for x either, so if you picked B, 8, you'd be wrong as well. Remember to refer to the question! The question asks for $3x$. So we need to divide $9x$ by 3:

$$9x = 72 \qquad \text{from above}$$
$$3x = 24 \qquad \text{dividing by 3}$$

Thus, the answer is D.

Always check the question again before choosing your answer. Doing all the right work but then getting the wrong answer can be seriously depressing. So make sure you're answering the right question.

> ✓ **PERFECT SCORE TIP**
> Don't let reconfigurations of variables confuse you. For example, $x^2 + x = x(x + 1)$. If this seems too confusing for you, plug in real numbers for the variables.

6. Look for the Hidden Answer

On many ACT questions, the right answer is hidden in one way or another. An answer can be hidden by being written in an unexpected way. For example, you might work out a problem and get .5 as your answer, but then find that .5 isn't among the answer choices. Then you notice that one choice reads $\frac{1}{2}$. You've found the hidden answer! It pays to think flexibly about numbers.

There's another way the ACT can hide answers. **Many ACT questions have more than one possible right solution, though only one correct answer choice is given. The ACT will hide that answer by offering one of the less obvious possible answers to a question.**

Example

2. If $3x^2 + 5 = 17$, which of the following could be the value of x?

    A. −3
    B. −2
    C.   0
    D.   1
    E.   4

You quickly solve this very straightforward problem like so:

$$3x^2 + 5 = 17 \qquad \text{given}$$
$$3x^2 = 12 \qquad \text{by subtracting 5}$$
$$x^2 = 4 \qquad \text{dividing by 3}$$
$$x = 2 \qquad \text{taking square root of both sides}$$

Having gotten an answer, you confidently look for it among the choices. But 2 isn't a choice. The explanation? This question has two possible solutions, not just one. The square root of 4 can be either 2 or −2. Thus, B is the answer.

Keep in mind that though there's only one right answer choice for each question, that right answer may not be the one that occurs to you first. A common mistake is to pick an answer that seems sort of like the answer you're looking for, even when you know it's wrong. Don't settle for second best. If you don't find your answer, don't assume that you're wrong. Try to think of another right way to answer the question.

7. Guess Intelligently

An unanswered question is always wrong, but even a wild guess may be right. On the ACT, a guess can't hurt you, but it can help. In fact, smart guessing can make a big difference in your score. **Always** guess on every ACT question you can't answer. Never leave a question blank.

You'll be doing two different kinds of guessing during your two sweeps through any subject test:

1. Blind guessing (which you do mostly on questions you deem too hard or time-consuming even to try).
2. Strategic guessing (which you do mostly on questions that you do some work on but can't make headway with).

When you guess blindly, you just choose any letter you feel like choosing (many students like to choose B for Bart; few choose H for Homer). When you guess in a strategic way, on the other hand, you've usually done enough work on a question to eliminate at least one or two choices. If you can eliminate any choices, you'll up the odds of guessing correctly.

> **EXPERT TUTOR TIP**
> If you guess blindly, you have one chance in four (or one in five on the Math) of getting the question right. If you can eliminate one or two choices as definitely wrong, you can improve those odds.

Here are some fun facts about guessing: If you were to work on only half of the questions on the ACT but get them all right, then guess blindly on the other half of the questions, you would probably earn a composite ACT score of around 23 (assuming you had a statistically reasonable success rate on your guesses). A 23 would put you in roughly the top quarter of all those who take the ACT. It's a good score. And all you had to do was answer half the questions correctly.

On the other hand, if you were to hurry and finish all the questions but get only half of them right, you'd probably earn only a 19, which is below average.

How? Why are you better off answering half and getting them all right instead of answering all and getting only half right?

Here's the trick. The student who answers half the questions right and skips the others can still take guesses on the unanswered questions—and odds are this student will have enough correct guesses to move up four points, from a 19 to a 23. But the student who answers all the questions and gets half wrong doesn't have the luxury of taking guesses.

In short: **guess if you can't figure out an answer for any question!**

> **EXPERT TUTOR TIP**
> Get the points you deserve on the questions you can answer. But don't worry about the ones you have to guess on. Odds are good that you'll guess some correctly. And those correct guesses will increase your score just as much as if you'd figured out the answers.

8. Be Careful with the Answer Grid

Your ACT score is based on the answers you select on your answer grid. Even if you work out every question correctly, you'll get a low score if you misgrid your answers. So be careful! Don't disdain the process of filling in those little "bubbles" on the grid. Sure, it's mindless, but under time pressure, it's easy to lose control and make mistakes.

It's important to **develop a disciplined strategy for filling in the answer grid.** We find that it's smart to grid the answers in groups rather than one question at a time. What you should do is this: as you figure out each question in the test booklet, circle the answer choice you come up with. Then, transfer those answers to the answer grid in groups of five or more (until you get close to the end of the section, when you should start gridding answers one by one).

> **PERFECT SCORE TIP**
> I found it helpful to grid after each Reading passage and after every two pages of Math. Gridding too often can be distracting to your concentration, but there is nothing worse than running out of time to grid your answers.

Gridding in groups like this cuts down on errors because you can focus on this one task and do it right. It also saves time you'd otherwise spend moving papers around, finding your place, and redirecting your mind. Answering ACT questions takes deep, hard thinking. Filling out answer grids is easy, but you have to be careful, especially if you do a lot of skipping around. Shifting between hard thinking and careful book-keeping takes time and effort.

In English, Reading, and Science, the test is divided naturally into groups of questions— the passages. It makes the most sense to circle your answers in your test booklet as you work them out. Then, when you're finished with each passage and its questions, grid the answers as a group.

In Math, the strategy has to be different because the Math test isn't broken up into natural groups. Mark your answers in the test booklet, and then grid them when you reach the end of each page or two. Since there are usually about five math questions per page, you'll probably be gridding five or ten math answers at a time.

No matter what subject test you're working on, though, if you're near the end of a subject test, start gridding your answers one at a time. You don't want to be caught with ungridded answers when time is called.

During the test, the proctor should warn you when you have about five minutes left on each subject test. But don't depend on proctors! **Rely on your own watch.** When there are five minutes left on a subject test, start gridding your answers one by one. With a minute or two left, start filling in everything you've left blank. Remember: even one question left blank could cut your score.

> ✔ **PERFECT SCORE TIP**
> When gridding, don't be a hero and try to remember eight answers in your head and transfer them to your grid. Work deliberately, but one place you cannot afford to lose points is in gridding your answers.

9. Use the Letters of the Choices to Stay on Track

One oddity about the ACT is that even-numbered questions have F, G, H, J (and, in Math, K) as answer choices, rather than A, B, C, D (and, again, E in Math). This might be confusing at first, but you can make it work for you. **A common mistake with the answer grid is to accidentally enter an answer one row up or down. On the ACT, that won't happen if you pay attention to the letter in the answer.** If you're looking for an A and you see only F, G, H, J, and K, you'll know you're in the wrong row on the answer grid.

Another advantage of having answers F through K for even-numbered questions is that it makes you less nervous about patterns in the answers. It's common to start worrying if you've picked the same letter twice or three times in a row. Since the questions have different letters, this can't happen on the ACT. Of course, you could pick the first choice (A or F) for several questions in a row. This shouldn't worry you. It's common for the answers in the same position to be correct three times in a row, and even four times in a row isn't unheard of.

> ✔ **PERFECT SCORE TIP**
> Especially if you have time problems, realize that gridding does take time. Use an actual answer grid when you take a practice test to get a feel for whether you will have trouble finishing the actual test.

10. Keep Track of Time

During each subject test, you really have to pace yourself. On average, English, Reading, and Science questions should take about 30 seconds each. Math questions should average less than one minute each. Remember to take into account the fact that you'll probably be taking two passes through the questions.

> **EXPERT TUTOR TIP**
> Spend your test time wisely! English, Reading passages: about nine minutes each (including questions); Science passages: about five minutes each (including questions); Math questions: about 30–60 seconds each, depending on the difficulty.

Set your watch to 12:00 at the beginning of each subject test so it will be easy to check your time. Again, don't rely on proctors, even if they promise that they will dutifully call out the time every 15 minutes. Proctors get distracted once in a while.

More basic questions should take less time, and harder ones will probably take more. In Math, for instance, you need to go much faster than one per minute during your first sweep. But at the end, you may spend two or three minutes on each of the harder problems you work out.

TAKE CONTROL

You are the master of the test-taking experience. A common thread in all ten strategies is: take control. That's Kaplan's ACT Mind-Set. Do the questions in the order you want and in the way you want. Don't get bogged down or agonize. Remember, you don't earn points for suffering, but you do earn points for moving on to the next question and getting it right.

The ACT Is NOT School

You have spent at least 11 years in school at this point. There, you learned some techniques that won't help you on the ACT. (Want two good examples? "Don't guess on a test" and "If you show your work on math problems, you'll get partial credit.") Many of these school-driven methods don't work well on the ACT. In fact, they work *against* you.

On ACT test day, don't fall into the trap of familiar school habits. Test day is an exciting and stressful event. We strongly suggest that you practice using the ten strategies in this chapter so that you're rehearsed and confident for test day.

Just reading and understanding these strategies before the test doesn't mean you'll remember to do them effectively on test day. The ACT Mind-Set will work only if you use it, so practice!

As you practice, time yourself. Buy or borrow a digital watch, and get used to working with it so it doesn't beep at the wrong moment. Your cell phone will be turned off during the test, so you won't be able to use that as a timekeeper.

Practicing the various sections of the test at home and taking at least one entire Practice Test in one sitting are the best ways to make sure you're comfortable with the test and ready to get your highest scores on test day.

> **GO ONLINE**
> Before going on to the subject-specific workouts, take the online diagnostic quiz if you haven't already. You'll learn where to focus your study time.

BASIC STRATEGY REFERENCE SHEET
The Four Keys to ACT Success

1. LEARN THE TEST

- Learn the directions before test day.
- Become familiar with all the subject tests.
- Get a sense of the range of difficulty of the questions.

2. LEARN THE KAPLAN METHODS AND STRATEGIES

- Develop a plan of attack for each subject test.
- Develop a guessing strategy that works for you.
- Find "unofficial" ways of finding answers fast.

3. LEARN THE MATERIAL TESTED

- Bone up on weak areas.
- Find out what is and isn't part of the ACT knowledge base.
- Use the ACT Resources section to review important Math and English concepts.

4. PRACTICE, PRACTICE, PRACTICE

The Top Ten Strategies

1. Do question triage.

2. Put the material into a form you can understand and use.

3. Ignore irrelevant issues.

4. Check back.

5. Answer the right question.

6. Look for the hidden answer.

7. Guess intelligently.

8. Be careful with the answer grid.

9. Use the letters of the choices to stay on track.

10. Keep track of time.

▶ IF YOU LEARNED ONLY TWO THINGS IN THIS CHAPTER...

1. Remember the ACT Mind-Set: Take control of your test experience.

2. Know the four keys to ACT success and the top ten strategies.

Skill-Building Workouts

CHAPTER 4

English Workout 1: When in Doubt, Take It Out

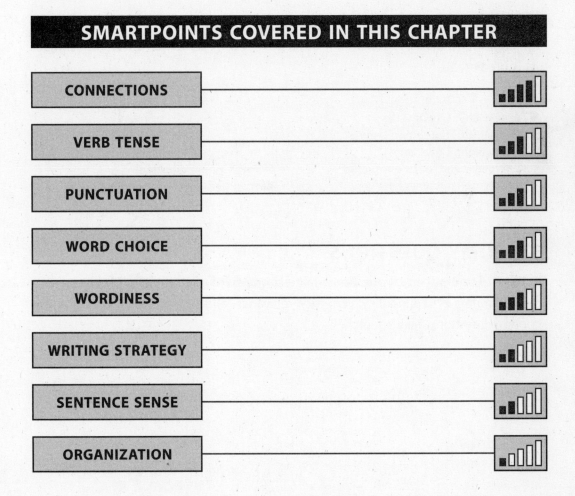

SMARTPOINTS COVERED IN THIS CHAPTER

| CONNECTIONS |
| VERB TENSE |
| PUNCTUATION |
| WORD CHOICE |
| WORDINESS |
| WRITING STRATEGY |
| SENTENCE SENSE |
| ORGANIZATION |

Think back to the last paper you had to write. Maybe your teacher assigned something like ten pages. You wrote and you wrote and ended up with six pages. It was the night before the paper had to be turned in; you were out of research and ideas. You knew what to do: pad it.

You're not alone. Almost all of us have padded papers at one time or another. The recipe for padding, in fact, is practically universal: You repeat yourself a few times. You trade short phrases for long-winded verbiage. You add a few offbeat ideas that don't really belong. Presto! Your six-page paper is transformed into a ten-page paper.

The ACT test makers know that most students pad. In fact, many of the English questions on the ACT are testing for the very same bad writing habits—long-windedness, repetitiousness, irrelevance—that padders tend to cultivate.

Once you know what ACT English is testing, you can easily avoid making these common English mistakes. More than any other part of the exam, the ACT English subject test is predictable.

 EXPERT TUTOR TIP
The ACT English test includes:
- 10 punctuation questions
- 12 grammar and usage questions
- 18 sentence structure questions
- 12 strategy questions
- 11 organization questions
- 12 style questions

ECONOMY QUESTIONS

On the ACT, more than 20 questions—almost one-third of all the English items—test your awareness of redundancy, verbosity, relevance, and similar issues. We call these Economy questions. Take a look.

Example

ACT ENGLISH: SHORTER IS OFTEN BETTER!

On recent ACTs, the shortest answer has been <u>correct,</u>
₁
<u>and absolutely right,</u> for about half of all English
₁

questions. Because this is <u>true,</u> a student who knows no
₂

English at all could earn—<u>and justly so—</u>an English
₃
subject score of about 15. Such a student could

compare the choices carefully and choose the <u>single</u>
₄
<u>shortest one</u> every time. Where the answers are the
₄
same length, the student could pick at random. On

recently published ACTs, guessing in this way would have

yielded between 35 and 38 correct answers out of 75

questions. Of course, you're going to <u>be doing</u> much
₅

better than that. You actually <u>are capable of speaking</u>
₆
<u>the English language.</u> You may not know every little
₆
rule of English usage, but you certainly know some-

thing. Obviously, getting the question right because

1. A. NO CHANGE
   B. correct
   C. right, that is, correct,
   D. correct, absolutely, and right,

2. F. NO CHANGE
   G. truthfully factual
   H. factually correct
   J. factual—and true too—

3. A. NO CHANGE
   B. —quite justly, in fact—
   C. and justify
   D. OMIT the underlined portion.

4. F. NO CHANGE
   G. singularly shortest one
   H. uniquely short item
   J. shortest one

5. A. NO CHANGE
   B. do
   C. achieve
   D. be achieving

6. F. NO CHANGE
   G. possess the capability of
      speaking English.
   H. possess the capability of
      speaking in the land called
      England.
   J. speak English.

you know the <u>right answer</u> is better than getting it
$\qquad$ 7

right because you guessed well.

     Still, you should always remember that the

ACT test makers <u>like</u> the shortest answers. Why?
$\qquad$ 8

Why should the ACT make life so easy for you?

<u>Why can't history or science classes in high school</u>
$\qquad$ 9

<u>be so easy?</u> Usually, the best way to write something
$\qquad$ 9

really is the shortest way to write it. The ACT can't

help that, <u>any more than you can help the fact that</u>
$\qquad$ 10

<u>you must take the ACT to get into college.</u> Good
$\qquad$ 10

7. A. NO CHANGE
   B. best choice to select
   C. most correct answer of the choices given
   D. answer considered as correct

8. F. NO CHANGE
   G. have a habit of liking
   H. habitually tend to like
   J. are in the habit of liking

9. A. NO CHANGE
   B. Why isn't history or science?
   C. History and science aren't so easy, either!
   D. OMIT the underlined portion.

10. F. NO CHANGE
    G. just as you are helpless to avoid the requirement of taking the ACT
    H. whether or not they'd want to
    J. OMIT the underlined portion and end the sentence with a period after *that*.

writing is concise and <u>clear</u>. There are many rules of
11
English, but many of them grow from one dominant

principle: use only the words you need to say what

you mean. 12

11. A. NO CHANGE

    B. clearly better

    C. translucent, like clear water

    D. clear. Thus it is short and to the point.

12. Suppose the author considers adding this final sentence: "Thus, if you can't say something nice, don't say anything at all." Would this be an effective conclusion for the paragraph?

    F. Yes, because this concept is needed to explain the meaning of the previous sentence.

    G. Yes, because it adds an uplifting moral tone to an otherwise depressing, amoral text.

    H. Yes, because this thought is relevant to the next paragraph.

    J. No, because the paragraph is not concerned with being nice.

Answers

1.	B	7.	A
2.	F	8.	F
3.	D	9.	D
4.	J	10.	J
5.	B	11.	A
6.	J	12.	J

The shortest answer happens to be correct in all 12 of the questions above. Note that OMIT, where it is an option, is the shortest answer since taking the material out leaves a shorter text than leaving anything in. In question 12, choice J is the shortest answer since it leaves the proposed final sentence off entirely.

Redundancy

In questions 1–4, the wrong (long) answers are redundant—they make the passage say the same thing twice. **The ACT is very strict about redundancy: Never let the text in a sentence repeat itself.**

Verbosity

In questions 5–8, the wrong (long) answers are verbose, which means overly wordy. They may have more words, but they are no clearer than the short answers and don't add meaning. **This is another rule the ACT is very strict about: the best way to write something is the shortest way, as long as it doesn't violate any rules of writing mechanics (like grammar or punctuation) or contain language that's either too formal or informal to match the style of the passage.**

> **EXPERT TUTOR TIP**
> On recent ACTs, the shortest answer has been correct on about one-half of all English questions.

Irrelevance

Questions 9–12 test relevance. The wrong (long) answers introduce irrelevant concepts. The paragraph is about ACT English questions and how to answer them—it's not about history or science classes, the necessity of taking the ACT, or that lovely translucence of clear water. **Omit the ideas that are not directly and logically tied in with the purpose of the paragraph or passage.**

With Economy questions, the shortest answer is correct with great frequency. If you suspect Economy is the tested issue, consider these questions:

- Is the underlined part redundant? Check the nonunderlined part of the passage to see if it contains words that repeat the meaning of the underlined part.
- Is the underlined part verbose? See if there is an answer choice that is shorter and still expresses the same meaning.
- Is the underlined part relevant? Ask yourself if it fits with the topic of the paragraph and the purpose of the passage as a whole.

Because the ACT values conciseness, remember: **when in doubt, take it out.**

> ✔ **PERFECT SCORE TIP**
> In English, every single word and sentence should have a unique purpose. If the underlined portion is not absolutely necessary, it is probably redundant or irrelevant.

Keep It Short—on All English Questions

Questions on which the lengths of the answers vary greatly and questions that contain the answer choice OMIT are usually Economy questions. For these questions, you should be especially inclined to choose the shortest choice. For the other questions, the shortest answer is not nearly as often correct.

As we'll see in later workouts, the other English questions mostly test your ability to spot nonsense, bad grammar, and bad punctuation. Even in these cases, the rule "when in doubt, take it out" still holds. Even for questions testing issues other than writing economy, some answer choices are wrong simply because they're too long.

Because the issue of writing economy is so important to English questions of all kinds, we've made it the linchpin for our recommended approach to the English subject test. **When approaching English questions, the very first question you should ask yourself is: "Does this stuff belong here? Can the passage or sentence work without it?"**

> **AVAILABLE ONLINE**
> The online companion includes two section-length ACT English Practice Tests. Hone your skills with these before tackling a full-length Practice Test.

Reading the Passage as You Go

Read the passage as far as you find necessary to answer each question, and then answer each one in turn. *Don't skip over sentences without questions in them*—you'll need to understand the whole passage when you answer the questions at the end.

> ☑️ **PERFECT SCORE TIP**
> Get into a "grammar mind-set." For the weeks before I took the ACT, I got used to noticing all the grammar mistakes in my life. While sometimes annoying to my family, immediately noticing agreement and other mistakes really helped me notice these mistakes on test day.

THE KAPLAN METHOD FOR ACT ENGLISH

Here's the Kaplan Method for ACT English questions.

STEP 1: Read until you have enough information to identify the issue.

Although the instructions on the ACT will tell you to read the whole passage and then answer the questions about it, our advice is to answer each question as soon as you've read far enough in the passage to do so. For some questions, you'll only need to read a sentence to find the issue. What's an "issue," you ask? Think of the issue as the reason the test makers included the question—what are you being tested on? Issues are not necessarily errors, because some sentences have no errors, and some English questions test your understanding of the passage as a whole.

STEP 2: Eliminate answer choices that do not address the issue.

Now that you've identified the issue that the question is testing, read through the answers to see which ones do not address the issue. Once these are eliminated, you may have one or two options left. Then move on to Step 3.

STEP 3: Plug in the remaining answer choices to select the most correct, concise, and relevant choice.

Finally, try out the remaining answer choices by "plugging" them into the sentence or paragraph and seeing how they work. This may mean reading the questions without the underlined phrase to see if OMIT is the best choice. The best choice will be grammatically correct, concise, and will make sense with the rest of the passage. This applies to any Big Picture questions, too.

Read the passage as far as you find necessary to answer each question, and then answer each one in turn. *Don't skip over sentences without questions in them*—you'll need to understand the whole passage when you answer the questions at the end.

Practice Being Economical

Now try the next practice passage, keeping in mind the approach you just learned.

THE OLDEST NFL TEAM

The Phoenix Cardinals are the oldest, most long-established, longest-playing football club in the National Football League (NFL). They began as the Racine Avenue Cardinals on Chicago's South Side sometime in the 1870s or 1880s, during the nineteenth century.

    At that time, the Cardinals were an amateur team that did not play for money. There was nothing in the world which so much as resembled pro football in those days. The Racine Avenue Cardinals played amateur ball all through the late 1800s and the game they played was football, no doubt about it.

1. A. NO CHANGE
    B. oldest
    C. most long-established
    D. longest-playing

2. F. NO CHANGE
    G. 1880s
    H. the nineteenth century
    J. during the 1880s

3. A. NO CHANGE
    B. that played for the pure joy of the sport.
    C. that played on a nonprofessional level.
    D. OMIT the underlined portion and end the sentence with a period.

4. F. NO CHANGE
    G. nothing anything like
    H. no such thing as
    J. not even a dream of

5. A. NO CHANGE
    B. no doubt about it.
    C. to be assured it was football.
    D. OMIT the underlined portion and end the sentence with a period.

None of the other clubs in the NFL was formed before the league itself was established in 1919. When the NFL was first established, the Cardinals remained aloof and thumbed their noses at it.
<u>6</u>
Professional football had a bad reputation, and

the Cardinals were greatly prideful of their
<u>7</u>
record as amateurs. However, in 1921, the Cardinals decided to join the NFL. They were required to play a "game to the death" with the Chicago Tigers (the Detroit Tigers are a baseball
<u>8</u>
team). Whichever team won would be allowed
<u>8</u>

to stay in Chicago; the other team would have
<u>9</u>
to move. The Cardinals won. The Tigers moved
<u>9</u>
away and soon went bankrupt. The Cardinals are thus the only NFL team that won their franchise on the football field.

Ironically, the team that fought to stay in Chicago eventually moved away. The Cardinals were rarely as successfully able to win games
<u>10</u>
or make money as the Chicago Bears, their
<u>10</u>

6. F. NO CHANGE
   G. aloof.
   H. aloof and tried to ignore it.
   J. off in their own corner.

7. A. NO CHANGE
   B. full of great pride
   C. proud
   D. gratefully proud

8. F. NO CHANGE
   G. (not to be confused with the Detroit Tigers, a baseball team).
   H. (not the more famous modern-day Detroit Tigers baseball team).
   J. OMIT the underlined portion and end the sentence with a period.

9. A. NO CHANGE
   B. be forced to move along
   C. be legally obliged, by injunction, to relocate their franchise
   D. be obligated to be moving out

10. F. NO CHANGE
    G. successful at winning
    H. winning or profitable, a team,
    J. successful

crosstown rivals. Fans gradually deserted the

Cardinals, so the team moved—to St. Louis in

1958 and to Phoenix in 1986, seeking a more

profitable market. Maybe Phoenix <u>is the place</u>
                                        11

<u>in which</u> the Cardinals are destined to stay.
  11

Some people say that the name "Cardinal" was

a nineteenth-century name for a mythical bird

that arose from its own ashes <u>in the fireplace,</u>
                                     12

and that the Cardinals date back to have begun

on Racine Avenue <u>(or maybe not).</u> Chicago was
                       13

proud to rise from its ashes like the mythical

Cardinal. The <u>name that is more common</u> for
                     14

11. A. NO CHANGE
    B. is the place at which
    C. is where
    D. OMIT the underlined portion.

12. F. NO CHANGE
    G. that had consumed it
    H. created by the fire that had
       consumed it
    J. OMIT the underlined portion.

13. A. NO CHANGE
    B. according to ironic legend.
    C. resulting from violations of the
       fire code and a cow in a barn.
    D. OMIT the underlined portion and
       end the sentence with a period.

14. F. NO CHANGE
    G. common name
    H. name that is famous
    J. common way of speaking

that mythical firebird is the Phoenix. ▢15

15. Suppose the author wishes to add a new paragraph at the end of the existing passage quickly summarizing the history of Canadian football. Would this be appropriate, in light of the content and style of the rest of the passage?

A. Yes, because it is only fair to mention Canadian football at least once in the passage.

B. Yes, because the Phoenix Cardinals now play Canadian football.

C. No, because the passage does not focus on sports history.

D. No, because the passage has nothing to do with Canadian football.

Answers

1.	B	9.	A
2.	G	10.	J
3.	D	11.	C
4.	H	12.	J
5.	D	13.	D
6.	G	14.	G
7.	C	15.	D
8.	J		

Did you notice anything about all of these questions? For the first 14, you only needed to read one sentence to answer each question. Imagine how long it would have taken to read the whole passage once and then go back and analyze each sentence. By using Step 1 of the Kaplan Method, you could take it one sentence at a time. Did you notice anything else? The correct answer usually made the sentence shorter and more concise. OMIT always makes the answer shorter but isn't always correct. In 11, if you omit the phrase "is the place in which," the sentence doesn't make any sense, meaning that you'd correct it in Step 3 of the three-step approach. (Note: This passage is not typical—most ACT passages don't consist exclusively of Economy questions—but we used this passage to drive home the point about choosing concise answers on the English subject test.)

> **EXPERT TUTOR TIP**
> Remember that OMIT is **always** the shortest answer.

Many students might object to answer J in question 10, because the word *successful* alone does not indicate the kind of success meant. Use common sense. Winning and making money would definitely make a professional football team successful. Thus, the concepts of winning and profitability are implicit in the notion that the Cardinals are (now) a successful team. **The ACT expects you to cut anything that isn't absolutely needed.**

> **PERFECT SCORE TIP**
> Do not defend something if the passage could make sense without it. The ACT will never ask you to add any unnecessary details or description.

▶ IF YOU LEARNED ONLY THREE THINGS IN THIS CHAPTER...

1. Read until you have enough information to identify the issue, eliminate choices that do NOT address the issue, and test each remaining choice to find the correct answer.

2. When approaching questions, ask yourself: Why did the test makers include this question? What issue is this question testing?

3. Many English questions test redundancy, verbosity, and irrelevance. Start with the shortest answer.

CHAPTER 5

English Workout 2: Make It Make Sense

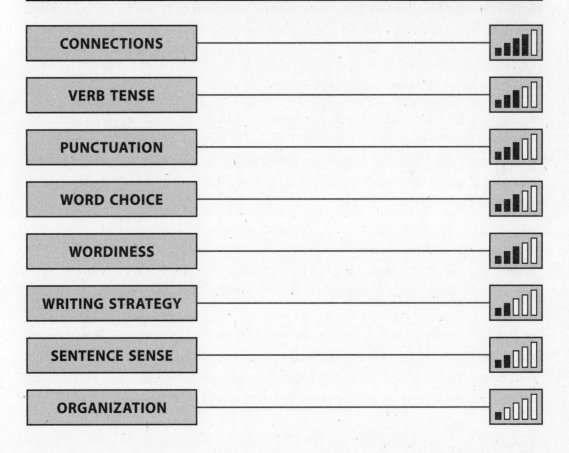

SMARTPOINTS COVERED IN THIS CHAPTER

- CONNECTIONS
- VERB TENSE
- PUNCTUATION
- WORD CHOICE
- WORDINESS
- WRITING STRATEGY
- SENTENCE SENSE
- ORGANIZATION

In English Workout 1, we saw that the ACT expects you to use your words efficiently and that, in fact, the shortest answer is correct remarkably often. Obviously, however, the shortest answer is sometimes wrong. What could make it wrong? It may not mean what it says.

Take this example: "Abraham Lincoln's father was a model of hardworking self-sufficiency. He was born in a log cabin he built with his own hands." Well, that's a cute trick, being born in a cabin you built yourself. Presumably, the writer means that Abe was born in a cabin that his father built. But the literal meaning of the example is that the father somehow managed to be born in a cabin that he himself had built.

It's possible, of course, to analyze this example in terms of the rules of apostrophe use and pronoun reference. But that's not practical for the ACT, even for a student who has good grammar skills. There isn't time to carefully analyze every question, consider all the rules involved, and decide on an answer. You have to do 75 English questions in only 45 minutes—that's almost 2 questions per minute.

But there *is* plenty of time to approach examples like this one in a more pragmatic way. Ask yourself, *Do these words make sense?*

For the ACT, it's important to care. You need to adjust your mind-set. After deciding whether or not the selection in a question is concise and relevant (Step 1 in the three-step method), the next step is to make sure that the sentence *says* exactly what it's supposed to *mean*. If it doesn't, your job is to make it do so. In other words, make it make sense.

> ☑ **PERFECT SCORE TIP**
> If you can't find a mistake in an underlined sentence, consider logic. A sentence may sound like English but actually have a logical inconsistency, which makes it not make sense.

We at Kaplan have a name for questions that test errors of meaning—**Sense questions.** Once you get the hang of them, these questions can actually be fun. They're often funny once you see them. The following passage gives examples of the most common kinds of Sense questions you'll find on the ACT.

> ☑ **PERFECT SCORE TIP**
> In the Reading section, skimming and not noting small problems is a good thing. In English, you must pay close attention to all words near the underlined part.

Passage I

ROBINSON CRUSOE: FICTION AND FACT

Most people—even those who've never read
Daniel Defoe's *Robinson Crusoe*—are familiar
with the strange story of the sailor shipwrecked
on a far-flung Pacific island. Relatively few of
them, however, know that Crusoe's <u>story. It was</u>
                                          1
actually based on the real-life adventures of a
Scottish seaman, Alexander Selkirk. Selkirk
came to the Pacific as a member of a 1703
privateering expedition led by a captain named
William Dampier. During the voyage, Selkirk
became dissatisfied with conditions aboard ship.
<u>After a bitter quarrel with his captain, he put</u>
                        2
<u>Selkirk ashore</u> on tiny Mas a Tierra, one of the
        2
islands of Juan Fernandez, off the coast of Chile.
Stranded, Selkirk lived there alone—in much

the <u>same manner as</u> Defoe's Crusoe—until 1709,
        3
when he was finally rescued by another English
privateer. Upon his return to England, Selkirk

found himself a <u>celebrity, his</u> strange tale had
                    4

1. A. NO CHANGE
    B. story: was
    C. story, was
    D. story was

2. F. NO CHANGE
    G. Quarreling with his captain, the
        boat was put ashore
    H. Having quarreled with his captain,
        Selkirk was put ashore
    J. Having quarreled with his captain,
        they put Selkirk ashore

3. A. NO CHANGE
    B. same manner that
    C. identical manner that
    D. identical way as

4. F. NO CHANGE
    G. celebrity, but his
    H. celebrity. His
    J. celebrity his

already become the talk of pubs and coffeehouses throughout the British Isles. The story even reached the ears of Richard Steele, who featured it in his periodical, *The Tatler*. Eventually, <u>he became</u> the subject of a best-selling book,
5
A Cruizing Voyage Round the World, by Woodes

5. A. NO CHANGE
   B. Selkirk became
   C. his became
   D. he becomes

Rogers. <u>While</u> there is some evidence that Defoe,
6
a journalist, may actually have interviewed Selkirk personally, most literary historians believe that it was the reprinting of the Rogers book in 1718 that served as the real stimulus for Defoe's novel.

6. F. NO CHANGE
   G. But since
   H. And therefore
   J. OMIT the underlined portion and start the sentence with *There*.

In *Crusoe*, which <u>has been published</u> in
7
1719, Defoe took substantial liberties with the Selkirk story. For example, while Selkirk's

7. A. NO CHANGE
   B. was published
   C. had been published
   D. will have been published

presence on the island was of course <u>known for</u>
8
<u>many people</u> (certainly everyone in the crew
8
that stranded him there), no one in the novel is aware of Crusoe's survival of the wreck and presence on the island. Moreover, while Selkirk's exile lasted just six years, Crusoe's goes on for a much more dramatic, though less credible, twenty-eight <u>(over four times as long)</u>. However,
9
Defoe's most blatant embellishment of the tale is the invention of the character of Friday, for whom there was no counterpart whatsoever in the real-life story.

8. F. NO CHANGE
   G. widely known among people
   H. known about many people
   J. known to many people

9. A. NO CHANGE
   B. (much longer)
   C. (a much longer time, of course)
   D. OMIT the underlined portion.

<u>Because of</u> its basis in fact, *Robinson*
         10

Crusoe is often regarded as the first major novel

in English literature. <u>Still popular today, contem-
                                                    11

porary audiences enjoyed the book as well.</u>
                            11

In fact, two sequels, in which Crusoe returns

to the island after his rescue, were eventually

<u>published. Though</u> to little acclaim. Meanwhile,
       12

Selkirk himself never <u>gave a hoot about returning</u>
                                            13

to the island that had made him famous.

Legend has it that he never gave up his eccentric

living habits, spending his last years in a cave

teaching alley cats to dance in his spare time.

One wonders if even Defoe himself could have

invented a more fitting end to the bizarre story

of his shipwrecked sailor.

10. F. NO CHANGE
    G. Despite
    H. Resulting from
    J. As a consequence of

11. A. NO CHANGE
    B. Still read today, Defoe's contemporaries also enjoyed it.
    C. Viewed by many even then as a classic, the book is still popular to this day.
    D. Much read in its day, modern audiences still find the book compelling.

12. F. NO CHANGE
    G. published, though
    H. published although
    J. published; although

13. A. NO CHANGE
    B. evinced himself as desirous of returning
    C. could whip up a head of steam to return
    D. expressed any desire to return

Questions 14–15 ask about the preceding passage as a whole.

14. Considering the tone and subject matter of the preceding paragraphs, is the last sentence an appropriate way to end the essay?

F. Yes, because it is necessary to shed some doubt on Defoe's creativity.

G. Yes, because the essay is about the relationship between the real Selkirk and Defoe's fictionalized version of him.

H. No, because there is nothing "bizarre" about Selkirk's story as it is related in the essay.

J. No, because the focus of the essay is more on Selkirk himself than on Defoe's fictionalized version of him.

15. This essay would be most appropriate as part of a:

A. scholarly study of 18th-century maritime history.

B. study of the geography of the islands off of Chile.

C. history of privateering in the Pacific.

D. popular history of English literature.

Answers

1.	D	9.	D
2.	H	10.	G
3.	A	11.	C
4.	H	12.	G
5.	B	13.	D
6.	F	14.	G
7.	B	15.	D
8.	J		

Please note that in the explanations that follow, we treat the questions not in numerical order but rather in groups according to the tested issue. We do this to help you better understand the concepts behind the questions. The more easily you can spot the tested issue—the concept the ACT requires you to understand to answer the question correctly—the more confident you'll feel on test day.

Sense Questions vs. Economy Questions

Most of the time, we don't usually care much if an author isn't clear. We have learned to interpret what the writer meant to say and move on. On the ACT, test takers *must* care and make sure that what is written is the same as what the author meant. Sense questions may seem harder than the Economy questions—the shortest answers aren't necessarily right.

Step 1 is all you needed in question numbers 1, 3, 7, 9, 10, and 13. "When in doubt, take it out" worked for these. As we saw in English Workout 1, questions that include an OMIT option, and those in which some of the answers are much longer than others, are usually testing writing economy.

In the rest of the questions in this passage, the answers differ in other ways. They may join or fragment sentences, rearrange things, or add words that affect the meaning of the sentences. When the answers are all about the same length, as in most of the questions here, the question is more likely to test sense. Consider the shortest answer first, but don't be as quick to select it and move on. Think about the effect each choice has on the *meaning* of the sentence, and pick longer answers if the shortest one doesn't make sense.

GRAMMAR RULES AND SENSE QUESTIONS

.∎◻◻◻ SENTENCE SENSE

.∎∎∎◻ CONNECTIONS

The ACT test makers include questions like those in Passage I to test many different rules of writing mechanics. Though it's *not necessary* to think about rules to answer the questions, being familiar with them will help. **The more ways to think about a question you have, the more likely you are to find the right answer.**

> **EXPERT TUTOR TIP**
> Students tend to reject informal writing as incorrect, but ACT passages are written at various levels of formality. Some are as stiff as textbooks. Others are as casual as a talk with friends. Pay attention to the tone of the words. Are they serious? Are they laid-back? Stay with the author's tone. Don't **always** stay formal.

We'll discuss some of these examples in groups based on what they're designed to test. That way we can briefly discuss the rules and also show you how the basic strategic approach of "make it make sense" can get you the answers without a lot of technical analysis. Let's start with **question 1.**

Completeness

.∎∎∎◻ CONNECTIONS

.∎◻◻◻ SENTENCE SENSE

.∎∎◻◻ PUNCTUATION

Question 1 tests sentence sense.

Rule at work: Every sentence must contain a subject and a predicate verb and express a complete thought.

> ...Relatively few of them, however, know
>
> that Crusoe's <u>story. It was</u> actually based
>   1
> on the real-life adventures of a Scottish
>
> Scottish seaman, Alexander Selkirk.

1. A. NO CHANGE
   B. story: was
   C. story, was
   D. story was

If the underlined section for question 1 were left as it is, the second sentence of the passage would be incomplete. It wouldn't make sense. "Relatively few people know that Crusoe's story" what? To make it make sense, you've got to continue the sentence so it can tell us what few people know about Crusoe's story. The three alternatives all do that, but choice B introduces a nonsensical colon, while choice C adds a comma when there's no pause in the sentence. Choice D, however, continues the sentence—adding nothing unnecessary but making it complete.

When you are testing a sentence for completeness, don't just look to see if it has a subject and verb.

Question 12 tests the same concept:

...In fact, two sequels, in which Crusoe returns to the island after his rescue, were eventually published. Though to little acclaim.
12

12. F. NO CHANGE
    G. published, though
    H. published although
    J. published; although

Here, the fragment should be more obvious, since the clause that's trying to pass itself off as a sentence—"Though to little acclaim"—contains neither a subject nor a verb. That's the technical reason it's wrong, and if you recognized this, great. On a more intuitive level, it just doesn't make sense to say, as a complete thought: "Though to little acclaim."

Clearly, that fragment has to be connected to the sentence before it, so choices F and J are wrong, since both would leave the fragment isolated. Choice H goes too far in the other direction, omitting any punctuation at all between the fragment and the main body of the sentence, and that's no good. The correct choice, G, does just what we need it to do: it connects the fragment logically to the main sentence, but it provides a comma to represent the pause between the two.

Sentence Structure

Rule at work: A sentence can have two thoughts, but they must be combined correctly (see below). If none of the answer choices does this, select the choice that creates two separate sentences.

...Upon his return to England, Selkirk found himself a celebrity, his strange tale had already become the talk of pubs and coffeehouses throughout the British Isles.
4

4. F. NO CHANGE
   G. celebrity, but his
   H. celebrity. His
   J. celebrity his

Here we have two complete thoughts: (1) Selkirk found himself a celebrity upon his return, and (2) his tale was bandied about the pubs and coffeehouses. You can't just run these two complete thoughts together with a comma, as the underlined portion does. And you certainly can't just run them together *without* a comma or anything else, as choice J does. You can relate the two thoughts with a comma and a linking word (*and*, for instance), but choice G's inclusion of the word *but* makes no sense. It implies a contrast, while the two complete thoughts are actually very similar. Thus, you should create two sentences, one for each thought. That's what correct choice H does.

Rule at work: There are three ways to connect complete thoughts.

1. Use a semicolon.
2. Use a comma with a FANBOYS (For, And, Nor, But, Or, Yet, So) conjunction.
3. Make one of the two thoughts *in*complete (or dependent).

Working with these three possibilities for question 4, you might have seen any of these correct answer choices:

1. Selkirk found himself a celebrity*;* his strange tale had already...
2. Selkirk found himself a celebrity*, **for*** his strange tale had already...
3. Selkirk found himself a celebrity ***because*** his strange tale had already...

> ✓ **PERFECT SCORE TIP**
> If considering independent versus dependent clauses seems too confusing for you, just think, "If I put a period in the middle of this sentence and did not change any words, would the two new sentences make sense?" If the answer is yes, the sentence is a run-on.

Modifiers

▁▃▅▇ SENTENCE SENSE

Question 2 tests modifier problems:

...After a bitter quarrel with his captain,
—————————————————————————————
                    2

he put Selkirk ashore on tiny Mas a Tierra,
————————————————————————
              2

one of the islands of Juan Fernandez...

2. F. NO CHANGE
   G. Quarreling with his captain, the boat was put ashore
   H. Having quarreled with his captain, Selkirk was put ashore
   J. Having quarreled with his captain, they put Selkirk ashore

Rule at work: A modifier, or describer, is any word or group of words that describes another. Any and all describers must clearly relate to (be close to) whatever they are referring to.

> ☑ **PERFECT SCORE TIP**
> Misplaced modifiers are a common ACT trick. If multiple answers sound right to you, consider, "Is every modifying phrase placed near the word it logically modifies?"

Sentences become confused if a descriptive word, phrase, or clause is separated from the verb, noun, pronoun, etc. that it should be connected to. In the underlined portion of question 2, the phrase "after a bitter quarrel with his captain" should describe the person (or pronoun) that follows next. It doesn't.

The *he* who put Selkirk ashore must be the captain, but it can't be the captain who had "a bitter quarrel with his captain." That doesn't make sense (unless the captain quarrels with himself). Put the thing modified next to the thing modifying it. The person who quarreled with his captain was Selkirk—not the boat and not *they*, whoever *they* are—so choice H is correct.

If you recognized the problem with question 2 as a misplaced modifier, that's great. Fantastic, even. However, you didn't have to know the technicalities to get the right answer here. You just had to make the sentence make sense.

Question 11 tests a similar problem:

...<u>Still popular today, contemporary</u>
               11
<u>audiences enjoyed the book as well.</u>
               11

11. A. NO CHANGE
    B. Still read today, Defoe's contemporaries also enjoyed it.
    C. Viewed by many even then as a classic, the book is still popular to this day.
    D. Much read in its day, modern audiences still find the book compelling.

The way the sentence is written, it basically means that contemporary audiences are "still popular today." That doesn't make sense. The *intended* meaning is that the *book* is still popular today, as it was then. Choice C fixes the sense problem by putting its modifier—"viewed by many even then as a classic"—next to the thing it modifies—"the book." Notice that the other choices all misplace their modifiers in the same way, making them modify "Defoe's contemporaries" (in B) and "modern audiences" (in choice D).

EXPERT TUTOR TIP
Sentences should make sense. You'll be richly rewarded on test day if you learn to recognize misplaced modifiers, ambiguous pronouns, and correct sentence structure.

As a rule of thumb, you should **always** make sure that modifiers are as close as possible to the things they describe.

Idiom (Accepted Word Form and Choice)

.▄▆▐▌▌ WORD CHOICE

Rule at work: The correct preposition can vary depending on the sense of the sentence. Many phrases in English are correct because people have agreed to use them in a certain way. No overall rules apply. To master these, listen to what sounds right, or if English is not your native language, remember them one by one.

Question 3 tests idiom, or accepted uses of English words. Many words have special rules.

...Stranded, Selkirk lived there alone—

in much the <u>same manner as</u> Defoe's
                    3

Crusoe—until 1709, when he was

finally rescued by another...

3. A. NO CHANGE
    B. same manner that
    C. identical manner that
    D. identical way as

The sentence as written actually makes sense. Selkirk lived in "much the same as" Defoe's Crusoe. The idiom "much the same" calls for *as* to complete the comparison between Selkirk's and Crusoe's ways of life. Note how choices B and C would create completeness problems—in much the same (or identical) manner that Defoe's Crusoe what? Choice D, meanwhile, sounds strange. In English, we just don't say "in much the identical way as" because the word *identical* is an absolute. You can't be more or partially identical; you either are or aren't identical to something else. Even if you didn't analyze choice D this carefully, it should have just sounded wrong to your ear. (In English Workout 3, we'll show you how "trusting your ear" can be a great way to get correct answers on the English subject test.)

Question 8 tests another idiom problem:

…For example, while Selkirk's presence on the island was of course <u>known for</u>
₈
<u>many people</u> (certainly everyone in the
₈
crew that stranded him there), no one in the novel is aware of Crusoe's survival of the wreck and presence on the island.

8. F. NO CHANGE
   G. widely known among people
   H. known about many people
   J. known to many people

The underlined portion as written is unidiomatic. Selkirk's presence wasn't known *for* many people—it was known *by,* or known *to,* many people. When you're known *for* something, that means you have a reputation for doing such and such. That makes no sense in this context. Choice J *does* make sense, since it points out that Selkirk's presence on the island was known *to* many people—that is, it was something that many people knew about. Choice G is unidiomatic; we just wouldn't say "among people" here, since it's not specific enough. That sounds as if we're talking about people as a species. Choice H would have been acceptable if it had read "known about *by* many people," but without the *by,* the correction just wouldn't make sense.

> ✔ **PERFECT SCORE TIP**
> If you are a native English speaker, the key to idioms is really trusting your ear. Chances are, incorrect idioms will jump out at you if you trust what you hear.

Idiom is a tough topic if you're not a native speaker. You have to think very carefully about the meaning of every word. But if you *are* a native speaker, **use your many years of hearing English as a guide.** Choose the correction that makes sense and doesn't sound weird.

Pronouns

▪▫▫ **WORD CHOICE**

▪▫▫ **SENTENCE SENSE**

▪▫▫ **ORGANIZATION**

Rule at work: A pronoun must agree with the person or thing it is referring to, in person, gender, and number (singular or plural). The reference must be clear; if there is *any* confusion, the sentence must be fixed.

Sometimes, the test will throw you a sentence in which the meaning of a pronoun is unclear. You won't be sure to whom or what the pronoun is referring. That's the kind of problem you were given in **question 5:**

...The story even reached the ears of Richard Steele, who featured it in his periodical, *The Tatler*. Eventually, he became the subject of a best-selling book...

5. A. NO CHANGE
   B. Selkirk became
   C. his became
   D. he becomes

The *intended* meaning of the pronoun *he* here is Selkirk. But what's the closest male name to the pronoun? Richard Steele, the publisher of *The Tatler*. Your job is to make it clear whom the pronoun is referring to. Choice B takes care of the problem by naming Selkirk explicitly. Choice C would create a sense problem—his *what* became the subject of a book? Meanwhile, D shifts the verb tense into the present, which makes no sense since this book was written over 250 years ago!

> ✓ **PERFECT SCORE TIP**
> Ambiguous pronouns are never right. If *he* or *they* are used, make sure it is obvious whom these pronouns are describing.

Mistakes of sense often involve pronouns. Make a habit of checking every underlined pronoun as you go along. What does the pronoun stand for? Can you tell? If not, there's an error. Does it make sense? If not, there's an error. Make sure it's perfectly clear to what or to whom all pronouns refer.

Logic

📊 **WORD CHOICE**
📊 **SENTENCE SENSE**
📊 **ORGANIZATION**

Think about words like *therefore, despite, however,* and *because*. Such words are structural clues. They serve as signposts in the passage to let you know where the author is going and how all of the pieces logically fit together. If the author uses the structural clue *on the other hand,* that means a contrast is coming up; if he or she uses the clue *moreover,* that means that a continuation is coming up—an addition that is more or less in the same vein as what came before.

Many ACT English questions mix up the logic of a piece of writing by giving you the wrong structural clue or another logic word. That's what's tested in **question 10:**

...<u>Because of</u> its basis in fact,
     10
Robinson Crusoe is often regarded as

the first major novel in English literature.

10. F. NO CHANGE
    G. Despite
    H. Resulting from
    J. As a consequence of

As written, this sentence means that *Crusoe* was regarded as the first major novel because it was based on fact. But that makes no sense. If it was based on fact, that would work against its being regarded as a novel. There's a contrast between "basis in fact" (which implies nonfiction) and "first major novel" (which implies fiction). To show that contrast logically, you need a contrast word like *despite*. That's why choice G is correct here.

> **EXPERT TUTOR TIP**
> The ACT test makers love to include questions about transitions between clauses, sentences, and paragraphs. Learn to recognize the logic and direction of a piece of writing—this will help you on the English and Reading tests.

Question 6 also tests logic:

...the subject of a best-selling book,
A Cruizing Voyage Round the World,
by Woodes Rogers. <u>While</u> there is
           6
some evidence that Defoe, a journalist,
may actually have interviewed Selkirk
personally, most literary historians
believe that it was the reprinting of the
Rogers book in 1718 that served as the
real stimulus for Defoe's novel.

6. F. NO CHANGE
    G. But since
    H. And therefore
    J. OMIT the underlined portion and start the sentence with *There.*

The structural clue should convey a sense of contrast with the previous sentence. Even though Defoe may have interviewed Selkirk, many believe Defoe's main source was the book by Rogers. *While* provides the needed contrast, making NO CHANGE the correct answer.

Choices G and H have *since* and *therefore* which are cause-and-effect words, which make no sense in context. Choice J omits a key word and creates a run-on sentence—two independent clauses that are combined improperly. Remember, don't pick OMIT simply because it's there!

Verb Usage

▪▪▫▫▫ **VERB TENSE**

▪▫▪▫▫ **WORD CHOICE**

▪▫▫▫▫ **SENTENCE SENSE**

Rules at work:

1. Use the simplest tense possible. In most cases, the present, past, and future tenses are all you need.

2. Change tenses only if the sentence doesn't make sense as written.

3. Make sure the verb is singular if it has a singular subject and plural if the subject is plural.

Verbs have an annoying habit of changing form depending on who's doing the action and when that person is doing it. Example: "I *hate* verbs; he *hates* verbs; and we both *have hated* verbs ever since we were kids." **You have to be very careful to make sure verbs match their subject and the tense of the surrounding context.**

…In *Crusoe*, which <u>has been published</u> in 1719, Defoe took substantial liberties with the Selkirk story.

7.
  A. NO CHANGE
  B. was published
  C. had been published
  D. will have been published

The publication of *Robinson Crusoe* is something that took place in 1719—the past, in other words. So the underlined portion, which puts the verb in the present perfect tense, is flawed. Choices C and D, meanwhile, would put the verb into tenses normally used to convey a complex time relationship. Choice C makes it seem as if publication of the book happened before Defoe took his liberties with the story, but that's nonsensical. The liberties were taken in the writing of the book. Choice D, meanwhile, does strange things with the time sequence. The book was published in the past; Defoe also took his substantial liberties in the same past. So just use the simple past tense, choice B.

Tone

▂▃▅ **WORD CHOICE**

▂▃▅ **WRITING STRATEGY**

Rule at work: Every writer of an ACT English passage has a voice, or tone. This voice is usually either casual (conversational) or factual (informational). Be sure to make choices that fit the author's voice.

As we said earlier, the passages in the English subject test vary in tone. Some are formal, others are informal. Usually, you'll know which is which without having to think about it. If a passage contains slang, a few exclamation points, and a joke or two, the tone is informal; if it sounds like something from a textbook, the tone is probably formal.

Good style requires that the tone of a piece of writing be at the same level throughout. Sometimes the underlined portion might not fit the tone of the rest of the passage. If so, it's up to you to correct it. Look at **question 13**:

…Meanwhile, Selkirk himself never <u>gave a hoot about returning</u> to the island that had made him famous.

13. A. NO CHANGE
    B. evinced himself as desirous of returning
    C. could whip up a head of steam to return
    D. expressed any desire to return

Selkirk "never gave a hoot" about going back? No way! Slang doesn't belong in this passage. Choose D because it uses a straightforward, factual tone that fits the passage. The NO CHANGE choice is silly. Choice B is too wordy and formal. Choice C is also slang.

> **EXPERT TUTOR TIP**
> Don't pick an answer just because it sounds "fancy." Pick commonsense, everyday words that express the meaning the author intends. Don't worry if it sounds plain.

NONSTANDARD-FORMAT QUESTIONS

..ıll WRITING STRATEGY

.ıll ORGANIZATION

The Nonstandard-Format questions ask about the passage as a whole. Keep in mind the main point of the passage—the gist—as well as the overall tone and style. For an entire passage to make sense, it has to be consistent throughout, both in content and in tone and style.

Judging the Passage

Question 14 asks you to judge the passage. Was the last sentence an appropriate ending or not?

14. Considering the tone and subject matter of the preceding paragraphs, is the last sentence an appropriate way to end the essay?

   F. Yes, because it is necessary to shed some doubt on Defoe's creativity.

   G. Yes, because the essay is about the relationship between the real Selkirk and Defoe's fictionalized version of him.

   H. No, because there is nothing bizarre about Selkirk's story as it is related in the essay.

   J. No, because the focus of the essay is more on Selkirk himself than on Defoe's fictionalized version of him.

Think of the passage as a whole. It has been comparing Selkirk's real life with the one that Defoe made up for the character of Robinson Crusoe. Therefore, ending in this way, with an ironic reference wondering whether Defoe could have written a more fitting end to Selkirk's life, is perfectly appropriate. The answer to the question is yes (eliminating choices H and J). Choice G restates the point of the passage and is the best answer.

Reading Comprehension Questions

If you thought **question 15** looked like a Reading question hiding in the English part of the exam, you were right. As mentioned in ACT Basics, one reason that you should keep thinking about what the passage means—rather than focusing on picky rules of grammar or punctuation—is that **the English section includes some questions that test your reading comprehension skills.**

15. This essay would be most appropriate as part of a:

    A. scholarly study of 18th-century maritime history.

    B. study of the geography of the islands off of Chile.

    C. history of privateering in the Pacific.

    D. popular history of English literature.

What was this passage principally about? How Defoe's *Robinson Crusoe* was loosely based on the life of a real shipwrecked sailor, Alexander Selkirk. Would that kind of thing belong in a study of geography (choice B)? No. The focus is on the fictionalization of a historical life, not on the physical features of the islands off Chile. The passage isn't principally about privateering or maritime history either, so choices C and A are wrong as well. This passage is about the relationship between a true story and a famous fictionalized story. Its tone isn't overly scholarly, so it probably belongs in a popular history of English literature (choice D).

Structure and Purpose

The English section will also have questions that test your grasp of overall structure and purpose in a piece of prose. The test makers scramble the order of the sentences in a paragraph (or of the paragraphs in a passage). The question then asks you to decide on the best order for the scrambled parts. Take a look at this new question:

[1] Only recently has new evidence led many scientists to question the accepted division between birds and dinosaurs. [2] Traditionally, they have been placed in entirely separate classes within the subphylum *Vertebrata*. [3] Birds and dinosaurs don't have many obvious similarities. [4] Birds formed the class *Aves*, while dinosaurs constituted two orders, *Saurischia* and *Ornithischia*, within the class *Reptilia*.

16. To best fulfill the author's purpose, the order of the sentences in the paragraph should be:

    F. 1, 2, 3, 4.

    G. 2, 3, 4, 1.

    H. 3, 2, 4, 1.

    J. 3, 2, 1, 4.

Here again, the goal is to make it make sense. All of the sentences in this paragraph relate to the differences between birds and dinosaurs. Sentence 3 best introduces this idea. Notice that two of the answer choices begin with sentence 3—H and J. The other two can be eliminated.

Look again at the logic of the sentences. Because sentence 4 elaborates on the distinction introduced in sentence 2, sentence 4 should immediately follow sentence 2. Only choice H has them in that order, so H looks like the answer.

Just to check, you'll want to read the entire paragraph in the order suggested by choice H. And if you do, you'll notice that the paragraph makes perfect sense, with sentence 3 introducing the topic, sentences 2 and 4 showing how that topic has been traditionally viewed, and sentence 1 coming in naturally to show how that traditional view is no longer valid.

For questions like this, it's usually a good idea to start by trying to figure out the first (and sometimes the last) sentence because first and last sentences usually have the most obvious functions in an ACT-style paragraph.

EXPERT TUTOR TIP

If you don't know where to start on an organization question, look at the answers that begin with the same number (H and J), compare the two, and eliminate one or both answers.

▶ IF YOU LEARNED ONLY TWO THINGS IN THIS CHAPTER...

1. Consider the meaning of a sentence. If it doesn't make sense, there's probably a grammatical mistake. The correct answer will make sense.

2. Nonstandard-Format questions ask you to judge the passage and consider it as a whole. You may be asked about paragraph structure and function.

CHAPTER 6

English Workout 3: Look and Listen

In the first two English Workouts, we discussed English questions that hinged on economy and sense. There are some English questions—we call them Technicality questions—that may seem harder because they test for the technical rules of grammar, requiring you to correct errors that don't necessarily harm the economy or sense of the sentence. Don't worry. You don't have to be a grammar whiz to get these questions right. Luckily, you can often detect these errors because they "sound funny." **Most of the time on the ACT, it's safe to trust your ear.**

LISTEN TO THE CHOICES

Which of the following "sounds right" and which "sounds funny"?

- Bob doesn't know the value of the house he lives in.
- Bob don't know the value of the house he lives in.

The first sounds a lot better, right? For many of these questions, all you need to do is "listen" carefully in this way.

> **EXPERT TUTOR TIP**
> You can spot questions that test grammar rules because the answers are roughly the same length. Read the sentences carefully, looking and listening for clues to the error.

Your ear can help you determine the tone of a passage. For example, if the passage starts off "You'll just love Bermuda—great beaches, good living…" it won't end like this: "and an infinitely fascinating array of flora and fauna which may conceivably exceed, in range and scope, that of any alternative…" It's too formal. Pick something like this: "You'll just love Bermuda—great beaches, good living, and lots of awesome plants and animals."

> ✓ **PERFECT SCORE TIP**
> The best preparation for the English sections is really to enter a grammar "hyper mode" where you recognize grammar mistakes around you. If you are used to doing this in everyday life, common verb or agreement errors will pop out to you on the test.

Although ACT passages differ in level of formality, they all are designed to test standard English—the kind used by people in most of America. Test takers who speak regional or ethnic dialects may therefore find it more difficult to follow their ears on some ACT questions. In much of the South, for instance, it's common to use the word *in* with the word *rate,* like this: "Mortality declined *in* a rate of almost 2 percent per year." Most speakers of English, however, use the word *at* with *rate,* like this: "Mortality declined *at* a rate of…" Fortunately, ACT questions testing issues like this are rare. Even if you do speak a nonstandard dialect, you probably know what standard English sounds like. The dialect used on most television and radio programs would be considered standard.

In the following short passage, use your eyes and ears.

Passage II

THE HISTORY OF HALLOWEEN

Halloween was first celebrated <u>among various</u> Celtic
                                        1
tribes in Ireland in the fifth century B.C. It traditionally took place on the official last day of summer—October

<u>31, and</u> was named "All-Hallows' Eve." It was believed
  2
that all persons who had died during the previous year returned on this day to select persons or animals to inhabit for the next twelve months, until they could

<u>pass peaceful</u> into the afterlife.
  3

On All-Hallows' Eve, the Celts <u>were dressing</u> up as
                                        4
demons and monsters to frighten the spirits and tried

1. A. NO CHANGE
   B. among varied
   C. between the various
   D. between various

2. F. NO CHANGE
   G. 31—and
   H. 31. And
   J. 31; and

3. A. NO CHANGE
   B. pass peacefully
   C. passed peacefully
   D. be passing peaceful

4. F. NO CHANGE
   G. were dressed
   H. dressed
   J. are dressed

to make their homes <u>as coldest</u> as possible to prevent any
₅
stray ghosts from crossing their thresholds. Late at night,
the townspeople typically gathered outside the village,
where a druidic priest would light a huge bonfire to
frighten away ghosts and to honor the sun god for the
past summer's harvest. Any villager <u>whom was</u> suspected
₆

of being possessed would be captured, after which <u>they</u>
₇
might be sacrificed in the bonfire as a warning to other
spirits seeking to possess the living. When the Romans
invaded the British Isles, they adopted Celtic—not
Saxon—Halloween rituals, but they outlawed human
sacrifice in A.D. 61. Instead, they used effigies for their
sacrifices. In time, as <u>belief in</u> spirit possession waned,
₈

Halloween rituals lost their serious aspect and <u>had been</u>
₉
instead performed for amusement.

   Irish immigrants, fleeing from the potato famine

in the 1840s, <u>brought there</u> Halloween customs to the
₁₀
United States. In New England, Halloween became a
night of costumes and practical jokes. Some favorite

5. A. NO CHANGE
    B. colder
    C. coldest
    D. as cold

6. F. NO CHANGE
    G. whom were
    H. who was
    J. who were

7. A. NO CHANGE
    B. it
    C. he or she
    D. those

8. F. NO CHANGE
    G. belief for
    H. believing about
    J. belief of

9. A. NO CHANGE
    B. having been
    C. have been
    D. were

10. F. NO CHANGE
    G. brought they're
    H. brought their
    J. their brought-in

pranks <u>included unhinging</u> front gates and overturning
₁₁
outhouses. The Irish also introduced the custom of
carving jack-o'-lanterns. The ancient Celts probably
began the tradition by hollowing out a large turnip,
carving it with a demon's face, and lighting it from
inside with a candle. Since there were <u>far less</u> turnips in
₁₂
New England than in Ireland, the Irish immigrants were
forced to settle for pumpkins.

Gradually, Halloween celebrations spread to other
regions of the United States. Halloween has been a
popular holiday ever since, <u>although these days it's</u>
₁₃

principal celebrants are children <u>rather than</u> adults.
₁₄

11. A. NO CHANGE
    B. include unhinging
    C. had included unhinged
    D. includes unhinged

12. F. NO CHANGE
    G. lots less
    H. not as much
    J. far fewer

13. A. NO CHANGE
    B. although these days its
    C. while now it's
    D. while not it is

14. F. NO CHANGE
    G. rather then
    H. rather
    J. else then

Key to Passage II

	Answer	Issue
1.	A	*among/between* distinction
2.	G	commas and dashes mixed
3.	B	use of adjectives and adverbs
4.	H	wrong verb tense
5.	D	comparative/superlative
6.	H	*who/whom* confusion
7.	C	pronoun usage error
8.	F	preposition usage
9.	D	tense problem with *to be*
10.	H	*they're/there/their* mix-up
11.	A	wrong verb tense
12.	J	*less/fewer* confusion
13.	B	*it's/its* confusion
14.	F	*then/than* confusion

GRAMMAR RULES TO KNOW

The rest of this workout is designed to help you build your own "flag list" of common errors on the ACT that your ear might not catch. Consider each classic error. If it seems like common sense to you (or, better, if the error just sounds like bad English to you, while the correction sounds like good English), you probably don't have to add it to your flag list. On the other hand, if it doesn't seem obvious, add it to your list.

As we'll see, making things match works in two ways. Some rules force you to match one part of the sentence with another part. Other rules force you to match the right word or word form with the intended meaning.

> ✓ **PERFECT SCORE TIP**
> Depending on if the people around you use correct grammar, your ear may or may not give you correct answers. Even if you generally have correct grammar, knowing the rules will help make you more confident in yourself. So be sure to review the grammar rules in this section.

RULE 1: Number Agreement

The most tested agreement rule on the ACT is this: Singular nouns must match with singular verbs and pronouns, and plural nouns must match with plural verbs and pronouns. A common error in this area involves the use of the word *they*. It's plural, but in everyday speech, we often use it as a singular.

WRONG: "If a student won't study, they won't do well."

PROBLEM: A *student* (singular) and *they* (plural) don't agree.

CORRECTION: "If students won't study, they won't do well," or "If a student won't study, he or she won't do well."

> ✔ **PERFECT SCORE TIP**
> Take out surrounding words and just say the subject and the verb. Other words can hide verb mistakes, but a verb that doesn't match its subject will become clearer if you just say it after its subject.

RULE 2: Pronouns in Compounds

Another common agreement or matching error concerns compounds, which are phrases that join two words with *and* or *or*.

WRONG: "The fool gave the wrong tickets to Bob and I."

PROBLEM: *I* is a subject; it can't be the object of the preposition *to*.

CORRECTION: "The fool gave the wrong tickets to Bob and me."

Hint: Try dropping the rest of the compound (Bob and). "The fool gave the wrong tickets to I" should sound funny to you.

RULE 3: Commas or Dashes (Parenthetical Phrases)

Parenthetical phrases must begin and end with the same punctuation mark. Such phrases can be recognized because without them the sentence would still be complete. For instance: "Bob, on his way to the store, saw a large lizard in the street." If you dropped the phrase "on his way to the store," the sentence would still be complete. Thus, this phrase is parenthetical. It could be marked off with commas, parentheses, or dashes. But the same mark is needed at both ends of the phrase.

WRONG: "Bob—on his way to the store, saw a lizard."

PROBLEM: The parenthetical phrase starts with a dash but finishes with a comma.

CORRECTION: "Bob, on his way to the store, saw a lizard."

RULE 4: Commas (Run-Ons and Comma Splices)

You can't combine two sentences into one with a comma (though you can with a semicolon or conjunction).

WRONG:	"Ed's a slacker, Sara isn't."
PROBLEM:	Two sentences are spliced together with a comma.
CORRECTION:	"Ed's a slacker, but Sara isn't." Or "Ed's a slacker; Sara isn't." Or "Ed, unlike Sara, is a slacker."

RULE 5: Fragments

This rule goes hand in hand with the previous one. **A sentence must have at least one "major event."** A fragment is writing that could be a subordinate part of a sentence but not a whole sentence itself.

WRONG:	"Emily listened to music. While she studied."
PROBLEM:	"She studied" would be a sentence, but *while* makes this a fragment.
CORRECTION:	"Emily listened to music while she studied."

RULE 6: Punctuation

The ACT doesn't test tricky rules of punctuation. However, it does expect you to know what the punctuation marks mean and to match their use to their meanings. Here are some common punctuation marks and their meanings:

Use a **comma** (,) or **commas** to do the following:

- Set off items in a list of three or more items
- Combine two independent clauses with a FANBOYS conjunction (For, And, Nor, But, Or, Yet, So)
- Set off an introductory phrase from the rest of the sentence
- Separate nonessential information (something that could be considered a parenthetical phrase) from the rest of the sentence

Use a **semicolon** (;) to do the following:

- Combine two independent clauses when a FANBOYS word is not present
- Separate items in a series or list if those items already include commas

Use a **colon** (:) to introduce or emphasize a short phrase, quotation, example, explanation, or list.

Use a **dash** (—) or **dashes** to set off an explanatory or parenthetical phrase in a sentence.

Use an **apostrophe** (') to do the following:

- Indicate the possessive form of a noun
- Stand in for a missing letter or letters in a contraction

> **EXPERT TUTOR TIP**
> Most test takers need some review of punctuation. Brush up on your skills with English Review for the ACT on your online syllabus.

RULE 7: *-ly* Endings (Adverbs and Adjectives)

The ACT expects you to understand the difference between adverbs (which often end in *-ly*) and adjectives. The two are similar because they're both modifiers. They modify, refer to, or describe another word or phrase in the sentence. Nouns and pronouns must be modified by adjectives, while other words, especially verbs and adjectives themselves, must be modified by adverbs.

WRONG: "Anna is an extreme gifted child, and she speaks beautiful too."

PROBLEM: *Extreme* and *beautiful* are adjectives, but they're supposed to modify an adjective (*gifted*) and a verb (*speaks*) here, so they should be adverbs.

CORRECTION: "Anna is an extremely gifted child, and she speaks beautifully too."

RULE 8: *Good* or *Well*

In everyday speech, we often confuse the words *good* and *well*. But *good* is an adjective (it modifies a noun or pronoun); *well* is an adverb (it can modify verbs and adjectives).

WRONG: "Joe did good on the ACT."

PROBLEM: *Good* is an adjective, but here it's modifying a verb (*did*), so use an adverb.

CORRECTION: "Joe did well on the ACT."

One exception: *well* can also be used as an adjective when it means "healthy." So: "Joe was well again by the morning of the ACT" is correct, even though *well* is modifying the noun *Joe*.

> ☑ **PERFECT SCORE TIP**
> Perhaps the most ingrained grammar mistake is the answer of "Good" to the question, "How are you doing?" Especially when it comes to *good* vs. *well*, do not trust your ear, as it is often wrong. Just remember *good* is an adjective and will modify a noun while *well* modifies a verb.

RULE 9: *Lie, Lay, Laid, Lain*

The words *lay* and *lie* are easy to confuse because they look alike and have similar meanings. The key difference in meaning is point of view. If the speaker is doing something without a direct object, he is *lying*. If the speaker is doing it to something else, he is *laying*. For example, "I will go lie down" (not *lay* down), but "I will lay this pencil on the desk" (not *lie* it).

It gets worse. The past tense of *lay* is *laid*. That's not too hard. The confusing word is *lie*. The past tense of *lie* is *lay*; when used for special tenses (with the words *had, have,* or *been,* for example), the form is *lain*. Thus, you'd say, "I lay down" (meaning you, yourself, took a rest at some time in the past) or "I have lain down for a nap every afternoon for years now." You'd say, "I laid that pencil on the desk yesterday, just as I have laid it on the desk every day for years now."

Don't confuse *lie* with the word *lie* that relates to dishonesty. The past tense of *lie* (meaning to tell an untruth) is *lied*. The following example uses all the various forms correctly:

> "I lied. I said that I had lain down, but I hadn't. In fact, I had just laid the pencil down. After I lied, though, I lay down to repent for having lied."

Try not to get bogged down with *lie* and *lay*. If you don't get it, don't sweat it. It will account for one question if it appears at all.

RULE 10: *In, Of, To, For* (Idiomatic Preposition Use)

Whenever you see a preposition, double-check to make sure it makes sense and that it matches with the other words. Many words require particular prepositions.

WRONG:	"She tried to instill on me a respect to the law." "I want to protect you in all dangers."
PROBLEM:	The prepositions don't match the verbs.
CORRECTION:	"She tried to instill in me a respect for the law." "I want to protect you from all dangers."

RULE 11: *Who* or *Whom*

Many students fear the words *who* and *whom* more than any other grammatical conundrum. Fear no more. There's an easy way to remember when to use them: they work the same way *he* and *him* work. Turn the sentence into a question as we've done in the example below. If the answer to the question is *he,* the form should be *who.* If the answer is *him,* the form should be *whom.* Notice that the *ms* go together.

WRONG:	"Always remember who you're speaking to."
PROBLEM:	*Who* is wrong. Ask: Speaking to who? Speaking to him, not to he. So it should be *whom.*
CORRECTION:	"Always remember whom you're speaking to."

Some students try to avoid the who/whom problem by using the word *which* instead. Don't. It's not nice to call people "whiches." **Never** use the word *which* for a person.

> ✔ **PERFECT SCORE TIP**
> The Kaplan strategy for distinguishing between *who* and *whom* was very helpful for me. I substituted *he* and *him,* and a difficult grammar concept became manageable.

RULE 12: *Its* or *It's* (Apostrophe Use)

Apostrophes are used primarily for two purposes: possessives and contractions. When you make a *noun* (not a pronoun) possessive by adding an *s,* you use an apostrophe. Examples: *Bob's, the water's, a noodle's.* You **NEVER** use an apostrophe to make a pronoun possessive—pronouns have special possessive forms. You'd never write *her's.* When you run two words together to form a single word, you use an apostrophe to join them. For example: *you'd, he's, they're.*

Apostrophes also have a few unusual uses, but luckily they're almost **never** tested on the ACT. So master the basics and you're in good shape. The most common apostrophe issue on the ACT is usage of the words *its* and *it's.* A good way to remember which is which is that *its* and *it's* follow the same rule as do *his* and *he's.* Both *its* and *his* are possessive pronouns—so they have *no* apostrophes. Both *it's* and *he's* are contractions—so they *do* have apostrophes.

WRONG:	"The company claims its illegal to use it's name that way."
PROBLEM:	*It's* is a contraction of *it is; its* is the possessive form of *it.*
CORRECTION:	"The company claims it's illegal to use its name that way."

> ✓ **PERFECT SCORE TIP**
> Distinguishing *its* from *it's* was very important on my test. It is not a difficult concept, but it may help you get several questions correct on the ACT.

RULE 13: *There, Their,* or *They're* and *Are* or *Our* (Proper Word Usage)

Some students confuse the words *there, their,* and *they're.* **Remember that contractions use apostrophes—so *they're* is the contraction for *they are.*** You can tell which is *there* because it's spelled like *here,* and the words *here* and *there* match. (*Their* means "of or belonging to them"; you'll just have to remember that one the old-fashioned way.)

Students also frequently confuse the words *are* (a verb) and *our* (a possessive). You can remember that *our* is spelled like *your,* which is also possessive.

RULE 14: *Sang, Sung, Brang, Brung,* etc. (Verb Forms)

When the answers differ because of different forms of the same or similar verbs (for example, *live, lives, lived*), ask yourself *who* did it and *when* did they do it? We would say "I now live" but "he now lives." In these sentences, the *who* is different—and so the verb changes. Similarly, we would say "I now live" but "I lived in the past." In these sentences, the *when* is different—so the verb changes.

Most verbs are regular in this way, with only the endings *s* and *d* to worry about. You use the *s* when the subject is *he, she,* or *it* and the time is now (present tense). You use the *d* for times in the past. For times in the future, or several steps backward in time, there are no special endings. You use the words *will, will have, have,* and *had* for these time sequences. "I *will* live. I *will have* lived for 25 years by the time the next century begins. I *had* lived in Nebraska, but we moved. I *have* lived in Indiana since then."

However, a few verbs are irregular. They have special forms. For example, we say *sang* rather than *singed* and *have sung* rather than *have singed* or *have sang.* Each of these verbs must be learned separately.

One irregular verb commonly tested on the ACT is *bring.*

WRONG:	"I've brung my umbrella to work."
PROBLEM:	*Brang* and *brung* aren't used in standard English.
CORRECTION:	"I've brought my umbrella to work."

RULE 15: *Be* and *Was* (Forms of the Verb *To Be*)

The ACT tests the use of proper verb forms, especially of the verb *to be*. You must use the following forms. Memorize them if you have to:

Present Tense:	I *am*, we *are*, you *are*, they *are*, he/she/it *is*
Past Tense:	I *was*, we *were*, you *were*, they *were*, he/she/it *was*
Future Tense:	I/we/you/they/he/she/it *will be*
Perfect Tense:	I/we/you *have been*, he/she/it *has been*
Past Perfect:	I/we/you/he/she/it *had been*
Future Perfect:	I/we/you/he/she/it *will have been*

You decide which form (*am, are, is, were, was, will be, have been, had been, will have been*) is correct by determining what the subject is and what the tense is. (*Tense* refers to time: present, past, or future.) In many dialects, the words *be* and *was* are used instead of the special forms given. For example, many speakers might say, "They *be* going home" or "They *was* going home." On the ACT, the correct form is "They *are* (or *were*) going home."

✓ **PERFECT SCORE TIP**
The verb *to be* is commonly conjugated incorrectly in everyday life. Review the rules and make a concerted effort to use them correctly when speaking—it will pay off on test day.

RULE 16: *-ing* Endings (Unidiomatic Verb Use)

Don't use *-ing* endings where they aren't needed. They are used to indicate repeated or continuous action and shouldn't be used for a single action that occurs once.

WRONG:	"When I left for the store, I was forgetting my list."
PROBLEM:	The *-ing* ending isn't necessary.
CORRECTION:	"When I left for the store, I forgot my list."

RULE 17: -er and -est, More, and Most (Comparatives and Superlatives)

Whenever you see the endings -er or -est, or the words more or most, double-check to make sure they're used correctly. Words with -er or with more should be used to compare only two things. If there are more than two things involved, use -est or most.

WRONG:	"Bob is the fastest of the two runners."
PROBLEM:	The comparison is between just two things, so -est is inappropriate.
CORRECTION:	"Bob is the faster of the two runners."

Don't use the words more or most if you can use the endings instead. Say "I think vanilla is tastier than chocolate," not "I think vanilla is more tasty than chocolate." Never use both more or most **and** an ending. Don't say "Of the five flavors of frozen yogurt I've eaten, strawberry delight is the most tastiest." Just say it's "the tastiest."

A note on than and then: Than is used in comparisons such as "Bob is faster than Jim." Then refers to time, as in "Bob ran and then stopped."

RULE 18: Between or Among

Make sure that you use the word between only when there are two things involved. When there are more than two things, or an unknown number of things, use among.

WRONG:	"I will walk among the two halves of the class." "I will walk between the many students in class."
PROBLEM:	Use between for two things and among for more than two.
CORRECTION:	"I will walk between the two halves of the class." "I will walk among the many students in class."

RULE 19: Less or Fewer

Make sure that you use the word less only for uncountable things. When things can be counted, they are fewer.

WRONG:	"I have fewer water than I thought, so I can fill less buckets."
PROBLEM:	You can count buckets; you can't count water.
CORRECTION:	"I have less water than I thought, so I can fill fewer buckets."

HINT: People are **always** countable, so use fewer when writing about them.

GO ONLINE

For a more thorough account of the grammar points you should know for the ACT, refer to the English Review for the ACT section of your online syllabus.

▶ IF YOU LEARNED ONLY THREE THINGS IN THIS CHAPTER...

1. You can recognize some grammar mistakes because they sound strange. Listening is a great tool in the English section.

2. Other grammar mistakes break rules in context. To find these, you must read the sentence carefully to determine the correct punctuation, word, phrase, or clause.

3. Grammar rules tested by the ACT are relatively few. Refer to the quick outline provided in this chapter to learn them.

CHAPTER 7

Math Workout 1: The End Justifies the Means

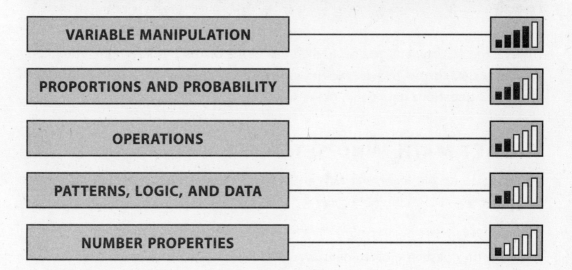

SMARTPOINTS COVERED IN THIS CHAPTER

VARIABLE MANIPULATION

PROPORTIONS AND PROBABILITY

OPERATIONS

PATTERNS, LOGIC, AND DATA

NUMBER PROPERTIES

Your goal on the Math subject test is to get as many correct answers as you can in 60 minutes. It doesn't matter what you do (short of cheating, naturally) to get those correct answers.

You don't have to do every problem the way your math teacher would. **Be open to clever and original solution methods.** All that matters is that your methods be quick and that they get you a solid number of correct answers. How many correct answers you need depends on what kind of score you're aiming for, but chances are you don't have to get so many right as you might think to get a good score. Yes, it's a tough test, but it's graded on a curve.

> **EXPERT TUTOR TIP**
> Here's how to use this chapter if you don't have much time. Learn the Kaplan Method for ACT Math, trying the sample questions that follow. Read the sidebars throughout the whole chapter for quick ACT Math strategy tips.

As we've pointed out, the ACT is different from the typical high school test. On a typical high school math test, you get a series of problems just like the ones you've been doing in class. Because you're being tested on a relatively narrow scope of topics, you're expected to get almost every question right.

ACT Math is different. The scope of what's tested is deliberately wide so that every student will get an opportunity to demonstrate his or her strengths, wherever they may lie.

> **PERFECT SCORE TIP**
> Remember that no one will be checking your method of doing problems. Don't feel compelled to do unnecessary algebra when you know a simpler way to solve the problem.

The average ACT student gets fewer than half of the Math questions right. **You need only about 40 correct answers to get your Math score over 25—just 2 right out of every 3 questions gets you a great score!**

THE ACT MATH MIND-SET

According to an old legend at MIT, a physics professor once asked the following question on a final exam: *How could a barometer be used to determine the height of a tower?*

To answer the question, most students worked out complex equations based on the fact that air pressure (which is what a barometer measures) decreases at higher altitudes. But one student made three suggestions instead:

1. Measure the length of the barometer, then use the barometer as a ruler and measure the tower.
2. Drop the barometer and time its fall, keeping in mind that the acceleration of falling objects is about 32 ft/sec^2.
3. Find the person who built the tower and say, "I'll give you a nice barometer if you tell me how tall your tower is."

Guess which student got an A…

On the ACT, as in college and beyond, you'll sometimes be called upon to do more than merely regurgitate memorized facts and unquestioningly follow prepackaged procedures. True, some ACT Math questions are straightforward: as soon as you understand what the question's asking, you know what to do. But more challenging—and more fun (really)—are the ACT Math questions that aren't what they seem at first glance. These are the questions that call for creative solutions.

EXPERT TUTOR TIP
The ACT Math test includes:
- 24 pre-algebra and elementary algebra questions (corresponding roughly to the 100 Key Math Concepts for the ACT, #1–65)
- 10 intermediate algebra questions (100 Key Math Concepts for the ACT, #66–70)
- 8 coordinate geometry questions (100 Key Math Concepts for the ACT, #71–77)
- 14 plane geometry questions (100 Key Math Concepts for the ACT, #78–95)
- 4 trigonometry questions (100 Key Math Concepts for the ACT, #96–100)

Don't Be Obedient

On the ACT, there's no partial credit. All that matters is the right answer. It makes no difference how you find it. In fact, as we'll see, it's sometimes safer and faster if you don't do ACT problems the "right" way—the way you've been taught in school. For a lot of ACT Math problems, there's more than one way to find the answer. And many of these other ways are faster than the so-called right way.

If you do every problem the way your algebra teacher would want you to, you may earn his or her undying gratitude, but you won't achieve your goal of getting as many correct answers as possible. **You don't have time to use the textbook approach on every question.** You don't have time to write out every step.

✓ PERFECT SCORE TIP
Learn the correct amount of work to write down on math problems. Writing down some steps will help lessen your confusion, but writing too much will make it harder for you to find the right answer.

Pick Numbers

Sometimes you can get stuck on an algebra problem because it's too general or abstract. A good way to get a handle on such a problem is to make it more explicit by temporarily substituting numbers for the variables.

Example

1. If a is an odd integer and b is an even integer, which of the following must be odd?

    A. $2a + b$

    B. $a + 2b$

    C. ab

    D. a^2b

    E. ab^2

$$3 + 2(2)$$
$$3 + 4 = 7$$

Rather than try to think this one through abstractly, it's easier to pick numbers for a and b. There are rules that predict the evenness or oddness of sums, differences, and products, but there's no need to memorize those rules. When it comes to adding, subtracting, and multiplying evens and odds, what happens with one pair of numbers generally happens with all similar pairs.

Just say, for the time being, that $a = 1$ and $b = 2$. Plug those values into the answer choices, and there's a good chance only one choice will be odd:

    A. $2a + b = 2(1) + 2 = 4$

    B. $a + 2b = 1 + 2(2) = 5$

    C. $ab = (1)(2) = 2$

    D. $a^2b = (1)^2(2) = 2$

    E. $ab^2 = (1)(2)^2 = 4$

Choice B was the only odd one for $a = 1$ and $b = 2$, so it *must* be the one that's odd no matter *what* odd number a and even number b actually stand for.

Backsolve

With some ACT Math problems, it may actually be easier to try out each answer choice until you find the one that works, rather than attempt to solve the problem and then look among the choices for the answer. Because this approach involves working backward from the answer choices to the question stem, it's called backsolving.

Example

2. All 200 tickets were sold for a particular concert. Some tickets cost $10 apiece, and the others cost $5 apiece. If total ticket sales were $1,750, how many of the more expensive tickets were sold?

    F.   20

    G.   75

    H.   100

    J.   150

    K.   175

$$1750 = 10(75) + 5(75)$$

There are ways to solve this problem by setting up an equation or two, but if you're not comfortable with the algebraic approach to this one, why not just try out each answer choice?

Start with choice H. If 100 tickets went for $10, then the other 100 went for $5. 100 at $10 is $1,000, and 100 tickets at $5 is $500, for a total of $1,500—too small. There must have been more than 100 $10 tickets.

Which answer do we try next? Because F and G are even smaller than H, try choice J next. If 150 tickets went for $10, then the other 50 went for $5. So 150 tickets at $10 is $1,500, and 50 tickets at $5 is $250, for a total of $1,750—that's it! The answer is J. On test day, the answers will also go in order from smallest to largest (or largest to smallest) allowing you to eliminate wrong answers without trying them out.

Backsolving your way to the answer may not be a method you'd show your algebra teacher with pride—but your algebra teacher won't be watching on test day. Remember, all that matters is right answers—it doesn't matter how you get them.

> **EXPERT TUTOR TIP**
> You will not get credit for anything you write under "DO YOUR FIGURING HERE." You get credit only for answers correctly gridded into the bubbles on your answer sheet.

Be a Thinker—Not a Number Cruncher

One reason you're given limited time for the Math subject test is that the ACT is testing your ability to think, not your willingness to do a lot of mindless calculations. So one of your guiding principles for ACT Math should be: **work less, but think harder.**

If you want to get the best score you can, be on the lookout for quicker ways to solve problems. Here's an example that could take a lot more time than it needs to:

Example

3. When $\frac{4}{11}$ is converted to a decimal, the 50th digit after the decimal point is:

   A. 2

   B. 3

   C. 4

   D. 5

   E. 6

It seems that when you convert $\frac{4}{11}$ to a decimal, there are at least 50 digits after the decimal point. The question asks for the 50th. One way to answer this question would be to divide 11 into 4, carrying the division out to 50 decimal places. That method would work, but it would take forever. It's not worth spending that much time on one question.

No ACT Math question should take more than a minute to solve. There has to be a faster way to solve this problem. There must be some kind of pattern you can take advantage of, some kind of pattern with a decimal. How about a *repeating* decimal?!

In fact, that's exactly what you have here. The decimal equivalent of $\frac{4}{11}$ is 0.3636363636…

The 1st, 3rd, 5th, 7th, and 9th digits are each 3. The 2nd, 4th, 6th, 8th, and 10th digits are each 6. Put simply, odd-numbered digits are 3s and even-numbered digits are 6s. The 50th digit is an even-numbered digit, so it's a 6 and the answer is E.

What looked at first glance like a fractions and decimals problem turned out to be something of an odds and evens problem. If you don't use creative shortcuts on problems like this one, you'll get bogged down, you'll run out of time, and you won't get a lot of correct answers.

> **EXPERT TUTOR TIP**
> Underlining what the question is asking will help you to make sure you choose the correct answer.

Question 3 demonstrates how the ACT designs problems to reward clever thinking and to punish students who blindly "go through the motions." But how do you get yourself into a creative mind-set on the Math test? For one thing, you have to take the time to understand thoroughly each problem you decide to work on. Most students are so nervous about time that they skim each math problem and almost immediately start computing with their pencils. But that's the wrong way of thinking. **Sometimes you have to *take* time to *save* time.** A few extra moments spent understanding a math problem can save many extra moments of computation or other drudgery.

> ☑ **PERFECT SCORE TIP**
> As will be discussed later, a calculator can be your biggest aid or your greatest weakness. Use it to eliminate timely and costly calculation mistakes but not as a substitute for thinking about a problem.

THE KAPLAN METHOD FOR ACT MATH

At Kaplan, we've developed this take-time-to-save-time philosophy into a method for ACT Math problems. The approach is designed to help you find the fast, inventive solutions that the ACT rewards. The steps are:

STEP 1: What Is the Question?

Focus first on the question stem (the part before the answer choices), and make sure you understand the problem. Sometimes you'll want to read the stem twice or rephrase it in a way you can better understand. Think to yourself: "What kind of problem is this? What am I looking for?"

To understand an ACT Math problem, you first have to understand the language. Mathematicians are generally very precise in their use of language. They choose their words carefully and mean exactly what they say. You don't need to memorize definitions (you'll **never** have to recite one on the ACT), but you do need to understand what the question writer means.

> ☑ **PERFECT SCORE TIP**
> Understanding the question is key. I know how tempting it is to start looking at answer choices before you really know what the question is looking for, but I promise this will not help you.

STEP 2: What Information Am I Given?

Now that you know what the question is asking, you need to figure out how to get from the problem to the answer. The best way to approach problems on the ACT is to ask yourself two things:

1. What information is provided in the question stem? Look at what information you're given along with what the question is asking. Do you have all of the information you need to answer the question like you would in a straightforward arithmetic or algebra problem? Are there additional computations you need to make in order to get to the answer? Note to yourself what information you have and what you may still need.

2. In what format do the answers appear? Take a quick look at the answers—not to choose an answer yet, just to check out the format of your options. This will help you organize your thinking. For example, you may think that you need to solve for x in an equation, but then you see that all of the answers are given in terms of x, so you don't actually need to find x, just come up with a formula. Additionally, if you are given information in fractions and see answers in decimals, you'll know that you need to convert from one to the other at some point.

For some questions, it will be clear to you what information you have and what you may need to do to find the answer. For others, you may not have all of the information you need and will need to do some computations before you can answer the question. That brings us to Step 3.

STEP 3: What Can I Do with the Information?

Think for a moment and decide on a plan of attack. Don't start crunching numbers until you've given the problem a little thought. There are three ways to solve the problem:

1. Use your math skills. If you know what to do, go for it!

2. Picking numbers. Are there variables in the answer choices that you can pick numbers for?

3. Backsolving. Are there numbers in the answer choices that you can use to figure out which one has to be the correct answer?

> **EXPERT TUTOR TIP**
> Examine the diagram if you are given one, or make your own.

STEP 4: Am I Finished?

Once you get an answer, check the question again. Have you fully answered the question? Some questions may require several steps, and you may miss the last step if you don't check before you select. The test makers know to offer tempting answer choices for students who don't recheck the question. For example, you may need to find the area of a circle and you've only determined the radius—and the radius might be an answer choice! Since you will have identified the question in Step 1, double-checking that you're finished should take only a few seconds, and it can make a real difference on test day. Once you're sure, circle the answer in your test book and fill in the answer grid.

If you are stuck, skip the problem on the first pass through the test. Get all your easy points first! When you come back, if you still don't know how to approach the problem, try guessing strategically. In other words, are there any answer choices that you know couldn't possibly be the answer? Eliminate as many as you can before you choose an answer. Each answer choice you eliminate gets you one step closer to the correct answer!

Each of these steps can happen in a matter of seconds; it may not always be clear when you've finished with one step and moved on to the next. Sometimes you'll know how to attack a problem the instant you read and understand it.

> **GO ONLINE**
> You can find the Kaplan Method for ACT Math on your downloadable study sheet, for review on the go.

Using the Kaplan Method

Here's how the Kaplan Method could be applied to question 3.

STEP 1: What Is the Question?

First, we made sure we understood what the problem was asking for: the 50th digit after the decimal point in the decimal equivalent of a certain fraction. Because we knew what *digit* and *decimal equivalent* meant, it took only a second to understand what the problem was asking.

STEP 2: What Information Am I Given?

In this case, you were given a fraction and were asked to convert it into a decimal and find the 50th digit after the decimal point. The answers were all single digits from 2 to 6.

STEP 3: What Can I Do with the Information?

Most crucially, we analyzed the situation and thought about a plan of attack before we tried to solve the problem. We realized that the obvious method would take too long, so we figured out a creative approach that got us an answer of 6 in just a few seconds.

STEP 4: Am I Finished?

Before choosing an answer, we reread the question to be sure that we had answered it fully. In this case, the question was pretty straightforward, but others may not be.

Finally, we looked at the answer choices, found 6, and selected choice E.

The Kaplan Method isn't a rigid procedure; it's a set of guidelines that will keep you on track, moving quickly, and evading pitfalls.

Example

4. If the sum of five consecutive even integers is equal to their product, what is the greatest of the five integers?

   F. 4
   G. 10
   H. 14
   J. 16
   K. 20

STEP 1: What Is the Question?

Before you can begin to solve this problem, you have to figure out what it's asking. You'll need to know the meanings of *sum, product, consecutive, even,* and *integer.* Put the question stem into words you can understand. What the question stem is really saying here is that when you add up these five consecutive even integers, you get the same thing as when you multiply them.

STEP 2: What Information Am I Given?

We are not given any numbers in the problem, but we *are* told that we'll be working with consecutive even integers. The difference between each integer in this series will be 2. A quick glance at the answer choices and we see that they are all positive. Good to know.

STEP 3: What Can I Do with the Information?

How are we going to figure out what these five numbers are? We could set up an equation:

$$x + (x - 2) + (x - 4) + (x - 6) + (x - 8) = x(x - 2)(x - 4)(x - 6)(x - 8)$$

But there's no way you'll have time to solve an equation like this! So don't even try. Come up with a better way.

Let's stop and think logically about this one for a moment. When we think about sums and products, it's natural to think mostly of positive integers. With positive integers, we would generally expect the product to be *greater* than the sum.

But what about negative integers? Hmm. Well, the sum of five negatives is negative, and the product of five negatives is also negative. Generally the product will be "more negative" than the sum, so with negative integers, the product will be less than the sum.

So when will the product and sum be the same? How about right at the boundary of positive and negative—that is, around 0? The five consecutive even integers with equal product and sum are: –4, –2, 0, 2, and 4.

$$(-4) \times (-2) \times 0 \times 2 \times 4 = (-4) + (-2) + 0 + 2 + 4$$

The product and sum are both 0. Ha! We've done it!

How to backsolve: The question asks which is the greatest of the integers, so you start with the greatest answer choice: K. If the largest number is 20, then the other numbers must be 18, 16, 14, 12. Their sum is $20 + 18 + 16 + 14 + 12 = 80$. 20 times 18 is already 360, so we know that choice K is not correct and that it is WAY too big! Let's try the next smallest choice, H (14). We want to add: $14 + 12 + 10 + 8 + 6 = 50$. Still too big, because 10 times 6 is already 60. So let's try 4, choice F. $4 + 2 + 0 + (-2) + (-4) = 4 \times 2 \times 0 \times (-2) \times (-4) = 0$. It works!

> **EXPERT TUTOR TIP**
> If you don't have any idea how to solve this problem, ask yourself, "Can I pick numbers? Can I backsolve?" There are numbers in the answer choices, so you should backsolve.

STEP 4: Am I Finished?

We found the answer by thinking logically about the question and confirmed our answer by backsolving. The question asks for the greatest of five integers, which is 4, choice F. If you didn't read the question carefully, you might be tempted to look for the sum and product of the five integers—fortunately, that's not an option, but for other questions, a tempting answer may be a choice.

You've probably encountered every math term that appears on the ACT sometime in your high school math career, but you may not remember exactly what every one of them means. The Math Glossary in the ACT Resources section of your online syllabus is a complete but compact list of the terminology you need for ACT Math problems. Look it over. Jot down the terms you're not sure of for future reference. And be sure to use the online glossary to look up any unfamiliar term you encounter while practicing with ACT Math questions.

> ☑ **PERFECT SCORE TIP**
> Math is one section where actual knowledge of material is necessary. If any terms you read here are unfamiliar to you, learn them! Don't waste precious easy points because you don't know the definition of basic terms.

Definition Alert

As you refresh your memory of key terminology, watch out for technicalities. Here are a few examples of such technicalities (by the way, these are great for stumping your know-it-all friends):

- *Integers* **include 0 and negative whole numbers.** If a question says "*x* and *y* are integers," it's not ruling out numbers like 0 and –1.

- *Evens and odds* **include 0 and negative whole numbers.** Zero and –2 are even numbers; –1 is an odd number.

- *Prime numbers* **do not include 1.** The technical definition of a prime number is a positive integer with exactly two distinct positive integer factors. Two is prime because it has exactly two positive factors: 1 and 2. It's also the smallest, and the only even, prime number. Four is not prime because it has three positive factors (1, 2, and 4)—too many! And 1 is not prime because it has only one positive factor (1)—too few!

- *Remainders* **are integers.** If a question asks for the remainder when 15 is divided by 2, don't say "15 divided by 2 is 7.5, so the remainder is .5." What you should say is: "15 divided by 2 is 7 with a remainder of 1."

- *The $\sqrt{}$ symbol represents the positive square root only.* The equation $x^2 = 9$ has two solutions: 3 and –3. But when you see $\sqrt{9}$, it means positive 3 only.

- *Rectangles* **include squares.** The definition of a rectangle is a four-sided figure with four right angles. It doesn't matter if the length and width are the same or not—if it has four right angles, it's a rectangle. When a question refers to "rectangle ABCD," it's not ruling out a square.

Example

5. What is the value of $x^2 + 3x - 9$ when $x = -3$?

    A. −27
    B. −9
    C. −6
    D. 0
    E. 9

$$(-3)^2 + 3(-3) - 9$$
$$9 + (-9) - 9$$
$$-9$$

STEP 1: What Is the Question?

You've probably seen dozens of problems just like this. If so, then you realize right away that what it's asking is, "What do you get when you plug $x = -3$ into $x^2 + 3x - 9$?"

STEP 2: What Information Am I Given?

In this question, we're given an algebra problem and a value for x. We're given three negative integers for answer choices, along with 0 and 3.

STEP 3: What Can I Do with the Information?

Because we have a value for x, we can just plug it into the algebra problem and solve:

$$x^2 + 3x - 9 = (-3)^2 + 3(-3) - 9$$
$$= 9 + (-9) - 9$$
$$= -9$$

STEP 4: Am I Finished?

Rereading the problem tells us we've done exactly what it asked; our answer, −9, is choice B.

So this is a case where you knew exactly what to do as soon as you understood what the question was asking. Sometimes you're not so lucky. Let's look at a case where the method of solution is not so obvious, even after you understand the stem:

▗▖▗▖ **NUMBER PROPERTIES**

Example

6. Which is the greatest of the numbers 1^{50}, 50^1, 2^{25}, 25^2, 4^{10}?

    F. 1^{50}

    G. 50^1

    (H.) 2^{25}

    J. 25^2

    K. 4^{10}

STEP 1: What Is the Question?

It's not hard to figure out what the question is asking: which of five numbers is the greatest? But the five numbers are all written as powers, some of which we don't have time to calculate. Yikes! How are we going to compare them?

STEP 2: What Information Am I Given?

Here you're given five integers of different values with exponents of different values. Since you're asked to find the greatest of the numbers, you can't rely on the answers to be in ascending value as they usually are for ACT questions—that would be too easy.

STEP 3: What Can I Do with the Information?

If all the powers had the same base or the same exponent, or if they could all be rewritten with a common base or exponent, we could compare all five at once. As it is, though, we should take two at a time.

> ◎ **KAPLAN'S TARGET STRATEGY**
> Step 3 is where you'll be doing most of your serious thinking. The other two Math Workouts will address this step in greater detail.

Compare 1^{50} and 50^1 to start: $1^{50} = 1$, while $50^1 = 50$, so there's no way choice F could be the biggest.

Next, compare 50^1 and 2^{25}. We don't have time to calculate 2^{25}, but we can see that it doesn't take anywhere near 25 factors of 2 to get over 50. In fact, 2^6 is 64, already more than 50, so 2^{25} is much more than 50. That eliminates G.

Choice J, 25^2, doesn't take too long to calculate: $25 \times 25 = 625$. How does that compare to 2^{25}? Once again, with a little thought, we realize that it doesn't take 25 factors of 2 to get over 625. That eliminates J.

The last comparison is easy because choice K, 4^{10}, can be rewritten as $(2^2)^{10} = 2^{20}$, which is clearly less than 2^{25}. That eliminates choice K.

> **EXPERT TUTOR TIP**
> Whenever plugging negative numbers into your calculator, always make sure to put them in parentheses. Not using them will lead to a wrong answer!

STEP 4: Am I Finished?

Check the question—we were asked for the greatest of the numbers. The answer is H and we are finished.

> **EXPERT TUTOR TIP**
> Use your calculator to fly right through Example 6. If you don't use a calculator all the time in school, start practicing so you are familiar with it by test day.

Know When to Skip

At any time during the four-step process, you could choose to cut bait and skip the question. **Almost everyone should skip at least some questions the first time through.**

> **EXPERT TUTOR TIP**
> The fastest way to a higher score on the ACT is to get all your easy points first—skip those hard problems, and go back to them later if you have time.

If you know your own strengths and weaknesses, you can sometimes choose to skip a question while still in Step 1: Understand. For example, suppose you **never** studied trigonometry. Maybe you think that a secant is something that sailors sing while climbing up the yardarms. Well, the ACT includes exactly four trigonometry questions, and it's not hard to spot them. Why waste a second on such questions? Skip them! You don't need those four measly questions to get a great score. And since you know a second visit later won't help any, you might as well go ahead and make some random guesses.

KAPLAN'S TWO-PASS PLAN FOR ACT MATH

We recommend that you plan two passes through the Math test.

- **First pass:** Examine each problem in order. Do every problem you understand. Don't skip too hastily—sometimes it takes a few seconds of thought to see how to do something—but don't get bogged down. Never spend more than a minute on any question in the first pass. This first pass should take about 45 minutes.

- **Second pass:** Use the last 15 minutes to go back to the questions that stumped you the first time. Sometimes a fresh look is all you need—after going away and then coming back, you'll sometimes suddenly see what to do. In most cases, though, you'll still be stumped by the question stem, so it's time to give the answer choices a try. Work by process of elimination, and guess. Be sure to select an answer for every question, even if it's just a blind guess.

It can be harder to decide when to skip a question if you understand it, but then get stuck in Step 2: Analyze. Suppose you just don't see how to solve it. Don't give up too quickly. Sometimes it takes 30 seconds or so before you see the light. But don't get bogged down either. Never spend more than a minute on a question the first time through the section. No single question is worth it. Be prepared to leave a question and come back to it later. Often, on the second try, you'll see something you didn't see before. That old lightbulb will light up over your head and you'll be on your way.

Of course, eventually, you're going to grid in an answer choice for every question, even the ones you don't understand. **The first time through the section, you should concentrate on the questions you understand.**

EXPERT TUTOR TIP
Making two passes through the Math test means you'll never run out of time before seeing every question.

Don't plan on visiting a question a third time; it's inefficient to go back and forth that much. Every time you leave a question and come back to it, you have to take at least a few seconds to refamiliarize yourself with the problem. **Always** grid in an answer choice on the second pass—even if it's just a wild guess. At the end of the second pass, every question should be answered.

Don't worry if you don't work on every question in the section. The average ACT test taker gets fewer than half of the problems right. You can score in the top quarter of all ACT test takers if you can do just half of the problems on the test, get every single one of them right, and guess blindly on the other half. If you did just one-third of the problems and got every one right, then guessed blindly on the other 40 problems, you would still earn an average score.

> ✓ **PERFECT SCORE TIP**
> I skipped multiple questions on my first time through. When I returned to them the second time, I found that they often became clearer to me. It is possible to get a very good score even if the solution to every problem does not pop out at you.

Don't Make Careless Mistakes

Most students don't worry much about careless errors. Because in school (where you show your work) you can earn partial credit, many students think that careless errors somehow "don't count." Not so on the ACT. There are only so many problems you'll know how to do. Some of the problems will be impossible for you, so you'll make or break your score on the problems you can do. You can't afford to miss one easy problem!

Unless math is a very strong area for you, the best way to maximize your score is to work on the questions you deserve to get correct. Don't worry about getting to every problem (though, of course, you should mark an answer for every problem on your answer grid, even if it's a blind guess).

Even if math is a strong area for you, don't get complacent on easy problems—that causes careless errors. For strong students, the easy problems may be the most challenging. You have to find a way to answer them quickly and accurately in order to have time for the tougher ones. You won't have time for the hard problems unless you save some time on the easy ones.

Here's a question that's not hard to understand but is hard to solve if you don't remember the rules for simplifying and adding radicals:

⢀⣿⣿ NUMBER PROPERTIES

Example

7. $\dfrac{\sqrt{32} + \sqrt{24}}{\sqrt{8}} = ?$

    A. $\sqrt{7}$

    B. $\sqrt{2} + \sqrt{3}$

    C. $2 + \sqrt{3}$

    D. $\sqrt{2} + 3$

    E. 7

STEP 1: What Is the Question?

The question wants you to simplify the given expression, which includes three radicals. In other words, turn the radicals into numbers you can use, then work out the fraction.

> **✓ PERFECT SCORE TIP**
> Sometimes radicals can be intimidating. Remember that even if you forget the rules, there are simpler ways to deal with them, such as using known radicals to estimate, or if worse comes to worst, using your calculator to get estimates.

STEP 2: What Information Am I Given?

You're given a fraction with numbers under a radical in the numerator and denominator. If you looked at the problem and had no idea what to do, a glance at the answers would help. The answers are not given in fractional terms so you know you can simplify the fraction to eliminate the denominator. Additionally, the choices include the numbers 7, 2, and 3, either alone or under radicals. Think about how the numbers under the radicals can be factored into those numbers as you approach Step 3.

STEP 3: What Can I Do with the Information?

The best way to solve this problem would be to apply the rules of radicals—but what if you don't remember them? Don't give up; you can still guesstimate. In the question stem, the numbers under the radicals are not too far away from perfect squares. You could round $\sqrt{32}$ off to $\sqrt{36}$, which is 6. You could round $\sqrt{24}$ to $\sqrt{25}$, which is 5. And you could round $\sqrt{8}$ off to $\sqrt{9}$, which is 3. So the expression is now

$\frac{6+5}{3}$, which is $3\frac{2}{3}$. That's just a guesstimate, of course—the actual value might be something a bit less or a bit more than that.

> **EXPERT TUTOR TIP**
> This problem can also be solved using a calculator. If you plug this into your calcula-tor, you get 3.73. Then put each of the answer choices into your calculator to see which one matches.

STEP 4: Am I Finished?

Reread the question, then look at the answer choices. Choice A ($\sqrt{7}$) is less than 3, so it's too small. Choice B ($\sqrt{2} + \sqrt{3}$) is about 1.4 + 1.7, or just barely more than 3, so it seems a little small, too. Choice C ($2 + \sqrt{3}$) is about 2 + 1.7, or about 3.7—that's very close to our guesstimate! We still have to check the other choices. Choice D ($\sqrt{2} + 3$) is about 1.4 + 3, or 4.4—too big. And choice E, 7, is obviously way too big. Looks like our best bet is choice C—and C in fact is the correct answer.

> **PERFECT SCORE TIP**
> My biggest problem on the Math section was trying to go too fast. In practice, I would often get questions wrong simply because I went too fast and missed an important word in the question or made an arithmetic mistake. These mistakes are not worth it—trust me.

TO CALCULATE OR NOT TO CALCULATE

You are permitted to use a calculator on the Math section. The good news is that you never *absolutely need* to use a calculator on the ACT. No Math question requires messy or tedious calculations. But while the calculator can't answer questions for you, it can keep you from making computational errors on questions you know how to solve. The bad news, however, is that a calculator can actually cost you time if you overuse it. Take a look at this example:

Example

8. The sum of all the integers from 1 to 44, inclusive, is subtracted from the sum of all the integers from 7 to 50, inclusive. What is the result?

    F.   6

    G.   44

    H.   50

    J. 264

    K. 300

You could add all the integers from 1 through 44, and then all the integers from 7 through 50, and then subtract the first sum from the second. And then punch in all the numbers into the calculator. And then hope you didn't hit any wrong buttons.

But that's the long way…and the *wrong* way. That way involves hitting over 250 keys on your calculator. It'll take too long, and you're too likely to make a mistake. The amount of computation involved in solving this problem tells you that there must be an easier way. Remember, no ACT problem absolutely requires the use of a calculator.

Look at the problem again: a calculator *can* help you on this question, but you have to think first. Both sums contain the same number of consecutive integers, and each integer in the first sum has a corresponding integer 6 greater than it in the second sum. Here's the scratchwork:

$$
\begin{array}{cc}
1 & 7 \\
+2 & +8 \\
+3 & +9 \\
\cdot & \cdot \\
\cdot & \cdot \\
\cdot & \cdot \\
+42 & +48 \\
+43 & +49 \\
+44 & +50 \\
\end{array}
$$

This means there are 44 pairs of integers which are each 6 apart. So the total difference between the two sums will be the difference between each pair of integers times the number of pairs. Now you can pull out your calculator, punch in "6 × 44 =," and get the correct answer of 264 with little or no time wasted. Mark J in your test booklet and move on.

EXPERT TUTOR TIP
If a problem seems to involve a lot of calculation, look for a quicker way. Try to spot a pattern that will help you save some time.

Of course, there will be many situations on the ACT in which using a calculator can save you time. Here's a trig question that's much easier with a calculator:

Example

9. sin 495° =

A. $-\dfrac{\sqrt{2}}{2}$

B. $-\dfrac{1}{2}$

C. $\dfrac{1}{2}$

D. $\dfrac{\sqrt{2}}{2}$

E. $\dfrac{3\sqrt{2}}{2}$

Without a calculator, this is a very difficult problem. To find a trigonometric function of an angle greater than or equal to 90°, sketch a circle of radius 1 which is centered at the origin of the coordinate grid. Start from the point (1, 0) and rotate the appropriate number of degrees counterclockwise. When you rotate counterclockwise 495°, you rotate 360° (which brings you back to where you started), and then an additional 135°. That puts you midway into the second quadrant. Now you need to know whether sine is positive or negative in the second quadrant. Pretty scary, huh?

> ☑ **PERFECT SCORE TIP**
> One of my biggest weaknesses is simple arithmetic, so my calculator was very helpful in eliminating these mistakes. Still, I had to be sure that I had a plan for how to do most problems without a calculator, and then use it just to check my math.

With a calculator, this problem becomes simple. Just punch in "sin 495°" and you get 0.7071067811865. Choices A and B are negative, so they're out, and 0.7071067811865 is clearly not equal to $\dfrac{1}{2}$, so choice C is also wrong. That leaves only choices D or E. Now, with respect to choice E: $\sqrt{2}$ is greater than 1, so if you multiply it by another number greater than 1 (namely $\dfrac{3}{2}$), the result is obviously greater than 1. So you can eliminate choice E, leaving D as the correct answer. With a calculator, you can get this question right without really understanding it.

> **EXPERT TUTOR TIP**
> When doing trig functions, make sure that your calculator is in degree mode—unless the answers contain π, in which case you have to use radians.

The key to effective calculator use is practice, so don't run out the night before the test to buy a fancy new calculator. If you don't already have a calculator (and intend to use one on the test), buy one now. Unless you're studying math or science in college, you won't need anything more complex than trig functions. You're better off bringing a straightforward model you're familiar with than an esoteric model you don't know how to use.

Practicing with your calculator is the best way to get a sense of where it can help and save time. Here's a brief guide to spotting those calculator-friendly Math questions.

Example

10. $(7.3 + 0.8) - 3(1.98 + 0.69) =$

   F. -0.99
   G. -0.09
   H. 0
   J. 0.09
   K. 0.99

This problem basically involves straightforward computation, so you'd be right if you reached for your calculator. However, if you just start punching the numbers in as they appear in the question, you will come up with the wrong answer. When you're performing a string of computations, you know that you need to follow the right order of operations. The problem is, your calculator might not know this. Some calculators have parentheses keys and do follow the order of operations, so it's important to know your calculator and what its capabilities are. See 100 Key Math Concepts for the ACT, #7 for further explanation of PEMDAS.

> **EXPERT TUTOR TIP**
> Some calculators automatically follow the proper order of operations, but others don't. Know before test day what your calculator can and cannot do.

If your calculator doesn't follow the order of operations, you'd need to perform the operations within parentheses separately and proceed carefully from there. You'd get $8.1 - 3(2.67)$. Multiplication comes before subtraction, so you'd get $8.1 - 8.01$, and then finally 0.09, choice J.

Example

11. A certain bank issues three-letter identification codes to its customers. If each letter can be used only once per code, how many different codes are possible?

  A.   26

  B.   78

  C.   326

  D. 15,600

  E. 17,576

Just manipulating the numbers in this problem will get you nowhere, but once you arrive at the setup, a calculator is very useful.

For the first letter in the code, you can choose any of the 26 letters in the alphabet. For the second letter, you can choose from all the letters in the alphabet except the one you used in the first spot, so there are 26 – 1 = 25 possibilities. For the third, there are 26 – 2 = 24 possibilities. So the total number of different codes possible is equal to 26 × 25 × 24. Using your calculator, you find that there are 15,600 codes—choice D.

Example

12. Which of the following fractions is greater than 0.68 and less than 0.72?

  F. $\dfrac{5}{9}$

  G. $\dfrac{7}{11}$

  H. $\dfrac{2}{3}$

  J. $\dfrac{5}{7}$

  K. $\dfrac{3}{4}$

Here, you have to convert the fractions to decimals and see which one falls in the range of values given in the question. If you're familiar with common decimal/fraction conversions, you might know that choice K, $\dfrac{3}{4}$, is equal to 0.75 (too large) and choice H, $\dfrac{2}{3}$, is approximately 0.67 (too small). But you'd still have to check out the other three choices. Your calculator can make short work of this, showing you that choice F, $\dfrac{5}{9}$, equals $0.\overline{55}$; choice G, $\dfrac{7}{11}$, equals $.\overline{63}$; and choice J, $\dfrac{5}{7}$, is approximately 0.71. Only 0.71 falls between 0.68 and 0.72, so choice J is correct.

GO ONLINE
Your downloadable study sheet contains key math formulas and concepts.

▶ IF YOU LEARNED ONLY FOUR THINGS IN THIS CHAPTER...

1. Look for the quickest ways to solve problems. Sometimes this requires creative thinking.

2. Use the answer choices to help you. If you are stuck, can you plug numbers in for the variables or use the numbers in the answer choices to get to the correct answer?

3. Follow Kaplan's Two-Pass Plan: Skip problems that are more difficult, and come back to them after you've finished the easy ones.

4. Practice with your calculator so you are comfortable using it—and understand when it is faster not to use it.

CHAPTER 8

Math Workout 2: Shake It Up!

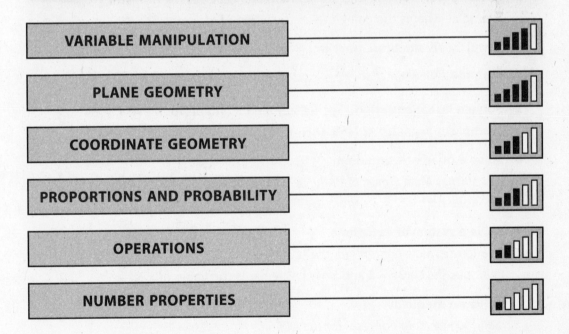

SMARTPOINTS COVERED IN THIS CHAPTER

- VARIABLE MANIPULATION
- PLANE GEOMETRY
- COORDINATE GEOMETRY
- PROPORTIONS AND PROBABILITY
- OPERATIONS
- NUMBER PROPERTIES

The main idea of Math Workout 1 was: Don't jump in headfirst and start crunching numbers until you've given a problem some thought. Make sure you know what you're doing—*and* that what you're doing won't take too long.

As we saw in Math Workout 1, sometimes you'll know how to proceed as soon as you understand the question. A good number of ACT algebra and coordinate geometry questions are straightforward textbook questions you may already be prepared for.

TEN TEXTBOOK ALGEBRA AND COORDINATE GEOMETRY QUESTIONS

░▎▎▎▊▏ VARIABLE MANIPULATION

░▎▎▊▏▏ COORDINATE GEOMETRY

When you take the ACT, you can be sure you'll see some of the following questions with only slight variations. You'll find answers and explanations for these questions in the 100 Key Math Concepts for the ACT section.

1. **Evaluate an algebraic expression.** *(See 100 Key Math Concepts for the ACT, #52)*
   Example: If $x = -2$, then $x^2 + 5x - 6 = ?$

2. **Multiply binomials.** *(See 100 Key Math Concepts for the ACT, #56)*
   Example: $(x + 3)(x + 4) = ?$

3. **Factor a polynomial.** *(See 100 Key Math Concepts for the ACT, #61)*
   Example: What is the complete factorization of $x^2 - 5x + 6$?

4. **Simplify an algebraic fraction.** *(See 100 Key Math Concepts for the ACT, #62)*
   Example: For all $x \neq \pm 63$, $\dfrac{x^2 - x - 12}{x^2 - 9} = ?$

5. **Solve a linear equation.** *(See 100 Key Math Concepts for the ACT, #63)*
   Example: If $5x - 12 = -2x + 9$, then $x = ?$

6. **Solve a quadratic equation.**
   (See 100 Key Math Concepts for the ACT, #66)
   Example: If $x^2 + 12 = 7x$, what are the two possible values of x?

7. **Solve a system of equations.**
   (See 100 Key Math Concepts for the ACT, #67)
   Example: If $4x + 3y = 8$ and $x + y = 3$, what is the value of x?

8. **Solve an inequality.**
   (See 100 Key Math Concepts for the ACT, #69)
   Example: What are all the values of x for which $-5x + 7 < -3$?

9. **Find the distance between two points in the (x, y) coordinate plane.**
   (See 100 Key Math Concepts for the ACT, #71)
   Example: What is the distance between the points with (x, y) coordinates $(-2, 2)$ and $(1, -2)$?

10. **Find the slope of a line from its equation.**
    (See 100 Key Math Concepts for the ACT, #73)
    Example: What is the slope of the line with the equation $2x + 3y = 4$?

These questions are all straightforward and traditional. They could have come out of a high school algebra textbook, so do these questions the way you were taught. In case you'd like to review them, you'll find all the standard approaches succinctly summarized in 100 Key Math Concepts for the ACT. We're not so concerned in these workouts with problems you may already know how to solve. Here, we're going to focus on several situations where the quick and reliable solution method is not so obvious.

> **GO ONLINE**
> Get more coordinate geometry practice with the online workshop and quiz available through your online syllabus.

> **PERFECT SCORE TIP**
> Basic algebra is a must-know for ACT Math. If any of these concepts seem unfamiliar to you, be sure to read about them in the 100 Key Math Concepts.

THREE WAYS TO SHAKE IT UP

It's bound to happen at some point on test day. You look at a math problem and you don't see what to do. Don't freak out. Think about the problem for a few seconds before you give up. **When you don't see the quick and reliable approach right away, shake the problem up a little.** Try one of these "shake-it-up" techniques:

1. **Restate.**
2. **Remove the disguise.**
3. **Try eyeballing.**

1. Restate the Problem

Often, the way to get over that stymied feeling is to change your perspective. Have you ever watched people playing Scrabble®? In their search to form high-scoring words with the letters on their seven tiles, they continually move the tiles around in their racks. Sometimes a good word becomes apparent only after rearranging the tiles. One might not see the seven-letter word in this arrangement:

        R E B A G L A

But reverse the tiles and a word almost reveals itself:

        A L G A B E R

The tiles can spell ALGEBRA.

The same gimmick works on the ACT, too. **When you get stuck, try looking at the problem from a different angle.** Try rearranging the numbers, changing fractions to decimals, factoring, multiplying out, or redrawing the diagram—anything that might give you the fresh perspective you need to uncover a good solution method.

Here's a question you might not know what to do with at first glance:

OPERATIONS

Example

1. Which of the following is equivalent to $7^{77} - 7^{76}$?

    A. 7

    B. 7^{77-76}

    C. $7^{77 \div 76}$

    D. $7(77 - 76)$

    E. $7^{76}(6)$

Here's a hint: *Think of an easier problem testing the same principles.* The important thing to look for is the basic relationships involved—here, we have exponents and subtraction. That subtraction sign causes trouble, because none of the ordinary rules of exponents (see 100 Key Math Concepts for the ACT, #47–48) seem to apply when there is subtraction of unlike terms.

Another hint: How would you work with $x^2 - x$? Most test takers could come up with another expression for $x^2 - x$: they'd factor to $x(x - 1)$. Or if the problem asked for $x^{77} - x^{76}$, they'd factor to $x^{76}(x - 1)$. The rule is no different for 7 than for x. Factoring out the 7^{76} gives you: $7^{76}(7 - 1)$, which is $7^{76}(6)$, or choice E.

> **EXPERT TUTOR TIP**
> If you are using a graphing calculator, you can use your calculator to solve Example 1.

Sometimes an ACT algebra question will include an expression that isn't of much use in its given form. The breakthrough in such a case may be to restate the expression by either simplifying it or factoring it.

> **PERFECT SCORE TIP**
> If the first way you think of to solve a problem is not working, don't be afraid to try a different one. Often, rephrasing a problem you are stuck on will make it become clearer.

.₀₀₀₀ NUMBER PROPERTIES

Example

2. If $\frac{x}{2} - \frac{x}{6}$ is an integer, which of the following statements must be true?

   F. x is positive.

   G. x is odd.

   H. x is even.

   J. x is a multiple of 3.

   K. x is a multiple of 6.

Re-express: $\frac{x}{2} - \frac{x}{6} = \frac{3x}{6} - \frac{x}{6} = \frac{2x}{6} = \frac{x}{3}$

This form of the expression tells us a lot more. If $\frac{x}{3}$ is an integer, then x is equal to three times an integer:

$$\frac{x}{3} = \text{an integer}$$

$$x = 3 \times \text{an integer}$$

In other words, x is a multiple of 3, choice J.

2. Remove the Disguise

Sometimes it's hard to see the quick and reliable method immediately because the true nature of the problem is hidden behind a disguise. Look at this example:

.₀₀₀₀ VARIABLE MANIPULATION

Example

3. What are the (x, y) coordinates of the point of intersection of the line representing the equation $5x + 2y = 4$ and the line representing the equation $x - 2y = 8$?

   A. $(2, 3)$

   B. $(-2, 3)$

   C. $(2, -3)$

   D. $(-3, 2)$

   E. $(3, -2)$

This may look like a coordinate geometry question, but do you really have to graph the lines to find the point of intersection? Remember, the ACT is looking for creative thinkers, not mindless calculators! Think about it for a moment—what's the special significance of the point of intersection, the one point that the two lines have in common? That's the one point whose coordinates will satisfy *both* equations.

> **EXPERT TUTOR TIP**
>
> Although this question turned out not to be a real coordinate geometry problem, the test makers do have a soft spot in their hearts for coordinate geometry. Typically 8 or more of the 60 Math questions involve coordinate geometry. It's hard to get a top score without getting at least some of these questions right. Use 100 Key Math Concepts for the ACT #71–77 to review the relevant rules and formulas.

So what we realize now is that this is not a coordinate geometry question at all, but a system-of-equations question. All it's really asking you to do is solve the pair of equations for *x* and *y*. The question has nothing to do with slopes, intercepts, axes, or quadrants. It's a pure algebra question in disguise.

Now that we know we're looking at a system of equations, the method of solution presents itself more clearly. The first equation has $a + 2y$, and the second equation has $a - 2y$. If we just add the equations, the *y* terms cancel:

$$
\begin{array}{r}
5x + 2y = 4 \\
\underline{x - 2y = 8} \\
6x = 12
\end{array}
$$

If $6x = 12$, then $x = 2$. Plug that back into either of the original equations, and you'll find that $y = -3$. The point of intersection is $(2, -3)$, and the answer is C.

> **EXPERT TUTOR TIP**
>
> When you have a system of equations, you can solve it by:
> - Combination
> - Substitution
> - Graphing
>
> The previous example demonstrates combination.

▁▃▅▇ VARIABLE MANIPULATION

Example

4. A geometer uses the following formula to estimate the area A of the shaded portion of a circle, as shown in the figure below, when only the height h and the length of the chord c are known:

$$A = \frac{2ch}{3} + \frac{h^3}{2c}$$

What is the geometer's estimate of the area, in square inches, of the shaded region if the height is 2 inches and the length of the chord is 6 inches?

F. 6

G. $6\frac{2}{3}$

H. $7\frac{1}{2}$

J. $8\frac{2}{3}$

K. 12

At first glance, this looks like a horrendously esoteric geometry question. Who ever heard of such a formula? But when you think about the question a bit, you realize that you don't really have to understand the formula. You certainly don't have to remember it—it's right there in the question.

> **EXPERT TUTOR TIP**
> If you look at this problem and you freak out the first time through the test, skip it. Hopefully you'll realize how easy it is on your second pass. Don't waste valuable time freaking out about one problem.

In fact, this is not really a geometry question at all. It's just an "evaluate the algebraic expression" question in disguise. All you have to do is plug the given values $h = 2$ and $c = 6$ into the formula:

$$A = \frac{2ch}{3} + \frac{h^3}{2c}$$

$$= \frac{2(6)(2)}{3} + \frac{(2)^3}{2(6)}$$

$$= 8 + \frac{2}{3} = 8\frac{2}{3}$$

Choice J is correct.

The people who wrote this question wanted you to freak out at first sight and give up. Don't give up on a question too quickly just because it looks like it's testing something you never saw before. In many such cases, it's really a familiar problem in disguise.

3. Stuck? Try Eyeballing

There is another simple but powerful strategy that should give you at least a 50-50 chance on almost any diagram question: **When in doubt, use your eyes. Trust common sense and careful thinking; don't worry if you've forgotten most of the geometry you ever knew.** For almost half of all diagram questions, you can get a reasonable answer without solving anything: just eyeball it.

The Math directions say, "Illustrative figures are NOT necessarily drawn to scale," but in fact they almost **always** are. You're never really *supposed* to just eyeball the figure, but it makes a lot more sense than random guessing. Occasionally, eyeballing can help you narrow down the choices.

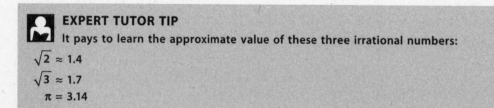

EXPERT TUTOR TIP
It pays to learn the approximate value of these three irrational numbers:
$\sqrt{2} \approx 1.4$
$\sqrt{3} \approx 1.7$
$\pi = 3.14$

Here's a difficult geometry question that you might just decide to eyeball:

.ııI0 PLANE GEOMETRY

Example

5. In the figure below, points *A*, *B*, and *C* lie on a circle centered at *O*. Triangle *AOC* is equilateral, and the length of *OC* is 3 inches. What is the length, in inches, of arc *ABC* ?

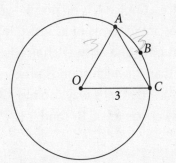

A. 3

B. π

C. 2π

D. 3π

E. 6π

STEP 1: What Is the Question?

There's an equilateral triangle that connects the center and two points on the circumference of a circle. You're looking for the length of the arc that goes from *A* to *C*.

STEP 2: What Information Am I Given?

You know the length of *OC* is 3 inches and that *AOC* is an *equilateral* triangle, that is, a triangle where all sides are equal lengths and all interior angles are 60 degrees. All but one of the answer choices are given in terms of π, so it's likely that a calculation with π would help you find the answer if you were to do a calculation using a formula. But read on, in Step 3 we'll show you that you don't actually need to use a formula to figure this one out!

STEP 3: What Can I Do with the Information?

What you're "supposed" to do to answer this question is recall and apply the formula for the length of an arc. But suppose you don't remember that formula (most people don't). Should you give up and take a wild guess?

No. You can eyeball it. Since you understand that *equilateral* means all sides are equal, you know that side $\overline{AC}$ is 3 inches long. Now look at arc *ABC* compared to side $\overline{AC}$. Suppose you were an ant, and you had to walk from *A* to *C*. If you walked along line segment $\overline{AC}$, it would be a 3-inch trip. About how long a walk would it be along arc *ABC*? Clearly more, but not much more, than 3 inches.

STEP 4: Am I Finished?

Now look at the answer choices. Choice A is no good—you know the arc is more than 3 inches. All the other choices are in terms of π. Just think of π as "a bit more than 3," and you will quickly see that only one answer choice is in the right ballpark. Choice B—π—would be a bit more than 3, which sounds pretty good. Choice C—2π—would be something more than 6. Already that's way too big. Choices D and E are even bigger. It sure looks like the answer has to be B—and it is.

> **GO ONLINE**
> If you have forgotten any of the geometry terms discussed in this workout, look them up in the Math Glossary of your online syllabus.

Not many ACT students would be able to solve question 5 the textbook way. If you could, great! Solving the problem is **always** more reliable than eyeballing. But when you *don't* know how to solve a diagram problem, or if you think it would take forever to get an answer, eyeballing and eliminating answer choices sure beat wild guessing. Sometimes, as with question 5, you might even be able to narrow the choices down to the one that's probably correct.

> **EXPERT TUTOR TIP**
> Answer choices are in order. If the first number you try doesn't work, the process of plugging in that first number might tell you whether you'll need a smaller or a larger number. So when backsolving, start with the middle choice (C or H) to be safe.

TYPICAL STORY PROBLEMS

We find that about one-third of the questions on the Math test are Story Problems. Though some Story Problems present unique situations that must be analyzed on the spot, others are just variations on familiar themes.

Percent Problems

In Percent Problems, you're usually given two numbers and asked to find a third. The key is to identify what you have and what you're looking for. In other words, identify the part, the percent, and the whole.

 EXPERT TUTOR TIP
Be prepared: Problems involving percentages, averages, ratios, and probability appear frequently on the ACT Math test.

Put the numbers and the unknown into the general form:

Part = Percent × Whole

Usually the part is associated with the word *is*, and the whole is associated with the word *of*.

PROPORTIONS AND PROBABILITY

Example

6. In a group of 250 students, 40 are seniors. What percentage of the group are seniors?

    F. 1.6%

    G. 6.25%

    H. 10%

    J. 16%

    K. 40%

The percent is what we're looking for ("What percentage..."); the whole is 250 ("...of the group..."); and the part is 40 ("...are seniors"). Plug these into the general formula:

Part = Percent × Whole

$40 = 250x$

$x = \dfrac{40}{250} = .16 = 16\%$

The answer is J.

Many ACT Percent Problems concern percent change. To increase a number by a certain percent, calculate that percent of the original number and add it on. To decrease a number by a certain percent, calculate that percent of the original number and then subtract. For example, to answer the question, "What number is 30 percent greater than 80?" first find 30 percent of 80—that's 24—and add that on to 80: 80 + 24 = 104.

> **EXPERT TUTOR TIP**
>
> When a quantity is increased or decreased by a percent *more than once*, you cannot simply add and subtract the percents to get the answer. In this kind of percent problem:
>
> - The first percent change is a percent of the starting amount.
> - The second percent change is a percent of the new amount.

The ACT has ways of complicating percent change problems. Especially tricky are problems with multiple changes, such as a percent increase followed by another percent increase or a percent increase followed by a percent decrease.

PROPORTIONS AND PROBABILITY

Example

7. If a positive number is increased by 70 percent, and then the result is decreased by 50 percent, which of the following accurately describes the net change?

   A. A 20 percent decrease

   B. A 15 percent decrease

   C. A 12 percent increase

   D. A 20 percent increase

   E. A 120 percent increase

To get a handle on this one, pick a number. Suppose the original number is 100. After a 70 percent increase, it rises to 170. That number, 170, is decreased by 50 percent, which means it's reduced by half to 85. The net change from 100 to 85 is a 15 percent decrease—choice B.

> ✓ **PERFECT SCORE TIP**
>
> One of the most common mistakes on percentages is thinking that taking 25 percent off twice is the same as taking 50 percent off—it is not. To avoid this, try pretending you began with 100 dollars and then doing the percentage manipulations in the question.

Average Problems

Instead of giving you a list of values to plug into the average formula, ACT Average Problems often put a slight spin on the question. They tell you the average of a group of terms and ask you to find the value of the missing term. Here's a classic example:

.ıı⌷⌷ PROPORTIONS AND PROBABILITY

Example

8. To earn a B for the semester, Linda needs an average of at least 80 on the five tests. Her average for the first four test scores is 79. What is the minimum score she must get on the fifth test to earn a B for the semester?

F. 80

G. 81

H. 82

J. 83

K. 84

The key to almost every Average Problem is to use the sum. Sums can be combined much more readily than averages. An average of 80 on five tests is more usefully thought of as a combined score of 400. To get a B for the semester, Linda's five test scores have to add up to 400 or more. The first four scores add up to $4 \times 79 = 316$. She needs another 84 to get that 316 up to 400. The answer is K.

> **👤 EXPERT TUTOR TIP**
> Backsolving is a fast way to work through average problems. Question 8 asks for the minimum score, so start with 80. Try plugging that in for the fifth test score.

Weighted Average Problems

Another spin ACT test makers put on Average Problems is to give you an average for part of a group and an average for the rest of the group, and then ask for the combined average.

.ıı⌷⌷ PROPORTIONS AND PROBABILITY

Example

9. In a class of 10 boys and 15 girls, the boys' average score on the final exam was 80 and the girls' average score was 90. What was the average score for the whole class?

A. 83

B. 84

C. 85

D. 86

E. 87

Don't just average 80 and 90 to get 85. That would work only if the class had exactly the same number of girls as boys. In this case, there are more girls, so they carry more weight in the overall class average. In other words, the class average should be somewhat closer to 90 (the girls' average) than to 80 (the boys' average).

As usual with averages, the key is to use the sum. The average score for the whole class is the total of the 25 individual scores divided by 25. We don't have 25 scores to add up, but we can use the boys' average and the girls' average to get two subtotals.

If 10 boys average 80, then their 10 scores add up to 10×80, or 800. If 15 girls average 90, then their 15 scores add up to 15×90, or 1,350. Add the boys' total to the girls' total: $800 + 1,350 = 2,150$. That's the class total, which can be divided by 25 to get the class average: $\frac{2,150}{25} = 86$. The answer is D.

Probability Problems

Probabilities are part-to-whole ratios. The whole is the total number of possible outcomes. The part is the number of favorable outcomes. For example, if a drawer contains two black ties and five other ties and you want a black tie, the total number of possible outcomes is 7 (the total number of ties), and the number of favorable outcomes is 2 (the number of black ties). The probability of choosing a black tie at random is $\frac{2}{7}$.

> **EXPERT TUTOR TIP**
> The probability of what *will* happen is not affected by what already *has* happened. Whenever you flip a coin, the probability is $\frac{1}{2}$ that it will be heads. Even if you flip the coin and get heads 10 times in a row, the probability is still $\frac{1}{2}$ on the 11th flip. Of course, the odds against 11 heads in a row are huge, but once the first 10 flips are history they're no longer relevant.

WHAT TO DO NEXT

Because more than half the Math questions on the ACT involve algebra, it's a good idea to solidify your understanding of the basics before test day. Focus on #52–70 in 100 Key Math Concepts for the ACT. Keep things in perspective. **Geometry questions are important, too, but algebra questions are more important.**

> ## IF YOU LEARNED ONLY THREE THINGS IN THIS CHAPTER...

1. You should be familiar with the ten textbook algebra and coordinate geometry problems.

2. Some ACT Math problems will be disguised so that their method of solution isn't obvious.

3. Be familiar with the formulas for calculating percentages and averages.

CHAPTER 9

Math Workout 3: Figuring It Out

SMARTPOINTS COVERED IN THIS CHAPTER

| PLANE GEOMETRY | |
| COORDINATE GEOMETRY | |

Every ACT Math subject test has about 14 geometry questions and exactly four trigonometry questions. Depending on what kind of score you're aiming for, you don't need to spend too much time working on trigonometry problems, but you definitely want to spend some time brushing up on your geometry skills.

Fortunately, a good number of the geometry questions are straightforward. Nothing is distorted or disguised. With these questions, you know what to do—if you know your geometry—the instant you understand them.

TEN TEXTBOOK GEOMETRY QUESTIONS

PLANE GEOMETRY

COORDINATE GEOMETRY

Here's a set of ten such questions. When you take the ACT, you will see quite a few questions just like these—possibly reworded and certainly with different numbers and figures. Use these questions to find out how well you remember your geometry.

> ✓ **PERFECT SCORE TIP**
> If you are aiming for a top Math score, you will need the trig questions. Luckily, normally three of the four can be answered simply by knowing SOHCAHTOA (sin = opposite/hypotenuse, cos = adjacent/hypotenuse, tan = opposite/adjacent). I took the ACT before taking trigonometry and did not think the trig questions were much to worry about. Still, if the trig sections look hard to you—review them. That one question can be really important if you are looking for a very high score.

Example

1. In the figure below, line t crosses parallel lines m and n. What is the degree measure of $\angle x$?

A. 40
B. 50
C. 60
D. 130
E. 140

2. What is the slope of the line perpendicular to the equation $4x + 3y = 9$?

F. $-\dfrac{4}{3}$

G. $-\dfrac{3}{4}$

H. $\dfrac{4}{3}$

J. $\dfrac{3}{4}$

K. 3

3. In the figure below, $\angle B$ is a right angle and the lengths of AB, BC, and CD are given in units. What is the area of $\triangle ACD$, in square units?

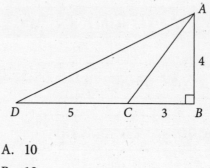

A. 10
B. 12
C. 16
D. 20
E. 32

4. In the figure below, △ABC is similar to △DEF. ∠A corresponds to ∠D, ∠B corresponds to ∠E, and ∠C corresponds to ∠F. If the given lengths are of the same unit of measure, what is the value of x?

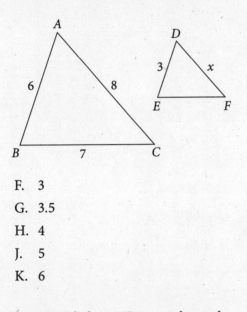

F. 3

G. 3.5

H. 4

J. 5

K. 6

5. In △ABC below, ∠B is a right angle. If $\overline{AB}$ is 1 unit long and $\overline{BC}$ is 2 units long, how many units long is $\overline{AC}$?

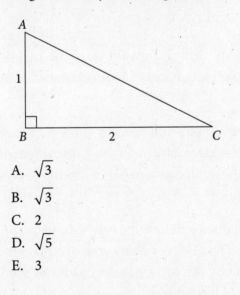

A. $\sqrt{3}$

B. $\sqrt{3}$

C. 2

D. $\sqrt{5}$

E. 3

6. Point P (–3, 5) and point Q (0, 1) are points on the x-y coordinate plane. What is the distance between points P and Q?

F. 4

G. 5

H. 6

J. 7

K. 8

7. In the figure below, $\overline{BE}$ is perpendicular to $\overline{AD}$, and the lengths of $\overline{AB}$, $\overline{BC}$, $\overline{CD}$, and $\overline{BE}$ are given in inches. What is the area, in square inches, of trapezoid ABCD ?

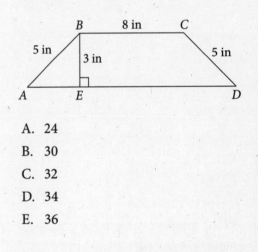

A. 24

B. 30

C. 32

D. 34

E. 36

8. What is the area, in square inches, of a circle with a diameter of 8 inches?

F.   4π

G.   8π

H. 16π

J. 32π

K. 64π

9. In the circle centered at O in the figure below, the measure of $\angle AOB$ is 40°. If $\overline{OA}$ is 9 units long, how many units long is minor arc AB?

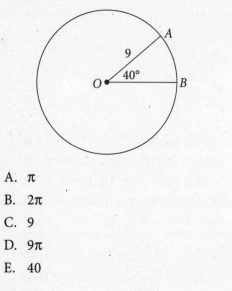

A. π

B. 2π

C. 9

D. 9π

E. 40

10. In the figure below, $ABCD$ is a square and $\overline{AB}$ is a diameter of the circle centered at O. If $\overline{AD}$ is 10 units long, what is the area, in square units, of the shaded region?

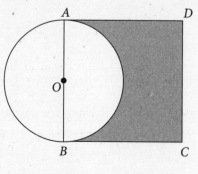

F. $100 - 50\pi$

G. $100 - 25\pi$

H. $100 - \dfrac{25\pi}{2}$

J. $100 - 10\pi$

K. $100 - 5\pi$

Scoring

10 correct: You have a solid grounding in geometry. Straightforward textbook geometry questions are no problem for you. Skip ahead to the section called Tackling More Complex Geometry questions.

8–9 correct: You have a pretty good grasp of the geometry you need to know for the ACT. Before moving on to the discussion of more complex geometry, read the explanations that follow for the questions you got wrong, and study the appropriate pages of the 100 Key Math Concepts for the ACT section at the back of this book.

0–7 correct: You have gaps in your knowledge of geometry. Before you can hope to get much out of our discussion of more complex geometry, you had better solidify your geometry foundations. Look at the explanations that follow, and study the corresponding pages of the 100 Key Math Concepts for the ACT section at the back of this book.

Answers

1.	E	6.	G
2.	J	7.	E
3.	A	8.	H
4.	H	9.	B
5.	D	10.	H

Answers and Explanations

1. When a transversal crosses parallel lines, the four acute angles formed are all equal, the four obtuse angles formed are all equal, and any angles that are not equal are supplementary. The angle marked x is obtuse, so it's supplementary to the given 40° angle. $180 - 40 = 140$. The answer is E. (*100 Key Math Concepts for the ACT, #79*)

2. First, you need to put the equation you are given into $y = mx + b$ form. When you do this, you can see that the slope of this line is $-\frac{4}{3}$. We are looking for the slope of the line perpendicular to this line. That means that we need the opposite reciprocal slope, which is $\frac{3}{4}$, choice J.

3. The formula for the area of a triangle is $A = \frac{1}{2}bh$. To apply this formula, you need the base and the height. Here, you can use CD for the base and AB for the height. So: Area $= \frac{1}{2}(CD)(AB) = \frac{1}{2}(5)(4) = 10$. The answer is A. (*100 Key Math Concepts for the ACT, #83*)

4. In similar triangles, corresponding sides are proportional. DE corresponds to AB, and DF corresponds to AC, so we can set up this proportion:

$$\frac{AB}{DE} = \frac{AC}{DF}$$

$$\frac{6}{3} = \frac{8}{x}$$

$$6x = 3 \times 8$$

$$6x = 24$$

$$x = 4$$

The answer is H. (*100 Key Math Concepts for the ACT, #82*)

5. The Pythagorean theorem says: $(\text{leg}_1)^2 + (\text{leg}_2)^2 = (\text{hypotenuse})^2$. Here, the legs have lengths of 1 and 2, so plug them into the formula:

$$(1)^2 + (2)^2 = (\text{hypotenuse})^2$$
$$1 + 4 = x^2$$
$$x^2 = 5$$
$$x = \sqrt{5}$$

The answer is D. (*100 Key Math Concepts for the ACT, #84*)

6. There are a couple of ways to solve a distance problem. If you can remember the formula, great! Plug the coordinates into the distance formula:

$$\sqrt{(x_1 - x_2)^2 + (y_2 - y_1)^2}$$

to get

$$\sqrt{(0 - (-3))^2 + (1 - 5)^2} = \sqrt{(-3)^2 + (4)^2} = \sqrt{9 + 16} = \sqrt{25} = 5$$

If you can't, you can still get this problem correct. Draw a quick graph and plot the two points that you are given. See if you can make a triangle once you draw the points, and then determine the lengths of the two legs. You will need to solve for the hypotenuse, but you know how to do this—the Pythagorean theorem! You might also recognize the Pythagorean triplet (3-4-5). Any way you solve it, you will get 5, choice G.

7. The formula for the area of a trapezoid is $A = \left(\dfrac{b_1 + b_2}{2}\right)h$, where b_1 and b_2 are the lengths of the parallel sides. You could think of it as the height times the average of the bases. You're given the height (3 inches), one base (8 inches), and enough information to figure out the other base. Notice that $\triangle ABE$ is a 3-4-5 triangle, so $AE = 4$ inches. And if you were to drop an altitude down from point C, you'd get another 3-4-5 triangle on the right:

EXPERT TUTOR TIP

If you don't remember the formula for the area of a trapezoid, break it into shapes that you do know the area formulas for—triangles and a rectangle.

Now you can see that the bottom base is 16 inches. Plug these numbers into the formula:

$$A = \left(\frac{b_1 + b_2}{2}\right)h$$

$$= \left(\frac{8 + 16}{2}\right) \times 3$$

$$= 12 \times 3 = 36$$

The answer is E. (*100 Key Math Concepts for the ACT, #87*)

8. The formula for the area of a circle is $A = \pi r^2$, where r is the radius. If the diameter is 8 inches, then the radius is 4 inches, which we plug into the formula:

$$A = \pi r^2$$

$$= \pi(4)^2$$

$$= 16\pi$$

The answer is H. (*100 Key Math Concepts for the ACT, #91*)

9. The central angle of minor arc AB is 40°, which is $\frac{1}{9}$ of the whole circle's 360°. The length of minor arc AB, therefore, is $\frac{1}{9}$ of the whole circle's circumference.

$$C = 2\pi r = 2\pi(9) = 18\pi$$

$$\frac{1}{9}C = \frac{1}{9}(18\pi) = 2\pi$$

The answer is B. (*100 Key Math Concepts for the ACT, #90*)

> **EXPERT TUTOR TIP**
> The length of an arc is only a fraction of the length around the circle (the circumference). The fraction is the angle divided by 360.

10. The shaded region is equal to the area of the square minus the area of the semicircle. The area of the square is $10 \times 10 = 100$. The radius of the circle is half of 10, or 5, so the area of the whole circle is $\pi(5)^2 = 25\pi$, and the area of the semicircle is $\frac{25\pi}{2}$. The square minus the semicircle, then, is: $100 - \frac{25\pi}{2}$. The answer is H. (*100 Key Math Concepts for the ACT, #87, #91*)

TACKLING MORE COMPLEX GEOMETRY QUESTIONS

Not all ACT geometry questions are straightforward. The test writers have ways of further complicating them. It's not **always** obvious at first what the question is getting at. Sometimes you really have to think about the figure and the given information before that lightbulb goes on in your head. Often, the inspiration that brings illumination is finding the hidden information.

 PLANE GEOMETRY

Example

1. In the figure below, $\triangle ABC$ is a right triangle and $\overline{AC}$ is perpendicular to $\overline{BD}$. If $\overline{AB}$ is 6 units long, and $\overline{AC}$ is 10 units long, how many units long is $\overline{AD}$?

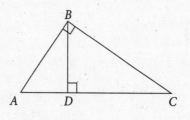

   A. 3
   B. $2\sqrt{3}$
   C. 3.6
   D. 4
   E. $3\sqrt{2}$

> ✓ **PERFECT SCORE TIP**
> If the question gives you lengths of sides, write them on the diagram. I found this often made solutions or other hints more obvious to me.

At first, this looks like a Pythagorean theorem question. In fact, the two given sides of $\triangle ABC$ identify it as the 6-8-10 version of the 3-4-5 special right triangle. (*100 Key Math Concepts for the ACT*, #85) So we know that $\overline{BC} = 8$. So what? How's that going to help us find $\overline{AD}$?

> ✓ **PERFECT SCORE TIP**
> If you are stuck on a triangle problem, the two most common solutions involve either the Pythagorean theorem or similar triangles, so be sure to look for ways to use either of those.

The inspiration here is to realize that this is a "similar triangles" problem. We don't see the word *similar* anywhere in the question stem, but the stem and the figure combined actually tell us that all three triangles in the figure—ΔABC, ΔADB, and ΔBDC—are similar. We know the triangles are similar because they all have the same three angles. Here are the three triangles separated and oriented to show the correspondences:

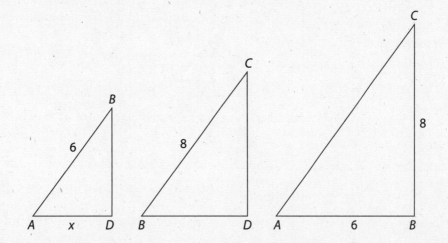

In this orientation, it's easy to set up the proportion that will solve the problem:

$$\frac{10}{6} = \frac{6}{x}$$

$$10x = 36$$

$$x = 3.6$$

The answer is C.

PLANE GEOMETRY

Example

2. In the figure below, the area of the circle centered at O is 25π, and $\overline{AC}$ is perpendicular to $\overline{OB}$. If $\overline{AC}$ is 8 units long, how many units long is $\overline{BD}$?

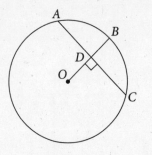

F. 2

G. 2.5

H. 3

J. 3.125

K. 4

This is a tough one. It's not easy to see how to get *BD* from the given information. You can use the area—25π—to figure out the radius, and then you'd know the length of *OB*:

$$\text{Area} = \pi r^2$$
$$25\pi = \pi r^2$$
$$25 = r^2$$
$$r = 5$$

So you know $\overline{OB} = 5$, but what about $\overline{BD}$? If you knew $\overline{OD}$, you could subtract that from $\overline{OB}$ to get what you want. But do you know $\overline{OD}$? This is the place where most people get stuck.

The inspiration that will lead to a solution is that you can take advantage of the right angle at *D*. Look what happens when you take a pencil and physically add $\overline{OA}$ and $\overline{OC}$ to the figure:

> **EXPERT TUTOR TIP**
> The radius will be the key to solving almost any ACT problem involving circles. If you get stuck, try drawing a radius to see if that helps you.

Δ*OAD* and Δ*OCD* are right triangles. And when we write in the lengths, we discover some special right triangles:

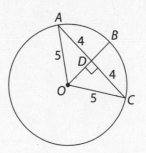

Now it's apparent that $\overline{OD} = 3$. Since $\overline{OB} = 5$, $\overline{BD}$ is 5 – 3 = 2. The answer is F.

Figureless Problems

Some ACT geometry problems present an extra challenge because they don't provide a figure. You have to figure it out for yourself. Try this one:

⊞⊞ PLANE GEOMETRY

Example

3. If one side of a right triangle is 3 units long, and a second side is 4 units long, which of the following could be the length, in units, of the third side?

    A. 1

    B. 2

    C. $\sqrt{7}$

    D. $3\sqrt{2}$

    E. $3\sqrt{3}$

The key to solving most figureless problems is to sketch a diagram, but sometimes the test makers deliberately give you less information than you might like. Question 3 is the perfect example—it gives you two sides of a right triangle and asks for the third. Sounds familiar. And the two sides it gives you—3 and 4—*really* sound familiar. It's a 3-4-5, right?

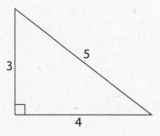

So the answer's 5…

Whoops! There's no 5 among the answer choices! What's going on?!

Better check back. Notice that the question asks, "Which of the following *could* be the length…" That *could* is crucial. It suggests that there's more than one possibility. Our answer of 5 was too obvious. There's another one somewhere.

✓ PERFECT SCORE TIP

Remember that there are multiple ways to draw diagrams. If the one you picked isn't working, try another instead of trying to do weird manipulations to an incorrect picture.

Can you think of another way of sketching the figure with the same given information? Who says that the 3 and 4 have to be the two legs? Look at what happens when you make one of them—the larger one, of course—the *hypotenuse*:

This is not a 3-4-5 triangle, because in a 3-4-5, the 3 and the 4 are the legs. This is no special right triangle; to figure out the length of the third side, resort to the Pythagorean theorem:

$$(\text{leg}_1)^2 + (\text{leg}_2)^2 = (\text{hypotenuse})^2$$
$$3^2 + x^2 = 4^2$$
$$9 + x^2 = 16$$
$$x^2 = 7$$
$$x = \sqrt{7}$$

The answer is C.

Many Steps and Many Concepts

Some of the toughest ACT geometry questions are ones that take many steps to solve and combine many different geometry concepts. The following is an example:

.ıılll PLANE GEOMETRY

Example

4. In the figure below, $\overline{AB}$ is tangent to the circle at A. If the circumference of the circle is 12π units and $\overline{OB}$ is 12 units long, what is the area, in square units, of the shaded region?

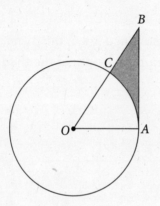

F. $18\sqrt{3} - 6\pi$

G. $24\sqrt{3} - 6\pi$

H. $18\sqrt{3} - 2\pi$

J. $12\pi - 12$

K. $243 - 2\pi$

This is about as hard as they come on the ACT. It is by no means clear how the given information—the circumference of the circle and the length of $\overline{OB}$ —will lead you to the area of the shaded region.

So what do you do? Give up? No. *Don't* give up immediately unless you're really short on time or you know for sure you can't do the problem.

So then should you just plow ahead blindly and figure out every length, angle, and area you can and see where that leads you? *Well, not exactly.* It would be better to be more systematic.

The key to success with a circuitous problem like this is to focus on your destination—what you're looking for—and think about what you need to get there. Then go back to the given information and see what you can do to get you going in the right direction. Think about where you're headed before you take even one step; otherwise, you may just have to backtrack.

Your goal in question 4 is to find the area of the shaded region. That region is a shape that has no name, let alone an area formula. Like most shaded regions, this one is in fact the difference between two familiar shapes with names and area formulas. Think of the shaded region in question 4 as:

(the area of $\triangle AOB$) – (the area of sector AOC)

So now you know you need to figure out the area of the triangle and the area of the sector.

First, the triangle. You are explicitly given $\overline{OB} = 12$. You are also given that $\overline{AB}$ is tangent to the circle at A, which tells you that $\overline{OA}$ is a radius and that $\angle OAB$ is a right angle. So if you can figure out the radius of the circle, you'll have two sides of a right triangle, which will enable you to figure out the third side, and then figure out the area.

You can get the radius from the given circumference. Plug what you know into the formula and solve for r:

$$\text{Circumference} = 2\pi r$$
$$12\pi = 2\pi r$$
$$r = \frac{12\pi}{2\pi} = 6$$
$$\overline{OA} = 6$$

Aha! So it turns out that $\triangle AOB$ is no ordinary right triangle. Since one leg—6—is exactly half the hypotenuse—12—you're looking at a 30°-60°-90° triangle. By applying the well-known side ratios (1:$\sqrt{3}$:2) for a 30°-60°-90° triangle (*100 Key Math Concepts for the ACT*, #85), you determine that $\overline{AB} = 6\sqrt{3}$. Now plug the lengths of the legs in for the base and altitude in the formula for the area of a triangle, and you'll get:

$$\text{Area} = \frac{1}{2}bh$$
$$= \frac{1}{2}(6\sqrt{3})(6)$$
$$= 18\sqrt{3}$$

Already it looks like the answer is going to be F or H—they're the choices that begin with $18\sqrt{3}$. You could just guess choice F or H and move on, but if you've come this far, you might as well go all the way.

Next, you need to determine the area of the sector. Fortunately, while working on the triangle, you figured out the two things you need to get the area of the sector: the radius of the circle (6) and the measure of the central angle (60°). The radius tells you that the area of the whole circle (πr^2) is 36π. And the central angle tells you that the sector is $\frac{60}{360}$, or $\frac{1}{6}$ of the circle. One-sixth of 36π is 6π. So the area of the shaded region is $18\sqrt{3} - 6\pi$, choice F.

GO ONLINE
Brush up on your trig. Try the online trigonometry workshop and test yourself with the online quiz.

▶ IF YOU LEARNED ONLY THREE THINGS IN THIS CHAPTER...

1. You should be familiar with the ten textbook geometry questions.

2. When dealing with "disguised" geometry questions, use the figure and the question stem to find the information you need. It may not be stated directly.

3. If a geometry question doesn't have a figure, it usually helps to draw one.

CHAPTER 10

Reading Workout 1: Know Where You're Going

Reading skills are crucial on every part of the ACT, not just on the Reading test. Savvy ACT-style reading is certainly useful for the English and Science tests. Even your work on many of the Math problems will benefit from the skills discussed as follows, so don't ignore the Reading Workouts, even if you think you're an ace reader.

The kind of reading rewarded by the ACT is special. You probably know how to do it already, but you may be reluctant to do it on a standardized test. You may think that success on a test like this requires that you read very slowly and deliberately, making sure you remember everything. Well, we at Kaplan have found that this kind of reading won't work on the ACT. In fact, it is a sure way to run out of time halfway through the Reading test.

 EXPERT TUTOR TIP
The ACT Reading test includes:
- One Prose Fiction passage with ten questions
- One Social Sciences passage with ten questions
- One Humanities passage with ten questions
- One Natural Sciences passage with ten questions

THE KEY TO ACTIVE ACT READING

The real key to ACT Reading is to read quickly but actively, getting a sense of the gist or main idea of the passage and seeing how everything fits together to support that main idea. You should constantly try to think ahead. Look for the general outline of the passage—determine how it's structured. Don't worry about the details. You'll come back for those later.

> ✔ **PERFECT SCORE TIP**
> Remember that on the ACT, the goal of reading is very different than it is in English class. No one is looking for original ideas or deep reading—just for you to get the main ideas.

Fast, active reading, of course, requires a little more mental energy than slow, passive reading, but it pays off. Those who dwell on details—who passively let the passage reveal itself at its own pace—are sure to run out of time. Don't be that kind of reader! Make the passage reveal itself to you on your schedule, by skimming the passage with an eye to structure rather than detail. Look for key words that tell you what the author is doing so that you can save yourself time. For instance, read examples very quickly, just glancing over the words. When an author says "for example," you know that what follows is an example of a general point. Do you need to understand that specific example? Maybe, maybe not. If you do, you can come back and read the verbiage when you're attacking the questions. You'll know exactly where the author gave an example of general point *x* (or whatever). If you *don't* need to know the example for any of the questions, great! You haven't wasted much time on something that won't get you a point.

> 👤 **EXPERT TUTOR TIP**
> Here's how to use this chapter if you don't have much time. Learn the Kaplan Method for ACT Reading. Try the sample passage that follows. Check your answers. If you need more help, go back and read the whole chapter.

You actually do this kind of "reading" all the time, and not just when you're reading a book or newspaper. When you watch TV or see a movie, for instance, you can often figure out much of what's going to happen in advance. You see the bad guys run out of a bank with bags of money in their hands, and you can guess that the next thing they'll do is get into a car and drive away in excess of the speed limit. You see a character in an old sitcom bragging to his friends about how great a driver he is, and you know that he's bound to get into a fender bender before the next commercial. **This ability to know where something is going is very valuable. Use it on the ACT.**

To help you know where an author is going, pay careful attention to structural clues. Words like *but, nevertheless,* and *moreover* help you get a sense of where a piece of writing is going. Look for signal phrases (like *clearly, as a result,* or *no one can deny that*) to determine the logic of the passage. The details, remember, you can come back for later, when you're doing the questions. **What's important in reading the passage is getting a sense of how those details fit together to express the point or points of the passage.**

> ✓ **PERFECT SCORE TIP**
> The key to ACT Reading is main ideas. At the end of every paragraph and passage, you should be able to give a very brief summary of what it was about. This will really help with the questions.

> 👤 **EXPERT TUTOR TIP**
> Read actively, with an eye toward where the author is going. Don't worry about remembering the details. You can (and should) always refer to them later.

Practice Knowing Where You're Going

In the following exercise, try to fill in the word or phrase that should come next. For most, there are many possible answers, so don't worry about getting the "right" answer.

1. You'd think that the recipe for a strawberry soufflé would be complicated, but my friend's version was _____.

2. I can't believe my good luck! The one time in my life I buy a lottery ticket, I _____.

3. A parked car burns no fuel and causes no pollution. Once the ignition is turned on, however, _____.

4. As their habitat is destroyed, wild animals _____.

5. The new word-processing program was far easier to use than the old one. Moreover, the accompanying instruction booklet explained the commands in a _____ way.

6. The new word-processing program was far easier to use than the old one. On the other hand, the accompanying instruction booklet explained the commands in a _____ way.

Answers

- In Sentence 1, the active reader would probably complete the sentence by saying that the friend's version was "actually quite simple" or something similar. How do you know what's coming next here? The structural clue *but* tips you off. *But* tells you that a contrast is coming up. You'd think the recipe would be complicated, *but* it's "actually quite simple."

- In Sentence 2, on the other hand, there's no real structural clue to help you out. However, the *meaning* of the sentence should make clear what's coming up. Because the speaker is marveling at his good luck, he must have won some money. A likely completion would be something like: The one time in my life I buy a lottery ticket, I "win the jackpot."

- In sentence 3, we have another contrast, signaled by the clue *however*. A parked car doesn't burn fuel or pollute, so the answer has to be something like "the car starts burning gas and polluting."

- Sentence 4 demonstrates again that you don't need explicit structural clues to stay ahead. Sometimes all you need is common sense. What do you think would happen to animals whose habitat had been destroyed? Would they thrive? Celebrate? Buy a condo in Florida? No, they'd probably "start dying out." They might even "become extinct."

- Sentences 5 and 6 show clearly how you can use an author's language to anticipate what point he or she is going to make next. Here, we have identical sentences, except for one small (but very important) difference. One of the sentences in question 5 includes the word *moreover*, indicating continuation or the addition of similar information. The blank should be something close to "in a clear and easy-to-understand" way. It makes sense that "The program was easy to use; moreover, the instructions were easy to understand." The connection in question 6, "on the other hand," indicates contrast. The sentences make sense only if you fill in the blank with "a confusing and unclear" way.

Create a Passage Map

The best way to read actively is to take quick notes, marking up the passage as you go. You don't have time to write extensively in the margin, nor do you want to underline too many sentences. After all, *if you underline everything, nothing stands out on the page.* Your goal is to create flags that wave at you when you are looking for the answers to the questions in the passage.

The fastest way to create your passage map is to follow the ABCs of Active Reading:

Abbreviate margin notes.
Bracket key sentences.
Circle key words and phrases.

Abbreviate margin notes. Develop your own shorthand notes, such as *opin* (opinion), *contr* (contrast or comparison), *hist* (history), *bio* (early years). You must be able to understand what you've written. Otherwise, the notes won't be helpful.

Bracket key sentences. These may (or may not) be the first and last sentences of a paragraph. You are looking for any sentences that express key themes, conclusions, or opinions (of either the author or of the characters in the passage). If you string these bracketed sentences together, you will have highlighted the author's train of thought.

Circle key words and phrases. These are the structural clues or flags (*however, therefore, on one hand…on the other hand*), as well as proper names, dates, key actions, etc.—the signposts of each paragraph. For example, if a passage were about child development, you'd want to circle the key ages discussed in each paragraph. Thus, circling *six months, one year, age two through five* would help you know where to look for the answers to questions about those ages.

> ✓ **PERFECT SCORE TIP**
> I found labeling each paragraph with its main topic helped me quickly know where to look when answering questions.

THE KAPLAN METHOD FOR ACT READING

These steps are tried-and-true. If you learn and practice them, you'll be able to read all four passages successfully and have time to answer all the questions. When test day rolls around, you'll be glad you've got these steps to follow.

The key to this section is being in control of timing—how much time you spend reading the passage (about three minutes) and answering the questions (an average of 30 seconds per question).

If you divide 40 questions into 35 minutes, you'll see that you have $8\frac{3}{4}$ minutes per passage. As you practice, it will be clear that one or two passages take more (or less) time than the others. So your goal is an average of just under 9 minutes per passage. How do you learn to do this? Practice. Practice. Practice.

For the ACT, however, you have a special purpose: to answer specific multiple-choice questions. And we've found that the best way to do that is to read each passage quickly and actively for general understanding, then refer to the passage to answer individual questions. Every ACT test taker can succeed by following the Kaplan Method:

STEP 1: Actively read the passage, taking notes as you go.

STEP 2: Examine the question stem, looking for clues.

STEP 3: Predict the answer and select the choice that best matches your prediction.

For most students, these three steps should together take up about nine minutes per passage. Spend three of those nine minutes on prereading. Spend the remaining time considering the questions and referring to the passage to check your answers. As we mentioned in the ACT Basics section, you'll probably want to take two sweeps through the questions for each passage, getting the doable ones the first time around, coming back for the harder ones.

STEP 1: Actively Read the Passage, Taking Notes as You Go

Read the whole passage before trying to answer the questions. Remember to "know where you're going," anticipating how the parts of the passage fit together. In this preread, the main goals are to:

- Understand the gist of the passage (the main idea)
- Take notes and create a road map of the passage

You may want to underline key points, jot down notes, circle structural clues— whatever it takes to accomplish the two goals above. It's a good idea to label each paragraph to fix in your mind how the paragraphs relate to one another and what aspect of the main idea is discussed in each. That could be your road map.

Two important reminders: The road map will be your guide to finding answers in the passage once you approach the questions. Do what works for you and don't get bogged down in the details. Most of the details in the passage aren't required for answering the questions, but you will want to keep straight who said what and why.

Most of the details in the passage aren't required for answering the questions, so why waste time worrying about them?

> **EXPERT TUTOR TIP**
> Mark up the passages! Have a system worked out in which you use different symbols to mean different things. For example, circle names, box numbers and dates, underline key sentences, and draw arrows to lists of details. Once you know your system, you can find the facts you are looking for faster.

STEP 2: Examine the Question Stem, Looking for Clues

Approaching the Reading questions requires self-discipline. Most test takers have an almost irresistible urge to immediately jump to the answer choices to see what "looks okay." That's not a good idea. Don't peek at the answer choices.

Read the question stem to identify what the test maker is asking. Which of the following is it about?

- A detail (what happened)
- The passage as a whole (the Big Idea)
- A conclusion (reading between the lines)
- A specific word or phrase used in the passage

Analyzing what the question stem is asking is very important because the test makers will offer you choices that don't answer the question at hand. It is easy to get the right answer—if you know what you are looking for.

How do you know what you're looking for? There will be clues in the question stem. These clues could be as straightforward as a line reference or as vague as the phrase "as stated in the passage." In both cases, though, you know that you'll be able to find the answer in the passage. That's where your notes come in handy.

In Reading, think about the question stem without looking at the choices. In most questions, you won't be able to remember exactly what the passage said about the matter in question. That's okay. In fact, even if you do think you remember, don't trust your memory. Instead refer to the passage.

Now's the time when your passage map comes to your aid. Your notes are all waiting to help you find the answers to the ten questions. Once you've found the right spot in the passage…

GO ONLINE
Refer to your downloadable study sheet to review the Kaplan Three-Step Method for ACT Reading—anywhere, anytime.

STEP 3: Predict the Answer and Select the Choice That Best Matches Your Prediction

It's extremely important in Reading to **make a habit of answering the question in your own words** (based on your checking of the passage) *before* looking at the answer choices. Predict before you pick. Most students waste enormous amounts of time thinking about answer choices in Reading. If you do that, you'll **never** finish, and you'll get so confused you'll probably get many questions wrong.

Once you have an answer in your head based on what you've read and rechecked in the passage, match it to one of the answer choices. Avoid trying to see if they "look right."

You don't want to think very hard about each choice if you can help it. They're intended to confuse you, after all, so don't think about them any more than you absolutely have to.

Now practice the Kaplan Method on the full-length ACT passage that follows. We're going to give you added incentive to use it by first showing you the questions *without* answer choices. That way you can practice the Kaplan Method for ACT Reading and won't be tempted to read the answers before answering the question in your own words. The same questions in ACT style, *with* answer choices, will follow the passage. But try to answer them in fill-in-the-blank format first.

Passage I

SOCIAL SCIENCE

This passage is taken from the book *History of Western Civilization, A Handbook,* ©1986 by William H. McNeill. Reprinted by permission of the University of Chicago Press.

By the tenth century most of northern Europe was divided into farming units known as manors…

Line (5) Almost always a manor comprised four parts: arable, meadow, waste, and the village area itself. The arable was of course the land which grew the crops on which the inhabitants of the manor subsisted. To maintain fertility and keep down weeds it (10) was necessary to fallow a part of the cultivated land each year. It was, therefore, usual (though not universal) to divide the arable into three fields. One such field was planted with winter grain, a second with spring (15) grain, and the third left fallow; the following year, the fallow field would be planted with winter grain, the field in which winter grain had been raised was planted with spring grain, and the third field left fallow. (20) By following such a rotation, the cycle was completed every three years. Since the fallow field had to be plowed twice in the year in order to keep down the weeds, and the others had to be plowed once, work for the (25) plow teams extended almost throughout the year. Plowing stopped only at times when all hands were needed to bring in the harvest, or when the soil was too wet to be plowed, or was frozen. The amount (30) of land that could be tilled was fixed fairly definitely by the number of plows and plow teams which the manor could muster; and official documents sometimes estimated the wealth and value of a manor in terms of the (35) number of plows it possessed.

The three great fields lay open, without fences, but were subdivided into numerous small strips (often one acre in size, i.e., the amount of one day's plowing) which (40) individual peasants "owned." The strips belonging to any one individual were scattered through the three fields in different parts, perhaps in order to assure that each peasant would have strips plowed (45) early and late, in fertile and infertile parts of the arable land.

Custom severely restricted the individual's rights over his land. The time for plowing and planting was fixed by custom (50) and each peasant had to conform, since he needed his neighbor's help to plow his strips and they needed his. Uniform cropping was imperative, since on a given day the village animals were turned into the fields to graze

(55) after the harvest had been gathered, and if some individual planted a crop which did not ripen as early as that of his neighbors, he had no means of defending his field from the hungry animals. If his crop ripened

(60) sooner, on the other hand, it could not be garnered without trampling neighboring fields. Moreover, the very idea of innovation was lacking: men did what custom prescribed, cooperated in the plowing and

(65) to some extent in the harvesting, and for many generations did not dream of trying to change.

The meadow was almost as important as the arable for the economy of the village.

(70) Hay from the meadow supported the indispensable draught animals through the winter. The idea that hay might be sown did not occur to men in medieval times; consequently they were compelled to rely on

(75) natural meadows alone. One result was that in many manors shortage of winter fodder for the plow teams was a constant danger. It was common practice to feed oxen on leaves picked from trees, and on straw from the

(80) grain harvest; but despite such supplements the draught animals often nearly starved in winter. In some cases oxen actually had to be carried out from their winter stalls to spring pastures until some of their strength

(85) was recovered and plowing could begin. Thus on many manors meadow land was even more valuable than the arable and was divided into much smaller strips (often the width of a scythe stroke).

(90) The waste provided summer pasture for various animals of the manor: pigs, geese, cattle, and sheep. The animals of the whole manor normally grazed together under the watchful eyes of some young children or

(95) other attendants who could keep them from wandering too far afield, and bring them back to the village at night. The waste also was the source of wood for fuel and for building purposes, and helped to supplement

(100) the food supply with such things as nuts, berries, honey, and rabbits...

The fourth segment of the manor was the village itself, usually located in the center of the arable near a source of

(105) drinking water, and perhaps along a road or path or footpath leading to the outside world. The cottages of medieval peasants were extremely humble, usually consisting of a single room, with earthen floor

(110) and thatched roof. Around each cottage normally lay a small garden in which various vegetables and sometimes fruit trees were planted. In the village streets chickens, ducks, and dogs picked up a precarious

(115) living.

QUESTIONS

1. The description of the near starvation of the oxen (lines 82–85) serves to:

2. According to the passage, the fact that the peasants' individual strips of land were unfenced subdivisions of larger fields required each peasant to:

3. According to the second paragraph (lines 4–35), the fallow part of the arable had to be plowed a total of how many times in any given calendar year?

4. The passage suggests that the practice of peasants owning strips "scattered through the three fields in different parts" (lines 42–43) was instituted in order to:

5. On the basis of the information in the passage, it may be inferred that people in medieval times did not think of sowing hay because:

6. As it is used in line 61, the word *garnered* means:

7. According to the passage, if one of the arable's three great fields were left fallow one year, it would be:

8. Which of the following conclusions is suggested by the fourth paragraph (lines 47–67)?

9. According to the passage, a manor's value might be judged according to the number of its plows because:

10. According to the passage, summer pasture for a manor's geese would be provided:

YOUR ANSWERS

1. The description of the near starvation of the oxen (lines 82–85) serves to:

   A. demonstrate how difficult life on the manor was in tenth century northern Europe.

   B. showcase how important work animals were to medieval manors.

   C. emphasize how important natural meadows were to feeding the work animals.

   D. explain why uniform cropping was a critical practice that ensured survival on the medieval manor.

2. According to the passage, the fact that the peasants' individual strips of land were unfenced subdivisions of larger fields required each peasant to:

   F. follow a fixed planting schedule so as to be able to harvest crops at the same time as the other peasants.

   G. harvest crops independently of his neighbors.

   H. limit the size of strips to what could be plowed in a single day.

   J. maintain small garden plots in order to provide his family with enough food.

3. According to the second paragraph (lines 4–35), the fallow part of the arable had to be plowed a total of how many times in any given calendar year?

   A. One

   B. Two

   C. Four

   D. Six

4. The passage suggests that the practice of peasants owning strips "scattered through the three fields in different parts" (lines 42–43) was instituted in order to:

   F. divide resources fairly evenly.

   G. preserve the wealth of elite land-owners.

   H. protect the three fields from overuse.

   J. force neighbors to work only their own lands.

5. On the basis of the information in the passage, it may be inferred that people in medieval times did not think of sowing hay because:

   A. hay sowing had not been done in the past.

   B. the need for more hay was not great enough to warrant the extra work.

   C. northern Europeans did not yet have the necessary farming techniques for successful hay cultivation.

   D. the tight schedule of cultivating the arable meant that the peasants had no time to cultivate extra crops.

6. As it is used in line 61, the word *garnered* means:

   F. planted.

   G. watered.

   H. gathered.

   J. plowed.

7. According to the passage, if one of the arable's three great fields were left fallow one year, it would be:

   A. left fallow for two more years in succession.

   B. planted the next year with winter grain only.

   C. planted the next year with spring grain only.

   D. planted with either winter or spring grain the next year.

8. Which of the following conclusions is suggested by the fourth paragraph (lines 47–67)?

   I. An individual was free to cultivate his own land in any way he wished.

   II. The manor was run according to tradition.

   III. Successful farming required cooperative methods.

   F. I and II only

   G. I and III only

   H. II and III only

   J. I, II, and III

9. According to the passage, a manor's value might be judged according to the number of its plows because:

   A. the more plows a manor had, the less land had to be left fallow.

   B. plows, while not in themselves valuable, symbolized great wealth.

   C. manors with sufficient plows could continue plowing throughout the year.

   D. the number of plows a manor owned determined how much land could be cultivated.

10. According to the passage, summer pasture for a manor's geese would be provided:

    F. next to cottages, within the village.

    G. on the fallow field of the arable.

    H. on the communal ground of the waste.

    J. on the whole of the meadow.

The Lay of the Land

Well, how'd you do? Did you remember to refer to the passage? You probably found that you had to do a more thorough check for some questions than for others.

This passage, like most nonfiction passages on the ACT, is organized in a fairly logical way around the main idea, which you might have expressed as "the structure and common practices of the medieval manor." Here's one possible road map you might have come up with:

- Paragraph 1 (just a single sentence, really): Intro to the topic of medieval manors (divided, as cited in the first sentence of next paragraph, into arable, meadow, waste, and village)
- Paragraphs 2, 3, and 4: Discussion of the arable and the practices associated with it
- Paragraph 5: Discussion of the meadow
- Paragraph 6: Discussion of the waste
- Paragraph 7: Discussion of the village

It should be obvious why, in your prereading step, you really need to get some sense of the layout of the passage like this. **Many questions don't contain specific line references to help you locate information, and if you don't have a road map of the passage in your head or on paper, you might get lost.**

Following is a key to the ten questions attached to this passage.

Key to Passage I

(NONFICTION—SOCIAL STUDIES)

	Answer	Refer to	Type	Comments
1.	C	Lines 68–89	Function	The entire paragraph supports this claim.
2.	F	Lines 52–59	Detail	"Uniform cropping was imperative…"
3.	B	Lines 21–23	Detail	Don't confuse fallow with planted fields.
4.	F	Lines 43–46	Inference	Every peasant got some fertile and some infertile land—inferably, to be fair to each.
5.	A	Lines 62–67, 72–75	Inference	No line reference, so you had to have a sense of the structure to find this.
6.	H	Lines 59–62	Vocab-in-Context	Use context. The crop is ripe, so it must be ready to be gathered.
7.	B	Lines 13–19	Detail	No line reference; otherwise, no problem.

8.	H	Lines 47–67	Inference	I: lines 47–52 say the opposite II: lines 48–52 III: lines 52–62 Statement I is false, so that means F, G, and J are wrong. That means H must be the answer.
9.	D	Lines 33–35	Detail	No line reference; number of plows = amount of land.
10.	H	Lines 90–92	Detail	Whole paragraph devoted to describing waste.

EXPERT TUTOR TIP

A few ACT questions—like question 8 in this passage—are Roman numeral questions. You're given three or four statements, each labeled with a Roman numeral. The idea is to treat each one as a true/false statement. Decide which statements are true, and then select the choice that includes only those statements. Often, you can save yourself some time on these questions. For instance, in question 8: Once you decide that Statement I is false, you can eliminate choices F, G, and J, all of which include Statement I. Thus, you can get your answer, choice H, without even looking at Statements II and III.

▶ IF YOU LEARNED ONLY THREE THINGS IN THIS CHAPTER...

1. Read the passage actively and take notes to create a passage map. Note the purpose of each paragraph and the passage overall.

2. Carefully read the question stems (*only*) to determine the type of question being asked.

3. Look for the correct answer in the passage—don't try to answer from memory. Predict an answer first, then look for the answer that best matches your prediction.

CHAPTER 11

Reading Workout 2: Look It Up!

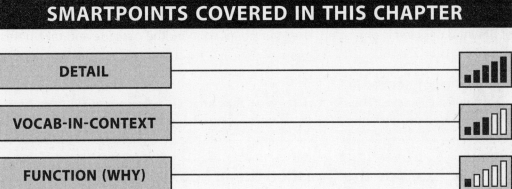

SMARTPOINTS COVERED IN THIS CHAPTER

DETAIL

VOCAB-IN-CONTEXT

FUNCTION (WHY)

INFERENCE

BIG PICTURE

In Reading Workout 1, we discussed general strategies for approaching ACT Reading. Now let's look more closely at the types of questions you'll encounter.

The three main types of Reading questions are:

SPECIFIC QUESTIONS

DETAIL

VOCAB-IN-CONTEXT

FUNCTION (WHY)

INFERENCE QUESTIONS

▁▂▃▄ **INFERENCE**

BIG PICTURE QUESTIONS

▁▂▃▄ **BIG PICTURE**

THE KAPLAN METHOD (AGAIN)

Don't forget to use the Kaplan Method for ACT Reading that we discussed in Reading Workout 1. Here's a reminder of how it works:

STEP 1: Actively Read the Passage, Taking Notes as You Go

In other words, quickly work through the passage (*before* trying to answer the questions) in less than three minutes. Read actively, and assemble a passage map or overall idea of how the passage is organized. Use your pencil to mark the passage and take notes.

> ✓ **PERFECT SCORE TIP**
> Prereading is much easier if you have an idea what the passage is about. Make sure to always read the brief intro provided at the beginning of each passage.

STEP 2: Examine the Question Stem, Looking for Clues

Before plunging into the answer choices, take a moment to understand what kind of question it is. They are:

- **Detail:** Asks about the "what" as stated in the passage
- **Vocab-in-Context:** Asks about the meaning of a word or words as used in context
- **Function:** Asks about why a word, sentence, or example is used in the passage
- **Inference:** Asks you to read between the lines to draw a conclusion that is not explicitly stated
- **Big Picture:** Asks about the overall point of the whole passage or of one paragraph

Refer to the passage to find the answer. You don't need to refer to the whole passage—just where the answer to a question can be found. Sometimes a line reference will be included in the question; otherwise, rely on your road map of the passage.

STEP 3: Predict the Answer and Select the Choice That Best Matches Your Prediction

Do this *before* looking at the answer choices. Then, with an answer in mind, it'll be easier to spot the correct choice.

IMPORTANT QUESTION TYPES

Try the following typical ACT nonfiction passage, this one from the Humanities. Afterward, we'll discuss selected questions from this set as examples of Specific Detail, Inference, and Big Picture questions.

Passage II

HUMANITIES

This passage is taken from the book *Invitation to the Theatre,* Third Edition, © 1985 by George Kernodle. Reprinted by permission of Wadsworth, a division of Thomson Learning.

Tragedy was the invention of the Greeks. In their Golden Age, the fifth century before Christ, they produced the world's greatest
Line dramatists, new forms of tragedy and
(5) comedy that have been models ever since, and a theatre that every age goes back to for rediscovery of some basic principles…

Since it derived from primitive religious rites, with masks and ceremonial costumes,
(10) and made use of music, dance, and poetry, the Greek drama was at the opposite pole from the modern realistic stage. In fact, probably no other theatre in history has made fuller use of the intensities of art. The
(15) masks, made of painted linen, wood, and plaster, brought down from primitive days the atmosphere of gods, heroes, and demons. Our nineteenth- and twentieth-century grandfathers thought masks must have been
(20) very artificial. Today, however, we appreciate their exciting intensity and can see that in a large theatre they were indispensable. If they allowed no fleeting change of expression during a single episode, they could give for
(25) each episode in turn more intense expression than any human face could. When

Oedipus comes back with bleeding eyes, the new mask could be more terrible than any facial makeup the audience could endure,
(30) yet in its sculpted intensity more beautiful than a real face.

Most essential of all intensities, and hardest for us to understand, was the chorus. Yet many playwrights today are
(35) trying to find some equivalent to do for a modern play what the chorus did for the Greeks. During the episodes played by the actors, the chorus would only provide a background of group response, enlarging
(40) and reverberating the emotions of the actors, sometimes protesting and opposing but in general serving as ideal spectators to stir and lead the reactions of the audience. But between episodes, with the actors out
(45) of the way, the chorus took over. We have only the words, not the music or dance, and some translations of the odes are in such formal, old-fashioned language that it is hard to guess that they were accom-
(50) panied by vigorous, sometimes even wild dances and symbolic actions that filled an orchestra which in some cities was sixty

to ninety feet in diameter. Sometimes the
chorus expressed simple horror or lament.

(55) Sometimes it chanted and acted out, in
unison and in precise formations of rows
and lines, the acts of violence the characters were enacting offstage. When Phaedra
rushes offstage in *Hippolytus* to hang herself

(60) from the rafters, the members of the chorus,
all fifteen of them, perform in mime and
chant the act of tying the rope and swinging
from the rafters. Sometimes the chorus tells
or reenacts an incident of history or legend

(65) that throws light on the situation in the play.

Sometimes the chorus puts into specific
action what is a general intention in the
mind of the main character. When Oedipus
resolves to hunt out the guilty person and

(70) cleanse the city, he is speaking metaphori-
cally, but the chorus invokes the gods of
vengeance and dances a wild pursuit.

On the printed page, the choral odes
seem static and formal, lyric and philosoph-

(75) ical, emotional letdowns that punctuate the
series of episodes, like intermissions between
two acts of a play. The reader who skips the
odes can get the main points of the play.
A few are worth reading as independent

(80) poems, notably the famous one in *Antigone*
beginning, "Many are the wonders of the
world, but none is more wonderful than
man." Some modern acting versions omit
the chorus or reduce it to a few background

(85) figures. Yet to the Greeks the odes were
certainly more than mere poetic interludes:
the wild Dionysian words and movements
evoked primitive levels of the subconscious
and at the same time served to transform

(90) primitive violence into charm and beauty
and to add philosophical reflections on the
meaning of human destiny.

For production today, we can only
improvise some partial equivalent. In Athens

(95) the entire population was familiar with
choral performances. Every year each of
the tribes entered a dithyramb in a contest,
rehearsing five hundred men and boys
for weeks. Some modern composers have

(100) tried to write dramatic music for choruses:
the most notable examples are the French
composer Darius Milhaud, in the primitive
rhythms, shouts, and chants of his operatic
version of the *Oresteia*; George Gershwin, in

(105) the Negro funeral scenes of *Porgy and Bess*;
and Kurt Weill, in the African choruses for
Lost in the Stars, the musical dramatiza-
tion of Alan Paton's novel, *Cry, the Beloved
Country*. For revivals of Greek tragedies we

(110) have not dared use much music beyond a
few phrases half shouted, half sung, and
drumbeats and suggestive melodies in the
background.

A quick preread of the passage should have given you a sense of its general organization:

- *First paragraph:* introduces the topic of Greek tragedy.
- *Second paragraph:* discusses use of masks (artificial but intense).
- *Third and fourth paragraphs:* discuss use of chorus (also artificial but intense).
- *Fifth paragraph:* expands discussion to choral odes.
- *Sixth paragraph:* concludes with discussion of how Greek tragedy is performed today and how it has influenced some modern art.

That's really all the road map you need going into the questions. Aside from that, you should take away the author's main point: Greek tragedy included many artificial devices, but these devices allowed it to rise to a high level of intensity.

1. Combined with the passage's additional information, the fact that some Greek orchestras were 60 to 90 feet across suggests that:

   A. few spectators were able to see the stage.
   B. no one performer could dominate a performance.
   C. choruses and masks helped overcome the distance between actors and audience.
   D. Greek tragedies lacked the emotional force of modern theatrical productions.

2. The phrase "fuller use of the intensities of art" (line 14) most nearly means:

   F. employment of brightly illuminated effects.
   G. good use of powerful, dramatic effects of music, dance, and poetry.
   H. the enjoyment of strong elements of effects on stage.
   J. the utilization of dramatic interactions.

3. The description of the chorus's enactment of Phaedra's offstage suicide (lines 58–63) shows that, in contrast to modern theater, ancient Greek theater was:

   A. more violent.
   B. more concerned with satisfying an audience.
   C. more apt to be historically accurate.
   D. less concerned with a realistic portrayal of events.

4. It can be inferred that one consequence of the Greeks' use of masks was that:

   F. the actors often had to change masks between episodes.
   G. the characters in the play could not convey emotion.
   H. the actors wearing masks played nonspeaking roles.
   J. good acting ability was not important to the Greeks.

5. Which of the following is supported by the information in the second paragraph (lines 8–31)?

   A. Masks in Greek drama combined artistic beauty with emotional intensity.

   B. The use of masks in Greek drama was better appreciated in the 19th century than it is now.

   C. Masks in Greek drama were used to portray gods but never human beings.

   D. Contemporary scholars seriously doubt the importance of masks to Greek theater.

6. The author indicates in lines 69–70 that Oedipus's resolution "to hunt out the guilty person and cleanse the city" was:

   F. at odds with what he actually does later in the performance.

   G. misinterpreted by the chorus.

   H. dramatized by the actions of the chorus.

   J. angrily condemned by the chorus.

7. According to the passage, when actors were present on stage, the chorus would:

   A. look on silently as spectators.

   B. inevitably agree with the actors' actions.

   C. communicate to the audience solely through mime.

   D. react to the performance as an audience might.

8. The main point of the fifth paragraph (lines 73–92) is that choral odes:

   F. should not be performed by modern choruses.

   G. have a meaning and beauty that are lost in modern adaptations.

   H. can be safely ignored by a modern-day reader.

   J. are only worthwhile in *Antigone*.

9. The passage suggests that modern revivals of Greek tragedies "have not dared use much music" (line 110) because:

   A. modern instruments would appear out of place.

   B. to do so would require a greater understanding of how choral odes were performed.

   C. music would distract the audience from listening to the words of choral odes.

   D. such music is considered far too primitive for modern audiences.

10. The author discusses *Porgy and Bess* and *Lost in the Stars* in order to:

   F. show how two modern plays reenact ancient Greek tragedies.

   G. demonstrate the use of music in modern plays.

   H. give examples of two modern-day playwrights who used musical choruses in their dramas.

   J. illustrate how music evokes subconscious emotions in modern-day plays.

Now let's take a look at selected questions, which fall into three categories.

Specific Questions

▁▃▅▇ DETAIL

▁▃▅▁ VOCAB-IN-CONTEXT

▁▃▁▁ FUNCTION

Questions 2, 6, 7, and 10 are typical Specific questions. Some Specific questions give you a line reference to help you out; others don't, forcing you either to start tearing your hair out (if you're an unprepared test taker) or else to seek out the answer based on your sense of how the passage is laid out (one of the two key reasons to preread the passage).

> **EXPERT TUTOR TIP**
> The answers are in the passage. Focus your attention on locating them. Your mind-set should be: "Find the answer," not "Remember the answer." Locate them using your trusty road map.

Question 2 is a Vocab-in-Context question. This stem refers to a word or phrase in the passage and asks you to select the answer that is closest to the meaning in *context*.

Read a little before line 12. Greek drama "made use of music, dance, and poetry" (line 10). This reference matches choice G, which is the correct answer.

Note: The best answer is not a direct definition of the words. Look instead for the answer that would make the most sense. To check your answer, plug it into the sentence.

Question 6 provides a line reference (lines 69–70), but to answer the question confidently, you should have also read a few lines *before* and a few lines *after* the cited lines. There, you would have read: "Sometimes the chorus puts into action what is a general intention in the mind of the main character. When Oedipus resolves…" Clearly, the Oedipus example is meant to illustrate the point about the chorus acting out a character's intentions. So choice H is correct—they are dramatizing (or acting out) Oedipus's resolution. (By the way, choice G might have been tempting, but there's no evidence that the chorus is misinterpreting, just that they're "putting a general intention into specific action.")

Question 7 is a Specific question *without* a line reference. Such questions are common on the ACT, and they require that you have a good sense of the structure of the passage as a whole so that you can locate the place where the question is answered. The mention of the chorus in the question should send you to paragraph 3. If you marked this paragraph with the ABC method we've discussed, a quick glance over should lead you to the sentence that begins on line 37, where the author claims that the chorus serves to "lead the reactions of the audience"—captured by choice D.

Question 10 is another type of Specific question: Function. These questions ask why an author uses a word, phrase, or detail in the passage. You can spot these questions because you'll see phrases like, "is used to," "is meant to," and "in order to" in the question stem.

Question 10 asks why the author mentions the modern plays *Porgy and Bess* and *Lost in the Stars* in the passage. It is important to remember that WHY something is discussed is different from WHAT is discussed. The road map after the passage and the topic sentences in lines 93–109 in the passage indicate the main idea for the final paragraph is the modern use of the chorus. Choice H is the right answer.

Note: While choices G and J may be true, they are not the reason why the author mentions these plays. Choice F is false—they are not reenactments of Greek tragedies.

Inference Questions

▂▃▅▇ **INFERENCE**

With Inference questions, your job is to combine ideas logically to make an inference—something that's not stated explicitly in the passage but that is definitely said implicitly. Often, you'll see a word like *suggest, infer, inference,* or *imply* in the question stem to tip you off.

To succeed on Inference questions, you have to read between the lines. Common sense is your best tool here. You use various bits of information in the passage as evidence for your own logical conclusion.

> ✓ **PERFECT SCORE TIP**
> While Inference questions will ask you to read between the lines, remember that they will never ask you to make conclusions outside the scope of the passage, so be sure all your answers have a basis in the reading.

Questions 1, 3, and **5** require that you combine information from more than one place in the passage. **Question 1** has no line references to help; a quick survey of the passage tells you that C is the only compatible answer. **Question 3** research might lead to a prediction of "the chorus emphasizes what's happening on stage," pointing

Part Two: Skill-Building Workouts
Reading Workout 2: Look It Up!

187

you to answer D. **Question 5** research leads you to the key word *intensity*, which you examined previously for question 2, and which appears in only one answer choice.

Note: The relationship between questions 2 and 5 is a good example of how answering one question can help you with the answer to another. Thus, you may find that if you skip a question the first time, you can answer it during a second pass.

Question 4 provides no line reference, but the mention of masks should have sent you to the second paragraph of the passage. Lines 23–24 explain that masks "allowed no fleeting change of expression during a single episode." Treat that as your first piece of evidence. Your second comes in lines 24–26: "they [the masks] could give for each episode in turn more intense expression than any human face could." Put those two pieces of evidence together—masks can't change expression *during* a single episode, but they can give expression for each episode *in turn*.

> **EXPERT TUTOR TIP**
> Making inferences often requires that you combine bits of information from different parts of the passage. Common sense will then lead you to an appropriate inference—one that's not too extreme.

Clearly, the actors must have changed masks between episodes so that they could express the different emotions that different episodes required. Choice F is correct.

One warning: Keep your inferences as close to the passage as possible. Don't make wild inferential leaps. An inference should follow naturally and inevitably from the evidence provided in the passage.

Big Picture Questions

BIG PICTURE

About one-third of the ACT Reading questions are Detail questions and most of the rest are Inference questions. But there are also a few questions that test your understanding of the theme, purpose, and organization of the passage as a whole. Big Picture questions tend to look for:

- **Main point or purpose of a passage or part of a passage**
- **Author's attitude or tone**
- **Logic underlying the author's argument**
- **Relationship between different parts of the passage**
- **Difference between fact and opinion**

One way to see the Big Picture is to read actively. As you read, ask yourself, "What's this all about? What's the point of this? Why is the author saying this?"

 EXPERT TUTOR TIP
If you're still stumped on a Big Picture question after reading the passage, try doing the Detail and Inference questions first. They can help you fill in the Big Picture.

Question 8 asks for the main idea of a particular paragraph—namely, the fifth—which our general outline indicates is the paragraph about choral odes. Skimming that paragraph, you find reference to how the odes seem to us modern people—"static and formal" (line 74), "like intermissions between two acts of a play" (lines 76–77). Later, the author states, by way of contrast (note the use of the clue word *yet*): "Yet to the Greeks the odes were certainly more than mere poetic interludes." Clearly, the author wants to contrast our modern static view of the odes with the Greeks' view of them as something more. That idea is best captured by choice G.

FIND AND PARAPHRASE...AND OTHER TIPS

The previous examples show that your real task in Reading is not what you might expect. **Your main job is to find the answers.** Perhaps a better name for the Reading subtest would be "find and paraphrase." But students tend to think that their task in Reading is to "comprehend and remember." That's the wrong mind-set.

Don't Be Afraid to Skip

Now that you've done a couple full-length passages and questions, you've probably encountered at least a few questions that you found unanswerable. **What do you do if you can't find the answer in the passage, or if you can find it but don't understand, or if you do understand but can't see an answer choice that makes sense? Skip the question.** Skipping is probably more important in Reading than in any other ACT subject test. Many students find it useful to skip as many as half of the questions on the first pass through a set of Reading questions. That's fine.

✓ **PERFECT SCORE TIP**
I found skipping questions during the first pass the most useful in Reading. Don't spend too much time on one question the first time through.

When you come back to a Reading question the second time, it usually makes sense to use the process of elimination. The first time around, you tried to find the *right* answer but you couldn't. So now try to identify the three *wrong* answers. Eliminating three choices is slower than finding one right choice, so don't make it your main strategy for Reading. However, it is a good way to try a second attack on a question.

Another thing to consider when attacking a question for a second time is that the right answer may have been hidden. Maybe it's written in an unexpected way, with different vocabulary, or maybe there is another good way that you haven't thought of to answer the question. Remember that it's still important to avoid getting bogged down when you come back to a question. **Be willing to admit that there are some problems you just can't answer. Guess if you have to.**

Here's a key to the Greek tragedy passage so that you can check the answers to the questions not discussed previously.

Key to Passage II
(NONFICTION—HUMANITIES)

	Answer	Refer to	Type	Comments
1.	C	Lines 20–22, 34–53	Inference	Q-stem emphasizes distance between audience and stage; masks and choruses help to enlarge the action so that it can be understood from a distance.
2.	G	Lines 8–26	Vocab-in-Context	Must make sense in context.
3.	D	Lines 58–62	Inference	Combine info from lines 8–12, 58–63, 85–92.
4.	F	Lines 23–26	Inference	Discussed above.
5.	A	Lines 8–31	Inference	Combine info from lines 12–14, 27–31.
6.	H	Lines 69–70	Detail	Don't overthink the answer.
7.	D	Lines 37–44	Detail	No line reference. Be careful.
8.	G	Lines 73–92	Big Picture	Which answer echoes the passage?
9.	B	Lines 107–111	Inference	Be sure to consult all your notes for the last paragraph.
10.	H	Lines 99–109	Function	"Some modern composers have tried to write dramatic music for choruses."

> ## IF YOU LEARNED ONLY THREE THINGS IN THIS CHAPTER...

1. Preread the passage and make a road map: know what each paragraph is saying.

2. Refer to your road map when you attack the questions, and **always** refer back to the passage to find the answer.

3. Reading questions can ask about specific details of a passage, what a passage implies, and its overall structure and argument.

CHAPTER 12

Reading Workout 3: Subject Matters

Now that you've learned the general approach to ACT Reading and the approach for each of the specific question types, let's look more closely at the two passage types that give students the most trouble—the Prose Fiction passage and the Natural Sciences passage.

The passage breakdown for the ACT Reading test is as follows:

- Prose Fiction—one passage per test
- Nonfiction—three passages per test, one each in:
  - **Social Sciences**
  - **Humanities**
  - **Natural Sciences**

Your approach will be essentially the same for all three nonfiction passages, since they're all well-organized essays. Your approach to the Prose Fiction passage, however, will be somewhat different.

What follows are two full ACT Reading passages—one Prose Fiction passage and one Natural Sciences passage (which, for convenience, we'll call just Science)—complete with questions. We'll talk about specific strategies for each, but just as importantly, we'll talk about how you can bring together everything you've learned so far and combine this knowledge into a plan of attack for *all* Reading passages. At the end of the workout, we'll also show you how to salvage a few extra points if you find yourself near the end of the test with not enough time to read the final passage.

> ✔ **PERFECT SCORE TIP**
> You do not have to read the four Reading passages in order! Figure out your best and start there. If prose is hard for you and takes a while, do it last even though it is first in the test book.

THE PROSE FICTION PASSAGE

The Prose Fiction passage differs from the three nonfiction passages in that it is not a well-structured essay designed to communicate ideas in a logical, orderly way. It is, usually, a story in which characters fully equipped with their own motivations and emotions interact with each other in revealing ways. For that reason, the Prose Fiction passage won't break down into an orderly outline or road map, so don't even try to characterize the function of each paragraph. Pay attention instead to the *story*.

In the Prose Fiction passage, almost all of the questions relate to the characters. Your job is to find the answers to the following questions:

- **Who are these people?** What are they like? How are they related to each other?

- **What is their state of mind?** Are they angry? Sad? Reflective? Excited?

- **What's going on?** What's happening on the surface? What's happening beneath the surface?

- **What's the author's attitude toward the characters?**

Most of the passages focus on one person or are written from the point of view of one of the characters. Figure out who this main character is and pay special attention to what he or she is like. **Read between the lines to determine unspoken emotions and attitudes. Little hints—a momentary frown, a pointed or sarcastic comment—are sometimes all you have to go on, so *pay attention*.** In fact, you'll probably want to spend more time prereading the Prose Fiction passage than you do any of the other three passages. It's important to get a good feel for the tone and style of the passage as a whole before going to the questions.

> 👤 **EXPERT TUTOR TIP**
> Fiction passages focus on the characters. Who are they? What are they like? What do they think about each other? Watch what they say and do in the passages.

Fortunately, the questions that accompany these passages tend to go more quickly than those for the other passages, so you'll be able to make up some of that time you lose reading the passage.

Make It a Movie in Your Head

Try to make the passage into a movie! Imagine the scenes, the characters, the events. In the Prose Fiction passage, it should be easy to imagine the story unfolding like a movie. Pay careful attention not only to what the characters say but also how they say it.

> ✔ **PERFECT SCORE TIP**
> I found imagining the prose passage as a movie very helpful. It helped keep me awake and engaged while reading it so I was more prepared for the questions.

And don't forget to read actively, as always. Don't just read and then react. Once you have an idea of the personality of the characters, you should be able to respond to the questions. What should you do if you are struggling to understand what's going on? Go to the questions and let the line and paragraph references guide you to important words, phrases, and sentences. One or two questions should help you discover the meaning of the passage. Don't forget to guess on a question you're not sure of.

The Real Thing: Practice Passage

What follows is a typical ACT Prose Fiction passage, complete with questions. Before trying it, you might want to glance back at the techniques discussed in our first Reading Workout. Review the Kaplan Reading Method. **Spend about three minutes prereading (a little more, actually, since this is the Prose Fiction passage). Then do whichever questions you can figure out quickly. Skip any hard or time-consuming problems and come back to them later.**

When you work on the questions, constantly refer to the passage. Plan to spend much more time with your eyeballs pointed at the passage than at the questions. And don't forget to answer the questions in your own words (based on what you've preread and reread in the passage) *before* you look at the answers.

Passage III

PROSE FICTION

This passage is excerpted from *Remains of the Day*, by Kazuo Ishiguro, © 1989 by Kazuo Ishiguro. Reprinted by permission of Alfred A. Knopf, a division of Random House, Inc. Reprinted in the UK by permission of Faber and Faber Ltd, publishers. Reprinted in Canada and Europe by permission of the author, c/o Rogers, Coleridge & White Ltd.

I recall a mist starting in as I crossed the lawn that afternoon. I was making my way up to the summer house for the purpose of clearing away the remains of his lordship's
(5) taking tea there with some guest a little while earlier. I can recall spotting from some distance... Miss Kenton's figure moving about inside the summerhouse. When I entered she had seated herself on one of the
(10) wicker chairs scattered around its interior, evidently engaged in some needlework. On closer inspection, I saw she was performing repairs to a cushion. I went about gathering up the various items of crockery from
(15) amidst the plants and the cane furniture, and as I did so, I believe we exchanged a few pleasantries, perhaps discussed one or two professional matters. For the truth was, it was extremely refreshing to be out in the
(20) summerhouse after many continuous days in the main building and neither of us was inclined to hurry with our tasks... In fact, I was looking out over the lawn to where the mist was thickening down around the poplar
(25) trees planted along the cart-track, when I finally introduced the topic of the previous year's dismissals. Perhaps a little predictably, I did so by saying:

"I was just thinking earlier, Miss Kenton.
(30) It's rather funny to remember now, but you know, only this time a year ago, you were still insisting you were going to resign. It rather amused me to think of it." When I finally turned to look at her, she was gazing
(35) through the glass at the great expanse of fog outside.

"You probably have no idea, Mr. Stevens," she said eventually, "how seriously I really thought of leaving this house. I felt so
(40) strongly about what happened. Had I been anyone worthy of any respect at all, I dare say I would have left Darlington Hall long ago." She paused for a while, and I turned my gaze back out to the poplar trees down
(45) in the distance. Then she continued in a tired voice: "It was cowardice, Mr. Stevens. Simple cowardice. Where could I have gone? I have no family. Only my aunt. I love her dearly, but I can't live with her for a day
(50) without feeling my whole life is wasting away. I did tell myself, of course, I would soon find some situation.

"But I was so frightened, Mr. Stevens. Whenever I thought of leaving, I just saw
(55) myself going out there and finding nobody who knew or cared about me. There, that's all my high principles amount to. I feel so ashamed of myself. But I just couldn't leave, Mr. Stevens. I just couldn't bring myself to
(60) leave."

Miss Kenton paused again and seemed to be deep in thought. I thus thought it opportune to relate at this point, as precisely as possible, what had taken place earlier
(65) between myself and Lord Darlington. I proceeded to do so and concluded by saying:

"What's done can hardly be undone. But it is at least a great comfort to hear his lordship declare so unequivocally that it
(70) was all a terrible misunderstanding. I just thought you'd like to know, Miss Kenton,

since I recall you were as distressed by the episode as I was."

"I'm sorry, Mr. Stevens," Miss Kenton
(75) said behind me in an entirely new voice, as though she had just been jolted from a dream, "I don't understand you." Then as I turned to her, she went on: "As I recall, you thought it was only right
(80) and proper that Ruth and Sarah be sent packing. You were positively cheerful about it."

"Now really, Miss Kenton, that is quite incorrect and unfair. The whole matter
(85) caused me great concern, great concern indeed. It is hardly the sort of thing I like to see happen in this house."

"Then why, Mr. Stevens, did you not tell me so at the time?"
(90)   I gave a laugh, but for a moment was rather at a loss for an answer. Before I could formulate one, Miss Kenton put down her sewing and said:

"Do you realize, Mr. Stevens, how
(95) much it would have meant to me if you had thought to share your feelings last year? You knew how upset I was when my girls were dismissed. Do you realize how much it would have helped me? Why, Mr.
(100) Stevens, why, why, why do you always have to pretend?"

I gave another laugh at the ridiculous turn the conversation had suddenly taken. "Really, Miss Kenton," I said, "I'm not sure
(105) I know what you mean. Pretend? Why, really...."

"I suffered so much over Ruth and Sarah leaving us. And I suffered all the more because I believed I suffered alone."

1. According to the passage, the author thinks Mr. Stevens is:

   A. worthy of respect.

   B. not considerate of Miss Kenton's feelings.

   C. too formal in his demeanor.

   D. disloyal to his friends.

2. The statement "Had I been anyone worthy of any respect at all, I dare say I would have left Darlington Hall long ago" (lines 40–44) can be interpreted to mean:

   F. no one at Darlington Hall truly respects Miss Kenton.

   G. Miss Kenton has little respect for Mr. Stevens.

   H. Miss Kenton feels she betrayed her principles by staying.

   J. Miss Kenton senses that Mr. Stevens feels superior to her.

3. According to the passage, the intent of Mr. Stevens's recollection of Miss Kenton's desire to resign (lines 29–33) is most likely to:

   A. open up a discussion of an event that had upset Miss Kenton.

   B. turn the conversation to the professional topic of furniture repair.

   C. indulge in nostalgic reminiscences of happier days.

   D. irritate Miss Kenton by mocking the seriousness of that desire.

4. Mr. Stevens gives "a laugh" (line 90) because he is suddenly:

   F. amused.

   G. insecure.

   H. suspicious.

   J. sarcastic.

5. The main point of Miss Kenton's references to her own family (lines 48–52) is that:

   A. she would have nowhere to turn if she left her job.

   B. children often reject those they should love.

   C. she was afraid of discovering that she did not love her aunt.

   D. life becomes very tedious when one visits relatives.

6. What is it that Mr. Stevens describes as "done" (line 66)?

   F. Lord Darlington's earlier conversation with him

   G. Miss Kenton's talk of leaving Darlington Hall

   H. Ruth and Sarah's dismissal

   J. Any talk of Miss Kenton's dismissal

7. As he is revealed in the passage, Mr. Stevens is:

   A. bored with their conversation in the summer house.

   B. increasingly hostile to Miss Kenton's depiction of his actions.

   C. uncomfortable with expressing his deep affection for Miss Kenton.

   D. unaware of how his past behavior had affected Miss Kenton.

8. Which of the following would be out of character for the narrator?

   I. Pointing out to Miss Kenton why she was unfairly characterizing his actions

   II. Spending time thinking about Miss Kenton's accusations

   III. Ridiculing Miss Kenton for poorly repairing the cushion

   F. I only

   G. II only

   H. I and II only

   J. III only

9. Miss Kenton interacts with Mr. Stevens in a way that can best be described as:

   A. sincere but formal.

   B. indifferent but polite.

   C. timid but angry.

   D. patronizing but kindly.

10. At the end of the passage, Miss Kenton asks, "Why, Mr. Stevens, why, why, why do you always have to pretend?" (lines 98–100) What specific action of Mr. Stevens does she have in mind?

    F. His apparent cheerfulness at Ruth and Sarah's dismissal

    G. His simulation of great affection for her

    H. His phony concern for her own future employment

    J. His empty expressions of sympathy for her own suffering

Answers and Explanations

Paragraphs in the Prose Fiction passage move the story forward. Your prereading road map should center on answers to four main questions about character, actions, and attitudes. They are:

1. **Who are these people?** The first paragraphs are peppered with hints about who these people are. Lines 3–6 discuss Mr. Stevens "clearing away the remains of his lordship's taking tea." Lines 12–13 describe Miss Kenton "performing repairs to a cushion." Lines 29–32 discuss her previous plans for resigning. Clearly, Mr. Stevens and Miss Kenton are servants (we later learn—in lines 64–65—that their employer is Lord Darlington).

2. **What is their state of mind?** We read of "the previous year's dismissals" (lines 26–27) and Miss Kenton's intentions to leave the house (lines 37–39) as a result of them. She "felt so strongly about what happened" (lines 39–40), but she was afraid to take the step of actually leaving in protest ("It was cowardice," she admits in line 46). It sounds like some other servants were dismissed unfairly last year and that this upset Miss Kenton. Apparently, Mr. Stevens also found the incident distressing (lines 71–72), but Miss Kenton hadn't realized this at the time.

3. **What's going on?** These are obviously very formal people, but there are strong emotions rumbling beneath the surface. It's clear that Miss Kenton is very upset because she didn't realize that Mr. Stevens disapproved of the dismissals, too ("Do you realize, Mr. Stevens, how much it would have meant to me if you had thought to share your feelings last year?"—lines 93–96. And later: "Why, Mr. Stevens, why, why, why do you always have to pretend?"—lines 98–100). We get the impression that Mr. Stevens is not a man who very readily shows his feelings and emotions—as Miss Kenton puts it, he always *pretends*.

4. **What is the author's attitude toward the characters?** Often, there will be a question asking about the author's point of view. Be careful here—don't confuse what the characters think about each other with what the author thinks. The two may not be the same.

Note: The first question here is about Writer's View. Your best bet is to skip the question and leave it for last.

Notice how many inference-type questions there are. This is typical of the Prose Fiction passage, where so much information is conveyed implicitly—between the lines. In most cases, you have to read around the specific line references in order to find your answer. If you've done your preread properly, however, you should be able to knock off most of the questions quickly.

Key to Passage III

(PROSE FICTION)

INFERENCE

BIG PICTURE

DETAIL

WRITER'S VIEW

	Answer	Refer to	Type	Comments
1.	B	First two paragraphs	Writer's View	Stevens says he was "amused" and thought it "funny" that she wanted to resign her position. Miss Kenton replies very seriously to his words, saying she doesn't understand him and how could he be so cheerful if he disapproved of the two firings. Miss Kenton has plainly suffered, and Mr. Stevens has not reacted kindly to her pain. The author's sympathy is with Miss Kenton, not Mr. Stevens.
2.	H	Lines 40–44, 55–56	Inference	"There, that's all my high principles amount to," she says.
3.	A	Lines 29–33, 60–65	Inference	Lines 60–65 show that Mr. Stevens has just been discussing this subject with Lord Darlington and now wants to discuss it with Miss Kenton.
4.	G	Lines 89–90	Inference	He is "at a loss for an answer" and clearly not laughing out of amusement.
5.	A	Lines 47–48	Detail	"Where could I have gone? I have no family."
6.	H	Lines 66–72	Detail	Refers to "the previous year's dismissals," first mentioned in lines 25–27.
7.	D	Throughout	Big Picture	Mr. Stevens's nervous laughs hint that he had no idea how deeply Miss Kenton was affected.
8.	J	Throughout	Inference	I: He does this in lines 82–86. II: He wishes to respond to the accusations in lines 78–81. III: This kind of blatant harshness would be uncharacteristic of so discreet and proper a man.
9.	A	Throughout	Big Picture	Miss Kenton freely expresses her feelings to him throughout, so she is sincere. But she **never** loses her formal language and demeanor.
10.	F	Lines 98–100, 73–81	Inference	She wishes that he "had thought to share [his] feelings"; she was under the impression that he was "positively cheerful about [the dismissals]."

THE NATURAL SCIENCES PASSAGE

The Science passage in the Reading subject test emphasizes reading. Here, it is more important understanding ideas than analyzing experiments and data.

Approaching the Science passage is really not any different from approaching the other nonfiction passages, since all are well-organized essays that lay out ideas in a straight-forward, logical way. However, you may be more likely to find unfamiliar vocabulary in Science passages. ***Don't panic.*** **Any unfamiliar terms will usually be defined in the passage or else will have definitions inferable from context.**

> ✔ **PERFECT SCORE TIP**
> Often, the Natural Science passage will be difficult and have a lot of unfamiliar scientific knowledge in it. Just remind yourself that you don't have to understand all the science behind it. The answer to almost every question is found in the passage and is within your grasp.

Don't Get Lost!

In the Science passage, it's easy to lose yourself in complex details. Don't do it. **It's _especially_ important not to get bogged down in the Science passage!** Many students try to understand and remember everything as they read, but that's not the right ACT mind-set. In your preread of the passage, just get the gist and the outline; don't sweat the details. As always, use line references in the questions when possible. They will lead you back to the details that are important. You'd be surprised how many questions you can answer on a passage you don't really understand.

The Real Thing: Practice Passage

The next passage is a typical ACT-style Science passage with questions. Attack it with the same Kaplan Method you use for other passages. Don't worry if you don't understand everything. Your only goal is to get a sense of the passage and its outline.

Passage IV

NATURAL SCIENCE

This passage is excerpted from *Light and Color in Nature and Art,* © 1983 by Samuel J. Williamson. Reprinted by permission of John Wiley & Sons, Inc.

Atoms can be excited in many ways other than by absorbing a photon. The element phosphorous spontaneously combines
Line with oxygen when exposed to air. There is
(5) a transfer of energy to the phosphorous electrons during this chemical reaction, which excites them to sufficiently high energy states that they can subsequently emit light when dropping into a lower
(10) state. This is an example of what is termed chemiluminescence, the emission of light as a result of chemical reaction.

A related effect is bioluminescence, when light is produced by chemical reactions
(15) associated with biological activity. Bioluminescence occurs in a variety of life forms and is more common in marine organisms than in terrestrial or freshwater life. Examples include certain bacteria, jellyfish,
(20) clams, fungi, worms, ants, and fireflies. There is considerable diversity in how light is produced. Most processes involve the reaction of a protein with oxygen, catalyzed by an enzyme. The protein varies
(25) from one organism to another, but all are grouped under the generic name luciferin. The enzymes are known as luciferase. Both words stem from the Latin lucifer meaning light-bearing. The various chemical steps
(30) leading to bioluminescence are yet to be explained in detail, but in some higher organisms the process is known to be activated by the nervous system.

The firefly is best understood. Its light organ is located near the end of
(35) the abdomen. Within it luciferin is combined with other atomic groups in a series of processes in which oxygen is converted into carbon dioxide. The sequence

culminates when the luciferin is split off
(40) from the rest, leaving it in an excited state. The excess energy is released as a photon. The peak in the emission spectrum lies between 550 and 600 nm depending on the type of luciferase. This flash produced
(45) by the simultaneous emission of many photons serves to attract mates, and females also use it to attract males of other species, which they devour.

Certain bacteria also produce light
(50) when stimulated by motion. This is why the breaking sea or a passing boat generate the greenish light seen in some bodies of water such as Phosphorescent Bay in Puerto Rico. Some fish have a symbiotic relationship
(55) with bacteria. The "flashlight fish" takes advantage of the light created by bacteria lodged beneath each eye. Certain other fish produce their own bioluminescence, which serves as identification. However, the
(60) biological advantage, if any, of bioluminescence in some other organisms such as fungi remains a mystery.

Triboluminescence is the emission of light when one hard object is sharply struck
(65) against another. This contact, when atom scrapes against atom, excites electrons and disrupts electrical bonds. Light is then created when the electrons find their way to lower states. Triboluminescence is not to be
(70) confused with the glow of small particles that may be broken off by the impact. Such "sparks" are seen as a result of their high temperature. Light given off by hot objects is known as thermoluminescence, or incandes
(75) cence.

Another form of thermoluminescence is the basis for dating ancient ceramic objects.

Quartz and other constituents of clay are continually irradiated by naturally occurring
(80) radioactive elements (e.g., uranium and thorium) and by cosmic rays. This produces defects in the material where electrons may be trapped. Heating pottery to 500°C releases the trapped electrons, which can
(85) then migrate back to their original atoms, where on returning to an atomic orbit they then emit a photon. The intensity of thermoluminescence is therefore a measure of the duration of irradiation since the time when
(90) the pottery had been previously fired.

Excitation is also possible by other means. The passage of an electrical current (electroluminescence) is one. The impact of high energy particles is another. The
(95) *aurora borealis* and its southern counterpart the *aurora australis* arise when a stream of high energy particles from the sun enters the Earth's upper atmosphere and literally shatters some of the molecules of
(100) the air. This leaves their atoms in excited states, and the light subsequently given off is characteristic of the atoms. Although the oxygen molecule, a major constituent of our atmosphere, has no emission in the visible,
(105) the oxygen atom can emit photons in either the red or green portions of the spectrum. Other atoms contribute to light at other wavelengths.

11. According to the information in the sixth paragraph (lines 76–90), the brighter the thermoluminescence of a heated piece of ancient pottery:

    A. the younger the piece is.

    B. the older the piece is.

    C. the less irradiation has occurred within the piece's clay.

    D. the fewer electrons have become trapped within the clay.

12. If an ancient ceramic bowl is heated to 500°C, light is emitted when certain electrons:

    F. release radioactive elements found in the clay.

    G. scrape against other electrons.

    H. become superheated.

    J. return to their former atoms.

13. Compared to bioluminescence, chemiluminescence is NOT produced by:

    A. organic proteins that have been catalyzed.

    B. a chemical reaction.

    C. any reaction involving oxygen.

    D. a change in energy states.

14. It can be inferred from the passage that the description of the firefly's production of light is a good example of the degree to which researchers understand:

    F. why light attracts fireflies.

    G. how a chemical process can trigger bioluminescence.

    H. how female fireflies attack male fireflies.

    J. how to measure the intensity of a firefly's bioluminescence.

15. In both chemiluminescence and bioluminescence, photons are emitted:

    A. as excess energy.

    B. only by certain marine organisms.

    C. only when luciferase is present.

    D. only when phosphorous is present.

16. Based on details in the passage, the word *excited* as used in line 1 means:

    F. split off from a molecule.

    G. agitated until glowing.

    H. raised to a higher energy level.

    J. heated to the point of disintegration.

17. In discussing the creation of the two kinds of aurora, the passage asserts that the oxygen molecule "has no emission in the visible [spectrum]" (line 104) but also states that "the oxygen atom can emit photons in either the red or the green portions of the spectrum" (lines 105–106). Is the passage logically consistent?

    A. Yes, because visible light is emitted after the oxygen molecules have been broken apart into oxygen atoms.

    B. Yes, because the passage presents factual information and therefore cannot be illogical.

    C. No, because the oxygen molecule forms the largest part of the atmosphere and scientific theories must account for its invisible emissions.

    D. No, because the writer has failed to adequately differentiate between the oxygen molecule's behavior and that of the oxygen atom.

18. Assume that two meteors have collided and shattered. Astronomers see both a burst of light and then a subsequent glow. Such a visual phenomenon could best be explained as the result of:

       I. chemiluminescence.

      II. triboluminescence.

      III. thermoluminescence.

    F. II only

    G. II and III only

    H. I and III only

    J. I, II, and III

19. Based on information presented in the passage, which of the following is a hypothesis, rather than a fact?

    A. Fireflies use bioluminescence to attract mates.

    B. Thermoluminescence and triboluminescence are two distinctly different kinds of light emission.

    C. A firefly's type of luciferase determines the peak of its light emission's intensity.

    D. All organisms that produce bioluminescence do so for some biological advantage.

20. According to the last paragraph (lines 91–108), both the *aurora borealis* and the *aurora australis*:

    F. arise from the effect of high energy particles on atoms.

    G. occur without the presence of oxygen.

    H. emit light due to the presence of electrical currents.

    J. are visible from the surface of the Earth.

Answers and Explanations

Feeling a little numb? Unless you're a real science buff, you probably found this passage a lot less exciting than the atoms did. And you may have found yourself adrift in a sea of bewildering terms—*chemiluminescence, luciferin, aurora australis.*

We hope, though, that you didn't panic. You could still get points—and lots of them—from this passage even if all that you took away from your preread was a sense that the passage was mainly about things in nature glowing when their atoms are excited. That, and a sense of a road map, was really all you needed. Most of the questions were answerable by referring to the appropriate lines in the passage and paraphrasing what you read there.

Here's a possible road map for the passage:

- **First paragraph:** Introduction of idea of excited atoms releasing photons (i.e., luminescence). Discusses *chemiluminescence* (resulting from a chemical reaction).
- **Second paragraph:** Discusses *bioluminescence* (associated with biological activity—that is, with things that are alive).
- **Third paragraph:** Example of *bioluminescence*—fireflies.
- **Fourth paragraph:** More examples of *bioluminescence*—sea life.
- **Fifth paragraph:** Discusses *triboluminescence* (things hitting each other) and *thermoluminescence* (hot objects).
- **Sixth paragraph:** Example of *thermoluminescence*—refired ceramic objects.
- **Seventh paragraph:** Concludes with discussion of *electroluminescence* (associated with electrical currents).

Basically, the author is giving us a rundown on the various kinds of luminescence in nature. When the questions ask about one kind or another, you simply refer to the appropriate paragraph and lines.

Following is a key to the answers for this passage. Notice how you could have gotten an answer to number 12, for instance, *even if you were totally confused*. If you found 500° in the passage (line 83), the sentence more or less spelled out the answer for you, requiring a minimum of paraphrasing.

Key to Passage IV

(NONFICTION—NATURAL SCIENCES)

▪▪▪▫ INFERENCE

▪▪▪▫ DETAIL

▪▪▫▫ BIG PICTURE

	Answer	Refer to	Type	Comments
11.	B	Lines 76–90	Inference	More time since last firing to trap more electrons, creating brighter glow
12.	J	Lines 76–87	Detail	"migrate back to their original atoms"
13.	A	Paragraph 2	Detail	Be careful with the reversal word NOT in the question. Organic means "having to do with life."
14.	G	Lines 22–33, 33–48	Inference	Remember, passage is about luminescence, not fireflies.
15.	A	Lines 4–12, 44–47	Inference	B and C aren't chemi-; D isn't bio-. Only A is both.
16.	H	Lines 2–12, 65–77	Detail	Lines 4–10 say it all.
17.	A	Lines 91–108	Detail	Note difference between oxygen molecule and oxygen atom.
18.	G	Lines 63–75	Inference	I: No, since no chemical reaction II: Yes, since impact reaction III: Yes, since "subsequent glow" (probably a heat reaction)
19.	D	Throughout	Big Picture	Any statement about "all organisms" is probably a hypothesis, since no one can verify what's true of every organism in existence.
20.	F	Lines 65–77	Detail	"a stream of high energy particles from the sun"

EMERGENCY STRATEGY FOR TEST DAY

If you have less than four minutes left and you've still got an entire passage untouched, you need to shift to last-minute strategies. Don't try to preread the passage; you'll just run out of time before you answer any questions. Instead, scan the questions without reading the passage and look first for the ones that mention line numbers or specific paragraphs. You can often get quick points on these questions by referring back to the passage as the question stem directs, reading a few lines around the reference, and taking your best shot.

Of course, the most important thing is to make sure you have gridded in at least a random guess on every question. If some of your blind guesses are right (as some of them statistically *should* be), they'll boost your score just as much as well-reasoned, thought-out answers would!

☑ **PERFECT SCORE TIP**
Remember that the most important thing to do on the ACT is to answer every question. Even if you have time trouble and don't finish a section—guess!

▶ **IF YOU LEARNED ONLY TWO THINGS IN THIS CHAPTER...**

1. In the Prose Fiction passage, concentrate on who the characters are and what they are doing. What are the characters' attitudes toward each other? What is the author's attitude toward the characters?

2. For Natural Science passages, ask yourself, "What's new?" in each paragraph. Don't get bogged down in details or terminology. All you need is the general idea of how the paragraphs fit together.

CHAPTER 13

Science Workout 1: Look for Patterns

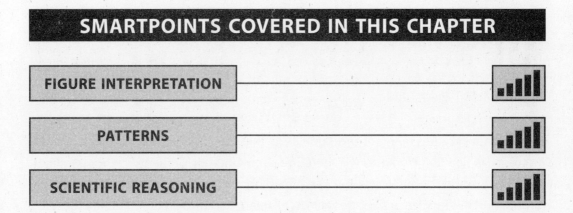

SMARTPOINTS COVERED IN THIS CHAPTER

FIGURE INTERPRETATION	
PATTERNS	
SCIENTIFIC REASONING	

The Science subject test causes a lot of unnecessary anxiety among ACT takers. Many people get so overwhelmed by the terminology and technicality of the passages that they just give up. What they fail to realize is that Science is a little like the reverse of Math. In Math, you'll remember, we said that many of the questions are difficult problems based on elementary principles. In Science, on the other hand, many of the questions are elementary problems based on difficult material. So it's important not to panic if you don't understand the passage in Science. You can often get many of the questions right on a passage, even if you find it virtually incomprehensible!

> **EXPERT TUTOR TIP**
> The ACT Science test covers biology, chemistry, Earth/space sciences, and physics. It includes:
> • Three Data Representation passages with five questions each
> • Three Experiment passages with six questions each
> • One Conflicting Viewpoints passage with seven questions

Many ACT takers also tend to rely too heavily on what they've learned in school when approaching the Science subject test. But as we've said, remembering facts is not the mind-set the ACT will reward. You couldn't possibly know the answers to ACT Science questions in advance: You have to pull them out of the passages. **All the information you need to answer the questions is right on the page.**

Worrying about science knowledge can be a problem no matter how good or bad your science background is. Students who have done poorly in science tend to panic because they think they don't know enough. Students who have done well in science might know **too** much. Some questions include wrong choices that are scientifically correct but don't relate to the passages. Choosing such answers will not earn you points on the ACT. Try not to rely primarily on your knowledge of science. Instead, use your ability to pull information from the passages.

> **EXPERT TUTOR TIP**
> Here's how to use this chapter if you don't have much time. Learn the Kaplan Method for ACT Science. Try the sample passage later in this chapter, then read the section called Reading Tables and Graphs.

ACT Science requires many of the same skills that ACT Reading does. The strategies discussed in Reading Workout I will therefore also work well for many Science passages. The most important difference between Reading and Science is that the details you have to find in the Science passages almost all relate to numbers or scientific processes, and they are often contained in graphs and tables rather than in paragraph form.

- **Reading graphs, tables, and research summaries.** Many questions involve accurately retrieving data from only one graph or table. Others involve combining knowledge from two different graphs or tables. Still others involve understanding experimental methods well enough to evaluate information contained in summaries of experiments.

- **Looking for patterns in the numbers that appear.** Do these numbers get bigger or smaller? Where are the highest numbers? The lowest? At what point do the numbers change? A little calculation is sometimes required, but not much. In Science, you won't be computing with numbers so much as thinking about what they mean.

In Science, as in Reading, it's crucial to consider the questions and at least try to answer them before looking at the answer choices. Refer to the passage to find the answer, and try to match it with one of the choices. **Use the process of elimination** as a fallback strategy for hard questions—but don't make it your main approach.

✓ **PERFECT SCORE TIP**

A common myth is that the ACT Science section is based on science knowledge. It is really another reading comprehension section, not a test of your scientific knowledge.

THE KAPLAN METHOD FOR ACT SCIENCE

STEP 1: Map the passage, identifying and marking the purpose, method, and results of the experiment.

STEP 2: Scan the figures, identifying variables and patterns.

STEP 3: Find support for the answer in the passage.

In Science, you have seven shorter passages to do instead of the four longer ones in Reading. Each passage should take you an average of five minutes to complete. We recommend using just about one minute or so to preread the passage, and then a total of about four minutes to consider the questions and refer to the passage (that's about 40 seconds per question). Notice that you spend less time prereading than in Reading.

STEP 1: Map the Passage, Identifying and Marking the Purpose, Method, and Results of the Experiment

As with the Reading test, you'll want to read and map the passage so you can easily find information once you attack the questions. Some of the material covered is extremely technical, and you'll just get frustrated trying to understand it completely. So it's crucial that you skim to get a general idea of what's going on and—just as importantly—to get a sense of where certain types of data can be found.

✓ **PERFECT SCORE TIP**

I often find the intro is the most useful part of the whole reading. Don't try to understand everything in them, but definitely make sure to read all the intros as they will give you background for the rest of the passages.

Almost all Science passages have the same general structure. They begin with an introduction—**always** read it first to orient yourself. Some passages relate to material you may have already studied in high school. If you're familiar with the concepts, you may not need to do more than skim the introduction. If not, you'll want to read it more carefully. But remember, don't focus on details. In the introduction, mark the *purpose* of the experiment. Whether you bracket it, circle it, or put a "P" next to it doesn't really matter. The only important thing is that somehow you note its location in case a question refers to it. The purpose will answer the question "Why was this experiment performed?"

After reviewing the introduction, quickly scan the rest of the passage. Take note of the *method* of the experiment(s). The method will answer the question "How was the experiment set up?" How is the information presented? Graphs? Diagrams? Are there experiments? What seems to be important? Size? Shape? Temperature? Speed? Chemical composition? Don't worry about details and don't try to remember it all. Plan to refer to the passage just as you would in Reading.

Example

> Scientists researching the relationship between birds and dinosaurs have chosen to carefully examine three fossils dating from the Jurassic period: an *archaeopteryx* (the oldest known bird) at the British Museum in London, a *compsognathus* (a dinosaur) at the Field Museum in Chicago, and a *teleosaurus* (a crocodile) at the National Museum in Beijing. All three creatures were about the same size as a turkey.

Remember to read actively. Ask yourself: Why would the scientists choose these three creatures? Since the scientists are studying birds and dinosaurs, the first two choices seem natural. But why should they include a crocodile? Maybe the National Museum in Beijing had a special deal on crocodile bones? More likely it's because crocodiles are somewhat like dinosaurs, but not extinct.

Finally, note the *results* of the experiment with an "R" next to the section—whether that's a paragraph, figure, or both. You don't need to fully comprehend the results just yet; you only need to indicate where they can be found so you can easily answer questions about them later.

STEP 2: Scan the Figures, Identifying Variables and Patterns

As you preread the passage, make sure you know what any tables and graphs in the passage are meant to represent. You only need to scan them to get a sense of what kind of data is contained in each graph and table, but don't read the data carefully yet. You may want to take note of general trends in the data, but don't waste time taking in information that may not be relevant to the questions. **Remember, your goal is to answer questions, not to learn and remember everything that goes on in the passage.**

> **EXPERT TUTOR TIP**
> If you need to know the meaning of a special scientific term, the test will usually define it. If the test doesn't tell you what a word means, you can usually figure it out from the context (or else you won't need to know it).

STEP 3: Find Support for the Answer in the Passage

Most of your time in Science will be spent considering questions and referring to the passage to find the answers. Here's where you should do most of your really careful reading. **It's essential that you understand exactly what the question is asking.** Then go back to the passage and get a sense of what the answer should be before looking at the choices.

There are three basic kinds of Science questions:

1. **Figure Interpretation questions.** For these questions, you'll almost certainly be going back to the graphs. They are usually among the easiest on the Science test. Knowing the headings of each figure will help make these questions that much easier.

2. **Patterns questions.** These are usually medium difficulty. You have to look beyond just the data that is presented in the figures to see what the patterns are in the data.

3. **Scientific Interpretation questions.** These questions are usually among the hardest on the test because they are based on what is in the text versus what is in the figures. Here, you must apply a scientific principle or identify ways of defending or attacking a principle. This includes making predictions based on a given theory or showing how a hypothesis might be strengthened or weakened by particular findings. (These questions will be especially important for the Conflicting Viewpoints passage, discussed in Science Workout 3.)

As we mentioned, one possible pitfall in answering the questions is relying too heavily on your own knowledge of science. In answering questions, use your knowledge of scientific *methods* and *procedures*. But don't rely heavily on any knowledge of specific facts. For example, the following question might have appeared with the previous passage excerpt:

.ııll **SCIENTIFIC REASONING**

Example

1. The dinosaur studied by the scientists, *compsognathus*, was:

     A. definitely a reptile.

     B. definitely a bird.

     C. about the size of a turkey.

     D. larger than *archaeopteryx* or *teleosaurus*.

If you know that dinosaurs are usually classified as reptiles, choice A would be very tempting. But it's wrong—the passage doesn't say that. In fact, if we had seen the rest of this passage, we would have learned that the researchers were questioning whether dinosaurs should be classified as reptiles or birds. What the passage *does* say is that all three of the creatures tested are turkey sized, making the correct choice C.

As in Reading, you have to be diligent about referring to the passage. Your prereading of the passage should have given you an idea of where particular kinds of data can be found. Sometimes the questions themselves will direct you to the right place.

Be careful not to mix up units when taking information from graphs, tables, and summaries. Don't confuse *decreases* and *increases*: Many questions will hinge on whether you can correctly identify the factors that decrease and the ones that increase. Incorrect answers will often put a *decrease* where an *increase* should be and vice versa. **Read the questions carefully!**

> **👤 EXPERT TUTOR TIP**
> Reading the question carefully is the most important step. If you miss a little word such as *not*, you will get the question wrong.

The answers to the Science questions are there in the passage. As mentioned in Step 2, don't rely too much on your own knowledge of science. Instead, think of paraphrasing the information in the passage.

> **✔ PERFECT SCORE TIP**
> The words *not* and *except* will show up in question stems, and missing them is an easy way to get a question wrong. Pay attention to these words and circle them when you see them.

Once you've paraphrased the information and matched it to an answer choice, double-check the question to make sure that you've actually answered the question asked.

Many of the questions in Science are reversal questions. Always look for words such as *not* and *except* in the questions.

READING TABLES AND GRAPHS

Most of the information in ACT Science passages is presented in tables or graphs, usually accompanied by explanatory material. Knowing how to read data from tables and graphs is critical to success on the Science subject test! In order to read most graphs and tables, ask yourself:

- What does the figure show?
- What are the units of measurement?
- What is the pattern in the data?

Let's say you saw the following graph in a Science passage:

- **What does the figure show?** Most graphs and tables have titles that tell you what they represent. For some, though, you may have to get that information from the introduction. Here, the graph is representing how cold or hot the air is at various altitudes above a certain Test Site #3.

- **What are the units of measurement?** Note that distance here is measured in *kilometers*, not miles or feet. Temperature is measured in degrees *Celsius*, not Fahrenheit.

- **What is the pattern in the data?** The pattern of the data in this graph is pretty clear. As you rise in altitude, the temperature drops—the higher the altitude, the lower the temperature. (As we'll see later, this kind of trend is called an *inverse variation*.)

The sloping line on the graph represents the various temperatures measured at the various altitudes. To find what the measured temperature was at, say, 2 km above sea level, find the 2 km point on the *x*-axis and trace your finger directly up from it until it hits the line. It does so at about the level of 3°C. In other words, at an altitude of 2 km above sea level at Test Site #3, the air temperature was about 3°C.

> **EXPERT TUTOR TIP**
> Get plenty of practice reading and interpreting data presented in graphs and tables. This is one of the most frequently tested topics in ACT Science.

Be careful with units of measurement. Most passages use the metric system, but a few may use traditional or British units of measure. You won't be expected to remember oddball unit conversions such as 8 furlongs = 1 mile or 2.54 cm = 1 in, and passages that use special units of measure, such as microns or parsecs, will define these units if necessary. But don't assume that all the units in the graphs match the units in the questions. For instance, try the following question:

 FIGURE INTERPRETATION

Example

2. At what altitude did the meteorologists measure an air temperature of 10°C?

    F. 1.4 m

    G. 140 m

    H. 1,400 m

    J. 14 km

Many test takers solving the problem above would find the point on the line at the level of 10°C on the *y*-axis, trace their fingers down to the *x*-axis, see that the altitude would be about halfway between 1 and 2 (a little closer to 1, maybe), and then quickly choose F. This is incorrect; F gives you 1.4 *meters*, while the graph figures are given in *kilometers*. Remember to translate the data! A kilometer is 1,000 meters, so 1.4 kilometers would be 1.4 times 1,000 meters = 1,400 meters. That's choice H.

You should follow a similar procedure with tables of information. For instance, in the introduction to the passage in which the following table might have appeared, you would have learned that scientists were trying to determine the effects of two pollutants (Pb and Hg, lead and mercury) on the trout population of a particular river.

Table 1

Location	Water Temperature (°C)	Presence of Pb (parts per million)	Presence of Hg (parts per million)	Population Density of Speckled Trout (# per 100 m³)
1	15.4	0	3	7.9
2	16.1	0	1	3.5
3	16.3	1	67	0
4	15.8	54	3	5.7
5	16.0	2	4	9.5

- **What does the figure show?** Here, each row represents the data from a different numbered location on the river. Each column represents different data: water temperature, presence of the first pollutant, presence of the second pollutant, population of one kind of trout.

- **What are the units of measurement?** Temperature is measured in degrees Celsius. The two pollutants are measured in parts per million (or ppm). The trout populations are measured in average number per 100 cubic meters of river.

- **What is the pattern in the data?** Glancing at the table, it looks like locations where the Hg concentration is high (as in Location 3), the trout population is virtually nonexistent. This would seem to indicate that trout find a high Hg concentration incompatible. But notice the location where the other pollutant is abundant—in Location 4. Here, the trout population seems to be more in line with other locations. That would seem to indicate that this other pollutant—Pb—is NOT quite so detrimental to trout populations (though we'd have to do more studies if it turned out that all of the trout in that location had three eyes).

How Tables and Graphs Relate

To really understand tables and graphs, it helps to see how the same information can be represented in both. For instance, look at the next table and graph:

CONCENTRATION OF *E. COLI* IN COOKING POOL B	
Distance from Effluent Pipe 3	**1,000s of *E. coli* per Centiliter**
0 m	0.4
5 m	5.6
10 m	27.6
15 m	14.0
20 m	7.5

Concentration of *E. coli* in Cooling Pool B

The previous table and graph represent the exact same data. And here's yet another way of depicting the same data, in a bar chart:

Concentration of *E. coli* in Cooling Pool B

Remember that data can be represented in many different ways. But however it appears in the passage, whether it be in tables, graphs, or charts, you'll have to read and translate it to answer the questions.

EXPERT TUTOR TIP
No matter what the figure looks like, you still ask yourself the same questions:
1. What does the figure show?
2. What are the units of measurement?
3. What is the pattern in the data?

PERFECT SCORE TIP
If you do not have much experience reading graphs—practice! Being able to read graphs is one of the most necessary skills on this section.

Look for Patterns and Trends

When you first examine a graph or table, don't focus on exact numbers. **Look for *patterns* in the numbers. But don't assume that there is *always* a pattern or trend:** Finding that there isn't a pattern is just as important as finding that there is one. When looking for patterns and trends, you should keep three things in mind:

1. EXTREMES

Extremes—or maximums and minimums—are merely the highest and lowest points that things reach. In tables, the minimums and maximums will be represented by relatively high and low numbers. In graphs, they will be represented by highs and lows on the *x*- and *y*-axes. In bar charts, they will be represented by the tallest and shortest bars.

Look back at Table 1. What location on the river has the maximum concentration of Hg? Of Pb? A glance at the numbers tells you that Location 3—with 67 ppm—represents the maximum for Hg, while Location 4—with 54 ppm—represents the maximum for Pb.

How can taking note of maximums and minimums help you spot patterns in the data? Look again at Table 1. Notice that the maximum concentration of Hg, 67 ppm, just happens to coincide with the *minimum* for trout population—0 per 100 m³. That's a good indication that there's some cause and effect going on here. Somehow, a maximum of Hg concentration correlates with a minimum of trout population. The obvious (though not airtight) conclusion is that a high concentration of Hg is detrimental to trout populations. And this kind of finding is much more evident when you look at maximums and minimums.

2. CRITICAL POINTS

To find out how critical points can help you evaluate data, take another look at the graph representing the concentration of *E. coli* (a common type of bacterium) in Cooling Pool B.

Concentration of *E. coli* in Cooling Pool B

Meters Distant from Effluent Pipe 3

Notice how the concentration is low very near Effluent Pipe 3. From there, it rises until about 10 meters away from the pipe, then it falls again, tapering off as you get farther from the pipe. There's a critical point, then, right around 10 meters from Effluent Pipe 3. Somehow, that vicinity is most conducive to the growth of *E. coli*. As you move closer to or farther away from that point, the concentration falls off. So, in looking to explain the data, you'd want to focus on that location—10 meters from the pipe. What is it about that location that's so special? What makes it the hot new place for *E. coli* to see and be seen?

3. RELATIONSHIPS

Being able to recognize relationships within a figure will lead directly to earning more points on test day. Look at the figure below.

Hours of Sunlight	Air Temperature (Fahrenheit)		
	Chamber 1	Chamber 2	Chamber 3
2	73.23	75.67	78.87
4	71.23	75.79	79.78
6	69.23	74.76	81.34
8	67.23	79.87	82.12
10	65.23	80.65	83.06

 EXPERT TUTOR TIP
Learn to recognize patterns in data, and you'll be able to answer most ACT Science questions on test day. Look for extremes, critical points, and variation.

What happens in Chamber 1? What do you think the temperature is going to be after 12 hours of sunlight? Do you notice the pattern? The temperature goes down by 2 degrees for every 2 hours of sunlight. The temperature is going to be 63.23 degrees.

As the number of hours of sunlight increases, what happens to the temperature in Chamber 2? When you look at the data, there doesn't appear to be a relationship. This is a valid answer.

Based on the data, what do you think the temperature will be after one hour of sunlight in Chamber 3? Well, as the number of hours of sunlight increase, the temperature in the chamber increases. So if you had to predict what would happen after only one hour of sunlight, then according to the table, it is going to be less than 78.87 degrees.

Before you tackle a real Science passage, let's review the Kaplan Method for the Science section. Note how similar it is to the steps for the Reading section. However, here you spend only one minute prereading (actively reading) the passage.

THE REAL THING: PRACTICE PASSAGE

Let's take a look at a full-fledged Science passage that requires these skills. Give yourself about seven minutes to do the passage and the questions (on the actual test, you'll want to move a bit faster).

Passage I

Although the effective acceleration due to gravity at the Earth's surface is often treated as a constant ($g = 9.80$ m/sec²), its actual value varies from place to place because of several factors.

First, a body on the surface of any rotating spheroid experiences an effective force perpendicular to the rotational axis and proportional to the speed of rotation. This centrifugal force, which counteracts gravity, varies with latitude, increasing from zero at the poles to a maximum at the equator. In addition, because the Earth "bulges" at the equator, a body at equatorial sea level is farther from the center of the Earth than is a body at polar sea level. Figure 1 shows the variation of mean values of g at sea level resulting from both effects; the contribution from "bulging" is about half that from rotation.

Figure 1

Measurements of g also vary depending on local rock density and altitude. Table 1 shows the effect of altitude on g at various points above sea level.

Table 1

Altitude above Sea Level (km)	g(m/sec²)
1	−0.0031
5	−0.0154
10	−0.0309
25	−0.0772
30	−0.1543

EXPERT TUTOR TIP

Don't forget to ask yourself:
1. What does the figure show?
2. What are the units of measurement?
3. What is the pattern in the data?

▁▃▅▇ FIGURE INTERPRETATION

Examples

3. If the Earth's density were uniform, at approximately what latitude would calculations using an estimated value at sea level of $g = 9.80$ m/sec² produce the least error?

   A. 0°

   B. 20°

   C. 40°

   D. 80°

4. According to Table 1, what would the change in gravity (in m/sec²) be at 2 km above sea level?

   F. −0.0001

   G. −0.0030

   H. −0.0081

   J. −0.0165

▁▃▅▇ PATTERNS

5. Given the information in the passage, which of the following figures most closely approximates the value of g at a point 10 km high along the equator?

   A. 9.75 m/sec²

   B. 9.80 m/sec²

   C. 9.81 m/sec²

   D. 9.87 m/sec²

6. Suppose that the Earth stopped rotating but still "bulged." Based on information from the passage, the value of g at sea level at the equator would be:

   F. exactly 9.80 m/sec².

   G. greater than 9.78 m/sec².

   H. exactly 9.78 m/sec².

   J. less than 9.78 m/sec².

7. According to the information in Figure 1, the value of g:

   A. changes by a greater average amount per degree latitude between 30° and 60° than it does near the equator or poles.

   B. changes by a greater average amount per degree latitude near the equator or poles than it does between 30° and 60°.

   C. increases by an average of 5.8 m/sec² per degree latitude from the equator to the poles.

   D. decreases by an average of 3.1×10^{-3} m/sec² per degree latitude from the equator to the poles.

Answers

1. A
2. H
3. C
4. H
5. A
6. G
7. A

Answers and Explanations

This was actually a relatively simple, straightforward Science passage, but the terminology may have been intimidating nonetheless. The introduction tells you that the issue here is gravity and how its pull (in other words, the acceleration due to gravity) changes because of several factors. Those factors—and the changes they cause—are represented in Figure 1 (which deals with the factor of latitude) and Table 1 (which deals with the factor of altitude).

Analyzing Figure 1, you should have seen that the graph is supposed to show how g (the acceleration due to gravity) is affected by latitude (i.e., north-south location on the globe). The higher the latitude (the greater the distance from the equator), the greater the value of g. As the curves at the beginning and ending of the line in Figure 1 tell you, the increase in g is slower near the equator and near the poles.

Notice how you could have answered **question 3** just by understanding Figure 1. Question 3 asks, assuming the Earth's density were uniform, "at what latitude would calculations using an estimated value at sea level of $g = 9.80$ m/sec^2 produce the least error?" First, figure out what that question is asking. You remember this question; we mentioned it in ACT Basics. It's simply asking you: Where would you get an actual value of g closest to 9.80 m/sec^2? Find 9.80 on the y-axis of the graph, follow across until you intersect with the curved line, and see where you are on the x-axis. That turns out to be about a third of the way from 30° to 60° latitude. In other words, choice C, 40°, is the answer.

> **EXPERT TUTOR TIP**
> Remember, you score points by answering the questions correctly, not by understanding the passages completely. You can get points on a Science passage, even if you don't understand it!

Question 4 is simply asking you to figure out the pattern in Table 1. To find out what the change in g at 2 km is, you would need to look at the table between 1 km and 5 km. There is only one answer choice that falls between the values of –0.0031 and –0.0154, and that is choice H, –0.0081.

We'll get to **question 5** soon.

Question 6 requires more applications of principles and is yet another question that can be answered by simply reading Figure 1. It asks you to suppose that rotation effects (one of the two factors affected by latitude) ceased, but that the Earth still bulged at the equator. What would be the value of g? Well, again, rotation tends to "counteract" gravity, so it would have a depressing effect on g. Without rotation, then, g would be less depressed—it would go up, in other words. That means (reading from Figure 1 again) that g at 0° latitude (the equator) would, in the absence of rotation, go up from its current value of 9.78. That's why choice G is correct.

Question 7 (not to get monotonous) can also be answered just by reading Figure 1. It asks you to describe what the graph tells you about the value of g. As we saw, the value rises slowly as you head away from 0° latitude (the equator), rises more rapidly in the middle latitudes, and slows down again near 90° latitude (the poles). That's best described by choice A. (Choice B gets it backwards—remember to read the choices carefully!) Choices C and D would involve you in some extensive calculations, at the end of which you'd realize that they were not true. But there's no reason to get that far. If you find yourself doing extensive calculation, you should know that you're on the wrong track. ACT Science will involve simple calculation only.

Notice how you could have answered four of the five questions with just a rudimentary grasp of the introduction and an understanding of how to read Figure 1 and Table 1.

The other question, **question 5**, requires that you read both Figure 1 and Table 1 properly. It asks for the value of g at the equator (that information comes from Figure 1), but at an altitude of 10 km above sea level (that information comes from Table 1). Figure 1 tells you that the value of g at the equator at sea level would be 9.78 m/sec². But at 10 km above sea level, according to Table 1, g would be slightly lower—0.0309 m/sec² lower to be precise. So 9.78 minus 0.0309 would be about 9.75 m/sec². That's choice A.

Look for Patterns

The previous passage and questions should convince you of one thing: to do well on Science, you have to be able to read graphs and tables, paying special attention to trends and patterns in the data. Sometimes that's all you need to do to get most of the points on a passage.

> ## ▶ IF YOU LEARNED ONLY THREE THINGS IN THIS CHAPTER...
>
> 1. The information you need is given in the passages—don't rely on your outside knowledge of science.
>
> 2. Approach Science passages like Reading passages: read and map the passage, focus on the question stem, and find the answer in the data or scenario given.
>
> 3. When reading graphs and tables, determine what's being represented, the units of measurement, and any patterns or trends.

CHAPTER 14

Science Workout 2: Think Like a Scientist

SMARTPOINTS COVERED IN THIS CHAPTER

FIGURE INTERPRETATION

SCIENTIFIC REASONING

In Science Workout 1, you learned that to succeed on the ACT Science subtest, you've got to be able to spot trends and patterns in the data of graphs and tables. But that's not all you need to do well. You've also got to learn how to think like a scientist. You don't have to know very much science (though it certainly helps), but you should at least be familiar with how scientists go about getting and testing knowledge.

HOW SCIENTISTS THINK

Scientists use two very different kinds of logic, which (to keep things nontechnical) we'll call:

1. **General-to-Specific Thinking**
2. **Specific-to-General Thinking**

General-to-Specific

In some cases, scientists have already discovered a law of nature and wish to apply their knowledge to a specific case. For example, a scientist may wish to know how fast a pebble (call it Pebble A) will be falling when it hits the ground three seconds after being dropped. There is a law of physics from which it can be determined that on Earth, falling objects accelerate at a rate of about 9.8 m/sec². The scientist could use this known general principle to calculate the specific information she needs: after three seconds, the object would be falling at a rate of about 3 sec × 9.8 m/sec², or roughly 30 m/sec. You could think of this kind of logic as *general-to-specific*. The scientist uses a *general* principle (the acceleration of any object falling on Earth) to find a *specific* fact (the speed of Pebble A).

> ✔ **PERFECT SCORE TIP**
> Most Science questions will give you data and ask you for conclusions, so focus on these skills.

Specific-to-General

But scientists use a different kind of thinking in order to discover a new law of nature. In this case, they examine many specific facts and then draw a general conclusion about what they've seen. For example, a scientist might watch hundreds of different kinds of frogs live and die and might notice that all of them developed from tadpoles. She might then announce a conclusion: all frogs develop from tadpoles. You could think of this kind of logic as *specific-to-general*. The scientist looks at many *specific* frogs to find a *general* rule about all frogs.

This conclusion is called a hypothesis, not a fact or a truth, because the scientist has not checked every single frog in the universe. She knows that there theoretically *could* be a frog somewhere that grows from pond scum or from a Dalmatian puppy. But until she finds such a frog, it is reasonable to think that her hypothesis is correct. Many hypotheses, in fact, are so well documented that they become the equivalent of laws of nature.

In your science classes in school, you mostly learn about general-to-specific thinking. Your teachers explain general rules of science to you and then expect you to apply these rules to answer questions and solve problems. Some ACT Science questions are like that as well. But a majority are not. **Most ACT Science questions test specific-to-general thinking.** The questions test your ability to see the kinds of patterns in specific data that, as a scientist, you would use to formulate your own general hypotheses. We did something like this in Science Workout 1, when we theorized—based on the trends we found in a table of data—that the pollutant Hg was in some way detrimental to trout populations.

> **EXPERT TUTOR TIP**
> Only one to three questions on the entire test will be based on your science knowledge. Everything else is based on what's in the passage.

HOW EXPERIMENTS WORK

Many ACT passages describe experiments and expect you to understand how they're designed. Experiments help scientists do specific-to-general thinking in a reliable and efficient way. Consider the tadpole researcher. In a real-world situation, what would probably happen is that she would notice some of the frogs develop from tadpoles and wonder if maybe they all did. Then she'd know what to look for and could check all the frogs systematically. This process contains the two basic steps of any experiment:

1. **Forming a hypothesis** (guessing that all frogs come from tadpoles)
2. **Testing a hypothesis** (checking the frogs to see if this guess was right)

Scientists are often interested in cause-and-effect relationships. Having formed her hypothesis about tadpoles, a scientist might wonder what *causes* a tadpole to become a frog. To test causal relationships, a special kind of experiment is needed. She must test one possible cause at a time in order to isolate which one actually produces the effect in question. For example, the scientist might inject tadpoles with several different kinds of hormones. Some of these tadpoles might die. Others might turn into frogs normally. But a few—those injected with Hormone X, say—might remain tadpoles for an indefinite time. One reasonable explanation is that Hormone X in some way inhibited whatever causes normal frog development. In other words, the scientist would hypothesize a causal relationship between Hormone X and frog development.

> **EXPERT TUTOR TIP**
> Many ACT Science questions ask you to determine the purpose of an experiment or to design one yourself. To figure out the purpose of an experiment, look to see what factor was allowed to change: That's what's being tested. To design an experiment yourself, keep everything constant except the factor you must investigate.

Method

The relationship between Hormone X and frog development, however, would not be demonstrated very well if the scientist also fed different diets to different tadpoles, kept some in warmer water, or allowed some to have more room to swim than others —or if she didn't also watch tadpoles who were injected with no hormones at all but who otherwise were kept under the same conditions as the treated tadpoles. Why? Because if the "eternal tadpoles" had diets that differed from that of the others, the scientist wouldn't know whether it was Hormone X or the special diet that kept the eternal tadpoles from becoming frogs. Moreover, if their water was warmer than that of the others, maybe it was the warmth that somehow kept the tadpoles from developing. And if she didn't watch untreated tadpoles (a control group), she couldn't be sure whether under the same conditions a normal, untreated tadpole would also remain undeveloped.

Thus, a scientist creating a well-designed experiment will:

- Ensure that there's a single variable (like Hormone X) that varies from test to test or group to group.
- Ensure that all other factors (diet, temperature, space, etc.) remain the same.
- Ensure that there is a control group (tadpoles who don't get any Hormone X at all) for comparison purposes.

Results

One of the advantages to knowing how experiments work is that you can tell what a researcher is trying to find out about by seeing what she allows to vary. That's what is being researched—in this case, Hormone X. Data about things other than hormones and tadpole-to-frog development would be outside the design of the experiment. Information about other factors might be interesting but could not be part of a scientific proof.

For example, if some of the injected tadpoles that did grow into frogs later actually turned into princes, the data from experiments about the hormone they were given would not prove what causes frogs to become princes. But this data *could* be used to design another experiment intended to explore what could make a frog become a prince.

Therefore, whenever you see an experiment in Science, you should ask yourself:

1. **What's the factor that's being varied?** That is what is being tested.
2. **What's the control group?** It's the group that has nothing special done to it.
3. **What do the results show?** What differences exist between the results for the control group and those for the other group(s)? Or between the results for one treated group and those for another differently treated group?

> ✔ **PERFECT SCORE TIP**
> I found the Kaplan Method for experiment questions very useful. It helped me focus on what components of the design were important and deserved my attention.

HANDLING EXPERIMENT QUESTIONS

Following is a full-fledged Science passage organized around two experiments. Use the Kaplan Method, but this time, ask yourself the previous three questions. Take about five or six minutes to do the passage and its questions.

Passage II

A *mutualistic* relationship between two species increases the chances of growth or survival for both of them. Several species of fungi called *mycorrhizae* form mutualistic relationships with the roots of plants. The benefits to each species are shown in the figure below.

Figure 1

Some of the plant species that require or benefit from the presence of mycorrhizal fungi are noted below.

Cannot survive without mycorrhizae	Grow better with mycorrhizae
All conifers	Citrus trees
Some deciduous trees (e.g., birch, beech)	Ericaceae (heath, rhododendrons, azaleas), grapes
Orchids	Soybeans

Agronomists investigated the effects of mycorrhizae on plant growth and survival in the following studies.

STUDY 1

Three four-acre plots were prepared with soil from a pine forest. The soil for Plot A was mixed with substantial quantities of cultured mycorrhizal fungi. The soil for Plot B contained only naturally occurring mycorrhizal fungi. The soil for Plot C was sterilized in order to kill any mycorrhizal fungi. Additionally, Plot C was lined with concrete. After planting, Plot C was covered with a fabric that filtered out microorganisms while permitting air and light to penetrate. 250 pine seedlings were planted in each of the three plots. All plots received the same amount of water. The six-month survival rates were recorded in the following table.

Table 1

	Number of seedlings alive after 6 months	Utilization of available K (average)	Utilization of available P (average)
Plot A	107	18%	62%
Plot B	34	10%	13%
Plot C	0	N/A	N/A

N/A = not applicable

STUDY 2

The roots of surviving seedlings from Plots A and B were analyzed to determine how efficiently they absorbed potassium (K) and phosphorus (P) from the soil. The results were added to Table 1.

1. The most likely purpose of the concrete liner was:

   A. to block the seedlings from sending out taproots to water below the plot.

   B. to prevent mycorrhizal fungi in the surrounding soil from colonizing the plot.

   C. to absorb potassium and phosphorus from the soil for later analysis.

   D. to provide a firm foundation for mycorrhizal fungi in the plot.

2. Mycorrhizae are highly susceptible to acid rain. Given the information from the passage, acid rain is probably most harmful to:

   F. wheat fields.

   G. birch forests.

   H. orange groves.

   J. grape vines.

3. In a third study, pine seedlings were planted in soil from a different location. The soil was prepared as in Study 1. This time, the survival rates for seedlings planted in Plot A and Plot B were almost identical to each other. Which of the following theories would NOT help to explain these results?

   A. Sterilization killed all the naturally occurring mycorrhizal fungi in the new soil.

   B. The new soil was so mineral-deficient that it could not sustain life.

   C. The new soil was naturally more fertile for pine seedlings than that used in Study 1.

   D. Large quantities of mycorrhizal fungi occurred naturally in the new soil.

4. According to the passage, in which of the following ways do plants benefit from mycorrhizal associations?

   I. More efficient sugar production
   II. Enhanced ability to survive drought
   III. Increased mineral absorption

   F. I only

   G. III only

   H. II and III only

   J. I, II, and III

5. Which of the following generalizations is supported by the results of Study 2?

   A. Mycorrhizal fungi are essential for the survival of pine seedlings.

   B. Growth rates for pine seedlings may be improved by adding mycorrhizal fungi to the soil.

   C. Mycorrhizal fungi contain minerals that are not normally found in pine forest soil.

   D. Pine seedlings cannot absorb all the potassium that is present in the soil.

Answers

1. B
2. G
3. A
4. H
5. D

Answers and Explanations

Notice how many diagrams and tables were used here. That's common in experiment passages, where information is given to you in a wide variety of forms. Typically, though, the experiments themselves are clearly labeled, as Study 1 and Study 2 were here.

A quick preread of the introduction would have revealed the topic of the experiments here—the "mutualistic relationship" between some fungi and some plant roots. The fungi are called mycorrhizae ("myco" for short). The first diagram just shows you who gets what out of this relationship. The benefit accruing to the plant (the arrow pointing to the word *plant*) is an increased ability to absorb water and minerals. The benefit accruing to the *fungus* (the other arrow) is the plant-synthesized sugars on which the fungus feeds. That's the mutual benefit that the myco association creates.

Notice, by the way, that reading this first diagram alone is enough to answer **question 4**. The question is asking: what do the plants get out of the association? And we just answered that—increased ability to absorb water and minerals. Statement III is obviously correct, but so is Statement II, because increased water absorption would indeed enhance the plant's ability to survive drought (a drought is a shortage of water, after all). Statement I, though, is a distortion. We know that the fungi benefit from sugars produced by the plants, but we don't have any evidence that the association actually causes plants to produce sugar more efficiently. So I is out; II and III are in, making choice H the answer.

CAN'T LIVE WITHOUT THOSE FUNGI

Let's get back to the passage. We've just learned who gets what out of the myco association. Now we get a table that shows what *kinds* of plants enter into such associations. Some (those in the first column) are so dependent on myco associations that they can't live without them. Others (those in the second column) merely grow better with them; presumably, they could live without them.

Here again is a question we can answer based solely on information in this one table. **Question 2** tells us that mycos are highly susceptible to acid rain, and then asks what kind of plant communities would be most harmed by acid rain. Well, if acid rain hurts mycos, then the plants that are most dependent on myco fungi (that is, the ones listed in the first column) would be the most harmed by acid rain. Of the four choices, only birch forests—choice G—correspond to something in column 1 of the table. Birch trees can't even *survive* without myco fungi, so anything that hurts myco fungi would inferably hurt birch forests. (Grapevines and orange groves would also be hurt by acid rain, but not as much, since they *can* survive without myco fungi; meanwhile, we're told nothing about wheat in the passage.)

STUDY 1

Now look at the first experiment. Three plots, each with differently treated soil, are planted with pine seedlings. Plot A gets soil with cultivated myco fungi, Plot B gets untreated soil with only naturally occurring myco fungi, and Plot C gets no myco fungi at all since the soil has been sterilized and isolated (via the concrete lining and the fabric covering). Now ask yourself the three important Experiment questions:

1. **Find the factor being varied.** The factor being varied is the amount of myco fungi in the soil. Plot A gets lots; Plot B gets just the normal amount; Plot C gets none at all. It's clear, then, that the scientists are testing the effects of myco fungi on the growth of pine seedlings.

2. **Identify the control group.** The plants in Plot B, since they get untreated soil. To learn the effects of the fungi, the scientists will then compare the results from fungi-rich Plot A with the control and the results from fungi-poor Plot C with the same control.

3. **Analyze the results.** The results are listed in the first column of the table. And they are decisive: no seedlings at all survived in Plot C, 34 did in Plot B, and 107 did in Plot A. The minimums and maximums coincide. Minimum fungi = minimum number of surviving seedlings; maximum fungi = maximum number of surviving seedlings. Clearly, there's a cause-and-effect relationship here. Myco fungi probably help pine seedlings survive.

Questions 1 and 3 can be answered solely on the basis of Study 1. **Question 1** is merely a procedural question: why the concrete liner in Plot C? Well, in the analysis of the experiment above, we saw that the factor being varied was the amount of myco fungi. Plot C was designed to have none at all. Thus, one can safely assume that the concrete liner was probably there to prevent any stray myco fungi from entering the sterilized soil—choice B.

Question 3 actually sets up an extra experiment based on Study 1. The soils were prepared in the exact same way, except that the soil came from a different location.

The results? The number of surviving seedlings from Plots A and B were almost identical. What can that mean? Well, Plot A was supposed to be the fungi-rich plot, whereas Plot B (the control) was supposed to be the fungi-normal plot. But here they have the same results. However, notice that we're *not* told what those results are; it could be that no seedlings survived in any plots this time around.

The question—a reversal question—is phrased so that the three wrong choices are things that *could* explain the results; the correct choice will be the one that *can't*. Choices B, C, and D all *can* explain the results, since they all show how similar results could have been obtained from Plots A and B. If the new soil just couldn't support life—fungi or no fungi—well, Plots A and B would have gotten similar results; namely, no seedlings survive. On the other end of the spectrum, choices C and D show how the two plots might have gotten similarly *high* survival rates. If there were lots of myco fungi naturally in this soil (that's choice D), then there wouldn't be all that much difference between the soils in Plots A and B. If the soil were naturally extremely fertile for the pine seedlings (that's choice C), there must have been lots of fungi naturally present in the soil because pine trees (conifers) don't grow without fungi. So all three of these answers would help to explain similar results in Plots A and B.

Choice A, however, wouldn't help, because it talks about the sterilized soil that's in Plot C. The soil in Plot C won't affect the results in Plots A and B, so choice A is the answer here—the factor that *doesn't* help to explain the results.

STUDY 2

This study takes the surviving seedlings from Plots A and B in Study 1 and just tests how much potassium (K) and phosphorus (P) the roots have used. The results are listed in the second and third columns of the table. (Notice the N/A—not applicable—for Plot C in these columns, since there were no surviving seedlings to test in Plot C!) The data shows much better utilization of both substances in the Plot A seedlings, the seedlings that grew in a fungi-rich soil. This data would tend to support a theory that the myco fungi aid in the utilization of K and P and that this in turn aids survival in pine seedlings.

The only question that hinges on Study 2 is **question 5**. It asks what generalization would be supported by the specific results of Study 2. Notice that Study 2 involved only measuring K and P. It did not involve survival rates (that was Study 1), so choice A can't be right. And *neither* study measured growth rates, so B is out. The minerals K and P were in the control group's soil, which was natural, untreated pine forest soil, so choice C is clearly unsupported.

But the *data* did show that not all of the potassium (K) could be absorbed by pine seedlings. Only 18 percent was absorbed in Plot A, while only 10 percent was absorbed in Plot B. That's a long way from 100 percent, so choice D is a safe generalization to make.

> **EXPERT TUTOR TIP**
> Many questions on experiment passages will be answerable based solely on the data contained in a single graph or table. You can get these points with relative ease, even if you don't have time for, or don't fully understand, the experiments.

THE REAL THING: PRACTICE PASSAGE

Now that we've taken you step-by-step through a Science passage based on an experiment, it's time to try one on your own. Give yourself about six minutes for the next passage and questions. This time the explanations at the end will be very short:

Passage III

The following flowchart shows the steps used by a chemist in testing sample solutions for positive ions of silver (Ag), lead (Pb), and mercury (Hg).

The following experiments were performed by the chemist:

EXPERIMENT 1

Hydrochloric acid (6 M HCl) was added to samples of four unknown solutions labeled 1, 2, 3, and 4. A white powder precipitated out of solutions 1, 2, and 3; no precipitate formed in solution 4.

EXPERIMENT 2

Each of the sample solutions from Experiment 1 was placed in a 100°C water bath for 15 minutes. The precipitate in solution 1 redissolved completely; solutions 2 and 3 still contained a white powder; solution 4 was unchanged. Solutions 2 and 3 were centrifuged to remove the precipitates, which were retained for further testing. Potassium chromate (K_2CrO_4) was then added to each sample. A bright yellow precipitate formed in solutions 1 and 2; none formed in solutions 3 or 4.

EXPERIMENT 3

The white powder centrifuged from solutions 2 and 3 in Experiment 2 was treated with aqueous ammonia (NH_3). The precipitate from solution 2 returned into solution, while that from solution 3 produced a gray powder.

▁▂▃▅ SCIENTIFIC REASONING

6. Which conclusion is best supported by the results of Experiment 1 alone?

   F. Silver ions are present only in solution 3.

   G. No ions are present in solution 4.

   H. Lead ions are present in solutions 1, 2, and 3.

   J. No positive ions of silver, mercury, or lead are present in solution 4.

▁▂▃▅ SCIENTIFIC REASONING

7. Based on the experimental results, which ions did solution 2 contain?

   A. Lead ions only

   B. Lead and silver ions only

   C. Silver and mercury ions only

   D. Silver ions only

▁▂▃▅ SCIENTIFIC REASONING

8. The yellow precipitate that formed in Experiment 2 was most likely:

   F. $AgCl$.

   G. Hg_2Cl_2.

   H. $PbCrO_4$.

   J. Ag_2CrO_4.

▁▂▃▅ FIGURE INTERPRETATION

9. The experimental results suggest that if lead chloride ($PbCl_2$) were treated with aqueous ammonia (NH_3), the results would be:

   A. a bright yellow precipitate.

   B. a light gray precipitate.

   C. a powdery white precipitate.

   D. impossible to determine from the information given.

.ɪɪɪ FIGURE INTERPRETATION

10. A student proposed that the analysis could be carried out more efficiently by heating the samples to 100°C before adding the 6 M HCl. This suggestion is:

    F. a bad idea; since $PbCl_2$ will not precipitate out of solution at this temperature, lead ions would be undetectable.

    G. a bad idea; the hot solutions could not be safely centrifuged.

    H. a good idea; the number of steps would be reduced from 3 to 2, saving much time and effort.

    J. a good idea; the chloride-forming reaction would proceed faster, eliminating the necessity for a 15-minute water bath.

Answers

6. J
7. B
8. H
9. D
10. F

Answers and Explanations

This experiment passage was somewhat different from the preceding one. In the mycorrhiza experiment, the scientists were thinking in specific-to-general terms (observing the growth of specific pine seedlings to come to a conclusion about the general effect of myco fungi on pine seedlings). In this series of experiments, the general principle is known—silver, lead, and mercury will precipitate or dissolve when certain things are done to them—and the scientists are using this principle to test certain substances in order to identify them. In fact, this is more like a procedure than an experiment, since there's no control group. But the same kind of experimental thinking—using the results of varying procedures to make reasonable inferences about what's happening—will get you your answers.

This passage also introduces the idea of a flowchart. Basically, the flowchart indicates an order of procedures. You follow the flowchart from top to bottom. The things in squares indicate what's done to a specimen; the things in diamonds indicate possible results.

Let's say you have an unknown substance. Following the flowchart, the first thing you do is add hydrochloric acid. If a white powder precipitates, that means there are positive ions of silver, lead, and/or mercury. (If nothing precipitates, the experiment is over; the substance is not of interest here.)

But, assuming you do get a white powder, how do you identify exactly which kind of white powder you have? You do the next procedure—heat it to 100°C. When you do this, any lead ions will dissolve, but any silver or mercury ions will remain as a powder. So the flowchart has to divide here.

If part of your specimen dissolved when heated, that doesn't necessarily mean you have lead ions. To test for that, you add K_2CrO_4. If a yellow powder forms, then you know you've got lead; if not, you've got something else.

But what about the other branch? That tells you what has to be done if you *do* have some powder remaining after heating. And what you do is add NH_3. If the powder dissolves, you've got silver ions. If it forms a gray powder, on the other hand, what you've got are mercury (Hg) ions.

The three experiments here are actually three parts of a single experiment or procedure, each one using the results of the former in the way outlined in the flowchart. The questions ask for results at various points in the procedure, so let's look at them briefly now.

Key to Passage III

	Answer	Refer to	Comments
6.	J	Experiment 1 only	If any Ag, Pb, or Hg ions were present, they would have precipitated out as powder. Note that G is too extreme (could be ions of a fourth type not within scope of the experiment). Not enough testing in Exp. 1 to determine F or H.
7.	B	All three experiments	Heating created leftover powder, so substance 2 has to have Ag or Hg or both—cut A. Addition of K_2CrO_4 left yellow precipitate, so it must contain Pb (cut C and D).
8.	H	Experiment 2	Must be lead-based, because Ag and Hg precipitates were already removed (cut F, G, and J).
9.	D	Flowchart	No evidence for what would happen—two different branches of the flowchart.
10.	F	Flowchart	If the solutions were heated first, and then the HCl was added, the $PbCl_2$ would never form; the chemist would not know whether lead ions were present.

As you've seen, not all experiments on the ACT Science subject test are specific-to-general experiments; some are general-to-specific procedures. But the same kind of strict thinking—manipulating factors to narrow down possibilities—can get you points, no matter what direction you're thinking in.

GO ONLINE
Review Science strategies on your downloadable study sheet.

EXPERT TUTOR TIP
If you get stuck on a problem, see what answer choices you can eliminate. The more you eliminate, the closer you are to the correct answer.

> **IF YOU LEARNED ONLY THREE THINGS IN THIS CHAPTER...**

1. When you encounter experiment questions, identify the factor being varied, the control group (if any), and how results vary between groups.

2. Look for Figure Interpretation questions first—they'll get you the quickest points.

3. Some scenarios ask you to make inferences about data (specific-to-general); others ask you to use general ideas to determine what will happen in a particular case (general-to-specific).

CHAPTER 15

Science Workout 3: Keep Your Viewpoints Straight

SMARTPOINTS COVERED IN THIS CHAPTER

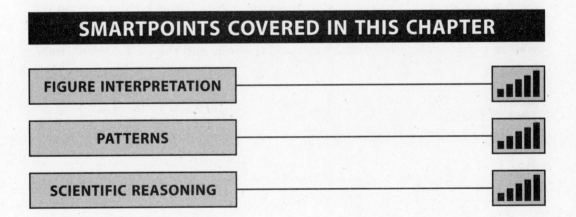

FIGURE INTERPRETATION

PATTERNS

SCIENTIFIC REASONING

On the Science test, you'll find one Conflicting Viewpoints passage, in which two scientists propose different theories about a particular scientific phenomenon. Often, the two theories are just differing interpretations of the same data; other times, each scientist offers his own data to support his own opinion. In either case, it's essential that you know more or less what theory each scientist is proposing and that you pay careful attention to how and where their theories differ.

In Science Workout 2, we talked about how scientists think, and you should bring all of that information to bear on the Conflicting Viewpoints passage. Because the scientists are disagreeing on interpretation, it's usually the case that they're engaging in specific-to-general thinking. They're each using specific data, sometimes the *same* specific data, but they're coming to very different general conclusions.

> **✔ PERFECT SCORE TIP**
> On the Conflicting Viewpoints passages, I found it helpful to briefly summarize each one—just like a Reading passage. This helped keep me focused and engaged in the passage.

Your job is *not* to figure out which scientist is right and which is wrong. Instead, you'll be tested on whether you *understand* each scientist's position and the thinking behind it.

PREREADING THE CONFLICTING VIEWPOINTS PASSAGE

When tackling the Conflicting Viewpoints passage, you'll probably want to spend a little more time than usual on the prereading step of the Kaplan Reading Method. As we saw on other Science passages, your goal in prereading is to get a general idea of what's going on so that you can focus when you do the questions. But we find that **it pays to spend a little extra time with the Conflicting Viewpoints passage in order to get a clearer idea of the opposing theories and the data behind them.**

> **👤 EXPERT TUTOR TIP**
> This passage is usually the hardest passage for students. Don't worry! There is only one passage like this, and you can save it for last if it is easier for you.

The passage will usually consist of a short introduction laying out the scientific issue in question, followed by the different viewpoints. Sometimes these viewpoints are presented under the headings Scientist 1 and Scientist 2, or Theory 1 and Theory 2, or Hypothesis 1 and Hypothesis 2.

A scientific viewpoint on the ACT will typically consist of two parts:

1. **A statement of the general theory**
2. **A summary of the data behind the theory**

Usually, the first line of each viewpoint expresses the general theory. Scientist 1's first sentence might be something like: *The universe will continue to expand indefinitely.* This is Scientist 1's viewpoint boiled down to a single statement. Scientist 2's first sentence might be: *The force of gravity will eventually force the universe to stop expanding and to begin contracting.* This is Scientist 2's viewpoint, and it clearly contradicts Scientist 1's opinion.

While it's important that you understand these basic statements of theory, it is just as important that you see how they oppose each other. In fact, you might want to circle the theory statement for each viewpoint, right there in the test booklet, to fix the two positions in your mind.

> ✓ **PERFECT SCORE TIP**
> I found it helpful to write down the opinions of each author (pro or con) so I didn't confuse them. If you confuse the two authors' opinions, you will lose valuable points, as most of the questions are based around you not mixing up their viewpoints.

After each statement of theory will come the data that's behind it. As we said, sometimes the scientists are just drawing different interpretations from the same data. But usually, each will have different supporting data. There are two different kinds of data:

1. **Data that supports the scientist's own theory**
2. **Data that weakens the opposing scientist's theory**

It's normally a good idea to identify the major points of data for each theory. You might underline a phrase or sentence that crystallizes each, or even take note of whether it primarily supports the scientist's own theory or shoots holes in the opposing theory.

Once you understand each scientist's theory and the data behind it, you'll be ready to move on to the questions. Remember that some of the questions will refer to only one of the viewpoints. **Whatever you do, *don't mix up the two viewpoints!*** A question asking about the data supporting Theory 2 may have wrong answers that perfectly describe the data for Theory 1. If you're careless, you can easily fall for one of these wrong answers.

THE REAL THING: PRACTICE PASSAGE

What follows is a full-fledged, ACT-style Conflicting Viewpoints passage. Give yourself six minutes or so to read the passage and do all seven questions.

Passage IV

Tektites are natural, glassy objects that range in size from the diameter of a grain of sand to that of a human fist. They are found in only a few well-defined areas, called strewn fields. Two theories about the origin of tektites are presented here.

SCIENTIST 1

Tektites almost certainly are extraterrestrial, probably lunar, in origin. Their forms show the characteristics of air-friction melting. In one study, flanged "flying saucer" shapes similar to those of australites (a common tektite form) were produced by ablating lenses of tektite glass in a heated airstream that simulated atmospheric entry.

Atmospheric forces also make terrestrial origin extremely improbable. Aerodynamic studies have shown that because of atmospheric density, tektite-like material ejected from the Earth's surface would never attain a velocity much higher than that of the surrounding air, and therefore would not be shaped by atmospheric friction. Most likely, tektites were formed either from meteorites or from lunar material ejected in volcanic eruptions.

Analysis of specimen #14425 from the *Apollo 12* lunar mission shows that the sample strongly resembles some of the tektites from the Australasian strewn field. Also, tektites contain only a small fraction of the water that is locked into the structure of terrestrial volcanic glass. And tektites never contain unmelted crystalline material; the otherwise similar terrestrial glass produced by some meteorite impacts **always** does.

SCIENTIST 2

Nonlocal origin is extremely unlikely, given the narrow distribution of tektite strewn fields. Even if a tightly focused jet of lunar matter were to strike the Earth, whatever was deflected by the atmosphere would remain in a solar orbit. The next time its orbit coincided with that of the Earth, some of the matter would be captured by Earth's gravity and fall over a wide area.

There are striking similarities not only between the composition of the Earth's crust and that of most tektites but also between the proportions of various gases found in the Earth's atmosphere and also the vesicles of certain tektites.

Tektites were probably formed by meteorite impacts. The shock wave produced by a major collision could temporarily displace the atmosphere above. Terrestrial material might then splatter to suborbital heights and undergo air-friction melting upon reentry. And tektite fields in the Ivory Coast and Ghana can be correlated with known impact craters.

📶 SCIENTIFIC REASONING

1. The discovery that many tektites contain unmelted, crystalline material would:

    A. tend to weaken Scientist 1's argument.

    B. tend to weaken Scientist 2's argument.

    C. be incompatible with both scientists' views.

    D. be irrelevant to the controversy.

2. Which of the following is a reason given by Scientist 2 for believing that tektites originate on the Earth?

    F. The density of the Earth's atmosphere would prevent any similar lunar or extraterrestrial material from reaching the Earth's surface.

    G. Tektites have a composition totally unlike that of any material ever brought back from the moon.

    H. Extraterrestrial material could not have been as widely dispersed as tektites are.

    J. Material ejected from the moon or beyond would eventually have been much more widely distributed on Earth.

3. Scientist 1 could best answer the point that some tektites have vesicles filled with gases in the same proportion as the Earth's atmosphere by:

    A. countering that not all tektites have such gas-filled vesicles.

    B. demonstrating that molten material would be likely to trap some gases while falling through the terrestrial atmosphere.

    C. suggesting that those gases might occur in the same proportions in the moon's atmosphere.

    D. showing that similar vesicles, filled with these gases in the same proportions, are also found in some terrestrial volcanic glass.

4. How did Scientist 2 answer the argument that tektite-like material ejected from the Earth could not reach a high enough velocity relative to the atmosphere to undergo air-friction melting?

    F. By asserting that a shock wave might cause a momentary change in atmosphere density, permitting subsequent aerodynamic heating

    G. By pointing out that periodic meteorite impacts have caused gradual changes in atmospheric density over the eons

    H. By attacking the validity of the aerodynamic studies cited by Scientist 1

    J. By referring to the correlation between tektite fields and known impact craters in the Ivory Coast and Ghana

5. The point of subjecting lenses of tektite glass to a heated airstream was to:

   A. determine their water content.

   B. see if gases became trapped in their vesicles.

   C. reproduce the effects of atmospheric entry.

   D. simulate the mechanism of meteorite formation.

6. Researchers could best counter the objections of Scientist 2 to Scientist 1's argument by:

   F. discovering some phenomenon that would quickly remove tektite-sized objects from orbit.

   G. proving that most common tektite shapes can be produced by aerodynamic heating.

   H. confirming that active volcanoes once existed on the moon.

   J. mapping the locations of all known tektite fields and impact craters.

7. Which of the following characteristics of tektites is LEAST consistent with the theory that tektites are of extraterrestrial origin?

   A. Low water content

   B. "Flying saucer" shapes

   C. Narrow distribution

   D. Absence of unmelted material

Answers

1. A
2. J
3. B
4. F
5. C
6. F
7. C

Answers and Explanations

Your preread of the introduction should have revealed the issue at hand—namely, tektites, which are small glassy objects found in certain areas known as strewn fields. The conflict is about the *origin* of these objects: In other words, where did they come from?

 EXPERT TUTOR TIP
Keep viewpoints straight:
1. Read the intro and Scientist 1 passage.
2. Answer questions that say Scientist 1.
3. Read Scientist 2 paragraph.
4. Answer Scientist 2 questions.
5. Answer any other questions.

Scientist 1's theory is expressed in his first sentence: "Tektites almost certainly are extraterrestrial, probably lunar, in origin." Put that into a form you can understand: Scientist 1 believes that tektites come from space, probably the moon. On the other hand, Scientist 2 has an opposing theory, also expressed in her first sentence: "Nonlocal origin is extremely unlikely." In other words, it's unlikely that tektites came from a nonlocal source; they probably came from a *local* source, i.e., right here on Earth. The conflict is clear. One says that tektites come from space; the other says they come from Earth. You might have even labeled the two positions "space origin" and "Earth origin."

Scientist 1 presents three points of data:

1. Tektite shapes show characteristics of "air-friction melting" (supporting the theory of space origin).

2. "Atmospheric forces" wouldn't be great enough to shape tektite-like material ejected from Earth's surface (weakening the theory of Earth origin).

3. Tektites resemble moon rocks gathered by *Apollo 12* but not Earth rocks (strengthening the theory of space origin).

Scientist 2 also presents three points of data:

1. Any matter coming from space would "fall over a wide area" instead of being concentrated in strewn fields (weakening the theory of space origin).

2. There are "striking similarities" between tektites and the composition of the Earth's crust (strengthening the theory of Earth origin).

3. "Meteorite impacts" could create shock waves, explaining how terrestrial material could undergo air-friction melting (strengthening the theory of Earth origin by counteracting Scientist 1's first point).

Obviously, you won't have time to write out the supporting data for each theory the way we've done above. But it is important to circle or bracket the key phrases in the data descriptions ("air-friction melting," *Apollo 12*," etc.) and number them. **What's important is that you have an idea of what data supports which theory.** The questions, once you get to them, will then force you to focus.

> **EXPERT TUTOR TIP**
> Active Reading in the Conflicting Viewpoints passage will make it easier to find the information you need to answer questions correctly.

Question 1 asks how it would affect the scientists' arguments if it were discovered that many tektites contain unmelted crystalline material. Well, Scientist 1 says that tektites never contain unmelted crystalline material and that the terrestrial glass produced by some meteorite impacts *always* does. Therefore, by showing a resemblance between tektites and Earth materials, this discovery would weaken Scientist 1's argument for extraterrestrial origin. **Choice A is correct.**

For **question 2**, you had to identify which answer choice was used by Scientist 2 to support the argument that tektites are terrestrial in origin. You should have been immediately drawn to choice J, which expresses what we've identified above as Scientist 2's first data point. Notice how choice F is a piece of evidence that Scientist 1 cites. (Remember not to confuse the viewpoints!) As for choice G, Scientist 2 says that tektites *do* resemble Earth materials, but never says that they *don't* resemble lunar materials. And choice H gets it backwards; Scientist 2 says that extraterrestrial material *would* be widely dispersed and that the tektites are *not* widely dispersed, rather than vice versa.

> **EXPERT TUTOR TIP**
> Many Conflicting Viewpoints questions relate to *evidence* (or *data*). You may be asked: What was presented? Why? Would it help or hurt a scientist's claim?

For **question 3**, you need to find the best way for Scientist 1 to counter the point that some tektites have vesicles filled with gases in the same proportion as the Earth's atmosphere. First, make sure you understand the meaning of that point. The idea that these gases must have been trapped in the vesicles (little holes) while the rock was actually being formed is being used by Scientist 2 to suggest that tektites are of terrestrial origin. Scientist 1 *could* say that not all tektites have such gas-filled vesicles—choice A—but that's not a great argument. If any reasonable number of them *do*, Scientist 1 would have to come up with an alternative explanation (Scientist 2 **never** claimed that *all* tektites contained these vesicles). But if, as choice B suggests, Scientist 1 could demonstrate that molten material would be likely to trap some terrestrial gases while falling through Earth's atmosphere, this would explain how tektites might have come from beyond Earth and still contain vesicles filled with Earth-like gases. Choice C is easy to eliminate if you know that the moon's atmosphere is extremely thin and totally different in composition from Earth's atmosphere. Unlike correct choice B, it doesn't explain how the trapped gas made it to Earth. Finally, since it's Scientist 2 who claims that tektites are terrestrial in origin, choice D, showing that similar gas-filled vesicles occur in some terrestrial volcanic glass, this wouldn't help Scientist 1 at all.

In **question 4**, you're asked how Scientist 2 answered the argument that tektite-like material ejected from the Earth could not reach a high enough velocity to undergo air-friction melting. Well, that was Scientist 2's third data point. The shock wave produced by a major meteorite collision could momentarily displace the atmosphere right above the impact site (meaning the air moved out of the way for a brief time). So when the splattered material reentered the atmosphere, it would undergo air-friction melting. That's basically what choice F says, making it the correct answer.

In **question 5**, the concept of subjecting lenses of tektite glass to a heated airstream was mentioned toward the beginning of Scientist 1's argument. The point was to simulate the entry of extraterrestrial tektite material through Earth's atmosphere, which is closest to choice C.

Question 6 shows again why it pays to keep each scientist's viewpoint straight. You can't counter the objections of Scientist 2 to Scientist 1's argument unless you know what Scientist 2 was objecting to. Scientist 2's first data point is the only one designed to shoot holes in the opposing viewpoint. There, Scientist 2 takes issue with the idea that lunar material could strike the Earth without being dispersed over a far wider area than the known strewn fields. But, as correct choice F says, if researchers found some force capable of removing tektite-sized objects from orbit *quickly*, it would demolish the objection that Scientist 2 raises in her first paragraph. The tektite material would strike the Earth or be pulled away quickly, instead of remaining in a solar orbit long enough to be captured by the Earth's gravity and subsequently be distributed over a wide area of the Earth.

Question 7 wasn't too tough if you read the question stem carefully. You want to find the tektite characteristic that is LEAST consistent with the theory that tektites came from the moon or beyond. This is Scientist 1's theory, so you want to pick the answer choice that doesn't go with his argument. Scientist 1's evidence *does* include tektites' low water content, "flying saucer" shapes, and absence of unmelted material. The only answer choice that he didn't mention was the narrow distribution of the strewn fields. And with good reason. That's part of Scientist 2's argument *against* an extraterrestrial origin. So the correct answer is choice C.

> **EXPERT TUTOR TIP**
> If a passage looks very difficult for you, skip it. Do the easy passages first, then come back to the passages that look like they are harder.

THE DEEP END: FACING TOUGH SCIENCE PASSAGES

Now we're going to do something very cruel. We're going to throw you a Science passage of such technical difficulty that you will want to go screaming for the exit before you finish reading it.

> **PERFECT SCORE TIP**
> I know how stressful the Science section can get. It is the fourth section, and you are given passages about things you could never hope to understand. Take a deep breath when you get to difficult Science questions, and remember that you have strategies to tackle them.

We're doing this for a reason. Sometimes on the ACT Science test, you'll find yourself encountering a bear of a passage—one that seems entirely incomprehensible. **The secret to success with these passages is: *don't panic.*** As we'll show you, you can get points on even the most difficult Science passage in the entire history of the ACT—as long as you keep your cool and approach it in a savvy, practical way. Here's the passage:

Passage V

Neutrinos (n) are subatomic particles that travel at approximately the speed of light. They can penetrate most matter, because they are electrically neutral and effectively massless.

Generally accepted theory holds that the nuclear reactions that power the sun create vast quantities of neutrinos as byproducts. Three proposed stages

(PPI, PPII, and PPIII) of the most important solar reaction are shown in Figure 1, along with their neutrino-producing subpaths. Equations for the subpaths are shown in Table 1, as are the predicted neutrino energies and fluxes.

Figure 1

Table 1

Subpath name	Subpath equation	Neutrino energy (MeV)	Expected flux on Earth ($10^{10}\,cm^{-2}\,sec^{-1}$)
p-p	$_1H^1 + _1H^1 \longrightarrow _1H^2 + \beta^+ + n$	0.42	6.06781
p-e-p	$_1H^1 + \beta^- + _1H^1 \longrightarrow _1H^2 + n$	1.44	0.01524
Be^7†	$_4Be^7 + \beta^- \longrightarrow _3Li^7 + n$	0.87	0.43924
Be^7††	$_4Be^7 + \beta^- \longrightarrow _3Li^7 + n$	0.38	0.04880
B^8	$_5B^8 \longrightarrow _4Be^8 + \beta^+ + n$	14.05*	0.00054

†Be^7 subpath 1
††Be^7 subpath 2

*Maximum

📊 FIGURE INTERPRETATION

8. According to the information presented in the passage, which of the following stages or subpaths should contribute the smallest portion of the total solar neutrino flux on Earth?

   F. p-p

   G. PPI

   H. PPII

   J. PPIII

📶 FIGURE INTERPRETATION

9. Of the neutrinos that are produced in the subpaths described in the passage, which type can have the greatest energy?

   A. n_1
   B. n_2
   C. n_3
   D. n_4

📶 PATTERNS

10. Based on the information presented in the passage, the percentage of solar neutrinos produced by Be^7 subpath 2 is approximately:

    F. 1.2%.
    G. 10%.
    H. 12%.
    J. 90%.

📶 FIGURE INTERPRETATION

11. Solar neutrinos are detected through a reaction with $_{37}Cl$ for which the minimum neutrino energy is approximately 0.8 MeV. Of the neutrinos discussed in the passage, this method would detect:

    A. all of the neutrinos produced in PPI and PPII.

    B. some of the neutrinos produced in PPI, PPII, and PPIII.

    C. only neutrinos produced in Be^7 subpath 1 of PPII.

    D. only neutrinos produced in PPIII.

📶 SCIENTIFIC REASONING

12. The symbol β represents a beta particle, a particle emitted during nuclear decay. Beta particles may be positively or negatively charged. During which of the following subpaths are beta particles emitted?

    I. p-p
    II. p-e-p
    III. B^8

    F. II only
    G. I and III only
    H. II and III only
    J. I, II, and III

Answers

8. J
9. D
10. F
11. B
12. G

Answers and Explanations

Confused? If you aren't, you should stick close to your phone, because the Nobel Prize committee will probably be calling sometime soon! On the other hand, if you *are* confused, don't sweat it. **As we said in ACT Basics, some ACT questions are so hard that even your *teachers* would have a hard time getting them correct.**

> ✔ **PERFECT SCORE TIP**
> The most important thing to remember for Science is that you do not have to understand everything that is said. For example, you do not have to have any idea whatsoever what PPIII is to answer question 8. In fact, they don't expect you to.

The good news is that you don't have to understand a passage to get a few questions right. Here's how you might have approached the previous passage:

GETTING POINTS EVEN IF YOU DON'T GET THE POINT

Your preread of the introduction should have told you that the passage is about neutrinos coming from the sun. But that may be all you were able to get from this gibberish. You may have been in a total fog looking at Figure 1 and Table 1. But if you didn't panic, you might have noticed a few things: First, that whatever Figure 1 illustrates, there are some really big parts and some really small parts. If you look at the *x*-axis of the chart, you'll see that, whatever PPI, PPII, and PPIII are, the first is 88 percent, the second only 12 percent, and the third only 0.01 percent.

Is that tiny, vague insight enough to get a point? Yes! Look at **question 8**. It asks which stage or subpath contributes the *smallest* portion of flux. Well, look for a small portion. PPIII's figure of 0.01 percent is a very small number, whatever it's supposed to be referring to, so PPIII would be a good guess here. And indeed, choice J is correct for question 8.

What about Table 1? This is a little easier to understand, especially if you ignore the column about subpath equations. But "neutrino energy" sounds like something we can comprehend. Apparently, each subpath produces a different level of neutrino energy. Some have high energy (like B^8, with 14.06), and some have low energy (like Be^7††, with only 0.38). Energy is mentioned in **question 9**. Which type of neutrinos can have the greatest energy? Well, if B^8 were a choice, we'd pick that. But the choices are ns, not Bs. Well, try to find B^8 somewhere in the other chart—Figure 1. There, we find it somehow associated with n_4 neutrinos. So take a gamble; choose n_4—which is choice D—for this question. If you did that, you'd still have gotten another point, still without really understanding much more than before.

You're hot; keep it going. **Question 10** refers to Be^7 subpath 2. You may have noticed in the note under Table 1 that the Be^7 with two little dagger marks signifies subpath 2. So far, so good. Notice that the choices are all percentages. Where are percentages mentioned? In Figure 1. So find Be^7 with two dagger marks in Figure 1. You find it in the area of PPII, which is 12 percent of the x-axis in that chart. But notice that Be^7 with two dagger marks represents only *part* of that part of the figure— 10 percent, to be exact. So 10 percent of 12 percent would be 1.2 percent. That's choice F. It's also the correct answer.

Things get a little harder with **question 11**, but you still might have gotten the answer if you used common sense. Here we get some mumbo jumbo about $_{37}Cl$, but the part of the question that should have caught your eye was the bit about a minimum neutrino energy of 0.8 MeV. Neutrino energy was represented in the third column of Table 1. According to that table, only three subpaths have an energy greater than 0.8—p-e-p (with 1.44), Be^7 with one dagger mark (with 0.87), and B^8 (the champion, with 14.06). Unfortunately, the answer choices aren't expressed in those terms; they're expressed in terms of PPI, II, and III, so we're going to have to translate from table to figure again, just as we did with **question 9**.

Take p-e-p first. That's part (but not all) of the PPI portion of Figure 1. Be^7 with one dagger mark, similarly, is part (but not all) of the PPII portion. And B^8 is all of the PPIII portion. So there are at least parts of PPI, PPII, and PPIII implicated here. That should have led you to choice B, which would have gotten you yet another point. Notice that choice A is inaccurate because it talks about *all* of something in PPI and PPII and doesn't mention PPIII at all. Choices C and D, meanwhile, seem too limited, since they only mention one of the PP areas (whatever they are). So B is definitely the right answer choice.

Finally, **question 12** talks about beta particles. Well, that little beta symbol appears only in the subpath equation column of Table 1. There, we find beta symbols in the equations for *all* of the subpaths in the table. That may have led you to believe that all three Roman numerals should be included, and no one would have blamed you for choosing choice J (I, II, and III). You would have been wrong, but you can't win them all when you're winging questions you don't really understand.

Of course, if you noticed that the question was asking for beta particles *emitted,* and if you knew that in the subpath equations everything *before* the arrow is what you start with while everything *after* the arrow is what you finish with, you might have been able to make a better guess. You would have realized that those equations with a beta symbol *before* the arrow were ones in which a beta particle was *absorbed,* while those with a beta symbol *after* the arrow were ones in which a beta particle was *emitted*. In that case, then, you would have seen that the equations for p-p and B^8 do have beta particles emitted, while the equation for p-e-p does not. That might have led you to choice G—I and III only—which is the correct answer.

Six questions, six points—and all without understanding the passage in any deep or thorough way. Of course, if you understand the mysteries of neutrino flux and p-e-p subpaths, congratulations. You're probably enough of a science whiz to ace the subject test anyway. But if you're like most ACT test takers, you won't understand everything the passages talk about. Sometimes you'll even find yourself totally lost.

The moral of the story, of course, is **don't give up on a passage just because you don't understand it.** You may not be able to get *every* point associated with the passage, but you may be able to get at least one or two (or three or four). Remember: The test is designed in such a way that you can *figure out* many of the questions, even if you don't know the subject area.

Let's conclude now with another quick point about getting quick points. If you're nearly out of time and you've still got a whole Science passage left, you need to shift to last-minute strategies. As in Reading, don't try to preread the passage, or you'll just run out of time before you answer any questions. Instead, scan the questions without reading the passage and look first for the ones that require only reading data off of a graph or table. You can often get a couple of quick points just by knowing how to find data quickly.

Again, the most important thing is to make sure you have gridded in at least a random guess on every question.

☑ **PERFECT SCORE TIP**
The advice that cannot be repeated enough times is to answer every question. If you are running out of time, be sure to guess on every answer. Even one lucky guess could boost your score.

> ## IF YOU LEARNED ONLY THREE THINGS IN THIS CHAPTER...

1. Each ACT Science test has one Conflicting Viewpoints passage in which two scientists debate an issue.

2. Spend more time prereading Conflicting Viewpoints passages. Determine each scientist's view and identify the supporting and undermining evidence.

3. You can get many Science questions right even when you don't understand the entire passage. Don't panic when faced with a tough passage.

CHAPTER 16

Writing Workout: Write What Counts

A growing number of colleges want an assessment of your written communication skills. If you consider yourself a good writer and are accustomed to scoring well on essays, there may be a temptation to skip this chapter. Don't—top scores are not given out easily, and writing a scored first draft in under a half hour is unlike most of your past writing experiences.

In addition, the ACT essay is not a typical essay that you are used to writing in school. For example: you are allowed (even encouraged) to use the first person *I* and *we* in your argument. Personal experiences are excellent ways to back up your position. If you need to embroider the facts a little to make your point, no one is going to fact-check your essay.

> **GO ONLINE**
> Your online companion contains two practice essay prompts (in addition to the one in this chapter). After you test yourself, evaluate your essays by comparing them to the model essays provided.

Let's start with the basics.

JUST THE FACTS

Writing has **always** been an essential skill for college success. The ACT includes an optional Writing test. Some colleges require it; others do not. **Before registering for the ACT, find out if the schools to which you're applying want applicants to take the Writing test.**

The ACT English test measures knowledge of effective writing skills, including grammar, punctuation, organization, and style. The Writing test complements that evaluation of technical skill with an example of your simple, direct writing.

How the ACT Essay Is Scored

Your essay will be graded on a holistic scale of 1–6 (6 being the best). Graders will be looking for an overall sense of your essay, not assigning separate scores for specific elements like grammar or organization. Two readers read and score each essay; then those scores are added together to arrive at your Writing subscore (from 2–12). If there's a difference of more than a point between the two readers' scores, your essay will be read by a third reader.

Statistically speaking, there will be few essays that score 6. If each grader gives your essay a 4 or 5, that will place you at the upper range of those taking the exam.

☑ **PERFECT SCORE TIP**
I suggest taking the Writing section if you think there is any chance a college you want to go to might want it. Being forced to retake such a long test sounds more painful than just preparing for Writing in the first place.

What Should I Do?

The readers realize you're writing under time pressure and so expect you to make some mistakes. **The facts in your essay are not important; readers are not checking your facts. Nor will they judge you on your opinions. They want to see how well you can communicate a relevant, coherent point of view.**

The test makers identify the following as the skills tested in the Writing test:

- **Answer the question in the prompt.** State a clear perspective on an issue.

- **Build an argument.** Assemble supporting evidence logically with relevant, specific points.

- **Maintain focus and organize your specific points logically.** Avoid digressions and be sure to draw everything together in a concluding paragraph.

- **Address the complexity of the issue.** Discuss BOTH sides of the argument. Don't ignore the opposite side.

- **Write clearly.** Make sure your argument is easy to follow. Grammar rules are not the point of the essay; however, errors that interfere with the essay's argument will hurt your score.

Can I Prepare for the Essay?

The underlying skill in the Writing test is speed. On the ACT, you have only 30 minutes, and you must accomplish a lot in that time. It takes practice to read the prompt, organize your position with relevant ideas and facts, write a concluding paragraph—and proofread!

> ✔ **PERFECT SCORE TIP**
> The key to the ACT essay really is clarity. The graders want to see if you can logically put together an argument, and they don't want to waste their time trying to decode cryptic language, so make your points clear and obvious.

Do You Need to Prepare for the Essay?

The ACT essay is not like other writing experiences. It's a first draft that will be graded. Not only must it be complete and well organized, but it must also be easy for a grader to see that it is complete and well organized (and the grader may spend as little as a minute reading your essay). That's a lot to do in 30 minutes, so preparation and practice are essential.

> **EXPERT TUTOR TIP**
> By the way, practicing the ACT essay also reinforces what you've learned for the English test and strengthens your Reading test skills: in Reading, you take an argument apart; in Writing, you put together an argument.

THE KAPLAN METHOD FOR THE ACT ESSAY

STEP 1: Prompt
STEP 2: Plan
STEP 3: Produce
STEP 4: Proofread

If you plan your essay and adhere to your plan when you write, the result will be solidly organized. Between now and test day, you can't drastically change your overall writing skills—and you probably don't need to. **If your plan is good, all you need to do in the writing and proofreading steps is draw on your strengths and avoid your weaknesses.** Get to know what those are as you practice.

Write what counts: To maximize your score, use the Kaplan Method to help you focus on writing what the scorers will look for—*and nothing else.*

Step	A High-Scoring Essay	A Low-Scoring Essay
Prompt	clearly develops a position on the prompt	does not clearly state a position
Plan	supports with concrete, relevant examples	is general, repetitious, or overly simplistic
Produce	maintains clear focus and organization	digresses or has weak organization
Proofread	shows competent use of language	contains errors that reduce clarity

Kaplan has found this approach useful in our many years of experience with hundreds of sample essay statements on a wide range of tests. Let's look at what the test makers tell you about how the essays are scored.

To score Level 4, you must:

- Answer the question

- Support ideas with examples

- Show logical thought and organization

- Avoid major or frequent errors that make your writing unclear

Organization and clarity are key to an above-average essay. If the reader can't follow your train of thought—if ideas aren't clearly organized or if grammatical errors, misspellings, and incorrect word choices make your writing unclear—you can't do well.

To score Level 5, all you have to add to a 4 is:

- Address the topic in depth

In other words, offer more examples and details. The test graders love specific examples, and the more concrete your examples are, the more they clarify your thinking and keep you focused.

To score Level 6, all you have to add to a 5 is:

- Make transitions smoother and show variety in syntax and vocabulary

Use words from the prompt to tie paragraphs together, rather than relying exclusively on connectors like *however* and *therefore*. Vary your sentence structure, sometimes using simple sentences and other times using compound and complex ones. Adding a few college-level vocabulary words will also boost your score.

Now let's apply the Kaplan Method to a practice prompt:

 EXPERT TUTOR TIP
Note that you can't earn a 5 or 6 (10 or 12) if you haven't met the basic requirements for a 4 (8). Think of the requirements as building blocks to higher scores.

STEP 1: Prompt

The ACT Writing prompt usually relates to a topic that is familiar to high school students. It will outline an issue that teenagers are likely to have an opinion on.

✓ **PERFECT SCORE TIP**
You must take a position on the Writing section. Graders like to see decisiveness no matter what the opinion may be. In other words, don't try to toe the line and support both pro and con—pick one.

If, by chance, the prompt describes a situation you feel strongly about, be sure to present your argument in a careful, thoughtful manner. Do NOT write an overly emotional response.

EXPERT TUTOR TIP
The assignment is not to write something vaguely inspired by the information given—that's where many good, creative writers go wrong.

Spend less than a minute reading the prompt on test day.

Here's an example of a typical ACT Writing prompt:

> In many high schools, the administration provides guidelines for the publication of student newspapers. These guidelines often determine which topics can and cannot be discussed in the newspaper and prohibit use of language that the administration deems inappropriate. Many administrators and teachers feel that these restrictions enable them to provide a safe learning environment for students. Others feel that any restriction on the student newspaper is a violation of freedom of speech. In your opinion, should high schools place restrictions on student newspapers?
>
> In your essay, take a position on this question. You may write about either one of the two points of view given, or you many present a different point of view on this question. Use specific reasons and examples to support your position.

STEP 2: Plan

Take five or six minutes to build a plan before you write. This step is critical—a successful plan leads directly to a high-scoring essay. Focus on what kinds of reasoning and examples you can use to support your position.

> ✓ **PERFECT SCORE TIP**
> Organization is the biggest gift you can give yourself on the essay. "Clever ideas" are nowhere near as important as having a solid road map that is obvious to the readers. To avoid wasting time, make sure you do not start writing without knowing your three points and how you will support them.

Note: If you find you have more examples for a position different from the one you thought you would take originally, *change your position*.

There is no one way to plan an essay. One method is to draw a large "T" on the page and align examples and ideas on either side of the line. So you might have the following notes on the prompt we started with in Step 1:

NEWSPAPERS IN SCHOOL

Safe learning environment (more control)	Freedom of speech (less control)
can have faculty advisor monitor coverage to make sure issues are clearly, fairly, and *tastefully* presented	add coverage of state, local elections, & discussion of school issues imp't to students
Administration can get its side heard, too.	help prepare students to be adults who know how to think and to vote
promotes safe discussion, improves student morale, and avoids protests	air debates about student rights ex. dress code ex. off-campus lunch privileges
	Students have rights and should be acknowledged.

Conclusion: Everyone benefits from freedom of speech in a school newspaper.

Information banks: Don't wait until test day to think of examples you can use to support your ideas. Regardless of what question is raised in the prompt, you will draw your support from the things you know best and are most comfortable writing about—things that you know a fair amount of concrete detail about.

Refresh your memory about your favorite or most memorable books, school subjects, historical events, personal experiences, activities—anything. By doing so, you strengthen mental connections to those ideas and details—that will make it easier to connect to the right examples on test day.

Structure your essay: Plan a clear introduction, a distinct middle section, and a strong conclusion. **Choose your best examples, decide in what order you'll handle them, and plan your paragraphs.**

With that in mind, we suggest:

- Use an effective *hook* to bring the reader in.
- Use regular *transitions* to provide the glue that holds your ideas together.
- End with a *bang* to make your essay memorable.

Using a "hook" means avoiding an essay that opens (as thousands of other essays will): "In my opinion, … because …" Try a more general statement that introduces one or more of the key words you will use from the prompt.

Using the "T" model presented earlier, you might use the following sentence:

A student newspaper should help students learn to think and express themselves.

A "bang" means a closing that ties the three example paragraphs together. A good choice can be a clear, succinct statement of your thesis in the essay or a vivid example that's right on point.

To conclude the planned "T" essay, you might finish with:

Both students and the administration would benefit from a school newspaper that covers a broad array of topics.

> ✔ **PERFECT SCORE TIP**
> Every reader is going to read thousands of essays, so make yours memorable. A good hook and interesting writing will help wake up your reader and boost your score.

Let's plan for our prompt using a paragraph-by-paragraph method. The answer we've chosen is this:

I agree that restrictions on student newspapers violate freedom of speech, and I also believe restrictions impede student learning.

This position clearly responds to the assignment, and adding some reasoning not taken directly from the prompt immediately tells the reader "I have ideas of my own."

Next, working with our proposed response, comb your memory or your imagination for supporting reasons and examples to use. We'll use:

Point: Student newspapers should mimic real life newspapers.

Point: Not being in the school paper doesn't mean it's not discussed.

Point: Students can avoid "harming" others as well as adults.

Point: Censorship is anti-democratic.

Fill in the details. Jot down any notes you need to ensure that you use the details you've developed, but don't take the time to write full sentences. When you have enough ideas for a few supporting paragraphs, decide what your introduction and conclusion will be and the order in which you'll discuss each supporting idea.

Here's our sample plan:

Para 1:   I agree with "free speech." Student newspapers should prepare for real life.

Para 2:   Press is treated specially in real life.

Para 3:   Potential harm not a good argument.

Para 4:   Censorship vs. democracy

Para 5:   Better to have discussion out in the open.

Para 6:   Restate thesis.

If you take our advice and use examples that are very familiar to you, you won't have to write much in your plan in order to remember the point being made. **Learn how brief you can make your notes and still not lose sight of what you mean to say.**

> **EXPERT TUTOR TIP**
> Save your best example for last and stress its relative importance.

A good plan:

- Responds to the prompt
- Has an introduction
- Has strong examples, usually one per paragraph
- Has a strong conclusion

In addition to writing practice essays, practice just making plans on your own whenever you have a few spare minutes, using ideas for changes in high school curriculum, events, lifestyle, and activities, such as: longer vs. shorter class sessions; students should/should not be allowed off campus during the school day; study halls should/should not be eliminated; vocational options vs. all college prep. The more you think in advance about how you might discuss a variety of potential issues, the easier it will be to write your ACT essay on test day.

STEP 3: Produce

Appearances count. In purely physical terms, your essay will make a better impression if you fill a significant portion of the space provided and if it is clearly divided into three to five reasonably equal paragraphs (except that the final paragraph can be short). **Use one paragraph for your introduction, one for each example or line of reasoning, and one for your conclusion so your essay will be easy for readers to follow.**

Write neatly. Graders will give you a zero if your essay is hard to read—and negative feelings affect holistic scoring. If your handwriting is a problem, print.

Stick with the plan. Resist any urge to introduce new ideas—no matter how good you think they are—or to digress from the central focus or organization of each paragraph.

> **EXPERT TUTOR TIP**
> The ACT essay isn't the place for creative writing. Make your writing direct, persuasive, and error-free. Give the graders what they are looking for.

Think twice, write once. Write mentally before you write on paper. If your essays are littered with misspellings and grammatical mistakes, you may get a low score simply because the reader cannot follow what you are trying to say.

Use topic sentences. Each paragraph should be organized around a topic sentence that you should finish in your mind before you start to write. These may begin:

- *I believe…*
- *One example…*
- *Another example…*
- *Another example…*
- *Therefore, we can conclude…*

You don't have to write it this way in the essay, but completing these sentences in your mind ensures that you focus on what idea organizes each paragraph.

> **PERFECT SCORE TIP**
> Topic sentences are very important in ACT essays. The reader should be able to read just the topic sentences of each paragraph and get your major arguments, so make sure these sentences are clear.

Choose words carefully. Use vocabulary that you know well. Inserting new or fancy words that you have learned recently often sticks out. The result of unfamiliar words in an essay is the opposite of what you want: awkward, confusing thoughts. Instead of impressing the graders, you have made a mess. Two more points here:

1. Avoid using *I* excessively.
2. Avoid slang.

Use transitions. Think about the relationship between ideas as you write, and spell them out clearly. This makes it easy for the readers to follow your reasoning, and they'll appreciate it. **Use key words from the prompt as well as the kinds of words you've learned about in Reading that indicate contrast, opinion, relative importance, and support.**

Essay length. While many poor essays can be quite long, there will be few 6 essays under about 300 words, so take this into consideration as you practice. The length of an essay is no measure of its quality. However, it's hard to develop an argument in depth—something the graders look for—in one or two short paragraphs. **Don't ramble, digress, or write off topic just to make your essay longer.** Practice writing organized essays with developed examples, and you'll find yourself writing more naturally.

Don't sweat the small stuff. Do not obsess over every little thing. If you cannot remember how to spell a word, do your best and just **keep going.** Even the top scoring essays can have minor errors. The essay readers understand that you are writing first drafts and have no time for research or revision.

STEP 4: Proofread

Always leave yourself two or three minutes to review your work—the time spent will definitely pay off. Very few of us can avoid the occasional confused sentence or omitted word when we write under pressure. Quickly review your essay to be sure your ideas are clearly stated.

Don't hesitate to make corrections on your essay—these are timed first drafts, not term papers. But keep it clear: use a single line through deletions and an asterisk to mark where text should be inserted.

> ✓ **PERFECT SCORE TIP**
> Do you notice that most of your sentences tend to be relatively simple and begin with a subject followed by a passive verb? This is a problem. Varying sentence structure and writing in active voice will not only make your essay more enjoyable, but can be the difference between a 5 and a 6.

You don't have time to look for every minor error or to revise substantially. Learn the types of mistakes you tend to make and look for them. Some of the most common mistakes in students' essays are those found in the English test questions.

COMMON ERRORS

- Omitted words
- Sentence fragments
- Subject-verb agreement or verb tense errors
- Misplaced modifiers
- Pronoun agreement errors
- Misused words—especially homonyms like *their* for *there* or *they're*
- Spelling errors

> **EXPERT TUTOR TIP**
> Use a caret ^ or an asterisk * to insert a word or words. Write a backward P or ¶ to create a new paragraph, and cross words out with one line. Don't make a mess!

COMMON STYLE PROBLEMS

- Choppy sentences (combine some)
- Too many long, complex sentences (break some up)
- Too many stuffy-sounding words (replace some with simple words)
- Too many simple words (add a few college-level words)

> **EXPERT TUTOR TIP**
> On test day, use 6–7 minutes for planning and 23–24 minutes for writing and proofreading. Try writing practice essays in 20 minutes to make the real essay seem easier.

KNOW THE SCORE: SAMPLE ESSAYS

The best way to be sure you've learned what the readers will look for is to try scoring some essays yourself.

> **EXPERT TUTOR TIP**
> Don't cheat yourself by reading our explanation without first deciding what holistic grade you would give the sample essay.

The graders will be scoring holistically, not checking off "points"—but to learn what makes a good essay, it may help to consider these questions, based on the test makers' scoring criteria:

- Does the author answer the question?
- Is the author's position clearly stated?
- Does the body of the essay support and develop the position taken?
- Are there at least three supporting paragraphs?
- Is the relevance of each supporting paragraph clear?
- Does the writer address the other side of the argument?
- Is the essay organized, with a clear introduction, middle, and end?
- Does the author start a new paragraph for each new idea?
- Is each sentence in a paragraph relevant to the point made in that paragraph?
- Are transitions clear?
- Is the essay easy to read? Is it engaging?
- Are sentences varied?
- Is vocabulary used effectively? Is college-level vocabulary used?

> **PERFECT SCORE TIP**
> I know it is tempting to copy the prompt in your essay. The readers will notice and you will be penalized! There is nothing worse than copying the prompt in your essay, as it is not only painfully obvious that you don't have your own ideas, but it wastes time and space, and readers will simply disregard it. Do not copy the prompt!

Let's look at a sample essay based on the prompt and plan we've been looking at.

Sample Essay 1

In many high schools, the administration has provided guidelines for the publication of student newspapers. These guidelines often determine which topics can and cannot be discussed in the newspaper, and prohibit what the administration deems inappropriate language. Many administrators and teachers feel that these restrictions enable them to provide a safe, appropriate learning environment for students. Others feel that any restriction on the student newspaper is a violation of freedom of speech. In my opinion, students should be free to write on any topic.

Firstly, restrictions will not stop certain topics being talked about. Students will always discuss topics that they are interested in. Second, students are more aware of what is or is not appropriate than the administration might think. A newspaper is there to tell news and students will therefore write about the news.

Finally and most importantly, a right such as freedom of speech should not be checked at the school door. Students not being able to cognizant and value rights such as these if they are not taught their importance in school. So high schools should not place restrictions on student newspapers.

Score: _____ /6

It should have been fairly easy to see that this isn't a strong essay. We'd give it a score of 2 out of 6. The author does state a clear opinion, but half of the essay is a direct copy of the prompt—the graders will notice this and won't be impressed by it. The time and space spent just quoting the prompt was completely wasted—it earned the writer zero points.

The rest of the essay is organized and uses transition words (*firstly* and *finally*). The author states her thesis, follows with three supporting reasons, and then a conclusion. However, none of this is discussed fully enough—no concrete details or examples are given. In the second paragraph, for instance, the author should have added an example demonstrating that students are aware of what is appropriate or an example of topics that students will discuss in the paper.

The language is understandable, but there are significant errors affecting clarity. For instance, the second sentence of paragraph 3 is a fragment—there is no verb. Some vocabulary words are used without a clear understanding of their meaning: In paragraph 3, "not being able to cognizant" is incorrect; perhaps the student meant "not being able to understand."

This essay looks like the writer couldn't think of good ideas, waited too long to start writing, and had to write in a hurry.

Let's try another better essay. Read quickly and select a score before reading our evaluation.

Sample Essay 2

Many high schools place restrictions on appropriate topics and language for student newspapers. Many people disagree with these restrictions. While arguments can be made for either side, I believe that newspapers, as part of the school, should be placed under guidelines of the school.

First, a high school necessarily has stricter rules than normal society. These rules are not in place to punish students. They protect them and providing a suitable learning environment. In this way, when students leave high school they will have grown from children to adults, ready to succeed in the larger world. For example, the strict time schedule, with exactly three or four minutes given between classes, prepares students for strict schedules in the broader world.

Second, students interested in journalism should have instruction in how to write and publish newspaper articles. A student newspaper, which for obvious reasons has limited scope, is a perfect laboratory for students to experiment with journalistic writing. The administration and faculty dedicated to the newspaper can guide students in choosing appropriate topics, such as student elections. Then they can write articles on politics in the future. Imagine a student whose high school teacher taught the proper techniques for reporting on the race for student council president, joining a major news organization and reporting on the United States Presidential election.

Lastly, students may not realize the harm which their writing may cause. In my school, a student discovered a teacher's affair and "reported" on it in a story on the student's TV network, before the school could interfere. The teacher's career was destroyed and his marriage fell apart. Perhaps he deserved it, but student television should not have been the vehicle that ruined his life. The student reporter felt terribly in the end, as she had not thought through the consequences of her story. The same consequences could occur in a student newspaper that was restricted by no guidelines from the school.

Therefore, while many people argue that freedom of speech is a right too precious to give up, it is more important to provide guidelines for young people.

Score: _____ /6

Okay, now how do you want to score this essay?

This sample exceeds the basic requirements for a 4; it's a 5.

This essay addresses the assignment. The writer's position is clear, and the personal example in the fourth paragraph provides good support. The organization is good, and the author uses transition words. Each paragraph discusses a different aspect of the writer's argument. Let's look at why it doesn't rate a 6.

Some of the support isn't explained enough. The second paragraph, for example, doesn't show the connection between strict schedules and restrictions on newspaper reporting—the subject of the essay. The idea, in paragraph 3, of a student growing up to be a presidential reporter is interesting, but it doesn't particularly address the idea of restrictions. The final paragraph doesn't tie back to the main argument about newspapers; it only generally mentions "guidelines for young people."

The author's writing is good, but unexceptional. There are a few examples of complex sentences. For example, in paragraph 3: "A student newspaper, which for obvious reasons has limited scope, is a perfect laboratory for students to experiment with journalistic writing." The essay includes grammar mistakes, however, such as in paragraph 2: "They protect them and providing a suitable learning environment." In paragraph 3, the sentence "Then they can write articles on politics in the future" includes the ambiguous *they*, which could refer to the administration and teachers or the students.

> **EXPERT TUTOR TIP**
> To get from a 4 to a 5, you need fully developed examples and logic. To get to a 6, you also need lively, mostly error-free writing.

Let's look at another essay. Read it quickly and decide how you would score it.

Sample Essay 3

School administrations and teachers who support restrictions believe that these restrictions are needed to form an appropriate learning environment. But I agree with those who oppose such restrictions because they violate freedom of speech and these limits impede student progress and success after high school.

Despite the true need for rules in high schools, newspapers should be exempt. Students need discipline in the form of detention for misbehavior or demerits for poor study, but the student newspaper should not be a part of that system. Rather, it should mimic "real world" journalism.

Student editors, usually seniors aged seventeen or eighteen, are well aware of the overall environment in which they publish, and understand what is or is not appropriate. High school should give students practice at being cognizant of the larger arena in which they act. The few negative incidents that free press will admittedly cause will teach students that in life, one must take responsibility for one's actions.

Therefore, the argument for freedom of speech in student newspapers advances substantial educational goals for students, as well as our unalienable right of freedom of speech. This right, however, is paramount. The American public school is an extension of the American government and community, and censorship is inconsistent with American democracy. Again, students need to be prepared for the world they will live in; depriving them of rights that are promoted in the greater community prepares students poorly for life after high school.

Finally, censoring information in the student newspaper will not remove the subject from student discussion. Rather, it will remove a balanced, informative viewpoint, and often make the "inappropriate" action more desirable and "cool." Placing restrictions on student newspapers would be a serious mistake that would hinder students from learning what it is to participate in a free society.

Score: _____ /6

Did you recognize this as an essay similar to the plan we did earlier?

Para 1: I agree with "free speech." Student newspapers should prepare for real life.

Para 2: Press is treated specially in real life.

Para 3: Potential harm not a good argument.

Para 4: Censorship vs. democracy

Para 5: Not discussing in press doesn't mean not discussing in school.

This essay is pretty good—it would earn a 4. The position is clearly stated, and some supporting reasoning is given.

However, the reasoning is too general and the writing is too ordinary to earn the top score. Let's see how it could be improved.

TURNING A 4 INTO A 6

The essay plunges right into the two points of view offered in the prompt. It could be improved by introducing the issue with a general statement, like:

Many students, parents, and school administrators are debating the proper role of student newspapers. Should their language and content be restricted?

In the last sentence of the first paragraph, the writer introduces some additional reasoning *not* included in the prompt. That's excellent, but it would be better to make it clear where the position from the prompt ends and the author's position begins, perhaps like this:

> But I agree with those who oppose such restrictions because they violate freedom of speech. I would further argue that these limits impede student progress and success after high school.

The second paragraph is relevant and organized—it covers one of the two positions offered in the prompt. But it would be better if the writer tied this argument more clearly to something specific in the prompt, perhaps with an opening sentence using language from the prompt, like:

> Some people claim that high school students need strict guidelines in order to prepare for life after school.

Moreover, at the end of the paragraph, the reference to mimicking "real world" journalism would be improved by telling the reader what "real world" journalism is:

> Rather, it should mimic "real world" journalism, which strives to provide valid, balanced reporting on events important to the public, or in this case the student body.

The third paragraph addresses the view in the prompt that students can cause harm by printing inappropriate articles. Again, it should be made clearer what part of the prompt this paragraph is responding to, with a first sentence like:

> Others believe that students may cause unintended harm with newspaper articles written on controversial subjects. I think that is laughable.

Paragraph four is pretty good, as is. It states clearly what the author considers the most important argument. The fifth paragraph raises good arguments, but leaves them undeveloped. It would be best to provide an example of what type of story would help promote "balanced, informative" discussion to counteract "inappropriate…cool" actions, like:

> For instance, a reporter for my high school paper researched and wrote an in-depth story on the increasing drug problem among students. The administration quickly intervened and stopped the story, declaring that drugs were an inappropriate topic for student discussion. This story, however, would have focused discussion on a crucial issue for students, so that they can make the right choice when offered drugs or when they see friends using drugs. Unfortunately, this is a situation most students will face, and they need to be prepared. Suppressing the story made drugs seem even more rebellious and mysterious and most importantly did not give students facts with which they could prepare.

This makes it clear why the writer saved this argument for the last—an important, detailed example.

Finally, since this writer offers a fair number of supporting ideas, it would also be a good idea to add some transitions that establish the relative importance of those ideas. For example, in the third paragraph:

> First of all, student editors, usually seniors aged seventeen or eighteen, are well aware of the overall environment in which they publish, and understand what is or is not appropriate. But even more importantly, high school should give students practice at being cognizant of the larger arena in which they act.

> **✔ PERFECT SCORE TIP**
> Remember that your personal opinion really is irrelevant. Write your essay on the topic you can support the best, as they will grade how you write not what you think.

Here's how this essay would look with the improvements we've suggested.

> Many students, parents, and school administrators are debating the proper role of student newspapers. Should their language and content be restricted? School administrations and teachers who support restrictions believe that these restrictions are needed to form an appropriate learning environment. But I agree with those who oppose such restrictions because they violate freedom of speech. I would further argue that these limits impede student progress and success after high school.

> Some people claim that high school students need strict guidelines in order to prepare for life after school. Despite the true need for rules in high schools, newspapers should be exempt. Students need discipline in the form of detention for misbehavior or demerits for poor study, but the student newspaper should not be a part of that system. Rather, it should mimic "real world" journalism, which strives to provide valid, balanced reporting on events important to the public, or in this case the student body.

> Others believe that students may cause unintended harm with newspaper articles written on controversial subjects. I think that is laughable. First of all, student editors, usually seniors aged seventeen or eighteen, are well aware of the overall environment in which they publish, and understand what is or is not appropriate. But even more importantly, high school should give students practice at being cognizant of the larger arena in which they act. The few negative incidents that free press will admittedly cause will teach students that in life, one must take responsibility for one's actions.

Therefore, the argument for freedom of speech in student newspapers advances substantial educational goals for students, as well as our unalienable right of freedom of speech. This right, however, is paramount. The American public school is an extension of the American government and community, and censorship is inconsistent with American democracy. Again, students need to be prepared for the world they will live in; depriving them of rights that are promoted in the greater community prepares students poorly for life after high school.

Finally, censoring information in the student newspaper will not remove the subject from student discussion. Rather, it will remove a balanced, informative viewpoint, and often make the "inappropriate" action more desirable and "cool." For instance, a reporter for my high school paper researched and wrote an in-depth story on the increasing drug problem among students. The administration quickly intervened and stopped the story, declaring that drugs were an inappropriate topic for student discussion. This story, however, would have focused discussion on a crucial issue for students so that they can make the right choice when offered drugs or when they see friends using drugs. Unfortunately, this is a situation most students will face, and they need to be prepared. Suppressing the story made drugs seem even more rebellious and mysterious and most importantly did not give students facts with which they could prepare.

Placing restrictions on student newspapers would be a serious mistake that would hinder students from learning what it is to participate in a free society.

This is now a 6 essay. It addresses the task both fully and concretely. It addresses both sides of the argument, refutes two opposing arguments, and then moves to the bulk of the author's own reasoning. The first paragraph introduces all the lines of reasoning that will be used, demonstrating to the reader that the writer knew right from the start where this essay was headed. The development of ideas is clear and logical and the paragraphs reflect this organization.

EXPERT TUTOR TIP
There are no right or wrong opinions. You can earn a 6 with an essay for or against the issue raised in the prompt.

The author shows a high level of skill with language. The transitions between paragraphs are clear and guide the reader through the reasoning. The sentence structure varies throughout the passage and is at times complex.

So what did we do to our 4 to make it a 6?

- We added examples and detail.
- We varied sentence structure and added stronger vocabulary (*strives*, *laughable*, *intervened*, and *suppressing*).
- While length alone doesn't make a 6, we've added detail to our original essay.
- The conclusion, rather than being lost in the fifth paragraph, is now a strong, independent statement that concisely sums up the writer's point of view.

Remember that your graders will be reading *holistically*. They will not be grading you by assigning points to particular aspects of your writing. However, as you practice essay writing, you can build an otherwise humdrum essay into a 6 by working on specific elements, with the net effect of giving your essay that 6 glow.

PREPARING FOR THE ESSAY

Information Banks

Don't wait until test day to think about what subjects you can draw on for your examples to create animated and engaging essays. Examples can be drawn from anywhere: your life experience, a story you saw on the news, etc. So prepare yourself by refreshing your memory about your favorite subjects—collect examples that can be used for a variety of topics.

Don't hesitate to use your examples broadly. If the topic is about school, that doesn't mean you have to use school-based examples. It's better to write about things that you are comfortable with and know a lot about—but be sure to make it clear how they are relevant to the topic.

Read Op-Ed Essays

Newspapers and blogs have op-ed (opinion-editorial) articles. These present arguments and opinions on a wide range of topics. Some will present their arguments well, others will not. Make a point of reading and evaluating them. Ask yourself:

- What is the author's point?
- How is it supported?
- Is the argument convincing? If not, why?

Follow a Practice Regimen

Don't try to cut corners. Learn the Kaplan Method and practice writing at least one essay a week; last minute cramming will not be effective. If you intend to maximize your score, you must establish and adhere to a practice schedule. Practice at the same time of day that you will be writing on test day.

Be hard on yourself. **Always** time yourself to internalize the necessary pacing. Don't allow yourself any extra minutes to complete an essay.

Never start to write until you have a complete plan, and then adhere to your plan.

Always reserve two minutes to look over the essay and make needed additions or corrections.

> ✔ **PERFECT SCORE TIP**
> Writing an essay fast can be very challenging if you are not used to it. If this scares you, practice! Go to a quiet place and give yourself 25 minutes to write a sample essay. Make sure you handwrite it, as you will have to on the test.

Self-Evaluation

After each practice essay, score yourself based on the guidelines provided. As part of your self-evaluation, determine which types of examples are most useful to you and what types of errors you make most often. Then analyze how well you followed the Kaplan Method in constructing your essays and what you might focus on to improve. Do you have a tendency to rush your plan, or do you find that you haven't left two minutes to proofread at the end? **Practice to make your pacing reliable.**

Get a Second Opinion

Ask someone else to read and critique your practice essays. If you know someone else who's taking the ACT, you might agree to assist each other in this way. Knowing whether another person can follow your reasoning is the single most important learning aid you can have for the essay.

> ✔ **PERFECT SCORE TIP**
> I really recommend getting a second opinion on practice essays. I know I write many things that I believe are clear but that others cannot understand. If you are not good at judging your own clarity and logic, have someone else help you.

If You're Not a "Writer"

While the essay is optional, many colleges require the ACT essay. Remember that the essay is set up so that *everyone* can do well on it. You don't have to be an expert writer to formulate a good argument and support it well. Plain, clear language will go a long way toward getting a good score.

> **EXPERT TUTOR TIP**
> If you're down to the wire, allow yourself a few minutes to plan and then write, based on that plan, no matter how much you wish you could think of other ideas. Remember that the essay tests your ability to convey those ideas—not the ideas themselves.

If English Is Your Second Language

The ACT essay can be a special challenge for the international student or ESL student here in the United States. On the ACT, you will be taking a position on the prompt, something that sometimes, but not **always**, happens on the TOEFL® (Test of English as a Foreign Language). However, plan your essay using all the tools in this chapter and write according to your plan. Make a special point of spending time proofreading your practice essays when you finish them, and edit anything that makes your writing unclear. There's a strong connection between your English reading skills and your writing skills, so keep reading as well (and don't forget to look for material for your information banks while you read).

PRACTICE ESSAY

Try out the Kaplan Method on the following essay prompt. After you're finished, read your essay, and if possible, have someone else read it as well. You can compare it to the model essay that follows the lined pages. Good luck!

Many city councils have introduced proposals that would give them the power to ban certain books from the children's and young adult sections of local public libraries. Some citizens support such proposals because they hope to limit young people's exposure to inappropriate materials. However, other people believe that these measures are equivalent to censorship. In your opinion, should the government have the right to restrict the materials available to young people in libraries?

In your essay, take a position on this question. You may write about either one of the two points of view given, or you may present a different point of view on this question. Use specific reasons and examples to support your position.

_____

_____

_____

_____

_____

_____

_____

_____

_____

_____

_____

_____

_____

_____

_____

_____

_____

_____

_____

_____

_____

_____

_____

_____

_____

Model Essay

Here's one possible way to approach this essay prompt. Remember that the opinion you express is less important than the way you present it. Notice how this response includes a logically arranged argument with specific examples.

In some districts, city councils and other governing bodies have suggested that they be given the power to ban certain teen and children's books from public libraries. While some citizens believe that it would be beneficial for an outside party to screen the books that are available to young people, others are upset at what they see as censorship of the library's offerings.

Leaving the question of censorship aside, I believe that decisions about which books are appropriate for young people should be left to the young people themselves and their parents, not to city councils or librarians. Young people's reading levels and maturity levels can vary dramatically even within the same age group, and parents are the best judges of what kinds of books are suitable for their children. The proposal to have the city council make these decisions also fails to take into account the huge variations in parents' own preferences for their children; the idea of inappropriateness is a very subjective one. While some parents may agree with the city council's decisions, others may feel that the city council bans too many books, or even too few. In the end, parents must be responsible for knowing what books their children are reading and making their own decisions about those books' appropriateness within the context of their own values.

Additionally, whether certain books are appropriate or not, it's unrealistic to think that removing "objectionable" material from public libraries will keep young people from ever encountering that kind of material. Between television, the Internet, and interactions with friends and classmates, young people encounter all sorts of situations that may not necessarily be age appropriate. It's understandable that adults are concerned, but trying to keep potentially objectionable books away from young readers doesn't ensure that they won't encounter the language or situations used in those books elsewhere. To my mind, the best solution is for adults to encourage young people to analyze these situations thoughtfully, ask questions, and form their own opinions, rather than trying to shield them from the realities of the world.

Finally, although certain books contain elements that some people may find offensive or upsetting, those elements don't necessarily outweigh the literary merits of the books in question. One example of this is *Huckleberry Finn*, which all of the students at my school read as a requirement in English classes. It is widely recognized as a classic of American literature, even though it also includes portrayals of African-American characters that many people find offensive. The historical context that is necessary to understand *The Diary of Anne Frank* may be upsetting to younger readers, but the diary is still a significant historical document. Many books with controversial content are still worth reading, and a policy that screens out books based on their potential to offend may exclude important works of literature from libraries.

In conclusion, I believe that the power to make determinations about a book's appropriateness should lie not with a city council or a librarian, but with young readers and their parents. The role of a library is to make information available, not to make or enforce judgments about what its patrons should or should not be reading.

▶ IF YOU LEARNED ONLY FOUR THINGS IN THIS CHAPTER...

1. You should be familiar with the Kaplan Method for the ACT Essay: pause to know the prompt, plan, produce, and proofread.

2. The Writing test asks you to take a position on the issue in the prompt. The best essays knock down the opposing arguments and positively support the side you take.

3. Support your view with relevant and clearly organized evidence. Examples will come from your own experiences.

4. Pacing is crucial to getting all your ideas on paper. Be sure to leave yourself two or three minutes to proofread.

PART THREE

Ready, Set, Go

CHAPTER 17

Strategic Summaries

ENGLISH TEST

The English subject test:

- Is 45 minutes long
- Includes five passages, representing a range of writing styles and levels of formality
- Consists of 75 questions, divided among the five passages, which test many points of grammar, punctuation, writing mechanics, usage, and rhetorical skills by proposing ways of expressing information underlined at various points in the passages; we divide the questions strategically into three groups:

    1. **Economy questions**
    2. **Sense questions**
    3. **Technicality questions**

There are also some Nonstandard-Format questions that require different strategies, as outlined in Special Strategies below.

The questions **do *not* get harder** as you proceed through the section.

> ✓ **PERFECT SCORE TIP**
> If you haven't read the rest of this book, remember two important things about the ACT—there is no guessing penalty, and the questions do not get harder as you go in the section.

Mind-Set

- **When in doubt, take it out.** Make sure that everything is written as concisely as possible. If you think something doesn't belong in a sentence, it probably doesn't, so choose an answer that leaves it out.
- **Make it make sense.** Make sure that each answer you choose creates a sentence or paragraph that is logical. Consider sentence formation, making sure that you

use complete sentences and not fragments. When connection words are tested, think about how ideas relate logically. For an answer choice to be right in ACT English, it must create a sentence that is logically *and* grammatically correct.

- **Trust your eyes and ear.** Mistakes in grammar often sound or look bad to your ear. Trust that instinct. Don't choose the answer that "sounds fancy," choose the one that "sounds right." Review the Grammar Rules to Know in English Workout 3.

The Kaplan Method

For each question, ask yourself three things. Note that you may actually have your answer before getting to all three questions:

STEP 1: Read until you have enough information to identify the issue. Don't read the whole passage before attacking the questions; instead, take the English test one sentence or issue at a time. As you approach each question, ask yourself, "What issue is this question testing?"

STEP 2: Eliminate choices that do NOT address the issue. Read through each answer to see if it addresses the issue you identified in Step 1. If not, cross it out and move on. Try to eliminate as many answer choices as possible. For those you don't eliminate…

STEP 3: Plug in the remaining choices, and choose the one that is most correct, concise, and relevant. The ACT test makers want short, simple, easy-to-understand prose. Make sure the answer you choose sounds right.

> ✓ **PERFECT SCORE TIP**
> On the English section, remember to get used to recognizing common errors and trusting your ear.

Special Strategies

A few questions will require you to rearrange the words in a sentence, the sentences in a paragraph, or even the paragraphs in a passage. Others may ask questions about the meaning of all or part of the passage, or about its structure. Your approach to these Nonstandard-Format questions should be:

1. **Determine your task.** What are you being asked to do?
2. **Consider the passage as a whole.** Read the sentences around the numbered question. You need to know the various points made there. Most passages will have a well-defined theme, laid out in a logical way. Choose the answer that

expresses this theme or the arrangement of elements that best continues the logical "flow" of the passage.

3. **Predict your answer.** As in Reading, you should have an idea of what the answer is before looking at the choices.

Timing

We recommend that you *not* skip around in the English subject test. Although you can certainly use the usual Two-Pass Approach, you might prefer to go straight from beginning to end, answering all of the questions as you go. Unlike in other sections, in English you'll usually have at least a sense of what the right answer should be rather quickly. Remember, even the correct answer will start to sound wrong if you think about it too much!

Set your watch to 12:00 at the beginning of the subject test. Although you should go faster if you can, here's roughly where you should be at the following checkpoints.

12:09 . . . . . One passage finished and answers gridded in

12:18 . . . . . Two passages finished and answers gridded in

12:27 . . . . . Three passages finished and answers gridded in

12:36 . . . . . Four passages finished and answers gridded in

12:45 . . . . . Five passages finished and answers for the entire section gridded in

Note that you should do at least some work on all 75 English questions, and make sure you have at least a guess gridded in for every question when time is called.

When You're Running Out of Time

If you have no time left even to read the last few questions, choose the shortest answer for each one. Remember that OMIT, when it appears, counts as the shortest answer.

Scoring

Your performance on the English subject test will be averaged into your ACT Composite Score, weighted equally with your scores on the other three major subject tests. You will also receive:

- English subject score—from 1 to 36—for the entire English subject test
- Usage/Mechanics subscore—from 1 to 18—based on your performance on the questions testing grammar, usage, punctuation, and sentence structure

- Rhetorical Skills subscore—from 1 to 18—based on your performance on the questions testing strategy, organization, and style

- Writing subscore—from 2 to 12—based on the optional Writing test

- Combined English-Writing score—from 1 to 36—if you take the optional Writing test

MATH TEST

The Math subject test:

- Is 60 minutes long

- Consists of 60 questions, which test your grasp of pre-algebra, algebra, coordinate geometry, plane geometry, and trigonometry; we break down the questions into the following three strategic categories:

    1. **Diagram questions**
    2. **Story questions**
    3. **Concept questions**

The math concepts **do get more advanced** as you proceed through the section.

Mind-Set

- **The end justifies the means.** That means getting as many correct answers as quickly as possible. If that means doing straightforward questions in a straightforward way, that's fine. But many questions can be solved faster by using Kaplan Methods, such as backsolving and picking numbers.

- **Take time to save time.** It sounds paradoxical, but to go your fastest on the Math test, you've got to slow down. Never dive in headlong, wildly crunching numbers or manipulating equations without first giving the problem some thought.

- **When in doubt, shake it up.** ACT Math questions are not always what they seem at first glance. Sometimes all you need is a new perspective to break through the disguise.

GO ONLINE
Find the Kaplan Method for approaching each section of the ACT on your downloadable study sheet.

The Kaplan Method

STEP 1: What is the question? First, focus on the question stem and make sure you understand the problem. Underlining what the question is asking might help you. If it is a word problem and you are completely lost, try taking notes. You will pull out the information that is necessary to solve the problem. Think to yourself: "What kind of problem is this? What am I looking for? What am I given?"

STEP 2: What information am I given? You're given information in the question stem and in the answer choices. Pay attention to the format of these to figure out the best approach to the question.

STEP 3: What can I do with the information?

- Think for a moment and decide on a plan of attack.

- **Straightforward math.** Do you know how to solve the problem using your math knowledge? Go for it!

- **Picking numbers.** Are there variables in the answer choices? If so, is there a way to pick numbers for the variable to help you get to the right answer?

- **Backsolving.** Are there numbers in the answer choices? What is the question asking for? (That is what the numbers in the answer choices represent.) Is there a way to use the answer choices to get to the right answer?

- **Guess strategically.** If you're really not sure, you can guess—you don't lose points for incorrect answers on the ACT. Try to eliminate as many incorrect choices as you can before guessing, and mark the question in your booklet so you can return to it at the end of the Math test and try again.

STEP 4: Am I finished? Before you select an answer, reread the question. Are you answering the right question? Did you miss any steps? Most importantly, does it match one of the answer choices? If so, circle the answer in your test book and fill in the appropriate bubble on your answer grid. If you are stuck, circle the problem in your test book and move on to get all your "easy" points first! Come back to this problem after you have gone through the entire test.

Special Strategies

We offer several recommendations for what to do when you get stuck. If after a few moments of thought you find you still can't come up with a reasonable way of doing the problem, try one of these techniques:

- **Restate.** When you get stuck, try looking at the problem from a different angle. Try rearranging the numbers, changing decimals to fractions, fractions to decimals, multiplying out numbers, factoring problems, redrawing a diagram, or anything that might help you to look at the problem a bit differently.

- **Remove the disguise.** Find out what the question is really asking—it might not be what the problem appears to ask at first. See Math Workout 2 for some examples!

- **Try eyeballing.** Even though the directions warn you that diagrams are "not necessarily" drawn to scale, eyeballing is a surprisingly effective guessing strategy. Unless a problem says "Note: Not drawn to scale," you can assume that it is drawn to scale! Use that to help you eliminate answer choices that you know are wrong!

> ✓ **PERFECT SCORE TIP**
> Remember that the textbook way to solve a problem is not always the best in Math. Try to simplify problems by plugging in numbers for variables and restating difficult problems.

Timing

Remember the Two-Pass Approach. **Spend about 45 minutes on your first pass through the Math subject test: Do the easier questions, guess on the questions you know you'll never get, and mark the tough ones that you'll want to come back to.** Spend the last 15 minutes picking up those questions that you skipped on the first pass.

We recommend that you grid your answers at the end of every page or two. In the last five minutes or so, start gridding your answers one by one. And make sure that you have an answer (even if it's a blind guess) gridded for every question by the time the test is over.

Don't worry if you have to guess on a lot of the Math questions. You can miss a lot of questions on the subject test and still get a great score. **Remember that the average ACT test taker gets fewer than half the Math questions right!**

When You're Running Out of Time

If at some point you realize you have more questions left than you have time for, be willing to skip around, looking for questions you understand right away. Pick your spots. Concentrate on the questions you have the best chance of correctly answering. Just be sure to grid an answer—even if it's just a wild guess—for every question.

Scoring

Your performance on the Math subject test will be averaged into your ACT Composite Score, equally weighted with your scores on the other three major subject tests. You will also receive:

- Math subject score—from 1 to 36—for the entire Math subject test
- Pre-Algebra/Elementary Algebra subscore—from 1 to 18
- Intermediate Algebra/Coordinate Geometry subscore—from 1 to 18
- Plane Geometry/Trigonometry subscore—from 1 to 18

READING TEST

The Reading subject test:

- Is 35 minutes long
- Includes four passages:
  - Three Nonfiction passages (one each in Social Science, Humanities, and Natural Science, though there is no significant difference among them except subject matter)
  - One Prose Fiction passage (an excerpt from a short story or novel)
- Consists of 40 questions, 10 on each passage, which include:
  - Detail questions
    - Specific Information
    - Vocab-in-Context
    - Function (Why)
  - Inference questions
  - Big Picture questions

The questions do *not* get harder as you go through the section.

> ☑ **PERFECT SCORE TIP**
> On the Reading section, remember to be able to summarize each paragraph and passage after prereading so you have a road map to help you with answering questions.

Mind-Set

- **Know where the passage is going.** Read the passages actively, and pay attention to structural clues and key words and sentences. The easiest way to do this is to create a road map.

- **Conquer the questions.** Look up the answers; don't be tempted by the choices.

The Kaplan Method

STEP 1: Actively read the passage, taking notes as you go. Try to understand the gist of the passage. Get a sense of the overall structure of the passage. Create a road map to make referring back easier.

STEP 2: Examine the question stem, looking for clues. Understand the question first, without looking at the answer choices that are offered. Remember that many wrong choices are designed to mislead test takers who just jump past the question stem and start comparing choices to each other.

STEP 3: Predict the answer and select the choice that best matches your prediction. Always refer to the passage before answering the question. If the question includes line references, read around them. Only then look at the choices. Make sure your answer matches the passage in meaning.

Answer the question in your own words before looking at the choices and match your answer with one of the choices. Having an answer in mind will keep you from falling for tempting but wrong answers—predict before you peek!

> **EXPERT TUTOR TIP**
> Once you've finished reading a passage and its questions, put it out of your mind. There's no connection at all between passages, so don't carry your stress or doubt to the next one. Approach each passage as if it were the only one. Stay active and confident—you're doing great!

Special Strategies

THE PROSE FICTION PASSAGE

When you preread the passage, pay attention to the characters, especially the main character. Read between the lines to determine unspoken emotions and attitudes. Ask yourself:

- **Who are these people?** What are they like? How do the characters relate to each other?

- **What is their state of mind?** Are they angry, sad, reflective, excited?

- **What's going on?** What's happening on the surface? What's happening beneath the surface?

- **What is the author's attitude toward the characters?** What words indicate a particular tone? Do any phrases suggest the author is either approving of or critical of one of the characters?

NONFICTION PASSAGES

Don't be thrown by unfamiliar vocabulary or topics. The Natural Science passage may take you into strange territory. Everything you need to know will be covered in the passage. If you find a difficult term, odds are the definition will be given to you in context (or else it simply might not matter what the word means). You can still get lots of questions right, even if you don't fully understand the passage. Remember, you can find all the answers in the passage.

Timing

You might want to take a few seconds at the beginning of the subject test to page through the passages, gauging the difficulty of each one. At first glance, you may wish to skip an entire passage if it seems very difficult.

We recommend that you treat each passage and its questions as a block. Take two passes through each block before moving on to the next. (Skip around if you like, but watch your answer grid if you do!) Get the easy questions on the first pass through and save the tougher ones for the second pass. Just make sure to keep track of time.

Set your watch to 12:00 at the beginning of the subject test. Although you should go faster if you can, here's roughly where you should be at the following checkpoints:

12:09 . . . . . One passage finished and answers gridded in

12:18 . . . . . Two passages finished and answers gridded in

12:27 . . . . . Three passages finished and answers gridded in

12:35 . . . . . Four passages finished and answers for entire section gridded in

Take about 30 seconds (average) per question. Some questions take more time than others (ones with Roman numerals in them and ones that have EXCEPT are examples). If you feel the need to spend a lot of time to get the right answer, don't. Either guess, or skip and come back. (Don't forget to do so.)

Do the best you can to finish all four passages, but don't panic if you don't. Develop a fallback position to use, if you fall short (see the tips that follow). If, during practice, you often don't get to *many* of the questions, approach all the passages this way:

1. **Learn to spot the easier questions and answer these quickly.**
2. **Address the ones you might be able to get with more research.**
3. **Guess randomly on the ones you would need lots of time for.**

Note: If you are a slow reader and have trouble with the ABCs of Active Reading, this method may help.

Don't panic if you can't finish all four passages. Make sure you do a good job on at least three passages—and remember to grid answers (even if they're blind guesses) for all questions by the end. Even if you try all four passages, you probably won't really work on all 40 questions. For many questions, you'll just have to guess. Just make sure you guess on the tough ones and actually work on the easy ones!

When You're Running Out of Time

If you have less than five minutes left for the last passage, do the following:

1. **Look for questions with specific line references and do them.**
2. **Refer to the cited location in the passage and answer the question as best you can, based on what you see there.**
3. **Make sure you have gridded in an answer for every question before time is called.**

Scoring

Your performance on the Reading subject test will be averaged into your ACT Composite Score, weighted equally with your scores on the other three major subject tests. You will also receive:

- Reading subject score—from 1 to 36—for the entire Reading subject test
- Social Science/Sciences subscore—from 1 to 18—based on your performance on the nonfiction passages drawn from Social Studies and Natural Sciences
- Arts/Literature subscore—from 1 to 18—based on your performance on the Non-fiction passage (drawn from the Humanities) and on the Prose Fiction passage

SCIENCE TEST

The Science subject test:

- Is 35 minutes long
- Includes seven passages or sets of scientific information, involving graphs, tables, and research summaries, and typically, one of the passages involves two conflicting viewpoints on a single scientific issue
- Consists of 40 questions, divided among the seven passages. We divide the questions strategically into three categories:

    1. **Figure Interpretation questions**
    2. **Patterns questions**
    3. **Scientific Reasoning questions**

The questions **do *not* get harder** as you proceed through the section.

Mind-Set

- **Look for patterns.** Usually, the exact data contained in Science passages is not as important as are changes in the data. Look for extremes (maximums and minimums), critical points (points of change), and variation (direct and inverse).
- **Know your direction.** There are two kinds of scientific reasoning—general-to-specific and specific-to-general. **Always** be aware of when scientists are inferring a specific case from a general rule and when they are using specific data to form a (general) hypothesis.
- **Refer, don't remember.** Don't even think of trying to remember data. It's **always** there, right on the page, for you to refer to when needed.

The Kaplan Method

STEP 1: Map the passage, identifying and marking the purpose, method, and results of the experiment. What is being researched? What are the scientists varying? What are the scientists keeping constant? Don't get bogged down in the details, and don't worry about understanding everything.

STEP 2: Scan figures, identifying variables and patterns. You don't need to study these closely, just note what each figure is telling you about the purpose, methods, or results of the experiment. That way you'll know where to look when answering the questions.

Consider the question stem. Make sure you understand exactly what the question is asking. Get a sense of what the answer should be without looking at the choices, many of which are designed to mislead you if you're indecisive.

STEP 3: Find support for the answer in the passage. Always refer back to the passage before looking at the choices and selecting one. Make sure you read charts and graphs accurately and that you do not confuse different kinds of units. It helps to answer the question in your own words. Don't rely too much on your knowledge of science. Match your answer with one of the choices.

> ✓ **PERFECT SCORE TIP**
> Remember that you do not have to understand all the science in the Science section to do well, so don't let difficult concepts throw you.

Special Strategies

READING TABLES AND GRAPHS

When reading tables and graphs, you should ask yourself:

- What does the figure show?
- What are the units of measurement?
- What is the pattern in the data?

EXPERIMENTS

Remember how experiments work. There is typically (though not always) a control group plus an experimental group or groups. In a well-designed experiment, the only difference between the groups will be a variation in the factor that's being tested. Ask yourself:

- What's the factor that's being varied?
- What's the control group, if any?
- What do the results show? What differences exist between the results for one group and those for another?

CONFLICTING VIEWPOINTS PASSAGE

Spend a little more time than usual on the prereading step of this passage. Focus on the two points of view. What are the scientists arguing about? What do they agree on, if anything? What do they differ on? Identify the following for each scientist:

- **Basic theory statement** (usually the first sentence of each scientist's presentation)
- **Major pieces of data behind the theory** (keeping in mind whether each supports the scientist's own theory or weakens the opposing scientist's theory)

Timing

Some Science passages are a lot harder than others, and they're not arranged in order of difficulty, so you might want to **take a few seconds at the beginning of the subject test to page through the passages, gauging the difficulty of each one.** You may wish to skip an entire passage if it seems very difficult (but remember that a very difficult passage may have very easy questions).

As in Reading, treat each passage and its questions as a block, taking two passes through each block before moving on to the next. Get the easy questions on the first pass through and save the tougher ones for the second pass. Some questions will probably be impossible for you to answer; take an educated guess on these.

Set your watch to 12:00 at the beginning of the subject test. Although you should go faster if you can, here's where you should be at the following checkpoints:

12:05 . . . . . One passage finished and answers gridded in

12:10 . . . . . Two passages finished and answers gridded in

12:15 . . . . . Three passages finished and answers gridded in

12:20 . . . . . Four passages finished and answers gridded in

12:25 . . . . . Five passages finished and answers gridded in

12:30 . . . . . Six passages finished and answers gridded in

12:35 . . . . . Seven passages finished and answers for the entire section gridded in

Don't spend time agonizing over specific questions. Avoid thinking long and hard about the answer choices. If you've spent a minute or so on a question and don't seem to be making any headway, make your best guess and move on.

Don't panic if you can't finish all seven passages, but try to do a good job on at least five of them. Make sure you remember to grid answers (even if they're blind guesses) for all questions by the end.

When You're Running Out of Time

If you have fewer than three minutes left for the last passage, do the following:

1. **Look for questions that refer to specific experiments or to specific graphs or tables.**
2. **Refer to the cited location in the passage and answer the question as best you can, based on what you see there.**
3. **Make sure you have gridded in an answer for every question before time is called.**

Scoring

Your performance on the Science subject test will be averaged into your ACT Composite Score, weighted equally with your scores on the other three major subject tests. You will also receive:

- A Science subject score—from 1 to 36—for the entire Science subject test

Unlike the other three subject scores, the Science score is not divided into subscores.

WRITING TEST

The Writing test:

- Is optional (check with the schools to which you are applying and with your guidance counselor about whether you should take the test)
- Is 30 minutes long
- Includes just one prompt about which you must write an essay that must:
  - State a point of view on the issue
  - Support the point of view with concrete, relevant examples
  - Provide a clear and coherent argument, which includes a discussion of the opposite point of view

Mind-Set

Don't wait until test day to think of examples you can use to support your ideas. Regardless of what question is raised in the prompt, you will draw your support from the things you know best and are most comfortable writing about—things that you can describe in concrete detail.

Refresh your memory about school subjects, current events, personal experiences, and activities—anything. By doing so, you strengthen mental connections to those ideas and details—that will make it easier to connect to the right examples on test day.

The Kaplan Method

1. **Prompt.** Read about the issue and take a position on it. There is no right or wrong answer, but make sure you address the issue. In other words, answer the question.

2. **Plan.** Take up to six or seven minutes to plan the essay before you write. Focus on what kinds of reasoning and examples you can use to support your position. If you find you have more examples for a position different from the one you thought you would take, *change your position*.

3. **Produce.** Write your draft, sticking closely to your plan. The essay should have three to five well-developed paragraphs with topic sentences and supporting details. Include an introductory paragraph stating your position and a concluding paragraph. Write neatly.

4. **Proofread.** Always leave yourself two minutes to review your work—the time spent will definitely pay off. Very few of us can avoid the occasional confused sentence or omitted word when we write under pressure. Quickly review your essay to be sure your ideas are clearly stated.

> ✔ **PERFECT SCORE TIP**
> Remember to write a "textbook essay" with a clear structure, topic sentences, well-developed examples, and sentence variation.

Helpful Strategies

You must be very focused in order to write a complete, coherent essay in 30 minutes. During the planning stage, use one of the two following strategies:

1. **Draw a "T" and list your argument on either side of it** (your stance on one side and your arguments addressing the other side on the other). See page 262. This method will help you decide if you have enough to back up your stance. You may find you need to take the opposite point of view!

   OR

2. **List the topic of each paragraph** you plan to write, noting the segments of the argument that you want to make.

Stick to the plan as you write the essay. Don't change the plan in midstream if another idea suddenly comes to you; it might derail the essay. Keep your focus on the issue and don't digress.

Make the structure of your essay very easy for the reader to see. Have an introductory paragraph, two or three middle paragraphs, each focused on one example or bit of evidence, and a concluding paragraph.

Write neatly. Graders will give you a poor grade if it's hard to decipher. If your handwriting is a problem, print.

Timing

With only 30 minutes, efficient use of time is critical. Divide your time as follows:

6–7 minutes—Read the prompt and plan the essay.

20–21 minutes—Draft the essay, sticking to the plan.

3 minutes—Proofread and correct any errors.

When You're Running Out of Time

Running out of time doesn't mean only that you'll have to guess on the last few questions as it does on the other tests; it means your essay won't be as complete and coherent as it should be. If you do start running out of time, leave out one of your example paragraphs and go on to the concluding paragraph. Even when you're rushed, try to allow one to two minutes to proofread for errors that affect clarity.

Scoring

Two trained readers read and score each of your essays on a scale of 1–6; then those scores are added together to arrive at your Writing subscore (from 2–12). If there's a difference of more than a point between the two readers' scores, your essay will be read by a third reader. Readers evaluate the essays holistically, judging the overall quality of each, not assigning separate scores for specific elements like grammar or organization.

A combined English-Writing score will also be recorded. Two-thirds of this score is based on your English score and one-third is based on your Writing subscore. The combined English-Writing score does not count toward your composite score.

Statistically speaking, there will be few essays that score 12 out of 12. If each grader gives your essay a 4 or 5 (making your subscore 8 or 10), that will place you at the upper range of those taking the exam.

CHAPTER 18

Last-Minute Tips

Is it starting to feel like your whole life is a buildup to the ACT? You've known about it for years, you've worried about it for months, and now you've spent at least a few hours in solid preparation for it. As the test gets closer, you may find your anxiety is on the rise. Don't worry. After the preparation you've received from this book, you're in good shape for test day.

 PERFECT SCORE TIP
If it is close to the test and you know there is one specific section you are not prepared for, do as many practice problems from that section as possible. Practice really does bring you closer to perfection.

To calm any pretest jitters you may have (and assuming you've left yourself at least some breathing time before your ACT), let's go over a few last-minute strategies for the few days before and after the test.

EXPERT TUTOR TIP
If you have less than two weeks to prep for the ACT, read this chapter. It tells you how to use your time wisely before, during, and after the test.

THREE DAYS BEFORE THE TEST

- If you haven't already done so, take one of the full-length Practice Tests in this book under timed conditions. If you have already worked through all the tests in the book, try an actual published ACT (your guidance counselor might have one). You can also find practice questions on the official ACT website at www. actstudent.org.
- Try to use all of the techniques and tips you've learned in this book. Take control. Approach the test strategically and confidently.

WARNING: Don't take a full practice ACT unless you have at least 48 hours left before the test! Doing so will probably exhaust you, hurting your scoring potential on the actual test! You wouldn't run a marathon the day before the real thing, would you?

TWO DAYS BEFORE THE TEST

- **Go over the results of your Practice Test.** Don't worry too much about your score or whether you got a specific question right or wrong. Remember—the Practice Test doesn't count. But do examine your performance on specific questions with an eye to how you might get through each one faster and with greater accuracy on the actual test to come.

- **After reviewing your test, look over the Strategic Summaries.** If you feel a little shaky about any of the areas mentioned, quickly read the relevant workouts.

- **This is the last study day—review a couple of the more difficult principles we've covered, do a few more practice problems, and call it quits.** It doesn't pay to make yourself crazy right before the test. Besides, you've prepared. You'll do well.

> **EXPERT TUTOR TIP**
> Guard against being easily distracted during the test—by traffic outside or a sniffling neighbor. Try practicing in a coffee shop or with the door to your room open.

THE DAY BEFORE THE TEST

- **Don't study.**
- **Get together an "ACT survival kit" containing the following items:**
  - Watch (preferably digital)
  - At least three sharpened No. 2 pencils
  - Pencil sharpener
  - Two erasers
  - Photo ID card (if you're not taking the test at your high school, make sure your ID is official)
  - An approved calculator
  - Your admission ticket
  - Snack and a bottle of water—there's a break, and you'll probably get hungry
  - Confidence!

- **Know exactly where you're going and how you're getting there.** It's a good idea to visit your test center sometime before test day so that you know what to expect on the big day.

✔ **PERFECT SCORE TIP**
Make sure you prepare the things you will need the day before. It is not worth getting stressed the morning of because you cannot find your calculator or pencils.

- **Relax!** Read a good book, take a bubble bath, watch TV. Exercise can be a good idea early in the afternoon. Working out makes it easier to sleep when you're nervous, and it also makes many people feel better. Of course, don't work so hard that you can't get up the next day!

✔ **PERFECT SCORE TIP**
You have worked too hard for this test to give it all up by going out the night before. Relax the night before and get a good night's sleep so you are ready for the next morning.

- **Get a good night's sleep.** Go to bed early and allow for some extra time to get ready in the morning.

THE MORNING OF THE TEST

- **Eat breakfast.** Protein is brain food, but don't eat anything too heavy or greasy. Don't drink a lot of coffee if you're not used to it; bathroom breaks cut into your time, and too much caffeine—or any other kind of drug—is a bad idea.

✔ **PERFECT SCORE TIP**
Be sure to bring food for breaks, and eat a sufficient breakfast. I find foods such as peanut butter and raisins give me the lasting energy needed for such a grueling test. Be careful of eating sugar, as it only gives short-term energy.

- **Dress in layers** so that you can adjust to the temperature of the test room.
- **Read something.** Warm up your brain with a newspaper or a magazine. Don't let the ACT be the first thing you read that day.
- **Be sure to get there early.** Allow yourself extra time for traffic, mass-transit delays, and any other possible problems.
- **If you can, go to the test with a friend** (even if he or she isn't taking the test). It's nice to have somebody supporting you right up to the last minute.

DURING THE TEST

- **Don't get rattled.** If you find your confidence slipping, remind yourself how well you've prepared. You've followed the keys to ACT success, and you have practiced. You know the test; you know the strategies; you know the material tested. You're in great shape, as long as you relax!

- **Even if something goes really wrong, don't panic.** If the test booklet is defective—two pages are stuck together or the ink has run—try to stay calm. Raise your hand, and tell the proctor you need a new book. If you accidentally misgrid your answer page or put the answers in the wrong section, again, don't panic. Raise your hand, and tell the proctor. He or she might be able to arrange for you to regrid your test after it's over, when it won't cost you any time.

> ✓ **PERFECT SCORE TIP**
> Calm down during the test. Take a deep breath if you are getting stressed, and remember that you are prepared and have an arsenal of tools to help increase your chances of answering even the toughest problems.

Good luck! With all of your practice and Kaplan's strategies under your belt, we know you'll do great on the ACT.

AFTER THE TEST

Once the test is over, put it out of your mind. If you don't plan to take the ACT again, shelve this book and start thinking about more interesting things.

You might walk out of the ACT thinking that you blew it. This is a normal reaction. Lots of people—even the highest scorers—feel that way. You tend to remember the questions that stumped you, not the many that you knew. If you're really concerned, call us for advice. Also call us if you had any problems with your test experience—a proctor who called time early, a testing room whose temperature hovered just below freezing. We'll do everything we can to make sure that your rights as a test taker are preserved!

However, we're positive that you performed well and scored your best on the exam because you followed our ACT Premier Program. Be confident that you were prepared, and celebrate in the fact that the ACT is a distant memory.

If you want more help or just want to know more about the ACT, college admissions, or Kaplan prep courses for the ACT, give us a call at 800-KAP-TEST or visit us at www.kaptest.com. We're here to answer your questions and to help you in any way we can. Also, be sure to return one last time to your online syllabus and complete our survey. We're only as good as our successful students!

> ☑ **PERFECT SCORE TIP**
> Congratulations! You're done! Schedule something fun to do after the test as a reward for your hard work—and don't fret about score reports. Don't beat yourself up if you don't think you did your best.

PART FOUR

Practice Test and Explanations

Practice Test

HOW TO TAKE THIS PRACTICE TESTS

This Practice Test is a Kaplan-created test, similar to the actual ACT test. Before taking the Practice Test, find a quiet room where you can work uninterrupted for three and a half hours. Make sure you have a comfortable desk, your calculator, and several No. 2 pencils. Use the answer sheet to record your answers. Once you start the Practice Test, don't stop until you've finished. Remember: You can review any questions within a section, but you may not jump from one section to another.

You'll find the answers and explanations to the test questions immediately following the test.

ACT Practice Test
ANSWER SHEET

ENGLISH TEST

1. (A)(B)(C)(D)   11. (A)(B)(C)(D)   21. (A)(B)(C)(D)   31. (A)(B)(C)(D)   41. (A)(B)(C)(D)   51. (A)(B)(C)(D)   61. (A)(B)(C)(D)   71. (A)(B)(C)(D)
2. (F)(G)(H)(J)   12. (F)(G)(H)(J)   22. (F)(G)(H)(J)   32. (F)(G)(H)(J)   42. (F)(G)(H)(J)   52. (F)(G)(H)(J)   62. (F)(G)(H)(J)   72. (F)(G)(H)(J)
3. (A)(B)(C)(D)   13. (A)(B)(C)(D)   23. (A)(B)(C)(D)   33. (A)(B)(C)(D)   43. (A)(B)(C)(D)   53. (A)(B)(C)(D)   63. (A)(B)(C)(D)   73. (A)(B)(C)(D)
4. (F)(G)(H)(J)   14. (F)(G)(H)(J)   24. (F)(G)(H)(J)   34. (F)(G)(H)(J)   44. (F)(G)(H)(J)   54. (F)(G)(H)(J)   64. (F)(G)(H)(J)   74. (F)(G)(H)(J)
5. (A)(B)(C)(D)   15. (A)(B)(C)(D)   25. (A)(B)(C)(D)   35. (A)(B)(C)(D)   45. (A)(B)(C)(D)   55. (A)(B)(C)(D)   65. (A)(B)(C)(D)   75. (A)(B)(C)(D)
6. (F)(G)(H)(J)   16. (F)(G)(H)(J)   26. (F)(G)(H)(J)   36. (F)(G)(H)(J)   46. (F)(G)(H)(J)   56. (F)(G)(H)(J)   66. (F)(G)(H)(J)
7. (A)(B)(C)(D)   17. (A)(B)(C)(D)   27. (A)(B)(C)(D)   37. (A)(B)(C)(D)   47. (A)(B)(C)(D)   57. (A)(B)(C)(D)   67. (A)(B)(C)(D)
8. (F)(G)(H)(J)   18. (F)(G)(H)(J)   28. (F)(G)(H)(J)   38. (F)(G)(H)(J)   48. (F)(G)(H)(J)   58. (F)(G)(H)(J)   68. (F)(G)(H)(J)
9. (A)(B)(C)(D)   19. (A)(B)(C)(D)   29. (A)(B)(C)(D)   39. (A)(B)(C)(D)   49. (A)(B)(C)(D)   59. (A)(B)(C)(D)   69. (A)(B)(C)(D)
10. (F)(G)(H)(J)   20. (F)(G)(H)(J)   30. (F)(G)(H)(J)   40. (F)(G)(H)(J)   50. (F)(G)(H)(J)   60. (F)(G)(H)(J)   70. (F)(G)(H)(J)

MATH TEST

1. (A)(B)(C)(D)(E)   11. (A)(B)(C)(D)(E)   21. (A)(B)(C)(D)(E)   31. (A)(B)(C)(D)(E)   41. (A)(B)(C)(D)(E)   51. (A)(B)(C)(D)(E)
2. (F)(G)(H)(J)(K)   12. (F)(G)(H)(J)(K)   22. (F)(G)(H)(J)(K)   32. (F)(G)(H)(J)(K)   42. (F)(G)(H)(J)(K)   52. (F)(G)(H)(J)(K)
3. (A)(B)(C)(D)(E)   13. (A)(B)(C)(D)(E)   23. (A)(B)(C)(D)(E)   33. (A)(B)(C)(D)(E)   43. (A)(B)(C)(D)(E)   53. (A)(B)(C)(D)(E)
4. (F)(G)(H)(J)(K)   14. (F)(G)(H)(J)(K)   24. (F)(G)(H)(J)(K)   34. (F)(G)(H)(J)(K)   44. (F)(G)(H)(J)(K)   54. (F)(G)(H)(J)(K)
5. (A)(B)(C)(D)(E)   15. (A)(B)(C)(D)(E)   25. (A)(B)(C)(D)(E)   35. (A)(B)(C)(D)(E)   45. (A)(B)(C)(D)(E)   55. (A)(B)(C)(D)(E)
6. (F)(G)(H)(J)(K)   16. (F)(G)(H)(J)(K)   26. (F)(G)(H)(J)(K)   36. (F)(G)(H)(J)(K)   46. (F)(G)(H)(J)(K)   56. (F)(G)(H)(J)(K)
7. (A)(B)(C)(D)(E)   17. (A)(B)(C)(D)(E)   27. (A)(B)(C)(D)(E)   37. (A)(B)(C)(D)(E)   47. (A)(B)(C)(D)(E)   57. (A)(B)(C)(D)(E)
8. (F)(G)(H)(J)(K)   18. (F)(G)(H)(J)(K)   28. (F)(G)(H)(J)(K)   38. (F)(G)(H)(J)(K)   48. (F)(G)(H)(J)(K)   58. (F)(G)(H)(J)(K)
9. (A)(B)(C)(D)(E)   19. (A)(B)(C)(D)(E)   29. (A)(B)(C)(D)(E)   39. (A)(B)(C)(D)(E)   49. (A)(B)(C)(D)(E)   59. (A)(B)(C)(D)(E)
10. (F)(G)(H)(J)(K)   20. (F)(G)(H)(J)(K)   30. (F)(G)(H)(J)(K)   40. (F)(G)(H)(J)(K)   50. (F)(G)(H)(J)(K)   60. (F)(G)(H)(J)(K)

READING TEST

1. (A)(B)(C)(D)   6. (F)(G)(H)(J)   11. (A)(B)(C)(D)   16. (F)(G)(H)(J)   21. (A)(B)(C)(D)   26. (F)(G)(H)(J)   31. (A)(B)(C)(D)   36. (F)(G)(H)(J)
2. (F)(G)(H)(J)   7. (A)(B)(C)(D)   12. (F)(G)(H)(J)   17. (A)(B)(C)(D)   22. (F)(G)(H)(J)   27. (A)(B)(C)(D)   32. (F)(G)(H)(J)   37. (A)(B)(C)(D)
3. (A)(B)(C)(D)   8. (F)(G)(H)(J)   13. (A)(B)(C)(D)   18. (F)(G)(H)(J)   23. (A)(B)(C)(D)   28. (F)(G)(H)(J)   33. (A)(B)(C)(D)   38. (F)(G)(H)(J)
4. (F)(G)(H)(J)   9. (A)(B)(C)(D)   14. (F)(G)(H)(J)   19. (A)(B)(C)(D)   24. (F)(G)(H)(J)   29. (A)(B)(C)(D)   34. (F)(G)(H)(J)   39. (A)(B)(C)(D)
5. (A)(B)(C)(D)   10. (F)(G)(H)(J)   15. (A)(B)(C)(D)   20. (F)(G)(H)(J)   25. (A)(B)(C)(D)   30. (F)(G)(H)(J)   35. (A)(B)(C)(D)   40. (F)(G)(H)(J)

SCIENCE TEST

1. (A)(B)(C)(D)   6. (F)(G)(H)(J)   11. (A)(B)(C)(D)   16. (F)(G)(H)(J)   21. (A)(B)(C)(D)   26. (F)(G)(H)(J)   31. (A)(B)(C)(D)   36. (F)(G)(H)(J)
2. (F)(G)(H)(J)   7. (A)(B)(C)(D)   12. (F)(G)(H)(J)   17. (A)(B)(C)(D)   22. (F)(G)(H)(J)   27. (A)(B)(C)(D)   32. (F)(G)(H)(J)   37. (A)(B)(C)(D)
3. (A)(B)(C)(D)   8. (F)(G)(H)(J)   13. (A)(B)(C)(D)   18. (F)(G)(H)(J)   23. (A)(B)(C)(D)   28. (F)(G)(H)(J)   33. (A)(B)(C)(D)   38. (F)(G)(H)(J)
4. (F)(G)(H)(J)   9. (A)(B)(C)(D)   14. (F)(G)(H)(J)   19. (A)(B)(C)(D)   24. (F)(G)(H)(J)   29. (A)(B)(C)(D)   34. (F)(G)(H)(J)   39. (A)(B)(C)(D)
5. (A)(B)(C)(D)   10. (F)(G)(H)(J)   15. (A)(B)(C)(D)   20. (F)(G)(H)(J)   25. (A)(B)(C)(D)   30. (F)(G)(H)(J)   35. (A)(B)(C)(D)   40. (F)(G)(H)(J)

ENGLISH TEST

45 Minutes—75 Questions

Directions: In the following five passages, certain words and phrases are underlined and numbered. In the right-hand column are alternatives for each underlined portion. Select the one that best conveys the idea, creates the most grammatically correct sentence, or is the most consistent with the style and tone of the passage. If you decide that the original version is best, select NO CHANGE. You may also find questions that ask about the entire passage or a section of the passage. These questions will correspond to small numbered boxes in the text. For these questions, decide which choice best accomplishes the purpose set out in the question stem. After you've selected the best choice, fill in the corresponding oval in your Answer Grid. For some questions, you'll need to read the context in order to answer correctly. Be sure to read until you have enough information to determine the correct answer choice.

You will also find questions about a section of the passage or about the passage as a whole. These questions do not refer to an underlined portion of the passage, but rather are identified by a number or numbers in a box.

For each question, choose the alternative you consider best and fill in the corresponding oval on your answer document. Read each passage through once before you begin to answer the questions that accompany it. For many of the questions, you must read several sentences beyond the question to determine the answer. Be sure that you have read enough ahead each time you choose an alternative.

Passage I

ORIGINS OF URBAN LEGENDS

[1]

Since primitive times, societies have created,
1

and told legends. Even before the development
1

of written language, cultures would orally pass

down these popular stories.

1. A. NO CHANGE
   B. created then subsequently told
   C. created and told
   D. created, and told original

[2]

2 These stories served the dual purpose of entertaining audiences and of transmitting values

2. Suppose that the author wants to insert a sentence here to describe the different kinds of oral stories told by these societies. Which of the following sentences would best serve that purpose?

   F. These myths and tales varied in substance, from the humorous to the heroic.

   G. These myths and tales were often recited by paid storytellers.

   H. Unfortunately, no recording of the original myths and tales exists.

   J. Sometimes it took several evenings for the full story to be recited.

and beliefs from generation to generation. Indeed
                                         3
today we have many more permanent ways of handing down our beliefs to future generations, we continue to create and tell legends. In our technological society, a new form of folktale has emerged: the urban legend.
           4

3. A. NO CHANGE

   B. However,

   C. Indeed,

   D. Although

[3]

Urban legends are stories we all have heard; they are supposed to have really happened, but are never verifiable however. It seems that
                        5
the people involved can never be found. Researchers of the urban legend call the elusive participant in such supposed "real-life" events a FOAF—a Friend of a Friend.

4. F. NO CHANGE

   G. it is called the

   H. it being the

   J. known as the

5. A. NO CHANGE

   B. verifiable, however.

   C. verifiable, furthermore.

   D. verifiable.

[4]

Urban legends have some characteristic features. They are often humorous in nature

GO ON TO THE NEXT PAGE

with a surprise ending and a conclusion. One
                          ———————————————
                                  6
such legend is the tale of the hunter who was

returning home from an unsuccessful hunting

trip. On his way home, he accidentally hit and

killed a deer on a deserted highway. Even though

he knew it was illegal, he decided to keep the

deer, and he loads it in the back of his station
              ——————
                 7
wagon. As the hunter continued driving, the deer,

he was only temporarily knocked unconscious by
—————
  8
the car, woke up and began thrashing around.

The hunter panicked, stopped the car, ran to

the ditch, and watched the enraged deer destroy

his car.

[5]

One legend involves alligators in the sewer

systems of major metropolitan areas. According

to the story, before alligators were a protected

species, people vacationing in Florida purchased
——————————
     9
baby alligators to take home as souvenirs.

Between 1930 and 1940, nearly a million alligators
——————————————————————————————————————
                        10
in Florida were killed for the value of their skin,
——
                        10
used to make expensive leather products such as
——
                       10
boots and wallets. After the novelty of having a
————————————————
        10
pet alligator wore off, many people flushed their

baby souvenirs down toilets. Legend has it that

6. F. NO CHANGE
   G. ending.
   H. ending, which is a conclusion.
   J. ending or conclusion.

7. A. NO CHANGE
   B. loaded it in
   C. is loading it in
   D. had loaded it in

8. F. NO CHANGE
   G. which being
   H. that is
   J. which was

9. A. NO CHANGE
   B. species; people
   C. species. People
   D. species people

10. F. NO CHANGE
    G. Because their skin is used to make
       expensive leather products such as
       boots and wallets, nearly a million
       alligators in Florida were killed
       between 1930 and 1940.
    H. Killed between 1930 and 1940, the
       skin of nearly a million alligators
       from Florida was used to make
       expensive leather products such as
       boots and wallets.
    J. OMIT the underlined portion.

GO ON TO THE NEXT PAGE ▶

the baby alligators found a perfect growing and breeding environment in city sewer systems, where they thrive to this day on the ample supply of rats.

[6]

In addition to urban legends that are told from friend to friend, a growing number of urban legends are passed along through the Internet and email. One of the more popular stories are about a woman who was unwittingly charged
11
$100 for a cookie recipe she requested at an upscale restaurant. To get her money's worth,

11. A. NO CHANGE
     B. would be about
     C. is about
     D. is dealing with

this woman supposed copied the recipe for the
12
delicious cookies and forwarded it via email to everyone she knew.

12. F. NO CHANGE
     G. woman supposedly
     H. women supposedly
     J. women supposed to

[7]

Although today's technology enhances our ability to tell and retell urban legends, the Internet can also serve as a monitor of urban legends. Dedicated to commonly told urban
13
legends, research is done by many websites.
13
According to those websites, most legends, including the ones told here, have no basis in reality.

13. A. NO CHANGE
     B. Many websites are dedicated to researching the validity of commonly told urban legends.
     C. Researching the validity of commonly told urban legends, many websites are dedicated.
     D. OMIT the underlined portion.

GO ON TO THE NEXT PAGE

Questions 14–15 ask about the preceding passage as a whole.

---

14. The author wants to insert the following sentence:

    > Other urban legends seem to be designed to instill fear.

    What would be the most logical placement for this sentence?

    F. After the last sentence of paragraph 3

    G. After the second sentence of paragraph 4

    H. Before the first sentence of paragraph 5

    J. After the last sentence of paragraph 6

15. Suppose that the author had been assigned to write an essay comparing the purposes and topics of myths and legends in primitive societies and in our modern society. Would this essay fulfill that assignment?

    A. Yes, because the essay describes myths and legends from primitive societies and modern society.

    B. Yes, because the essay provides explanations of possible purposes and topics for myths and legends from primitive societies and modern society.

    C. No, because the essay does not provide enough information about the topics of the myths and legends in primitive societies to make a valid comparison.

    D. No, because the essay doesn't provide any information on the myths and legends of primitive societies.

GO ON TO THE NEXT PAGE

Passage II

HENRY DAVID THOREAU: A SUCCESSFUL LIFE

What does it mean to be successful? Do one
16
measure success by money? If I told you about

a man: working as a teacher, a land surveyor,
17
and a factory worker (never holding any of these

jobs for more than a few years), would that man

sound like a success to you? If I told you that he

spent two solitary years living alone in a small
18
cabin that he built for himself and that he spent

those years looking at plants and writing in a

diary—would you think of him as a celebrity

or an important figure? What if I told you that

he rarely ventured far from the town where he
19
was born, that he was thrown in jail for refusing

to pay his taxes, and that he died at the age of

forty-five? Do any of these facts seem to point

to a man whose life should be studied and

emulated?

You may already know about this man.

You may even have read some of his writings.

His name was: Henry David Thoreau, and he
20
was, in addition to the jobs listed above,

a poet, an essayist, a naturalist, and a social

critic. Although the facts listed about him may

16. F. NO CHANGE
    G. Does we
    H. Does one
    J. Did you

17. A. NO CHANGE
    B. man who worked
    C. man and worked
    D. man, which working

18. F. NO CHANGE
    G. two years living alone
    H. two solitary years all by himself
    J. a couple of lonely years living in solitude

19. A. NO CHANGE
    B. he is rarely venturing
    C. he has rare ventures
    D. this person was to venture rarely

20. F. NO CHANGE
    G. was Henry David Thoreau and he
    H. was: Henry David Thoreau; and he
    J. was Henry David Thoreau, and he

GO ON TO THE NEXT PAGE

not seem to add up to much, he <u>was, in fact a</u>
₂₁
tremendously influential person. Along with

writers such as Ralph Waldo Emerson, Mark

Twain, and Walt Whitman, Thoreau helped to

create the first literature and philosophy that

most people identify as <u>unique</u> American.
₂₂

In 1845, Thoreau built a <u>cabin. Near</u> Walden
₂₃
Pond and remained there for more than two

years, living alone, fending for himself, and

observing the nature around him. He kept

scrupulous notes in his diary, notes that he

later distilled into his most famous work titled

Walden. <u>*Walden* is read by many literature</u>
₂₄

<u>students today.</u>
₂₄

[1] To protest slavery, Thoreau refused to pay

his taxes in 1846. [2] Thoreau was a firm believer

in the abolition of slavery, and he objected to the

practice's extension into the new territories of the

West. [3] For this act of rebellion, he was thrown

in the Concord jail. [25]

21. A. NO CHANGE
    B. was, in fact, a
    C. was in fact a
    D. was in fact, a

22. F. NO CHANGE
    G. uniquely
    H. uniqueness
    J. the most unique

23. A. NO CHANGE
    B. cabin. On
    C. cabin, by
    D. cabin near

24. F. NO CHANGE
    G. This book is read by many literature students today.
    H. Today, many literature students read *Walden*.
    J. OMIT the underlined portion.

25. What is the most logical order of sentences in this paragraph?
    A. NO CHANGE
    B. 3, 2, 1
    C. 2, 1, 3
    D. 3, 1, 2

GO ON TO THE NEXT PAGE

Thoreau used his writing to spread his message of resistance and <u>activism; he published</u> 26 an essay entitled *Civil Disobedience* (also known as *Resistance to Civil Government*). In it, Thoreau laid out his argument for refusing to obey unjust laws.

Although Thoreau's life was very brief, <u>his</u> 27 works and his ideas continue to touch and influence people. Students all over the country— all over the world—continue to read his essays and hear his unique voice, urging them to lead lives of principle, individuality, and freedom. 28 To be able to live out the ideas that burn in

<u>the heart of a person</u>—surely that is the meaning 29 of success.

26. F. NO CHANGE
    G. activism, he published:
    H. activism, he published
    J. activism, he published,

27. A. NO CHANGE
    B. he's
    C. their
    D. those

28. The purpose of this paragraph is to:
    F. explain why Thoreau was put in jail.
    G. prove a point about people's conception of success.
    H. suggest that Thoreau may be misunderstood.
    J. discuss Thoreau's importance in today's world.

29. A. NO CHANGE
    B. one's heart
    C. the heart and soul of a person
    D. through the heart of a person

```
Question 30 asks about
the preceding passage as a whole.
```

30. By including questions throughout the entire first paragraph, the author allows the reader to:
    F. answer each question as the passage proceeds.
    G. think about the meaning of success.
    H. assess the quality of Thoreau's work.
    J. form an opinion about greed in modern society.

GO ON TO THE NEXT PAGE

Passage III

THE SLOTH: SLOW BUT NOT SLOTHFUL

[1]

More than half of the world's <u>currently living</u>
                                        31
<u>plant</u> and animal species live in tropical rain
  31
forests. Four square miles of a Central American
rain forest can be home to up to 1,500 different
species of flowering plants, 700 species of
trees, 400 species of birds, and 125 species of
mammals. Of these mammals, the sloth is one
of the most unusual.

[2]

Unlike most mammals, the sloth is usually
upside down. A sloth does just about everything
upside down, including sleeping, eating, mating,
and giving birth. <u>Its' unique</u> anatomy allows the
                      32
sloth to spend most of the time hanging from
one tree branch or another, high in the canopy
of a rain forest tree. About the size of a large
domestic <u>cat, the</u> sloth hangs from its unusually
            33

long limbs and long hooklike claws. <u>Specially</u>
                                        34
<u>designed for limbs, the sloth's muscles seem to</u>
                  34
<u>cling to things.</u>
      34

31. A. NO CHANGE
    B. currently existing plant
    C. living plant
    D. plant

32. F. NO CHANGE
    G. It's unique
    H. Its unique
    J. Its uniquely

33. A. NO CHANGE
    B. cat; the
    C. cat. The
    D. cat, but the

34. F. NO CHANGE
    G. The sloth's muscles seem to cling to
       things for specially designed limbs.
    H. The muscles in a sloth's limbs seem
       to be specially designed for clinging
       to things.
    J. OMIT the underlined portion.

GO ON TO THE NEXT PAGE ⟶

[3]

In fact, a sloth's limbs are so specific adapted
                                    35
to upside-down life that a sloth is essentially

incapable of walking on the ground. Instead,
                                       36
they must crawl or drag itself with its massive
36
claws. This makes it easy to see why the sloth

rarely leaves its home in the trees. Because it can
                                       37
not move swiftly on the ground, the sloth is an

excellent swimmer.

[4]

38 A sloth can hang upside down and,

without moving the rest of its body turn its face
                                    39

35. A. NO CHANGE
    B. so specific and
    C. so specified
    D. so specifically

36. F. NO CHANGE
    G. Instead, it
    H. However, they
    J. In addition, it

37. A. NO CHANGE
    B. Despite
    C. Similarly,
    D. Though

38. The author wants to insert a sentence
    here to help connect paragraph 3 and
    paragraph 4. Which of the following
    sentences would best serve that purpose?

    F. Of course, many other animals are
        also excellent swimmers.
    G. Another unique characteristic of the
        sloth is its flexibility.
    H. In addition to swimming, the sloth
        is an incredible climber.
    J. Flexibility is a trait that helps the
        sloth survive.

39. A. NO CHANGE
    B. body turns
    C. body, it has the capability of turning
    D. body, turn

180 degrees so that it <u>was looking</u> at the ground.
₄₀

A sloth can rotate its forelimbs in all directions,
so it can easily reach the leaves that make up
its diet. The sloth can also roll itself up into a
ball in order to <u>protect and defend itself from</u>
₄₁

predators. <u>The howler monkey, another inhabitant</u>
₄₂
<u>of the rain forest, is not as flexible as the sloth.</u>
₄₂

[5]

The best defense a sloth has from predators
such as jaguars and large snakes, though, is its
camouflage. During the rainy season, a sloth's
thick brown or gray fur is usually covered with
a coat of blue-green <u>algae. Which</u> helps it blend
₄₃
in with its forest surroundings. Another type
of camouflage is the sloth's incredibly slow
movement: it often moves less than 100 feet
during a 24-hour period.

[6]

It is this slow movement that earned the
sloth its name. *Sloth* is also a word for laziness
or an aversion to work. But even though it
sleeps an average of 15 hours a day, the sloth

40. F. NO CHANGE
    G. had been looking
    H. will have the ability to be looking
    J. can look

41. A. NO CHANGE
    B. protect itself and defend itself from
    C. protect itself so it won't be harmed by
    D. protect itself from

42. F. NO CHANGE
    G. Another inhabitant of the rain forest, the howler monkey, is not as flexible as the sloth.
    H. Not as flexible as the sloth is the howler monkey, another inhabitant of the rain forest.
    J. OMIT the underlined portion.

43. A. NO CHANGE
    B. algae, which
    C. algae, being that it
    D. algae

isn't necessarily lazy. It just moves, upside down, at its own slow pace through its world of rain forest trees. 44

44. The author is considering deleting the last sentence of paragraph 6. This change would:

 F. diminish the amount of information provided about the habits of the sloth.

 G. make the ending of the passage more abrupt.

 H. emphasize the slothful nature of the sloth.

 J. make the tone of the essay more consistent.

Question 45 asks about
the preceding passage as a whole.

---

45. The author wants to insert the following description:

> An observer could easily be tricked into thinking that a sloth was just a pile of decaying leaves.

What would be the most appropriate placement for this sentence?

 A. After the last sentence of paragraph 1

 B. After the third sentence of paragraph 2

 C. Before the last sentence of paragraph 5

 D. Before the first sentence of paragraph 6

 GO ON TO THE NEXT PAGE

Passage IV

FIRES IN YELLOWSTONE

During the summer of 1988, I watched Yellowstone National Park go up in flames. In June, fires ignited by lightning had been allowed
46
to burn unsuppressed because park officials expected that the usual summer rains would douse the flames. However, the rains never

will have come. A plentiful fuel supply of fallen
47
logs and pine needles was available, and winds of up to 100 mph whipped the spreading fires along and carried red-hot embers to other areas, creating new fires. By the time park officials succumbed to the pressure of public opinion and decide to try to extinguish the flames. It's too
48   49
late. The situation remained out of control in spite of the efforts of 9,000 firefighters who were using state-of-the-art equipment. By September, more than 720,000 acres of Yellowstone had been

affected by fire. Nature was only able to curb
50
the destruction; the smoke did not begin to clear
50
until the first snow arrived on September 11.

46. F. NO CHANGE
    G. fires having been ignited by lightning
    H. fires, the kind ignited by lightning,
    J. fires ignited and started by lightning

47. A. NO CHANGE
    B. came
    C. were coming
    D. have come

48. F. NO CHANGE
    G. are deciding
    H. decided
    J. OMIT the underlined portion.

49. A. NO CHANGE
    B. flames, it's
    C. flames, it was
    D. flames; it was

50. F. NO CHANGE
    G. Only curbing the destruction by able nature
    H. Only nature was able to curb the destruction
    J. Nature was able to curb only the destruction

GO ON TO THE NEXT PAGE

Being that I was an ecologist who has
<u>51</u>
studied forests for 20 years, I knew that this was

not nearly the tragedy it seemed to be. Large

fires are, after all, necessary <u>in order that the</u>
<u>52</u>
<u>continued health in the forest ecosystem be</u>
<u>52</u>
<u>maintained.</u> Fires thin out overcrowded areas
<u>52</u>
and allow the sun to reach species of plants

stunted by shade. Ash fertilizes the soil, and

fire smoke kills forest bacteria. In the case of

the lodgepole pine, fire is essential to reprodu-

tion: the <u>pines' cone</u> open only when exposed to
<u>53</u>
temperatures greater than 112 degrees.

The fires in Yellowstone did result in some

loss of wildlife, but overall, the region's animals

proved to be fire-tolerant and fire-adaptive.

<u>However,</u> large animals such as bison were often
<u>54</u>

seen <u>grazing, and</u> bedding down in meadows
<u>55</u>
near burning forests. Also, the fire posed little

threat to the members of any endangered animal

species in the park.

My confidence in the natural resilience of

the forest has been borne out in the years since

51. A. NO CHANGE
    B. Being that I am
    C. I'm
    D. As

52. F. NO CHANGE
    G. for the continued health of the
       forest ecosystem to be maintained
    H. in order to continue the mainte-
       nance of the health of the forest
       ecosystem
    J. for the continued health of the
       forest ecosystem

53. A. NO CHANGE
    B. pines cones'
    C. pine's cones
    D. pine's cone

54. F. NO CHANGE
    G. Clearly,
    H. In fact,
    J. Instead,

55. A. NO CHANGE
    B. grazing; and bedding
    C. grazing: and bedding
    D. grazing and bedding

the fires ravaged Yellowstone. Judged from recent
₅₆
pictures of the park the forest was not destroyed;
₅₆

56. F. NO CHANGE

   G. Recent pictures of the park show
   that

   H. Judging by the recent pictures of the
   park,

   J. As judged according to pictures
   taken of the park recently,

it was rejuvenated.
₅₇

57. A. NO CHANGE

   B. they

   C. the fires

   D. I

Questions 58–59 ask about the preceding passage as a whole.

---

58. The writer is considering inserting the
following true statement after the first
sentence of the second paragraph:

   Many more acres of forest burned in
   Alaska in 1988 than in Yellowstone
   Park.

   Would this addition be appropriate for
   the essay?

   F. Yes, the statement would add
   important information about the
   effects of large-scale forest fires.

   G. Yes, the statement would provide an
   informative contrast to the Yellowstone fire.

   H. No, the statement would not provide
   any additional information about
   the effect of the 1988 fire in Yellowstone.

   J. No, the statement would undermine
   the author's position as an authority
   on the subject of forest fires.

59. Suppose that the writer wishes to
provide additional support for the
claim that the fire posed little threat
to the members of any endangered
animal species in the park. Which of
the following additions would be most
effective?

   A. A list of the endangered animals
   known to inhabit the park

   B. A discussion of the particular
   vulnerability of endangered species
   of birds to forest fires

   C. An explanation of the relative
   infrequency of such an extensive
   series of forest fires

   D. A summary of reports of biolo-
   gists who monitored the activity
   of endangered species in the park
   during the fire

GO ON TO THE NEXT PAGE

Passage V

MY FIRST WHITE-WATER RAFTING TRIP

[1]

White-water rafting <u>being</u> a favorite pastime of
₆₀
mine for several years. I have drifted down many

challenging North American rivers, including

the Snake, the Green, and the <u>Salmon, and there</u>
₆₁
<u>are many other rivers in America as well.</u> I have
₆₁
spent some of my best moments in dangerous

rapids, yet nothing has matched the thrill I expe-

rienced facing my <u>first rapids, on the Deschutes</u>
₆₂
<u>River.</u>
₆₂

[2]

My father and I spent the morning floating

down a calm and peaceful stretch of the Deschutes

in his wooden MacKenzie river boat. This trip

<u>it being</u> the wooden boat's first time down rapids,
₆₃

as well as mine. <u>Rapids are rated according to a</u>
₆₄
<u>uniform scale of relative difficulty.</u>
₆₄

60. F. NO CHANGE
    G. have been
    H. has been
    J. was

61. A. NO CHANGE
    B. Salmon, just three of many rivers
       existing in North America.
    C. Salmon; many other rivers exist in
       North America.
    D. Salmon.

62. F. NO CHANGE
    G. first: rapids on the Deschutes River.
    H. first rapids; on the Deschutes River.
    J. first rapids on the Deschutes River.

63. A. NO CHANGE
    B. it happened that it was
    C. was
    D. being

64. F. NO CHANGE
    G. Rated according to a uniform scale,
       rapids are relatively difficult.
    H. (Rapids are rated according to a
       uniform scale of relative difficulty.)
    J. OMIT the underlined portion.

GO ON TO THE NEXT PAGE

[3]

Roaring, I was in the boat approaching
                    —
                    65

Whitehorse Rapids. I felt much like a novice skier
        —
        65

peering down her first steep slope: I was scared,

but even more excited. The water churned and
                                    —————
                                      66

covering me with a refreshing spray. My father,
—————
  66

towards the stern, controlled the oars. The

carefree expression he usually wore on the river

had been replaced and instead he adopted a
                   ———————————
                         67

look of intense concentration as he maneuvered

around boulders dotting our path. To release

tension, we began to holler like kids on a roller

coaster, our voices echoing across the water as
                                ————
                                 68

we lurched violently about.

[4]

Suddenly we came to a jarring halt and we
                                    ———
                                     69

stopped; the left side of the bow was wedged
—————
  69

on a large rock. A whirlpool whirled around

us; if we capsized, we would be sucked into the

undertow. Instinctively, I threw all of my weight

towards the right side of the tilting boat. Luckily,

65. A. NO CHANGE
    B. It roared, and the boat and I approached Whitehorse Rapids.
    C. While the roaring boat was approaching Whitehorse Rapids, I could hear the water.
    D. I could hear the water roar as we approached Whitehorse Rapids.

66. F. NO CHANGE
    G. churned, and covering me
    H. churning and covering me
    J. churned, covering me

67. A. NO CHANGE
    B. with
    C. by another countenance altogether:
    D. instead with another expression;

68. F. NO CHANGE
    G. throughout
    H. around
    J. from

69. A. NO CHANGE
    B. which stopped us
    C. and stopped
    D. OMIT the underlined portion.

GO ON TO THE NEXT PAGE ⟶

it was just enough force to dislodge us, and we
  70

continued on down for about ten more minutes

of spectacular rapids.

[5]

Later that day, we went through Buckskin

Mary Rapids and Boxcar Rapids. When we

pulled up on the bank that evening, we saw that

the boat had received its first scar: _that scar was a_
                                                        71

small hole on the upper bow from the boulder

we had wrestled with. In the years to come,

we went down many rapids and the boat

receiving many bruises, but Whitehorse is the
  72

most memorable rapids of all. [73]

70. F. NO CHANGE
    G. it's
    H. it is
    J. its

71. A. NO CHANGE
    B. that was a
    C. which was a
    D. a

72. F.   NO CHANGE
    G. received many
    H. received much
    J.   receives many

73. Which of the following concluding
    sentences would most effectively
    emphasize the final point made in this
    paragraph while retaining the style and
    tone of the narrative as a whole?

    A. The brutal calamities that it
        presented the unwary rafter were
        more than offset by its beguiling
        excitement.

    B. Perhaps it is true that your first
        close encounter with white water is
        your most intense.

    C. Or, if not the most memorable, then
        at least a very memorable one!

    D. Call me crazy or weird if you want,
        but white-water rafting is the sport
        for me.

GO ON TO THE NEXT PAGE ⟩

Questions 74–75 ask about the preceding passage as a whole.

74. The writer has been assigned to write an essay that focuses on the techniques of white-water rafting. Would this essay meet the requirements of that assignment?

F. No, because the essay's main focus is on a particular experience, not on techniques.

G. No, because the essay mostly deals with the relationship between father and daughter.

H. Yes, because specific rafting techniques are the essay's main focus.

J. Yes, because it presents a dramatic story of a day of white-water rafting.

75. Suppose that the writer wants to add the following sentence to the essay:

It was such a peaceful summer day that it was hard to believe dangerous rapids awaited us downstream.

What would be the most logical placement of this sentence?

A. After the last sentence of paragraph 1

B. After the last sentence of paragraph 2

C. Before the first sentence of paragraph 4

D. After the last sentence of paragraph 4

MATH TEST

60 Minutes—60 Questions

Directions: Solve each of the following problems, select the correct answer, and then fill in the corresponding oval on your Answer Grid.

Don't linger over problems that are too time-consuming. Do as many as you can, then come back to the others in the time permitted.

You may use a calculator on this test. Some questions, however, may be easier to answer without the use of a calculator.

Note: Unless the question says otherwise, assume all of the following:

1. Illustrative figures are *not* necessarily drawn to scale.
2. All geometric figures lie in a plane.
3. The term *line* indicates a straight line.
4. The term *average* indicates arithmetic mean.

---

1. In a recent survey, 14 people found their mayor to be "very competent." This number is exactly 20% of the people surveyed. How many people were surveyed?

    A. 28
    B. 35
    C. 56
    D. 70
    E. 84

DO YOUR FIGURING HERE.

2. A train traveled at a rate of 90 miles per hour for x hours, and then at a rate of 60 miles per hour for y hours. Which expression represents the train's average rate in miles per hour for the entire distance traveled?

   F. $\dfrac{540}{xy}$

   G. $\dfrac{90}{x} \times \dfrac{60}{y}$

   H. $\dfrac{90}{x} + \dfrac{60}{y}$

   J. $\dfrac{90x + 60y}{x + y}$

   K. $\dfrac{150}{x + y}$

3. In a certain string ensemble, the ratio of men to women is 5:3. If there are a total of 24 people in the ensemble, how many women are there?

   A. 12
   B. 11
   C. 10
   D. 9
   E. 8

4. If $x \neq 0$, and $x^2 - 3x = 6x$, then $x = $?

   F. -9
   G. -3
   H. $\sqrt{3}$
   J. 3
   K. 9

DO YOUR FIGURING HERE.

GO ON TO THE NEXT PAGE

5. The two overlapping circles below form three regions, as shown:

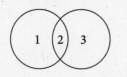

What is the maximum number of regions that can be formed by three overlapping circles?

A. 5

B. 6

C. 7

D. 8

E. 9

DO YOUR FIGURING HERE.

6. If $x^2 + 6x + 8 = 4 + 10x$, then x equals which of the following?

F. −2

G. −1

H. 0

J. 1

K. 2

7. Nine less than the number c is the same as the number d, and d less than twice c is 20. Which two equations could be used to determine the value of c and d?

A. $d - 9 = c$
   $d - 2c = 20$

B. $c - 9 = d$
   $2c - d = 20$

C. $c - 9 = d$
   $d - 2c = 20$

D. $9 - c = d$
   $2c - d = 20$

E. $9 - c = d$
   $2cd = 20$

GO ON TO THE NEXT PAGE

8. An ice cream parlor offers five flavors of ice cream and four different toppings (sprinkles, hot fudge, whipped cream, and butterscotch). There is a special offer that includes one flavor of ice cream and one topping, served in a cup, sugar cone, or waffle cone. How many ways are there to order ice cream with the special offer?

F.   4

G.   5

H. 12

J.   23

K. 60

DO YOUR FIGURING HERE.

9. At a recent audition for a school play, 1 out of 3 students who auditioned were asked to come to a second audition. After the second audition, 75% of those asked to the second audition were offered parts. If 18 students were offered parts, how many students went to the first audition?

A. 18

B. 24

C. 48

D. 56

E. 72

10. One number is 5 times another number and their sum is −60. What is the lesser of the two numbers?

F.   −5

G. −10

H. −12

J.   −48

K. − 50

11. In the figure below, which is composed of equilateral triangles, what is the greatest number of parallelograms that can be found?

DO YOUR FIGURING HERE.

    A. 6
    B. 9
    C. 12
    D. 15
    E. 18

12. The circle in the figure below is inscribed in a square with a perimeter of 16 inches. What is the area of the shaded region?

    F. 4π
    G. $16 - 2\pi$
    H. $16 - 4\pi$
    J. $8 - 2\pi$
    K. $8 - 4\pi$

13. How many positive integers less than 50 are multiples of 4 but *not* multiples of 6?

    A. 4
    B. 6
    C. 8
    D. 10
    E. 12

14. What is the value of $f(3)$ where $f(x) = (8 - 3x)$ $(x^2 - 2x - 15)$?

    F. −30

    G. −18

    H. 12

    J. 24

    K. 30

DO YOUR FIGURING HERE.

15. A class contains five juniors and five seniors. If one member of the class is assigned at random to present a paper on a certain subject, and another member of the class is randomly assigned to assist him, what is the probability that both will be juniors?

    A. $\dfrac{1}{10}$

    B. $\dfrac{1}{5}$

    C. $\dfrac{2}{9}$

    D. $\dfrac{2}{5}$

    E. $\dfrac{1}{2}$

16. In triangle XYZ below, $\overline{XS}$ and $\overline{SZ}$ are 3 and 12 units, respectively. If the area of triangle XYZ is 45 square units, how many units long is altitude $\overline{YS}$?

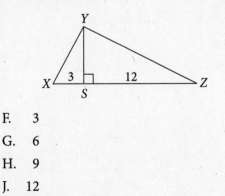

    F. 3

    G. 6

    H. 9

    J. 12

    K. 15

17. At which y-coordinate does the line
    described by the equation $6y - 3x = 18$
    intersect the y-axis?

    A. 2

    B. 3

    C. 6

    D. 9

    E. 18

DO YOUR FIGURING HERE.

18. If $x^2 - y^2 = 12$ and $x - y = 4$, what is the
    value of $x^2 + 2xy + y^2$?

    F. 3

    G. 8

    H. 9

    J. 12

    K. 16

19. What is the area in square units of the figure
    below?

    A. 147

    B. 108.5

    C. 91

    D. 60.5

    E. $39 + 7\sqrt{2}$

20. A carpenter is cutting wood to make a new bookcase with a board that is 12 feet long. If the carpenter cuts off three pieces, each of which is 17 inches long, how many inches long is the remaining fourth and final board? (A foot contains 12 inches.)

    F.   36
    G.   51
    H.   93
    J.   108
    K.   144

21. If $x^2 - 4x - 6 = 6$, what are the possible values for x?

    A.   4, 12
    B.   −6, 2
    C.   −6, −2
    D.   6, 2
    E.   6, −2

22. If −3 is a solution for the equation $x^2 + kx - 15 = 0$, what is the value of k?

    F.   5
    G.   2
    H.   −2
    J.   −5
    K.   Cannot be determined from the information given.

23. If the lengths, in inches, of all three sides of a triangle are integers, and one side is 7 inches long, what is the smallest possible perimeter of the triangle, in inches?

    A.   9
    B.   10
    C.   12
    D.   15
    E.   18

DO YOUR FIGURING HERE.

GO ON TO THE NEXT PAGE

DO YOUR FIGURING HERE.

24. If $0° < \theta < 90°$ and $\sin \theta = \dfrac{\sqrt{11}}{2\sqrt{3}}$, then $\cos \theta = ?$

    F. $\dfrac{1}{2\sqrt{3}}$

    G. $\dfrac{1}{\sqrt{11}}$

    H. $\dfrac{2}{\sqrt{3}}$

    J. $\dfrac{2\sqrt{3}}{\sqrt{11}}$

    K. $\dfrac{11}{2\sqrt{3}}$

25. Which of the following expressions is equivalent to $\dfrac{\sqrt{3+x}}{\sqrt{3-x}}$ for all x such that $-3 < x < 3$?

    A. $\dfrac{3-x}{3+x}$

    B. $\dfrac{3+x}{3-x}$

    C. $\dfrac{-3\sqrt{3+x}}{3-x}$

    D. $\dfrac{\sqrt{9-x^2}}{3-x}$

    E. $\dfrac{x^2-9}{3+x}$

26. In a certain cookie jar containing only macaroons and gingersnaps, the ratio of macaroons to gingersnaps is 2 to 5. Which of the following could be the total number of cookies in the cookie jar?

    F. 24
    G. 35
    H. 39
    J. 48
    K. 52

27. What is the sum of $\frac{3}{16}$ and .175?

    A. .3165
    B. .3500
    C. .3625
    D. .3750
    E. .3875

28. What is the maximum possible area, in square inches, of a rectangle with a perimeter of 20 inches?

    F. 15
    G. 20
    H. 25
    J. 30
    K. 40

DO YOUR FIGURING HERE.

GO ON TO THE NEXT PAGE

29. $\dfrac{\dfrac{3}{2} + \dfrac{7}{4}}{\left(\dfrac{15}{8} - \dfrac{3}{4}\right) - \left(\dfrac{4+3}{-4+3}\right)} = ?$

DO YOUR FIGURING HERE.

A. $\dfrac{3}{8}$

B. $\dfrac{2}{5}$

C. $\dfrac{9}{13}$

D. $\dfrac{5}{2}$

E. $\dfrac{8}{3}$

30. If $x - 15 = 7 - 5(x - 4)$, then $x = ?$

F. 0

G. 2

H. 4

J. 5

K. 7

31. The sketch below shows the dimensions of a flower garden. What is the area of this garden in square meters?

A. 31

B. 85

C. 99

D. 101

E. 117

32. What is the slope of the line described by the equation $6y - 3x = 18$?

    F. -2

    G. $-\dfrac{1}{2}$

    H. $\dfrac{1}{2}$

    J. 2

    K. 3

33. Line m passes through the point $(4, 3)$ in the standard (x, y) coordinate plane and is perpendicular to the line described by the equation $y = -\dfrac{4}{5}x + 6$. Which of the following equations describes line m?

    A. $y = \dfrac{5}{4}x - 2$

    B. $y = -\dfrac{5}{4}x + 6$

    C. $y = -\dfrac{4}{5}x - 2$

    D. $y = -\dfrac{4}{5}x + 2$

    E. $y = -\dfrac{5}{4}x - 2$

34. Line t in the standard (x, y) coordinate plane has a y-intercept of -3 and is parallel to the line having the equation $3x - 5y = 4$. Which of the following is an equation for line t?

    F. $y = -\dfrac{3}{5}x + 3$

    G. $y = -\dfrac{5}{3}x - 3$

    H. $y = \dfrac{3}{5}x + 3$

    J. $y = \dfrac{5}{3}x + 3$

    K. $y = \dfrac{3}{5}x - 3$

DO YOUR FIGURING HERE.

GO ON TO THE NEXT PAGE

35. If $y = mx + b$, which of the following equations expresses x in terms of y, m, and b?

    A. $x = \dfrac{y - b}{m}$

    B. $x = \dfrac{b - y}{m}$

    C. $x = \dfrac{y + b}{m}$

    D. $x = \dfrac{y}{m} - bx$

    E. $x = \dfrac{y}{m} + b$

36. In the figure below, $\overline{AB} = 20$, $\overline{BC} = 15$, and $\angle ADB$ and $\angle ABC$ are right angles. What is the length of $\overline{AD}$?

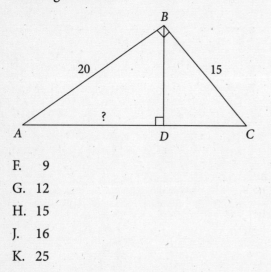

    F. 9
    G. 12
    H. 15
    J. 16
    K. 25

37. In the standard (x, y) coordinate plane shown in the figure below, points A and B lie on line m, and point C lies below it. The coordinates of points A, B, and C are $(0, 5)$, $(5, 5)$, and $(3, 3)$, respectively. What is the shortest possible distance from point C to a point on line m?

DO YOUR FIGURING HERE.

   A. 2

   B. $2\sqrt{2}$

   C. 3

   D. $\sqrt{13}$

   E. 5

38. For all $x \neq 8$, $\dfrac{x^2 - 11x + 24}{8 - x} = ?$

   F. $8 - x$

   G. $3 - x$

   H. $x - 3$

   J. $x - 8$

   K. $x - 11$

39. Points A and B lie in the standard (x, y) coordinate plane. The (x, y) coordinates of A are $(2, 1)$ and the (x, y) coordinates of B are $(-2, -2)$. What is the distance from A to B?

   A. $3\sqrt{2}$

   B. $3\sqrt{3}$

   C. 5

   D. 6

   E. 7

GO ON TO THE NEXT PAGE

40. In the figure below, $\overline{AB}$ and $\overline{CD}$ are both tangent to the circle as shown, and *ABCD* is a rectangle with side lengths 2*x* and 5*x* as shown. What is the area of the shaded region?

F. $10\pi x^2$

G. $10x^2 - \pi x^2$

H. $10x^2 - 2\pi x$

J. $9\pi x^2$

K. $6\pi x^2$

41. If $0° < \theta < 90°$ and $\cos \theta = \dfrac{5\sqrt{2}}{8}$, then $\tan \theta = ?$

A. $\dfrac{5}{\sqrt{7}}$

B. $\dfrac{\sqrt{7}}{5}$

C. $\dfrac{\sqrt{14}}{8}$

D. $\dfrac{8}{\sqrt{14}}$

E. $\dfrac{8}{5\sqrt{2}}$

DO YOUR FIGURING HERE.

GO ON TO THE NEXT PAGE

42. Consider fractions of the form $\frac{7}{n}$, where n is an integer. How many integer values of n make this fraction greater than .5 and less than .8?

F. 3

G. 4

H. 5

J. 6

K. 7

43. The circumference of circle X is 12π and the circumference of circle Y is 8π. What is the greatest possible distance between two points, one of which lies on the circumference of circle X and one of which lies on the circumference of circle Y?

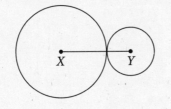

A. 6

B. 10

C. 20

D. 10π

E. 20π

44. $\sqrt{(x^2 + 4)^2} - (x + 2)(x - 2) = ?$

F. $2x^2$

G. $x^2 - 8$

H. $2(x - 2)$

J. 0

K. 8

GO ON TO THE NEXT PAGE

DO YOUR FIGURING HERE.

45. If $s = -3$, then $s^3 + 2s^2 + 2s = ?$

    A. -15

    B. -10

    C. -5

    D. 5

    E. 33

DO YOUR FIGURING HERE.

46. How many different numbers are solutions for the equation $2x + 6 = (x + 5)(x + 3)$?

    F. 0

    G. 1

    H. 2

    J. 3

    K. Infinitely many

47. In square $ABCD$ below, $\overline{AC} = 8$. What is the perimeter of $ABCD$?

    A. $4\sqrt{2}$

    B. 8

    C. $8\sqrt{2}$

    D. 16

    E. $16\sqrt{2}$

GO ON TO THE NEXT PAGE

48. The front surface of a fence panel is shown below with the lengths labeled representing inches. The panel is symmetrical along its center vertical axis. What is the surface area of the front surface of the panel in square inches?

DO YOUR FIGURING HERE.

F. 144

G. 132

H. 120

J. 80

K. $64 + 6\sqrt{5}$

49. In the figure below, O is the center of the circle, and C, D, and E are points on the circumference of the circle. If $\angle OCD$ measures 70° and $\angle OED$ measures 45°, what is the measure of $\angle CDE$?

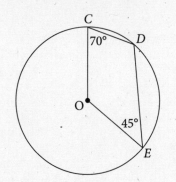

A. 25°

B. 45°

C. 70°

D. 90°

E. 115°

GO ON TO THE NEXT PAGE

50. Which of the following systems of equations does NOT have a solution?

    F. $x + 3y = 19$
       $3x + y = 6$

    G. $x + 3y = 19$
       $x - 3y = 13$

    H. $x - 3y = 19$
       $3x - y = 7$

    J. $x - 3y = 19$
       $3x + y = 6$

    K. $x + 3y = 6$
       $3x + 9y = 7$

51. What is the 46th digit to the right of the decimal point in the decimal equivalent of $\frac{1}{7}$?

    A. 1
    B. 2
    C. 4
    D. 7
    E. 8

52. Which of the following inequalities is equivalent to $-2 - 4x \le -6x$?

    F. $x \ge -2$
    G. $x \ge 1$
    H. $x \ge 2$
    J. $x \le -1$
    K. $x \le 1$

DO YOUR FIGURING HERE.

DO YOUR FIGURING HERE.

53. If $x > 0$ and $y > 0$, $\dfrac{\sqrt{x}}{x} + \dfrac{\sqrt{y}}{y}$ is equivalent to which of the following?

A. $\dfrac{2}{xy}$

B. $\dfrac{\sqrt{x} + \sqrt{y}}{\sqrt{xy}}$

C. $\dfrac{x + y}{xy}$

D. $\dfrac{\sqrt{x} + \sqrt{y}}{\sqrt{x + y}}$

E. $\dfrac{x + y}{\sqrt{xy}}$

54. In the diagram below, $\overline{CD}$, $\overline{BE}$, and $\overline{AF}$ are all parallel and are intersected by two transversals as shown. What is the length of $\overline{EF}$?

F. 2

G. 3

H. 4

J. 6

K. 9

55. What is the area, in square units, of the square whose vertices are located at the (x, y) coordinate points indicated in the figure below?

DO YOUR FIGURING HERE.

A. 9

B. 12

C. 16

D. 18

E. 24

56. Compared to the graph of $y = \cos \theta$, the graph of $y = 2 \cos \theta$ has:

   F. twice the period and the same amplitude.

   G. half the period and the same amplitude.

   H. twice the period and half the amplitude.

   J. half the amplitude and the same period.

   K. twice the amplitude and the same period.

57. Brandy has a collection of comic books. If she adds 15 to the number of comic books in her collection and multiplies the sum by 3, the result will be 65 less than 4 times the number of comic books in her collection. How many comic books are in her collection?

   A. 50

   B. 85

   C. 110

   D. 145

   E. 175

GO ON TO THE NEXT PAGE

58. One empty cylinder has three times the height and twice the diameter of another empty cylinder. How many fillings of the smaller cylinder would be equivalent to one filling of the larger cylinder?

(Note: The volume of a cylinder of radius r and height h is $\pi r^2 h$.)

F.   6

G. $6\sqrt{2}$

H. 12

J.   18

K. 24

DO YOUR FIGURING HERE.

59. What is the perimeter of a 30°-60°-90° triangle with a long leg of 12 inches?

A. $5\sqrt{3} + 12$

B. $4\sqrt{3} + 18$

C. $8\sqrt{3} + 18$

D. $12\sqrt{3} + 12$

E. $12\sqrt{3} + 18$

60. A baseball team scores an average of x points in its first n games and then scores y points in its next and final game of the season. Which of the following represents the team's average score for the entire season?

F. $x + \dfrac{y}{n}$

G. $x + \dfrac{y}{n+1}$

H. $\dfrac{x + ny}{n+1}$

J. $\dfrac{nx + y}{n+1}$

K. $\dfrac{n(x + y)}{n+1}$

IF YOU FINISH BEFORE TIME IS CALLED, YOU MAY CHECK YOUR WORK ON THIS SECTION ONLY. DO NOT TURN TO ANY OTHER SECTION IN THE TEST. **STOP**

READING TEST

35 Minutes—40 Questions

Directions: This test contains four passages, each followed by several questions. After reading each passage, select the best answer to each question and fill in the corresponding oval on your Answer Grid. You may refer to the passages while answering the questions.

Prose Fiction

This passage is adapted from the novel *Emma* by Jane Austen. It was originally published in 1815.

Emma Woodhouse, handsome, clever, and rich, with a comfortable home and happy disposition, seemed to unite some of the
Line best blessings of existence. She had lived
(5) nearly twenty-one years in the world with very little to distress or vex her. She was the youngest of the two daughters of a most affectionate, indulgent father, and had, in consequence of her sister's marriage, been
(10) mistress of his house from a very early period. Her mother had died too long ago for her to have more than an indistinct remembrance of her caresses, and her place had been taken by an excellent governess
(15) who had fallen little short of a mother in affection.

Sixteen years had Miss Taylor been in Mr. Woodhouse's family, less as a governess than a friend, very fond of both daughters,
(20) but particularly of Emma. Between them it was more the intimacy of sisters. Even before Miss Taylor had ceased to hold the nominal office of governess, the mildness of her temper had hardly allowed her
(25) to impose any restraint. The shadow of authority being now long passed away, they had been living together as friend and friend very mutually attached, and Emma doing just what she liked, highly esteeming Miss
(30) Taylor's judgment, but directed chiefly by

her own. The real evils, indeed, of Emma's situation were the power of having rather too much her own way, and a disposition to think a little too well of herself; these were
(35) the disadvantages which threatened alloy to her many enjoyments. The danger, however, was at present so unperceived, that they did not by any means rank as misfortunes with her.

(40) Sorrow came—a gentle sorrow—but not at all in the shape of any disagreeable consciousness. Miss Taylor married. It was Miss Taylor's loss which first brought grief. It was on the wedding-day of this beloved
(45) friend that Emma first sat in mournful thought of any continuance. The wedding over, and the bride-people gone, she and her father were left to dine together, with no prospect of a third to cheer a long evening.
(50) Her father composed himself to sleep after dinner, as usual, and she had then only to sit and think of what she had lost.

The marriage had every promise of happiness for her friend. Mr. Weston was
(55) a man of unexceptionable character, easy fortune, suitable age, and pleasant manners. There was some satisfaction in considering with what self-denying, generous friendship she had always wished and promoted the
(60) match, but it was a black morning's work for her. The want of Miss Taylor would be felt every hour of every day. She recalled her past kindness—the kindness, the affection of sixteen years—how she had taught her

GO ON TO THE NEXT PAGE ⟹

(65) and how she had played with her from five
years old—how she had devoted all her
powers to attach and amuse her in health—
and how she had nursed her through the
various illnesses of childhood. A large
(70) debt of gratitude was owing here, but the
intercourse of he last seven years, the equal
footing and perfect unreserve which had
soon followed Isabella's marriage, on their
being left to each other, was yet a dearer,
(75) tenderer recollection. She had been a friend
and companion such as few possessed:
intelligent, well-informed, useful, gentle,
knowing all the ways of the family, interested in all its concerns, and peculiarly
(80) interested in her, in every pleasure, every
scheme of hers—one to whom she could
speak every thought as it arose, and who
had such an affection for her as could never
find fault.

(85) How was she to bear the change? It was
true that her friend was going only half a
mile from them, but Emma was aware that
great must be the difference between a Mrs.
Weston, only half a mile from them, and
(90) a Miss Taylor in the house. With all her
advantages, natural and domestic, she was
now in great danger of suffering from intel-
lectual solitude.

1. According to the passage, what are the
   greatest disadvantages facing Emma?

   A. Her father is not a stimulating
      conversationalist, and she is bored.

   B. She is lonely and afraid that
      Mrs. Weston will not have a happy
      marriage.

   C. She is used to having her way too
      much, and she thinks too highly
      of herself.

   D. She misses the companionship
      of her mother, her sister, and
      Miss Taylor.

2. The name of Emma's sister is:

   F. Mrs. Weston.

   G. Isabella.

   H. Miss Taylor.

   J. Mrs. Woodhouse.

3. As described in the passage, Emma's
   relationship with Miss Taylor can be
   characterized as:

   A. similar to a mother-daughter
      relationship.

   B. similar to the relationship of sisters
      or best friends.

   C. weaker than Emma's relationship
      with her sister.

   D. stronger than Miss Taylor's relation-
      ship with her new husband.

4. As used in line 33, *disposition* can most
   closely be defined as:

   F. a tendency.

   G. control.

   H. placement.

   J. transfer.

GO ON TO THE NEXT PAGE ⇨

5. Which of the following are included in Emma's memories of her relationship with Miss Taylor?

   I. Miss Taylor taking care of Emma during childhood illnesses

   II. Miss Taylor entertaining Emma

   III. Miss Taylor teaching her mathematics

   IV. Miss Taylor scolding her for being selfish

   A. I, III, and IV only

   B. I and III only

   C. II, III, and IV only

   D. I and II only

6. It is most reasonable to infer from Emma's realization that "great must be the difference between a Mrs. Weston, only half a mile from them, and a Miss Taylor in the house" (lines 88–90) that:

   F. Miss Taylor will no longer be a part of Emma's life.

   G. Emma is happy about the marriage because now she will have more freedom.

   H. Emma regrets that her relationship with Miss Taylor will change.

   J. Emma believes that her relationship with Miss Taylor will become stronger.

7. Based on the passage, Emma could best be described as:

   A. sweet and naïve.

   B. self-centered and naïve.

   C. self-centered and headstrong.

   D. unappreciative and bitter.

8. The passage suggests that the quality Emma values most in a friend is:

   F. charisma.

   G. devotion.

   H. honesty.

   J. intelligence.

9. How does Emma view Mr. Weston?

   A. She thinks that he is an excellent match, and it required considerable self-sacrifice not to pursue him herself.

   B. She considers him to be a respectable if somewhat average match for her friend.

   C. She sees him as an intruder who has carried away her best friend in "a black morning's work" (line 60).

   D. She believes he is an indulgent, easily swayed man, reminiscent of her father.

10. From the passage, it can be inferred that Emma is accustomed to:

    F. behaving according to the wishes of her affectionate father.

    G. taking the advice of Miss Taylor when faced with deciding upon a course of action.

    H. doing as she pleases without permission from her father or governess.

    J. abiding by strict rules governing her behavior.

GO ON TO THE NEXT PAGE

Passage II

SOCIAL SCIENCE

This passage discusses different aspects of memory from a psychological perspective.

Learning and its result, memory, are processes by which we retain acquired information, emotions, and impressions that can influence our behavior. At the
(5) psychological level, memory is not a single process. Sensory memory, the first of three main systems of memory, describes the momentary lingering of perceptual information as it is initially sensed and briefly
(10) recorded. When an image strikes the eyes, it lingers in the visual system for an instant while the image is interpreted, and is quickly overwritten by new information. In the visual system this is called *iconic memory*, in
(15) the auditory system it is *echoic memory*, and in reference to touch it is *haptic memory*.

If sensory information is processed, it can move into the second main system of memory, working memory. This was once
(20) known as short-term memory (and that term is still popularly used). But working memory is viewed as a more accurate term, since this system not only stores information for short periods of time, but also enables the use
(25) and manipulation of information processed there. However, only a limited number of items can be held in working memory (the average for most people is seven), and decay of the memory occurs rapidly, although
(30) it can be held longer if the information is mentally or vocally repeated. Unless we make a conscious effort to retain it, a working memory may disappear forever.

Long-term memory is the most compre-
(35) hensive of the three, with apparently infinite capacity. Memories recorded in long-term memory are never lost, although at times there may be difficulty accessing them. There are three independent catego-
(40) ries of long-term memory which interact

extensively: *episodic* involves personal memories and details of daily life, and is closely identified with its time and place; *semantic* contains facts and general
(45) knowledge that are not tied to when or how they were learned; and *procedural* retains skills used to perform certain activities that eventually may not require conscious effort.

Although the main systems of memory
(50) are widely accepted, controversy continues about memory formation and retrieval. It was once believed that for a memory to enter long-term memory it must first be held in working memory. However, this idea
(55) has been challenged by an alternate theory suggesting that sensory memories can be directly entered into long-term memory through a pathway that runs parallel to, rather than in series with, working memory.
(60) Memories therefore can register simultaneously in both systems.

Likewise, all agree that the retrieval of long-term memories is facilitated by repetition, but there is no agreement about the
(65) accuracy of these memories. For many years, the scientific community viewed human memory as similar to computer memory, with the mind recording each detail just as it was presented. However,
(70) there is a growing consensus that our memory is sometimes flawed. An inference or assumption made by an individual when a memory is created may later be recalled as fact, or the mind may fill in details that
(75) were originally missing. Moreover, when we try to recall a particular memory, an unrelated memory may alter it through a process called interference. There is even evidence that an entirely false memory can
(80) be incorporated as a memory indistinguishable from true memories. Although for most purposes these discrepancies are harmless, concerns regarding the accuracy of human memory challenge the reliability of eyewit-
(85) ness testimony.

GO ON TO THE NEXT PAGE

11. The main purpose of the passage is to:

    A. describe the main memory systems and why they are increasingly controversial.

    B. describe the main memory systems and some views of memory formation and retrieval.

    C. demonstrate that early ideas about memory formation and retrieval were incorrect.

    D. demonstrate that theories about the main memory systems are incorrect.

12. Based on information in the passage, which of the following would be recalled from semantic long-term memory?

    F. Ballet steps

    G. A childhood birthday

    H. Multiplication tables

    J. Riding a bicycle

13. It can be reasonably inferred from the passage that, if a man in a car accident is unable to remember details of his life and family, but does remember how to perform his job, his:

    A. episodic memories have been lost.

    B. episodic memories have become inaccessible.

    C. procedural memories have been lost.

    D. procedural memories have become inaccessible.

14. The fact that the scientific community once viewed human memory as similar to computer memory is mentioned in the last paragraph in order to:

    F. illustrate that memory is now viewed as complex rather than mechanical.

    G. explain that memory is now viewed as an exact record of events.

    H. illustrate that memory is always inaccurate.

    J. explain that memories are formed the same way computers encode data.

15. A person reads, "The baseball hit the window," and when asked to recall the sentence, remembers, "The baseball broke the window." According to the passage, this is probably an example of:

    A. interference altering a memory.

    B. a memory that became inaccessible.

    C. a reader's assumption altering a memory.

    D. a completely false memory being created.

16. According to the passage, all the following are examples of episodic memory EXCEPT:

    F. the meal you ate last night.

    G. the name of an old classmate.

    H. the year your class won a trophy.

    J. the face of a stranger passed on the street.

GO ON TO THE NEXT PAGE

17. Based on information in the passage, the term *short-term memory* was most likely replaced with *working memory* in order to:

    A. refute the idea that memories in this category degrade quickly.

    B. emphasize that memories in this category can be manipulated.

    C. show that memories in this category become long-term memories.

    D. demonstrate that echoic memories are held in the visual system.

18. As it is used in the passage, the word *iconic* (line 14) most nearly means relating to:

    F. something sacred.

    G. a symbolic representation.

    H. visual sensory memory.

    J. a picture that represents a computer command.

19. According to the passage, most of the scientific community now agrees that:

    A. there are really four main categories of memory, not three.

    B. memories held in long-term memory remain forever.

    C. memories must be held in working memory before long-term memory.

    D. repetition does not affect the duration of memory.

20. According to the passage, which of the following is a characteristic of working memory?

    F. A slight echo in the ear

    G. Quick replacement by new sensory information

    H. Rapid forgetting

    J. Infinite capacity

GO ON TO THE NEXT PAGE

Passage III

HUMANITIES

This passage is excerpted from *A History of Women Artists*, © 1975 by Hugo Munsterberg; Clarkson N. Potter (a division of Random House, Inc.), publisher. Reprinted by permission of the author's family.

There can be little doubt that women artists have been most prominent in photography and that they have made their greatest
Line contribution in this field. One reason for
(5) this is not difficult to ascertain. As several historians of photography have pointed out, photography, being a new medium outside the traditional academic framework, was wide open to women and offered them
(10) opportunities that the older fields did not…

All these observations apply to the first woman to have achieved eminence in photography, and that is Julia Margaret Cameron… Born in 1815 in Calcutta into an
(15) upper-middle-class family and married to Charles Hay Cameron, a distinguished jurist and member of the Supreme Court of India, Julia Cameron was well-known as a brilliant conversationalist and a woman of person-
(20) ality and intellect who was unconventional to the point of eccentricity. Although the mother of six children, she adopted several more and still found time to be active in social causes and literary activities. After
(25) the Camerons settled in England in 1848 at Freshwater Bay on the Isle of Wight, she became the center of an artistic and literary circle that included such notable figures as the poet Alfred Lord Tennyson and the
(30) painter George Frederick Watts. Pursuing numerous activities and taking care of her large family, Mrs. Cameron might have been remembered as still another rather remarkable and colorful Victorian lady had it not
(35) been for the fact that, in 1863, her daughter presented her with photographic equipment, thinking her mother might enjoy taking pictures of her family and friends. Although forty-eight years old, Mrs. Cameron took
(40) up this new hobby with enormous enthusiasm and dedication. She was a complete beginner, but within a very few years she developed into one of the greatest photographers of her period and a giant in the
(45) history of photography. She worked ceaselessly as long as daylight lasted and mastered the technical processes of photography, at that time far more cumbersome than today, turning her coal house into a darkroom
(50) and her chicken house into a studio. To her, photography was a "divine art," and in it she found her vocation. In 1864, she wrote triumphantly under one of her photographs, "My First Success," and from then until her
(55) death in Ceylon in 1874, she devoted herself wholly to this art.

Working in a large format (her portrait studies are usually about 11 inches by 14 inches) and requiring a long exposure (on
(60) the average five minutes), she produced a large body of work that stands up as one of the notable artistic achievements of the Victorian period. The English art critic Roger Fry believed that her portraits were
(65) likely to outlive the works of artists who were her contemporaries. Her friend Watts, then a very celebrated portrait painter, inscribed on one of her photographs, "I wish I could paint such a picture as this." …Her
(70) work was widely exhibited, and she received gold, silver, and bronze medals in England, America, Germany, and Austria. No other female artist of the nineteenth century achieved such acclaim, and no other woman
(75) photographer has ever enjoyed such success.

Her work falls into two main categories on which her contemporaries and people today differ sharply. Victorian critics were particularly impressed by her allegorical
(80) pictures, many of them based on the poems of her friend and neighbor Tennyson…

GO ON TO THE NEXT PAGE ▷

Contemporary taste much prefers her portraits and finds her narrative scenes sentimental and sometimes in bad taste. Yet,
(85) not only Julia Cameron, but also the painters of that time loved to depict subjects such as *The Five Foolish Virgins* or *Pray God, Bring Father Safely Home*. Still, today her fame rests upon her portraits for, as she herself
(90) said, she was intent upon representing not only the outer likeness but also the inner greatness of the people she portrayed. Working with the utmost dedication, she produced photographs of such eminent
(95) Victorians as Tennyson, Browning, Carlyle, Trollope, Longfellow, Watts, Darwin, Ellen Terry, Sir John Herschel, who was a close friend of hers, and Mrs. Duckworth, the mother of Virginia Woolf.

21. Which of the following conclusions can be reasonably drawn from the passage's discussion of Julia Margaret Cameron?

    A. She was a traditional homemaker until she discovered photography.

    B. Her work holds a significant place in the history of photography.

    C. She was unable to achieve in her lifetime the artistic recognition she deserved.

    D. Her eccentricity has kept her from being taken seriously by modern critics of photography.

22. According to the passage, Cameron is most respected by modern critics for her:

    F. portraits.

    G. allegorical pictures.

    H. use of a large format.

    J. service in recording the faces of so many twentieth century figures.

23. The author uses which of the following methods to develop the second paragraph (lines 11–56)?

    A. A series of anecdotes depicting Cameron's energy and unconventionality

    B. A presentation of factual data demonstrating Cameron's importance in the history of photography

    C. A description of the author's personal acquaintance with Cameron

    D. A chronological account of Cameron's background and artistic growth

24. As it is used in the passage, *cumbersome* (line 48) most closely means:

    F. difficult to manage.

    G. expensive.

    H. intense.

    J. enjoyable.

25. When the author says that Cameron had found "her vocation" (line 52), his main point is that photography:

    A. offered Cameron an escape from the confines of conventional social life.

    B. became the main interest of her life.

    C. became her primary source of income.

    D. provided her with a way to express her religious beliefs.

GO ON TO THE NEXT PAGE

26. The main point of the third paragraph is that Cameron:

    F. achieved great artistic success during her lifetime.

    G. is the greatest photographer who ever lived.

    H. was considered a more important artist during her lifetime than she is now.

    J. revolutionized photographic methods in the Victorian era.

27. According to the passage, the art of photography offered women artists more opportunities than did other art forms because it:

    A. did not require expensive materials.

    B. allowed the artist to use family and friends for subject matter.

    C. was nontraditional.

    D. required little artistic skill.

28. *The Five Foolish Virgins* and *Pray God, Bring Father Safely Home* are examples of:

    F. portraits of celebrated Victorians.

    G. allegorical subjects of the sort that were popular during the Victorian era.

    H. photographs in which Cameron sought to show a subject's outer likeness and inner greatness.

    J. photographs by Cameron that were scoffed at by her contemporaries.

29. According to the passage, which of the following opinions of Cameron's work was held by Victorian critics but is NOT held by modern critics?

    A. Photographs should be based on poems.

    B. Her portraits are too sentimental.

    C. Narrative scenes are often in bad taste.

    D. Her allegorical pictures are her best work.

30. The author's treatment of Cameron's development as a photographer can best be described as:

    F. admiring.

    G. condescending.

    H. neutral.

    J. defensive.

Passage IV

NATURAL SCIENCE

This passage discusses aspects of the harbor seal's sensory systems.

The harbor seal, *Phoca vitulina*, lives amphibiously along the northern Atlantic and Pacific coasts. This extraordinary
Line mammal, which does most of its fishing at
(5) night when visibility is low and in places where noise levels are high, has developed several unique adaptations that have sharpened its acoustic and visual acuity. The need for such adaptations has been
(10) compounded by the varying behavior of sound and light in each of the two habitats of the harbor seal—land and water.

While the seal is on land, its ear operates much like the human ear, with sound waves
(15) traveling through air and entering the inner ear through the auditory canal. The directions from which sounds originate are distinguishable because the sound waves arrive at each inner ear at different times.
(20) In water, however, where sound waves travel faster than they do in air, the ability of the brain to differentiate arrival times between each ear is severely reduced. Yet it is crucial for the seal to be able to pinpoint the exact
(25) origins of sound in order to locate both its offspring and its prey. Therefore, the seal has developed an extremely sensitive quadraphonic hearing system, composed of a specialized band of tissue that extends
(30) down from the ear to the inner ear. In water, sound is conducted to the seal's inner ear by this special band of tissue, making it possible for the seal to identify the exact origins of sounds.

(35) The eye of the seal is also uniquely adapted to operate in both air and water. The human eye, adapted to function primarily in air, is equipped with a cornea, which aids in the refraction and focusing

(40) of light onto the retina. As a result, when a human eye is submerged in water, light rays are further refracted and the image is blurry. The seal's cornea, however, refracts light as water does. Therefore, in water, light
(45) rays are transmitted by the cornea without distortion, and are clearly focused on the retina. In air, however, the cornea is astigmatic, resulting in a distortion of incoming light rays. The seal compensates for this by
(50) having a stenopaic pupil, which constricts into a vertical slit. Since the astigmatism is most pronounced in the horizontal plane of the eye, the vertical pupil serves to minimize its effect on the seal's vision.

(55) Since the harbor seal hunts for food under conditions of low visibility, some scientists believe it has echolocation systems akin to those of bats, porpoises, and dolphins. This kind of natural radar involves
(60) the emission of high frequency sound pulses that reflect off obstacles such as predators, prey, or natural barriers. The reflections are received as sensory signals by the brain, which processes them into an image. The
(65) animal, blinded by unfavorable lighting conditions, is thus able to perceive its surroundings. Such echolocation by harbor seals is suggested by the fact that they emit "clicks," high frequency sounds produced in
(70) short, fast bursts that occur mostly at night, when visibility is low.

Finally, there is speculation that the seal's whiskers, or vibrissae, which are unusually well developed and highly
(75) sensitive to vibrations, act as additional sensory receptors. Scientists speculate that the vibrissae may sense wave disturbances produced by nearby moving fish, allowing the seal to home in on and capture prey.

GO ON TO THE NEXT PAGE

31. The harbor seal's eye compensates for the distortion of light rays on land by means of its:

    A. vibrissae.

    B. cornea.

    C. stenopaic pupil.

    D. echolocation.

32. The passage implies that a harbor seal's vision is:

    F. inferior to a human's vision in the water, but superior to it on land.

    G. superior to a human's vision in the water, but inferior to it on land.

    H. inferior to a human's vision both in the water and on land.

    J. equivalent to a human's vision both in the water and on land.

33. According to the passage, scientists think vibrissae help harbor seals to catch prey by:

    A. improving underwater vision.

    B. sensing vibrations in the air.

    C. camouflaging predator seals.

    D. detecting underwater movement.

34. According to the passage, the speed of sound in water is:

    F. faster than the speed of sound in air.

    G. slower than the speed of sound in air.

    H. the same as the speed of sound in air.

    J. unable to be determined exactly.

35. According to the passage, which of the following have contributed to the harbor seal's need to adapt its visual and acoustic senses?

    I. Night hunting
    II. The need to operate in two habitats
    III. A noisy environment

    A. I and II only

    B. II and III only

    C. I and III only

    D. I, II, and III

36. Which of the following claims expresses the writer's opinion and not a fact?

    F. The human eye is adapted to function primarily in air.

    G. When the seal is on land, its ear operates like a human ear.

    H. The "clicks" emitted by the harbor seal mean it uses echolocation.

    J. The need for adaptation is increased if an animal lives in two habitats.

37. The passage suggests that the harbor seal lives in:

    A. cold ocean waters with accessible coasts.

    B. all areas with abundant fish populations.

    C. most island and coastal regions.

    D. warm coastlines with exceptionally clear waters.

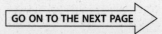 GO ON TO THE NEXT PAGE

38. According to the passage, a special band of tissue extending from the ear to the inner ear enables the harbor seal to:

    F. make its distinctive "clicking" sounds.

    G. find prey by echolocation.

    H. breathe underwater.

    J. determine where a sound originated.

39. The author compares harbor seal sensory organs to human sensory organs primarily in order to:

    A. point out similarities among mammals.

    B. explain how the seal's sensory organs function.

    C. prove that seals are more adaptively successful than humans.

    D. prove that humans are better adapted to their environment than seals.

40. According to the passage, one way in which seals differ from humans is:

    F. that sound waves enter the inner ear through the auditory canal.

    G. the degree of refraction of light by their corneas.

    H. they focus light rays on the retina.

    J. they have adapted to live in a certain environment.

SCIENCE TEST

35 Minutes—40 Questions

Directions: This test contains seven passages, each followed by several questions. After reading each passage, select the best answer to each question and fill in the corresponding oval on your Answer Grid. You may refer to the passages while answering the questions. You may NOT use a calculator on this test.

Passage I

The table below contains some physical properties of common optical materials. The refractive index of a material is a measure of the amount by which light is bent upon entering the material. The transmittance range is the range of wavelengths over which the material is transparent.

Table 1

Physical Properties of Optical Materials				
Material	Refractive index for light of 0.589 μm	Transmittance range (μm)	Useful range for prisms (μm)	Chemical resistance
Lithium fluoride	1.39	0.12–6	2.7–5.5	Poor
Calcium fluoride	1.43	0.12–12	5–9.4	Good
Sodium chloride	1.54	0.3–17	8–16	Poor
Quartz	1.54	0.20–3.3	0.20–2.7	Excellent
Potassium bromide	1.56	0.3–29	15–28	Poor
Flint glass*	1.66	0.35–2.2	0.35–2	Excellent
Cesium iodide	1.79	0.3–70	15–55	Poor

*Flint glass is lead oxide doped quartz.

1. According to the table, which material(s) will transmit light at 25 μm?

   A. Potassium bromide only
   B. Potassium bromide and cesium iodide
   C. Lithium fluoride and cesium iodide
   D. Lithium fluoride and flint glass

2. A scientist hypothesizes that any material with poor chemical resistance would have a transmittance range wider than 10 μm. The properties of which of the following materials contradicts this hypothesis?

   F. Lithium fluoride
   G. Flint glass
   H. Cesium iodide
   J. Quartz

GO ON TO THE NEXT PAGE

3. When light travels from one medium to another, total internal reflection can occur if the first medium has a higher refractive index than the second. Total internal reflection could occur if light were traveling from:

A. lithium fluoride to flint glass.

B. potassium bromide to cesium iodide.

C. quartz to potassium bromide.

D. flint glass to calcium fluoride.

4. Based on the information in the table, how is the transmittance range related to the useful prism range?

F. The transmittance range is always narrower than the useful prism range.

G. The transmittance range is narrower than or equal to the useful prism range.

H. The transmittance range increases as the useful prism range decreases.

J. The transmittance range is wider than and includes within it the useful prism range.

5. The addition of lead oxide to pure quartz has the effect of:

A. decreasing the transmittance range and the refractive index.

B. decreasing the transmittance range and increasing the refractive index.

C. increasing the transmittance range and the useful prism range.

D. increasing the transmittance range and decreasing the useful prism range.

GO ON TO THE NEXT PAGE

Passage II

Osmosis is the diffusion of a solvent (often water) across a semipermeable membrane from the side of the membrane with a lower concentration of dissolved material to the side with a higher concentration of dissolved material. The result of osmosis is an equilibrium—an even distribution—on both sides of the membrane. In order to prevent osmosis, external pressure must be applied to the side with the higher concentration of dissolved material. *Osmotic pressure* is the external pressure required to prevent osmosis. The apparatus shown below was used to measure osmotic pressure in the following experiments.

EXPERIMENT 1

Aqueous (water-based) solutions containing different concentrations of sucrose were placed in the closed side of the apparatus. The open side was filled with water. The sucrose solutions also contained a blue dye that binds to the sucrose. The osmotic pressure created by the piston was measured for each solution at various temperatures. The results are given in Table 1.

Table 1

Concentration of sucrose solution (mol/L)	Temperature K	Osmotic pressure (atm)
1.00	298.0	24.47
0.50	298.0	12.23
0.10	298.0	2.45
0.05	298.0	1.22
1.00	348.0	28.57
0.50	348.0	14.29
0.10	348.0	2.86
0.05	348.0	1.43

EXPERIMENT 2

Sucrose solutions of four different organic solvents were investigated in the same manner as in Experiment 1 with all trials at 298 K. The results are shown in Table 2.

Table 2

Solvent	Concentration of sucrose solution (mol/L)	Osmotic pressure (atm)
Ethanol	0.50	12.23
Ethanol	0.10	2.45
Acetone	0.50	12.23
Acetone	0.10	2.45
Diethyl ether	0.50	12.23
Diethyl ether	0.10	2.45
Methanol	0.50	12.23
Methanol	0.10	2.45

GO ON TO THE NEXT PAGE

6. According to the experimental results, osmotic pressure is dependent upon the:

F. solvent and temperature only.

G. solvent and concentration only.

H. temperature and concentration only.

J. solvent, temperature, and concentration.

7. According to Experiment 2, if methanol was used as a solvent, what pressure must be applied to a 0.5 mol/L solution of sucrose at 298 K to prevent osmosis?

A. 24.46 atm

B. 12.23 atm

C. 2.45 atm

D. 1.23 atm

8. A 0.10 mol/L aqueous sucrose solution is separated from an equal volume of pure water by a semipermeable membrane. If the solution is at a pressure of 1 atm and a temperature of 298 K:

F. water will diffuse across the semipermeable membrane from the sucrose solution side to the pure water side.

G. water will diffuse across the semipermeable membrane from the pure water side to the sucrose solution side.

H. water will not diffuse across the semipermeable membrane.

J. water will diffuse across the semipermeable membrane, but the direction of diffusion cannot be determined.

9. In Experiment 1, the scientists investigated the effect of:

A. solvent and concentration on osmotic pressure.

B. volume and temperature on osmotic pressure.

C. concentration and temperature on osmotic pressure.

D. temperature on atmospheric pressure.

10. Which of the following conclusions can be drawn from the experimental results?

I. Osmotic pressure is independent of the solvent used.

II. Osmotic pressure is only dependent upon the temperature of the system.

III. Osmosis occurs only when the osmotic pressure is exceeded.

F. I only

G. III only

H. I and II only

J. I and III only

11. What was the most likely purpose of the dye placed in the sucrose solutions in Experiments 1 and 2?

A. The dye showed when osmosis was completed.

B. The dye showed the presence of ions in the solutions.

C. The dye was used to make the experiment more colorful.

D. The dye was used to make the onset of osmosis visible.

GO ON TO THE NEXT PAGE

Passage III

A chemist investigating the influence of molecular weight and structure on the boiling point (transition from liquid to gaseous state) of different compounds recorded the data in the tables below. Two types of compounds were investigated: organic carbon compounds (shown in Table 1) and inorganic compounds (shown in Table 2).

Table 1

Straight-Chain Hydrocarbons		
Molecular formula	Molar weight* (g/mol)	Boiling point (°C)
CH_4	16	−162
C_2H_6	30	−88
C_3H_8	44	−42
C_4H_{10}	58	0
C_5H_{12}	72	36
C_8H_{18}	114	126
$C_{20}H_{42}$	282	345

*Molar weight is the weight of one mole, or an *Avogadro's Number* of molecules ($\approx 6 \times 10^{23}$), in grams.

Table 2

Other Substances (Polar and Non-Polar)		
Molecular formula	Molar weight (g/mol)	Boiling point (°C)
N_2*	28	−196
SiH_4*	32	−112
GeH_4*	77	−90
Br_2*	160	59
CO**	28	−192
PH_3**	34	−85
AsH_3**	78	−55
ICl**	162	97

*Non-Polar: molecule's charge is evenly distributed.

**Polar: molecule's negative and positive charges are partially separated.

12. Which of the following straight-chain hydrocarbons would NOT be a gas at room temperature?

F. C_2H_6

G. C_3H_8

H. C_4H_{10}

J. C_5H_{12}

13. Which of the following conclusions is supported by the observed results?

   I. Boiling point varies directly with molecular weight.

   II. Boiling point varies inversely with molecular weight.

   III. Boiling point is affected by molecular structure.

A. I only

B. II only

C. I and III only

D. II and III only

14. Based on the data in Table 1, the boiling point of the straight-chain hydrocarbon C_6H_{14} (molecular weight 86 g/mol) is most likely:

F. 30°C.

G. 70°C.

H. 130°C.

J. impossible to predict.

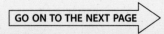
GO ON TO THE NEXT PAGE

15. Based on the data in Table 2, as molecular weight increases, the difference between the boiling points of polar and non-polar substances of similar molecular weight:

    A. increases.
    B. decreases.
    C. remains constant.
    D. varies randomly.

16. A polar substance with a boiling point of 0°C is likely to have a molar weight closest to which of the following:

    F. 58
    G. 80
    H. 108
    J. 132

Passage IV

A series of experiments was performed to study the environmental factors affecting the size and number of leaves on the *Cycas* plant.

EXPERIMENT 1

Five groups of 25 *Cycas* seedlings, all from 2–3 cm tall, were allowed to grow for 3 months, each group at a different humidity level. All of the groups were kept at 75°F and received 9 hours of sunlight a day. The average leaf lengths, widths, and densities are given in Table 1.

Table 1

% Humidity	Average length (cm)	Average width (cm)	Average density* (leaves/cm)
15	5.6	1.6	0.13
35	7.1	1.8	0.25
55	9.8	2.0	0.56
75	14.6	2.6	0.61
95	7.5	1.7	0.52

*Number of leaves per 1 cm of plant stalk

EXPERIMENT 2

Five new groups of 25 seedlings, all from 2–3 cm tall, were allowed to grow for 3 months, each group receiving different amounts of sunlight at a constant humidity of 55%. All other conditions were the same as in Experiment 1. The results are listed in Table 2.

Table 2

Sunlight (hrs/day)	Average length (cm)	Average width (cm)	Average density* (leaves/cm)
0	5.3	1.5	0.32
3	12.4	2.4	0.59
6	11.2	2.0	0.56
9	8.4	1.8	0.26
12	7.7	1.7	0.19

*Number of leaves per 1 cm of plant stalk

GO ON TO THE NEXT PAGE

EXPERIMENT 3

Five new groups of 25 seedlings, all from 2–3 cm tall, were allowed to grow at a constant humidity of 55% for 3 months at different daytime and nighttime temperatures. All other conditions were the same as in Experiment 1. The results are shown in Table 3.

Table 3

Day/night temperature (°F)	Average length (cm)	Average width (cm)	Average density* (leaves/cm)
85/85	6.8	1.5	0.28
85/65	12.3	2.1	0.53
65/85	8.1	1.7	0.33
75/75	7.1	1.9	0.45
65/65	8.3	1.7	0.39

*Number of leaves per 1 cm of plant stalk

17. Which of the following conclusions can be made based on the results of Experiment 2 alone?

   A. The seedlings do not require long daily periods of sunlight to grow.

   B. The average leaf density is independent of the humidity the seedlings receive.

   C. The seedlings need more water at night than during the day.

   D. The average length of the leaves increases as the amount of sunlight increases.

18. Seedlings grown at a 40% humidity level under the same conditions as in Experiment 1 would have average leaf widths closest to:

   F. 1.6 cm.

   G. 1.9 cm.

   H. 2.2 cm.

   J. 2.5 cm.

19. According to the experimental results, under which set of conditions would a *Cycas* seedling be most likely to produce the largest leaves?

   A. 95% humidity and 3 hours of sunlight

   B. 75% humidity and 3 hours of sunlight

   C. 95% humidity and 6 hours of sunlight

   D. 75% humidity and 6 hours of sunlight

20. Which variable remained constant throughout all of the experiments?

   F. The number of seedling groups

   G. The percent of humidity

   H. The daytime temperature

   J. The nighttime temperature

21. It was assumed in the design of the three experiments that all of the *Cycas* seedlings were:

   A. more than 5 cm tall.

   B. equally capable of germinating.

   C. equally capable of producing flowers.

   D. equally capable of further growth.

22. As a continuation of the three experiments listed, it would be most appropriate to next investigate:

   F. how many leaves over 6.0 cm long there are on each plant.

   G. which animals consume *Cycas* seedlings.

   H. how the mineral content of the soil affects the leaf size and density.

   J. what time of year the seedlings have the darkest coloring.

GO ON TO THE NEXT PAGE ⟩

Passage V

The resistance (R) of a conductor is the extent to which it opposes the flow of electricity. Resistance depends not only on the conductor's resistivity (ρ), but also on the conductor's length (L) and cross-sectional area (A). The resistivity of a conductor is a physical property of the material that varies with temperature.

A research team designing a new appliance was researching the best type of wire to use in a particular circuit. The most important consideration was the wire's resistance. The team studied the resistance of wires made from four metals—gold (Au), aluminum (Al), tungsten (W), and iron (Fe). Two lengths and two gauges (diameters) of each type of wire were tested at 20°C. The results are recorded in the following table.

10-gauge wire
A = 5.26 mm²

16-gauge wire
A = 1.31 mm²

2.59 mm

1.29 mm

Note: area of circle = πr²

Table 1

Material	Resistivity (mV–cm)	Length (cm)	Cross-sectional area (mm²)	Resistance (mV)
Au	2.44	1.0	5.26	46.4
Au	2.44	1.0	1.31	186.0
Au	2.44	2.0	5.26	92.8
Au	2.44	2.0	1.31	372.0
Al	2.83	1.0	5.26	53.8
Al	2.83	1.0	1.31	216.0
Al	2.83	2.0	5.26	107.6
Al	2.83	2.0	1.31	432.0
W	5.51	1.0	5.26	105.0
W	5.51	1.0	1.31	421.0
W	5.51	2.0	5.26	210.0
W	5.51	2.0	1.31	842.0
Fe	10.00	1.0	5.26	190.0
Fe	10.00	1.0	1.31	764.0
Fe	10.00	2.0	5.26	380.0
Fe	10.00	2.0	1.31	1,528.0

23. Of the wires tested, resistance increases for any given material as which parameter is decreased?

A. Length

B. Cross-sectional area

C. Resistivity

D. Gauge

24. Given the data in the table, which of the following best expresses resistance in terms of resistivity (ρ), cross-sectional area (A), and length (L)?

F. $\dfrac{\rho A}{L}$

G. $\dfrac{\rho L}{A}$

H. ρAL

J. $\dfrac{AL}{\rho}$

GO ON TO THE NEXT PAGE

25. Which of the following wires would have the highest resistance?

   A. A 1-cm aluminum wire with a cross-sectional area of 0.33 mm²

   B. A 2-cm aluminum wire with a cross-sectional area of 0.33 mm²

   C. A 1-cm tungsten wire with a cross-sectional area of 0.33 mm²

   D. A 2-cm tungsten wire with a cross-sectional area of 0.33 mm²

26. According to the information given, which of the following statements is (are) correct?

   I. 10-gauge wire has a larger diameter than 16-gauge wire.

   II. Gold has a higher resistivity than tungsten.

   III. Aluminum conducts electricity better than iron.

   F. I only

   G. II only

   H. III only

   J. I and III only

27. Which of the following graphs best represents the relationship between the resistivity of a tungsten wire and its length?

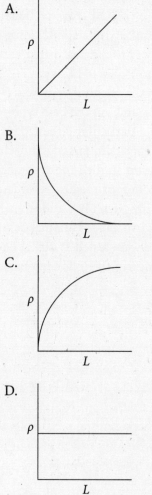

A.

B.

C.

D.

Passage VI

How does evolution occur? Two views are presented below.

SCIENTIST 1

Evolution occurs by natural selection. Random mutations are continually occurring in a species as it propagates. A number of these mutations result in traits that help the species adapt to environmental changes. Because these mutant traits are advantageous, the members of the species who possess them tend to survive and pass on their genes more often than those who do not have these traits. Therefore, the percentage of the population with an advantageous trait increases over time. Long necks evolved in giraffes by natural selection. The ancestors of giraffes had necks of various sizes; however, their average neck length was much shorter than the average neck length of modern-day giraffes. Since the food supply was limited, the individuals with necks on the long range of the spectrum had access to more food (the leaves of trees) and therefore were more likely to survive and pass on their traits than individuals with shorter necks. Therefore, the proportion of the individuals with long necks is slightly greater in each subsequent generation.

SCIENTIST 2

Evolution occurs by the inheritance of acquired characteristics. Characteristics that are acquired by an individual member of a species during its lifetime are passed on to its offspring. Therefore, each generation's traits are partially accounted for by all the changes that occurred in the individuals of the previous generation. This includes changes that occurred as a result of accidents, changes in the environment, overuse of muscles, etc. The evolution of long necks of giraffes is an example. Ancestors of giraffes had short necks and consequently had to stretch their necks to reach the leaves of trees that were their main source of food. This repeated stretching of their necks caused them to elongate slightly. This trait was passed on, so that the individuals of the next generation had slightly longer necks. Each subsequent generation also stretched their necks to feed; therefore, each generation had slightly longer necks than the previous generation.

GO ON TO THE NEXT PAGE ⇨

28. Both scientists agree that:

    F. the environment affects evolution.

    G. the individuals of a generation have identical traits.

    H. acquired characteristics are inherited.

    J. random mutations occur.

29. How would the two hypotheses be affected if it were found that all of the offspring of an individual with a missing leg due to an accident were born with a missing leg?

    A. It would support Scientist 1's hypothesis, because it is an example of random mutations occurring within a species.

    B. It would refute Scientist 1's hypothesis, because it is an example of random mutations occurring within a species.

    C. It would support Scientist 2's hypothesis, because it is an example of an acquired characteristic being passed on to the next generation.

    D. It would support Scientist 2's hypothesis, because it is an example of random mutations occurring within a species.

30. Which of the following characteristics can be inherited according to Scientist 2?

    I. Fur color

    II. Bodily scars resulting from a fight with another animal

    III. Poor vision

    F. I only

    G. II only

    H. I and III only

    J. I, II, and III

31. Scientist 1 believes that the evolution of the long neck of the giraffe:

    A. is an advantageous trait that resulted from overuse of neck muscles over many generations.

    B. is an advantageous trait that resulted from a random mutation.

    C. is an advantageous trait that resulted from a mutation that occurred in response to a change in the environment.

    D. is a disadvantageous trait that resulted from a random mutation.

32. The fundamental point of disagreement between the two scientists is whether:

    F. giraffes' ancestors had short necks.

    G. evolved traits come from random mutations or from the previous generation.

    H. the environment affects the evolution of a species.

    J. the extinction of a species could be the result of random mutations.

GO ON TO THE NEXT PAGE

33. Suppose evidence was found that suggested that before the discovery of fire, human skin lacked the nerve endings necessary to detect extreme heat. Which of the following pieces of information, if true, would most seriously weaken the hypothesis of Scientist 2?

   A. Human skin is capable of generating nerve endings with new functions during life.

   B. The total number of nerve endings in the skin of a human is determined at birth and remains constant until death.

   C. An excess of nerve endings that are sensitive to extreme heat is a relatively common human mutation.

   D. No evidence exists to suggest that an excess of nerve endings that are sensitive to heat could be acquired through mutation.

34. The average height of a full-grown person today is significantly greater than was the average height of a full-grown person 1,000 years ago. If it was proven that the increase in average height was due only to evolutionary changes, how would Scientist 1 most likely explain this increase?

   F. People genetically prone to growing taller have been more likely to produce offspring over the last 1,000 years.

   G. Over the last 1,000 years, improvements in nutrition and medicine have led to greater average growth over a person's lifetime, and this growth has been passed from one generation to the next.

   H. Increased height is not a trait that can be acquired through mutation.

   J. Measurements of average height were less accurate 1,000 years ago than they are today.

GO ON TO THE NEXT PAGE

Passage VII

Bovine spongiform encephalopathy (BSE) is caused by the spread of a misfolded protein that eventually kills infected cattle. BSE is diagnosed postmortem from the diseased cavities that appear in brain tissue and is associated with the use in cattle feed of ground-up meat from scrapie-infected sheep. A series of experiments was performed to determine the mode of transmission of BSE. The results are given in the table below.

EXPERIMENT 1

Sixty healthy cows were divided into two equal groups. Group A's feed included meat from scrapie-free sheep; and Group B's feed included meat from scrapie-infected sheep. Eighteen months later, the two groups were slaughtered and their brains examined for BSE cavities.

EXPERIMENT 2

Researchers injected ground-up sheep brains directly into the brains of two groups of 30 healthy cows. The cows in Group C received brains from scrapie-free sheep. The cows in Group D received brains from scrapie-infected sheep. Eighteen months later, both groups were slaughtered and their brains examined for diseased cavities.

Table 1

Group	Mode of transmission	Scrapie present	Number of cows infected with BSE*
A	feed	no	1
B	feed	yes	12
C	injection	no	0
D	injection	yes	3

*As determined visually by presence/absence of spongiform encephalopathy

35. Which of the following hypotheses was investigated in Experiment 1?

A. The injection of scrapie-infected sheep brains into cows' brains causes BSE.

B. The ingestion of wild grasses causes BSE.

C. The ingestion of scrapie-infected sheep meat causes scrapie.

D. The ingestion of scrapie-infected sheep meat causes BSE.

36. What is the purpose of Experiment 2?

F. To determine whether BSE can be transmitted by injection

G. To determine whether BSE can be transmitted by ingestion

H. To determine whether ingestion or injection is the primary mode of BSE transmission

J. To determine the healthiest diet for cows

37. Which of the following assumptions is made by the researchers in Experiments 1 and 2?

A. Cows do not suffer from scrapie.

B. A year and a half is a sufficient amount of time for BSE to develop in a cow.

C. Cows and sheep suffer from the same diseases.

D. Cows that eat scrapie-free sheep meat will not develop BSE.

GO ON TO THE NEXT PAGE

38. A researcher wishes to determine whether BSE can be transmitted through scrapie-infected goats. Which of the following experiments would best test this?

    F. Repeating Experiment 1, using a mixture of sheep and goat meat in Group C's feed

    G. Repeating Experiments 1 and 2, replacing sheep with healthy goats

    H. Repeating Experiments 1 and 2, replacing healthy sheep with healthy goats and scrapie-infected sheep with scrapie-infected goats

    J. Repeating Experiment 2, replacing healthy cows with healthy goats

39. What is the control group in Experiment 1?

    A. Group A
    B. Group B
    C. Group C
    D. Group D

40. Which of the following conclusions is (are) supported by the experiments?

    I. Cows that are exposed to scrapie-infected sheep are more likely to develop BSE than cows that are not.

    II. BSE is only transmitted by eating scrapie-infected sheep meat.

    III. A cow that eats scrapie-infected sheep meat is more likely to develop BSE than a cow that is injected with scrapie-infected sheep brains.

    F. II only
    G. III only
    H. I and III only
    J. II and III only

WRITING TEST

30 Minutes—1 Question

Directions: This is a test of your writing skills. You will have thirty (30) minutes to write an essay in English. Before you begin planning and writing your essay, read the writing prompt carefully to understand exactly what you are being asked to do. Your essay will be evaluated on the evidence it provides of your ability to express judgments by taking a position on the issue in the writing prompt; to maintain a focus on the topic throughout the essay; to develop a position by using logical reasoning and by supporting your ideas; to organize ideas in a logical way; and to use language clearly and effectively according to the conventions of standard written English. You may use the unlined pages in this test booklet to plan your essay. These pages will not be scored. *You must write your essay in pencil on the lined pages in the answer folder.* Your writing on those lined pages will be scored. You may not need all the lined pages, but to ensure you have enough room to finish, do NOT skip lines. You may write corrections or additions neatly between the lines of your essay, but do NOT write in the margins of the lined pages. *Illegible essays cannot be scored, so you must write (or print) clearly.*

If you finish before time is called, you may review your work. Lay your pencil down immediately when time called.

DO NOT OPEN THIS BOOKLET UNTIL TOLD TO DO SO.

GO ON TO THE NEXT PAGE

ACT Writing Test Prompt

While some high schools offer art and music courses to their students, these courses are not always mandatory. Some teachers, students, and parents think that schools should emphasize traditional academic subjects like math and science, as those skills will help the students more in the future when they join the workforce. Others feel that requiring all high school students to take classes in music or the visual arts would teach equally valuable skills that the students may not learn otherwise and would also help them do better in traditional academic subject areas. In your opinion, should art or music classes be mandatory for all high school students?

In your essay, take a position on this question. You may write about either one of the two points of view given, or you may present a different point of view on this question. Use specific reasons and examples to support your position.

Use this space to *plan* your essay. Your work here will not be graded. Write your essay on the lined pages that follow.

GO ON TO THE NEXT PAGE

GO ON TO THE NEXT PAGE

Practice Test One
ANSWER KEY

ENGLISH TEST

1. C	11. C	21. B	31. D	41. D	51. D	61. D	71. D
2. F	12. G	22. G	32. H	42. J	52. J	62. J	72. G
3. D	13. B	23. D	33. A	43. B	53. C	63. C	73. B
4. F	14. H	24. J	34. H	44. G	54. H	64. J	74. F
5. D	15. C	25. C	35. D	45. C	55. D	65. D	75. B
6. G	16. H	26. F	36. G	46. F	56. G	66. J	
7. B	17. B	27. A	37. D	47. B	57. A	67. B	
8. J	18. G	28. J	38. G	48. H	58. H	68. F	
9. A	19. A	29. B	39. D	49. C	59. D	69. D	
10. J	20. J	30. G	40. J	50. H	60. H	70. F	

MATH TEST

1. D	9. E	17. B	25. D	33. A	41. B	49. E	57. C
2. J	10. K	18. H	26. G	34. K	42. H	50. K	58. H
3. D	11. D	19. D	27. C	35. A	43. C	51. E	59. D
4. K	12. H	20. H	28. H	36. J	44. K	52. K	60. J
5. C	13. C	21. E	29. B	37. A	45. A	53. B	
6. K	14. H	22. H	30. K	38. G	46. G	54. G	
7. B	15. C	23. D	31. C	39. C	47. E	55. D	
8. K	16. G	24. F	32. H	40. G	48. G	56. K	

READING TEST

1. C	6. H	11. B	16. J	21. B	26. F	31. C	36. H
2. G	7. C	12. H	17. B	22. F	27. C	32. G	37. A
3. B	8. G	13. B	18. H	23. D	28. G	33. D	38. J
4. F	9. B	14. F	19. B	24. F	29. D	34. F	39. B
5. D	10. H	15. C	20. H	25. B	30. F	35. D	40. G

SCIENCE TEST

1. B	6. H	11. D	16. H	21. D	26. J	31. B	36. F
2. F	7. C	12. J	17. A	22. H	27. D	32. G	37. B
3. D	8. G	13. C	18. G	23. B	28. F	33. B	38. H
4. J	9. C	14. G	19. B	24. G	29. C	34. F	39. A
5. B	10. F	15. A	20. F	25. D	30. J	35. D	40. G

ANSWERS AND EXPLANATIONS

English Test

The questions fall into the following categories, according to the skills they test. If you notice that you're having trouble with particular categories, review the following:

1. REDUNDANCY: English Workout 1
2. RELEVANCE: English Workout 1
3. VERBOSITY: English Workout 1
4. JUDGING THE PASSAGE: English Workout 2
5. LOGIC: English Workout 2
6. MODIFIERS: English Workout 2
7. READING-TYPE QUESTIONS: English Workout 2
8. STRUCTURE AND PURPOSE: English Workout 2
9. TONE: English Workout 2
10. VERB USAGE: English Workout 2
11. COMPLETENESS: English Workouts 2 and 3
12. IDIOM: English Workouts 2 and 3
13. PRONOUNS: English Workouts 2 and 3
14. SENTENCE STRUCTURE: English Workouts 2 and 3
15. PUNCTUATION: English Workout 3

PASSAGE I

1. C
Punctuation
C is the most correct and concise answer choice. Choice A uses an unnecessary comma. Choice B is unnecessarily wordy. Choice D is redundant—if the societies created the legends, there is no need to describe the legends as original.

2. F
Structure and Purpose
The question stem gives an important clue to the best answer: the purpose of the inserted sentence is "to describe the different kinds" of stories. Choice F is the only choice that does this. Choice G explains how the stories were told. H explains why more is not known about the stories. Choice J describes the length of some stories.

3. D
Structure and Purpose
Answer choices A, B, and C create run-on sentences. Choice D describes a relationship that makes sense between our "many more permanent ways of handing down our beliefs" and the fact that "we continue to create and tell legends." It also creates a complete sentence.

4. F
Verbosity
Choices H and J are ungrammatical after a colon. Choices G, H, and J are unnecessarily wordy.

5. D
Redundancy
Choices A, B, and C are redundant or unnecessarily wordy. Because the contrasting word *but* is already used, *however* is repetitive and should be eliminated.

6. G
Redundancy

Choices F, H, and J are all redundant. The word *conclusion* is unnecessary because the word *ending* has already been used.

7. B
Verb Usage

Choice B is the only choice that stays consistent with the verb tense established by *knew* and *decided*.

8. J
Verb Usage

Choice F creates a run-on sentence and also makes it seem that the hunter, not the deer, "was only temporarily knocked unconscious by the car." Choices G and H use incorrect verb tenses.

9. A
Punctuation

Choice B is incorrect because the words preceding the semicolon could not be a complete sentence on their own. Choice C would create a sentence fragment. Choice D would create a run-on sentence.

10. J
Relevance

Regardless of the sequence of the words, the information provided in choices F, G, and H is irrelevant to the passage's topic of urban legends.

11. C
Verb Usage

The subject of the sentence is *One*, so the verb must be singular. Choices B and D use incorrect verb tenses.

12. G
Modifiers

Choice F creates a sentence that does not make sense. Choices H and J use the plural *women* instead of the singular *woman*.

13. B
Sentence Structure

Choice B most clearly expresses the idea that several websites research "the validity of commonly told urban legends." Because this information is relevant to the topic of urban legends, "OMIT the underlined portion" is not the best answer.

14. H
Structure and Purpose

Paragraph 4 describes an urban legend that is "humorous in nature." Paragraph 5 describes a rather frightening legend: alligators living underneath the city in the sewer system. The sentence "Other urban legends seem to be designed to instill fear" is an appropriate topic sentence for paragraph 5, and it also serves as a needed transition between paragraph 4 and paragraph 5.

15. C
Judging the Passage

Although the third and fourth sentences of paragraph 1 provide *some* general information about the purpose and topics of the myths and legends of primitive societies, no specifics are given. This makes choice C the best answer.

PASSAGE II

16. H
Verb Usage

Correct choices here could be *do you* or *does one*. The latter appears as an answer choice.

17. B
Punctuation
Choice A incorrectly uses a colon. Choices C and D are grammatically incorrect.

18. G
Redundancy
Solitary and *alone* are redundant in the same sentence. Choices H and J also have redundancy.

19. A
Modifiers
The underlined portion is clearest the way it is written.

20. J
Punctuation
The colon is incorrect, so eliminate choices F and H. Because it is a compound sentence, a comma is needed before *and*.

21. B
Sentence Structure
In fact is nonessential—it should be set off by commas.

22. G
Modifiers
American (an adjective) is the word being modified. Therefore, the adverb form of *unique* is needed.

23. D
Completeness
"Near Walden Pond…" is a long sentence fragment. The best way to fix the error is to simply combine the sentences by eliminating the period.

24. J
Logic
This paragraph and the ones that immediately follow outline Thoreau's life. His influence on the people of today is not discussed until the end of the essay. Therefore, the underlined sentence does not belong.

25. C
Logic
Sentence 3 logically follows sentence 1. Choice C is the only choice that lists this correct order.

26. F
Punctuation
There is one independent clause on each side of the semicolon, so the sentence is punctuated correctly. Choice G needs *and* after the comma to be correct. Choices H and J create run-on sentences.

27. A
Pronouns
A possessive pronoun is needed because the works belong to Thoreau. Eliminate choices B and D. Choice C relates to more than one person, so it is incorrect as well.

28. J
Judging the Passage
This paragraph discusses Thoreau's impact on modern society; only choice J expresses the correct topic.

29. B
Redundancy
Choices A, C, and D are excessively wordy.

30. G
Judging the Passage
The use of questions forces the reader to think about the answers. Choice F is too literal, and choice J is too broad for the topic of the essay. Choice H is incorrect because the author establishes the quality of Thoreau's work.

PASSAGE III

31. D
Redundancy

Because the word *live* is used later in the sentence, choices A, B, and C contain redundant information.

32. H
Pronouns

In this sentence, the *its* must be possessive because the *unique anatomy* belongs to the sloth. The word describing *anatomy* must be an adjective, not an adverb.

33. A
Punctuation

The comma is correctly used in choice A to separate the nonessential descriptive phrase "about the size of a large domestic cat" from the rest of the sentence.

34. H
Relevance

The information about the sloth's limbs is relevant to the topic, so it should not be omitted. Choice H clearly and directly expresses how the sloth's muscles are designed for clinging to things.

35. D
Modifiers

Adapted needs to be modified by an adverb, so D is the best choice.

36. G
Pronouns

Instead describes the right relationship between the two sentences. The pronouns must be consistent, and since *its* is already used in the sentence, G is the best choice.

37. D
Modifiers

D is the only choice that correctly describes the relationship between the sloth's inability to "move swiftly on the ground" and its ability to swim.

38. G
Judging the Passage

Choice G connects the sloth's unique characteristics discussed in paragraph 3 with the description of its flexibility in paragraph 4.

39. D
Punctuation

Choice D correctly uses the second comma necessary to separate the phrase "without moving the rest of its body" from the rest of the sentence. Choice C can be eliminated because it is unnecessarily wordy.

40. J
Verb Usage

J is the only choice that contains a verb tense consistent with the sentence.

41. D
Redundancy

Choices A, B, and C contain redundant information.

42. J
Relevance

This information about the howler monkey is irrelevant to the topic of the passage.

43. B
Sentence Structure

Choice A creates a sentence fragment. Choice C is unnecessarily wordy and awkward. Choice D creates a run-on sentence.

44. G
Judging the Passage
The last sentence aptly concludes the entire passage, and removing it would make the ending more abrupt.

45. C
Logic
The description of the sloth's *camouflage* is in paragraph 5.

PASSAGE IV

46. F
Verbosity
The underlined portion is best left as is. The other answer choices make the sentence unnecessarily wordy.

47. B
Verb Usage
The verb tense must agree with the tense that has been established up to this point. The passage is in the past tense, so choice B is correct.

48. H
Verb Usage
Like the answer to the previous question, the simple past tense is correct.

49. C
Verb Usage
Choice A creates a sentence fragment and uses an incorrect verb tense. Choice B also uses the wrong verb tense. Choice D incorrectly uses a semicolon, as the words preceding the semicolon do not constitute an independent clause.

50. H
Logic
In the context of the rest of the passage, only choice H makes sense. The firefighters' attempts to extinguish the flames failed; *only* nature could stop the fire with the first snowfall.

51. D
Verbosity
Choices A and B are unnecessarily wordy and awkward. Choice C creates a run-on sentence.

52. J
Verbosity
All of the other answer choices are unnecessarily wordy and/or repetitive.

53. C
Verb Usage
From the plural verb *open*, you can determine that the best answer will contain *cones*. This makes choice C the only possible answer, as the apostrophe is incorrectly used in choice B.

54. H
Logic
This is the only choice that makes sense in the context of the passage. The sighting of the large animals near burning forests is used as evidence that the animals of the region were "fire-tolerant and fire-adaptive."

55. D
Punctuation
The comma in choice A is unnecessary because the sentence has a list of only two examples, not three. The semicolon in choice B is incorrectly used because "and bedding down" does not begin an independent clause. The colon in choice C is incorrectly used because it is not being used to introduce or emphasize information.

56. G
Modifiers
The problem with "judging from recent pictures of the park" is that the phrase is modifying *forest*, and a forest obviously can't judge anything. The phrase would have been correct if the sentence read "judging from the recent

pictures of the park, I think that the forest was not destroyed." In this case, the phrase modifies *I*, the author, who is capable of judging. Choice G takes care of the problem by rewriting the sentence so that the modifying phrase is gone.

57. A
Pronouns
The pronoun refers to *forest*.

58. H
Judging the Passage
The introduction of information about fires in Alaska is unwarranted, so choices F and G can be eliminated. J is incorrect because the additional information would actually uphold the author's position as an authority.

59. D
Logic
The reports mentioned in choice D directly substantiate the author's claims much more than any of the other answer choices.

PASSAGE V

60. H
Verb Usage
Choice F creates a sentence fragment, and choice G incorrectly uses a plural verb with a singular subject. The verb tense of the paragraph makes H a better choice than J.

61. D
Relevance
The final part of the sentence, "…and there are many other rivers in America as well," is completely irrelevant to the rest of the sentence and the paragraph, in which the author discusses white-water rafting and the rivers she's rafted.

62. J
Punctuation
Choice F is wrong because *rapids* is essential information and should not be set off by commas. Choice G is wrong because what follows the colon is not an explanation. Choice H is incorrect because what follows the semicolon cannot stand alone as a sentence.

63. C
Completeness
Choices A and D create sentence fragments, and choice B is extremely awkward.

64. J
Relevance
This sentence is irrelevant to the topic of the passage.

65. D
Modifiers
This sentence makes it sound as though the author were roaring, not the rapids; *roaring* is a misplaced modifier. Choice B doesn't fix the problem because the reader has no idea what *it* refers to. Choice C has *the boat* roaring. D is the clearest choice.

66. J
Sentence Structure
The word *cover* must either be in past tense, or the structure of the sentence must change. Choice J does the latter.

67. B
Verbosity
Choice B is the simplest, most concise way of expressing the idea. Replacing "and instead he adopted" with "with" makes the sentence much less awkward.

68. F

Idioms

Choices G and J make it sound as though the author were in the water. Choice F expresses the idea more accurately than choice H does.

69. D

Redundancy

The phrase "and we stopped" is redundant because "we came to a jarring halt" says the same thing much more expressively. Omit the underlined portion.

70. F

Verb Usage

It was is fine here because the author is telling her story in the past tense. Choices G and H are the present tense, and J incorrectly introduces the possessive form.

71. D

Redundancy

The other answer choices are unnecessarily wordy; the simplest choice, D, is the best.

72. G

Verb Usage

The participle *receiving* has to be changed into a verb in the past tense, *received*, in order to be consistent with *went*. Choice G is correct as opposed to choice H because the number of bruises something has can be counted, which necessitates *many bruises*, not *much bruises*.

73. B

Logic

Choice A wouldn't work as a concluding sentence because its style and tone are off; nowhere in the passage does the writer use language such as "brutal calamities" and "beguiling excitement." Also, the writer and her father were not "unwary rafters." C contradicts the writer's main theme that nothing was as memorable

as her first ride through the rapids. The tone in D, "call me crazy or weird…," is much different from the writer's. Choice B is the choice that closely matches the author's style and tone while restating the main theme of the passage.

74. F

Structure and Purpose

This essay relates a personal experience of the writer: her first time rafting down the rapids. There is very little mention of the techniques of white-water rafting, so the essay would not meet the requirements of the assignment. Choice G is wrong because the essay does not focus on the relationship between father and daughter, but on their first rafting experience together.

75. B

Judging the Passage

The sentence foreshadows things to come, so it must appear toward the beginning of the essay. That eliminates choices C and D. The second paragraph is about the peaceful setting, so choice B is the most sensible answer.

Math Test

Answer explanations for the Math test refer to 100 Key Math Concepts for the ACT, found at the end of this book.

1. D

Percentages

Key Math Concepts for the ACT, #32. You know that 14 people are 20% of the total, and you need to find 100% of the total. You could set up an equation, or you could multiply 14 by 5, since 100% is 5 times as much as 20%. The number of people surveyed is 14 × 5, or 70.

2. J
Average Formula

Key Math Concepts for the ACT, #41. One safe way to answer this question is by picking numbers. For instance, if you let $x = 2$ and $y = 3$, the train would have traveled $90 \times 2 + 60 \times 3 = 360$ miles in 5 hours, or $\frac{360}{5} = 72$ miles per hour. If you then plug $x = 2$ and $y = 3$ into the answer choices, it's clear that the correct answer is J. No other answer choice equals 72 when $x = 2$ and $y = 3$.

3. D
Solving a Proportion

Key Math Concepts for the ACT, #38. If the ratio of men to women is 5:3, then the ratio of women to the total is $3:3 + 5 = 3:8$. Since you know the total number of string players is 24, you can set up the equation $\frac{3}{8} = \frac{x}{24}$ to find that $x = 9$. Also, without setting up the proportion, you could note that the total number of players is 3 times the ratio total, so the number of women will be 3 times the part of the ratio that represents women.

4. K
Evaluating an Expression

Key Math Concepts for the ACT, #52. In a pinch you could backsolve on this question, but this one is fairly easy to solve algebraically, like so:

$$x^2 - 3x = 6x$$
$$x^2 = 9x$$

Now you can divide both sides by x because $x \neq 0$:

$$\frac{x^2}{x} = \frac{9x}{x}$$
$$x = 9$$

5. C

With visual perception problems such as this one, the key is to play around with possibilities as you try to draw a solution. Eventually,

you should be able to come up with a picture like this:

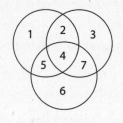

6. K
Evaluating an Expression

Key Math Concepts for the ACT, #52. This problem could be solved algebraically, but look at the answer choices. They are all simple numbers, making this a great opportunity for backsolving. Begin with choice H.

Plugging in 0, you get:

$$(0)^2 + 6(0) + 8 = 4 + 10(0)$$
$$8 = 4$$

Since 8 does not equal 4, you know this isn't the correct answer. But it is difficult to know which answer to try next. Should you aim higher or lower? If you're unsure of which direction to go, just try whatever looks easiest. Choice J, 1, looks like a good candidate:

$$(1)^2 + 6(1) + 8 = 4 + 10(1)$$
$$1 + 6 + 8 = 4 + 10$$
$$15 = 14$$

So choice J doesn't work either, but it looks like the numbers are getting closer, so you're going in the right direction. Try choice K just to be sure.

$$(2)^2 + 6(2) + 8 = 4 + 10(2)$$
$$4 + 12 + 8 = 4 + 20$$
$$24 = 24$$

Choice K is the correct answer.

7. B
Translating from English into Algebra

Key Math Concepts for the ACT, #65. Translate piece by piece:

"Nine less than c" indicates subtraction: $c - 9$.

"Nine less than c is the same as the number d": $c - 9 = d$. There's one equation.

"d less than" also indicates subtraction: $- d$.

"d less than twice c is 20": $2c - d = 20$. There's the second equation.

Choice B matches what we found.

8. K
Counting the Possibilities

Key Math Concepts for the ACT, #45. To determine the total number of possible arrangements on a question like this one, simply determine the number of possibilities for each component, and then multiply them together. There are 3 ways of serving the ice cream, 5 flavors, and 4 toppings. Therefore, there are $3 \times 5 \times 4 = 60$ ways to order ice cream, and choice K is correct.

9. E
Part-to-Part and Part-to-Whole Ratios

Key Math Concepts for the ACT, #37. Backsolving is a great technique to use for this problem. Start with C. The director asked 1 out of 3 students to come to the second audition and $\frac{1}{3}$ of 48 is 16, so 16 students were invited to a second audition. Then 75% of 16, which is $\frac{3}{4}(16)$ = 12 students were offered parts. The question states that 18 students were offered parts, so you already know that choice C is too small. (You can also, thus, eliminate choices A and B.) Since the director invited $\frac{1}{3}$ of the students to a second audition, the number of students at the first audition must be divisible by 3. (You can't have a fraction of a student.) That eliminates choice D, which leaves only choice E.

10. K
Multiplying/Dividing Signed Numbers

Key Math Concepts for the ACT, #6. Begin by translating the English into math: $x + 5x = -60$, $6x = -60$, so $x = -10$, and the two numbers are -10 and -50. Thus, the lesser number is -50.

By the way, this is where most people mess up. They forget that the lesser of two negative numbers is the negative number with the larger absolute value (since *less* means *to the left of* on the number line):

11. D
Special Quadrilaterals

Key Math Concepts for the ACT, #86. You're looking for the total number of parallelograms that can be found among the triangles, and parallelograms could be formed two ways from these triangles, either from two adjacent triangles or from four adjacent triangles, like so:

Begin by looking for the smaller parallelograms. If you look for parallelograms leaning in the same direction as the one we drew, you'll find three. But there are two other possible orientations for the smaller parallelogram; it could be flipped horizontally, or it could be rotated 90 degrees so that one triangle sits atop the other in the form of a diamond; both of these orientations also have three parallelograms, for a total of nine smaller parallelograms.

Now look for larger parallelograms. Perhaps the easiest way to count these is to look along the sides of the larger composite triangle. You should be able to spot two of the larger parallelograms along each side, one originating at each vertex, for a total of six larger parallelograms.

Thus, there are a total of 9 + 6 = 15 parallelograms in all.

12. H
Areas of Special Quadrilaterals/
Area of a Circle

Key Math Concepts for the ACT, #87, #91. The square has a perimeter of 16 inches, so each side of the square is 4 inches; the area of the square is, therefore, 16 square inches. If the side of the square is 4 inches, then the diameter of the circle is also 4 inches. The radius of the circle is then 2 inches. The area of the circle is 4π square inches. The area of the shaded region is then $16 - 4\pi$ square inches.

13. C
Factor/Multiple

Key Math Concepts for the ACT, #10. The safest strategy is simply to list out the possibilities. It's also helpful to realize that multiples of both 4 and 6 are multiples of 12 (the least common multiple between the two), so skip over all multiples of 12:

4, 8, ~~12~~, 16, 20, ~~24~~, 28, 32, ~~36~~, 40, 44, ~~48~~

So there are 8 in all.

14. H
Evaluating an Expression

Key Math Concepts for the ACT, #52. Don't be intimidated by the expression $f(x)$. In this case, you should just plug in the number that appears in the parentheses for the x in the expression they have given you.

So, if $f(x) = (8 - 3x)(x^2 - 2x - 15)$, $f(3) = [8 - 3(3)]$ $[(3)^2 - 2(3) - 15]$.

Once you get to this point, just remember PEMDAS.

$[8 - 3(3)][(3)^2 - 2(3) - 15] = (8 - 9)(9 - 6 - 15) =$ $(-1)(-12) = 12$, choice H.

15. C
Probability

Key Math Concepts for the ACT, #46. A class contains five juniors and five seniors. If one member of the class is assigned at random to present a paper on a certain subject, and another member of the class is randomly assigned to assist him, then:

The probability that the first student picked will be a junior $= \dfrac{\text{\# of Juniors}}{\text{Total \# of students}} = \dfrac{5}{10} = \dfrac{1}{2}$.

The probability that the second student picked will be a junior, given that the first student picked was a junior $= \dfrac{\text{\# of Juniors remaining}}{\text{Total \# of students remaining}}$.

So the probability that both students will be juniors $= \dfrac{1}{2} \times \dfrac{4}{9} = \dfrac{2}{9}$.

16. G
Area of a Triangle

Key Math Concepts for the ACT, #83. Since the formula to find the area of a triangle is $\dfrac{1}{2}$ (base)(height), you can plug in the base and area to find the height. You know that the area of this triangle is 45 units and that the base is 3 + 12 = 15. Let x be the length of altitude $\overline{YS}$. Plug these into the area formula to get $45 = \dfrac{15x}{2}$. Solve for x to get $x = 6$.

17. B
Using an Equation to Find an Intercept

Key Math Concepts for the ACT, #74. The y-coordinate is the point on which the x value is zero, so plug $x = 0$ into the equation:

$$6y - 3(0) = 18$$
$$6y = 18$$
$$y = 3$$

18. H
Solving a System of Equations

Key Math Concepts for the ACT, #67. This question involves common quadratics, so the key is to write these quadratic expressions in their other forms. For instance, $x^2 - y^2 = 12$, so $(x + y)(x - y) = 12$. Since $x - y = 4$, $(x + y)(4) = 12$, so $x + y = 3$. Finally, $x^2 + 2xy + y^2 = (x + y)^2 = (3)^2 = 9$.

19. D
Areas of Special Quadrilaterals/
Area of a Triangle

Key Math Concepts for the ACT, #87, #83. This shape must be divided into three simple shapes. By drawing downward two perpendicular line segments from the endpoints of the side which is 10 units long, you are left with a 3 × 10 rectangle, a triangle with a base of 4 and a height of 3, and a triangle with a base of 7 and a hypotenuse of $7\sqrt{2}$. The rectangle has an area of $3 \times 10 = 30$ square units. The smaller triangle has an area of $\frac{4 \times 3}{2} = 6$ square units. The larger triangle is a 45°-45°-90° triangle, so the height must be 7. Therefore, it has an area of $\frac{7 \times 7}{2} =$ 24.5 square units. The entire shape has an area of $6 + 30 + 24.5 = 60.5$ square units.

20. H
Translating from English into Algebra

Key Math Concepts for the ACT, #65. Although backsolving is certainly possible with this problem, it's probably quicker to solve with arithmetic. The board is 12 feet long, which means it is $12 \times 12 = 144$ inches. The carpenter cuts off $3 \times 17 = 51$ inches. That leaves $144 - 51 = 93$ inches.

21. E
Solving a Quadratic Equation

Key Math Concepts for the ACT, #66. To answer this question, begin by setting the right side of the equation equal to zero:

$$x^2 - 4x - 6 = 6$$
$$x^2 - 4x - 12 = 0$$

Now use reverse-FOIL to factor the left side of the equation:

$$(x - 6)(x + 2) = 0$$

Thus, either $x - 6 = 0$ or $x + 2 = 0$, so $x = 6$ or -2.

22. H
Solving a Quadratic Equation

Key Math Concepts for the ACT, #66. Here's another question that tests your understanding of FOIL, but you have to be careful. The question states that -3 is a possible solution for the equation $x^2 + kx - 15 = 0$, so in its factored form, one set of parentheses with a factor inside must be $(x + 3)$. Since the last term in the equation in its expanded form is -15, that means that the entire factored equation must read $(x + 3)(x - 5) = 0$, which in its expanded form is $x^2 - 2x - 15 = 0$. Thus, $k = -2$.

23. D

To solve this problem, you need to understand the triangle inequality theorem, which states: the sum of the lengths of any two sides of a triangle is always greater than the length of the third side. Therefore, the other sides of this triangle must add up to more than 7. You know from the problem that every side must be an integer. That means that the sides must add up to at least 8 inches (4 inches and 4 inches, or 7 inches and 1 inch, for example). The smallest possible perimeter is $7 + 8 = 15$.

24. F
Sine, Cosine, and Tangent of Acute Angles

Key Math Concepts for the ACT, #96. It's time to use SOHCAHTOA, and drawing a triangle might help as well. If the sine of θ (opposite side over hypotenuse) is $\frac{\sqrt{11}}{2\sqrt{3}}$, then one of the legs of the right triangle is $\sqrt{11}$, and the hypotenuse is $2\sqrt{3}$. Now apply the Pythagorean theorem to come up with the other (adjacent) leg: $(\sqrt{11})^2 + (n)^2 = (2\sqrt{3})^2$, so $11 + n^2 = 12$, which means that $n^2 = 1$, and $n = 1$. Thus, cosine (adjacent side over hypotenuse) θ is $\frac{1}{2\sqrt{3}}$.

25. D
Simplifying Square Roots

Key Math Concepts for the ACT, #49. Take a quick look at the answer choices before simplifying an expression like this one. Notice that none of these choices contain a radical sign in their denominators. So when you simplify the expression, try to eliminate that radical sign. Your calculations should look something like this:

$$\frac{\sqrt{3+x}}{\sqrt{3-x}} \times \frac{\sqrt{3-x}}{\sqrt{3-x}} = \frac{\sqrt{(3+x)(3-x)}}{\sqrt{(3-x)^2}} =$$

$$\frac{\sqrt{9-3x+3x-x^2}}{3-x} = \frac{\sqrt{9-x^2}}{3-x}$$

So choice D is correct.

26. G
Part-to-Part and Part-to-Whole Ratios

Key Math Concepts for the ACT, #37. If the ratio of the parts is 2:5, then the ratio total is 2 + 5 = 7. Thus, the actual total number of cookies must be a multiple of 7. The only choice that's a multiple of 7 is G, 35.

27. C
Converting Fractions to Decimals

Key Math Concepts for the ACT, #29. This question is a great opportunity to use your calculator. Notice that all your choices are decimals. In order to solve, convert $\frac{3}{16}$ into a decimal and add that to .175. $\frac{3}{16}$ = .1875, so the sum equals .1875 + .175 = .3625. So choice C is correct.

28. H
Areas of Special Quadrilaterals

Key Math Concepts for the ACT, #87. Remember that if you are given a perimeter for a rectangle, the rectangle with the greatest area for that perimeter will be a square. So we are looking for the area of a square with a perimeter of 20. The perimeter of a square equals $4s$, where s is the length of one side of the square. If $4s = 20$,

then $s = 5$. The area of the square equals $s^2 = 5^2 = 25$, choice H.

29. B
Adding/Subtracting, Multiplying/Dividing Fractions

Key Math Concepts for the ACT, #22, #23, #24. Be careful on this one. You can't start plugging numbers into your calculator without paying attention to the order of operations. This one is best solved on your own.

$$\frac{\frac{3}{2} + \frac{7}{4}}{\left(\frac{15}{8} - \frac{3}{4}\right) - \left(\frac{4+3}{-4+3}\right)} =$$

$$\frac{\frac{3}{2} + \frac{7}{4}}{\left(\frac{9}{8}\right) - \left(\frac{7}{-1}\right)} = \frac{\frac{13}{4}}{\frac{65}{8}} = \frac{13}{4} \times \frac{8}{65} = \frac{2}{5}$$

30. K
Solving a Linear Equation

Key Math Concepts for the ACT, #63. You could solve this algebraically for x as follows:

$$x - 15 = 7 - 5(x - 4)$$
$$x - 15 = 7 - 5x + 20$$
$$x - 15 = -5x + 27$$
$$6x = 42$$
$$x = 7$$

Remember also that if you are ever stuck, you can try to backsolve with the answer choices. Here, if you try them all out, only 7 works:

$$7 - 15 = 7 - 5(7 - 4)$$
$$-8 = 7 - 5(3)$$
$$-8 = 7 - 15$$
$$-8 = -8$$

31. C
Areas of Special Quadrilaterals, Area of a Triangle

Key Math Concepts for the ACT, #87, #83. Break strange figures like this one up into shapes that are more familiar and easier to handle. In this case, the quadrilateral can be split into a square and a right triangle. The square is 9 × 9, so the area of that part of the figure is 81 square meters. The right triangle has a height of 9 and a base of 4, so the area of the triangle would be $\frac{1}{2}bh = \frac{1}{2}(4 \times 9) = \frac{1}{2}(36) = 18$ square meters. So the total area of the figure is (81 + 18) square meters = 99 square meters, choice C.

32. H
Using an Equation to Find the Slope
Key Math Concepts for the ACT, #73. The easiest way to solve this question is to put it in the form $y = mx + b$, in which case m equals the slope. In other words, you want to isolate y:

$$6y - 3x = 18$$
$$6y = 3x + 18$$
$$y = \frac{3x + 18}{6}$$
$$y = \frac{1}{2}x + 3$$

So the slope equals $\frac{1}{2}$.

33. A
To answer this question, you have to know that perpendicular lines on the standard (x, y) coordinate plane have slopes that are negative reciprocals of each other. In other words, the line described by the equation $y = -\frac{4}{5}x + 6$ has a slope of $-\frac{4}{5}$, so a line perpendicular to it has a slope of $\frac{5}{4}$. This eliminates all choices but A. However, if you want to double-check, you can plug the coordinates you're given (4, 3) into the equation found in choice A.

$$3 = 54\ (4) - 2$$
$$3 = 5 - 2$$
$$3 = 3$$

34. K
Using an Equation to Find the Slope
Key Math Concepts for the ACT, #73. Since the problem gives you the y-intercept, it is easy to look at the answer choices and rule out choices F, H, and J. Put the equation from the question in slope-intercept form to find its slope:

$$3x - 5y = 4$$
$$-5y = -3x + 4$$
$$y = \frac{-3x + 4}{-5}$$
$$y = \frac{3}{5}x - \frac{4}{5}$$

Since line t is parallel, it has the same slope. This matches choice K.

35. A
Solving a Linear Equation
Key Math Concepts for the ACT, #63. To solve for x in the equation $y = mx + b$, isolate x on one side of the equation. Begin by subtracting b from both sides. You will be left with $y - b = mx$. Then divide both sides by m, and you will be left with $x = \frac{y - b}{m}$, choice A.

36. J
Special Right Triangles
Key Math Concepts for the ACT, #85. In this figure, there are many right triangles and many similar triangles. If you know to be on the look-out for 3-4-5 triangles, it should be easy to spot that triangle ABC has sides of 15-20-25, so $\overline{AC}$ is 25. Now turn your attention to triangle ABD. Since it's a right triangle that shares $\angle BAC$ with triangle ABC, it too must be a 3-4-5 triangle. So if the hypotenuse is 20, the shorter leg ($\overline{BD}$) must have a length of 12, and the longer leg ($\overline{AD}$) must have a length of 16.

37. A
The shortest distance to line m will be a line perpendicular to m. So the distance will be the

difference between the y-coordinates of point C and the nearest point on line m. Since every point on m has a y-coordinate of 5, and point C has a y-coordinate of 3, the difference is 2.

38. G

While you could try factoring the numerator, you'll find that you can't easily cancel out the denominator by doing so. Perhaps the easiest approach here is to pick numbers. Pick a simple number such as $x = 2$. Thus,

$$\frac{x^2 - 11x + 24}{8 - x} = \frac{(2)^2 - 11(2) + 24}{6} =$$

$$\frac{4 - 22 + 24}{6} = \frac{6}{6} = 1.$$

So 1 is your target number. When you plug $x = 2$ into the choices, the only choice that gives you 1 is G.

39. C
Finding the Distance between Two Points

Key Math Concepts for the ACT, #71.

The textbook method for this problem would be to use the distance formula but that's time-consuming. Instead, it may help you to draw a picture. Draw a right triangle into the coordinate plane as we've done above. Note that the distance between the two points represents the hypotenuse of the triangle. The legs of the triangle have lengths of 3 and 4, so the distance between the two points must be 5, choice C.

40. G
Areas of Special Quadrilaterals, Area of a Circle

Key Math Concepts for the ACT, #87, #91. To find the area of the shaded region, you must subtract the area of the circle from the area of the rectangle. Since the sides of the rectangle are $2x$ and $5x$, it has an area of $2x \times 5x = 10x^2$. By examining the diagram, you can see that the circle has a diameter of $2x$, so it has a radius of x. Its area is, therefore, πx^2. The shaded region, therefore, has an area of $10x^2 - \pi x^2$.

41. B
Sine, Cosine, and Tangent of Acute Angles

Key Math Concepts for the ACT, #96. Since you are not given a diagram for this problem, it's best to draw a quick sketch of a right triangle to help keep the sides separate in your mind. Mark one of the acute angles θ. Since $\cos \theta = \frac{5\sqrt{2}}{8}$, mark the adjacent side $5\sqrt{2}$ and the hypotenuse as 8. (Remember SOHCAHTOA.) Use the Pythagorean theorem to find that the side opposite θ is $\sqrt{14}$. The problem asks you to find $\tan \theta$. Tangent $= \frac{\text{opposite}}{\text{adjacent}}$, so $\tan \theta = \frac{\sqrt{14}}{5\sqrt{2}}$, which can be simplified to $\frac{\sqrt{7}}{5}$.

42. H

This question is one where your calculator can come in handy. Divide 7 by integer values for n, and look for values between .5 and .8. Begin by looking for the integer values of n where $\frac{7}{n}$ is greater than .5. If $n = 14$, then $\frac{7}{n} = .5$, so n must be less than 14. Work through values of n until you get to the point where $\frac{7}{n} \geq .8$. When $n = 9$, $\frac{7}{n} = .778$, but when $n = 8$, $\frac{7}{n} = .875$. So the integer values that work in this case are $n = 9, 10, 11, 12,$ and 13. Five integer values work, so choice H is correct.

43. C

The points are as far apart as possible when separated by a diameter of X and a diameter of Y.

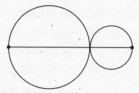

The circumference of a circle is $\pi \times$ (diameter), so the diameter of circle X is 12, and the diameter of circle Y is 8. The greatest possible distance between points then is $12 + 8 = 20$.

44. K

Adding and Subtracting Polynomials

Key Math Concepts for the ACT, #54. Begin by getting rid of the square root sign. If $y \geq 0$, then $\sqrt{y^2} = y$, so $\sqrt{(x^2 + 4)^2} = x^2 + 4$. $(x + 2)(x - 2) = x^2 - 4$, so you now have $(x^2 + 4) - (x^2 - 4) = ?$ Get rid of the parentheses, and you have $x^2 + 4 - x^2 + 4 = x^2 - x^2 + 4 + 4 = 8$.

45. A

Evaluating an Expression

Key Math Concepts for the ACT, #52. Here, you need to substitute -3 for s and solve. That gives you the expression $(-3)^3 + 2(-3)^2 + 2(-3)$, which equals $-27 + 18 - 6$, or -15. If you missed this problem, you probably made a mistake with the signs of the numbers.

46. G

Multiplying Binomials—FOIL

Key Math Concepts for the ACT, #56. Be careful on this one. Begin by simplifying the equation by FOILing one side:

$$2x + 6 = (x + 5)(x + 3)$$
$$2x + 6 = x^2 + 8x + 15$$

Then get the right side of the equation to equal zero: $x^2 + 6x + 9 = 0$.

The left side of this equation is the perfect square $(x + 3)^2$, so $(x + 3)^2 = 0$, which has only one solution, $x = -3$. Choice G is correct.

47. E

Pythagorean Theorem

Key Math Concepts for the ACT, #84. The textbook method for this would be to use the Pythagorean theorem to find the length of a side and then multiply that by 4, but there's an easier way: Eyeball it! The perimeter is greater than $\overline{AC}$, so you can get rid of choices A and B. It appears to be quite a bit greater than $\overline{AC}$, more than twice as great, so choices C and D are out as well. That only leaves choice E.

If you wanted to solve this the conventional way, since the perimeter is the sum of the lengths of all the sides of the square, you need to find the length of the square's sides. Let the length of each of the square's sides be x. $\overline{AC}$ divides the square into two right triangles, so we can apply the Pythagorean theorem: $\overline{AB}^2 + \overline{BC}^2 = \overline{AC}^2$. Since $\overline{AB}$ and $\overline{BC}$ are sides of the square, they have the same length. We can write that as $x^2 + x^2 = \overline{AC}^2$. $\overline{AC} = 8$, so $2x^2 = 8^2$, $2x^2 = 64$, $x^2 = 32$, $x = \sqrt{32} = \sqrt{16 \times 2} = 4\sqrt{2}$. So each side of the square is $4\sqrt{2}$, and the perimeter of the square is $4 \times 4\sqrt{2} = 16\sqrt{2}$.

48. G

Areas of Special Quadrilaterals, Area of a Triangle

Key Math Concepts for the ACT, #87, #83. To find the area of this complex shape, you could divide it into two simple shapes by drawing a line 30 inches up, parallel to the horizontal base. This leaves you with a 4×30 rectangle and a triangle with height of 6 and a base of 4. The rectangle has an area of $4 \times 30 = 120$ square inches, and the triangle has an area of $\frac{4 \times 6}{2} = 12$ square inches. That makes a total of $120 + 12 = 132$ square inches.

49. E
Interior Angles of a Triangle

Key Math Concepts for the ACT, #80. Triangles are the secret to solving this one. Drawing $\overline{OD}$ divides quadrilateral $OCDE$ into two triangles, OCD and ODE. Both triangles are isosceles because $\overline{OC}$, $\overline{OD}$, and $\overline{OE}$ are all radii of circle O. Angles ODC and OCD have equal measures, since they're opposite equal sides, so $\angle ODC$ measures 70°. Similarly, $\angle ODE$ measures 45°. Together, angles ODC and ODE make up $\angle CDE$, so its measure is 70° + 45° = 115°.

50. K
Solving a System of Equations

Key Math Concepts for the ACT, #67. Remember that lines intersect at the point that is a solution to both equations. So equations with no common solution don't intersect—they have the same slope and are parallel. To solve this problem, search through the answer choices to find the pair of equations representing lines with the same slope. If you write the equations in K in slope-intercept form, you'll get $y = -\frac{1}{3}x + 2$, $y = -\frac{1}{3}x + \frac{7}{9}$, so the slope is clearly the same for both equations.

51. E
Repeating Decimal

Key Math Concepts for the ACT, #30. To solve a repeating decimal question, begin by determining the pattern of the decimal on your calculator. $\frac{1}{7} = 0.142857142857\ldots$, so you know that this fraction repeats every 6 decimal places. Since we are looking for the 46th decimal place, we need to determine where in the 6-term pattern we would be at the 46th place. Divide 46 by 6, and look for the remainder. The remainder in this case is 4, so we are looking for the 4th term in the sequence, which is 8, choice E.

52. K
Solving an Inequality

Key Math Concepts for the ACT, #69. Remember that you treat an inequality exactly like an equality, except that you need to flip the sign when you multiply or divide by a negative number. In this problem, you start with the inequality $-2 - 4x \le -6x$. Add $4x$ to both sides to get $-2 \le -2x$. Divide by -2 and flip the sign to get $1 \ge x$, which matches choice K.

53. B
Adding/Subtracting Fractions

Key Math Concepts for the ACT, #22. For this problem, it would probably be easiest to pick numbers. Since you will be taking the square root of the numbers, it's easiest to pick perfect squares, like 4 and 9:

$$\frac{\sqrt{4}}{4} + \frac{\sqrt{9}}{9} = \frac{2}{4} + \frac{3}{9} = \frac{1}{2} + \frac{1}{3} = \frac{5}{6}$$

When you plug 4 and 9 into the answer choices, only B gives you $\frac{5}{6}$.

54. G
Parallel Lines and Transversals

Key Math Concepts for the ACT, #79. When transversals intersect parallel lines, corresponding line segments on the transversals are proportional. In other words, $\frac{\overline{DE}}{\overline{CB}} = \frac{\overline{EF}}{\overline{BA}}$. Thus, $\frac{6}{8} = \frac{\overline{EF}}{4}$, so $EF = 3$.

55. D
Area of a Triangle

Key Math Concepts for the ACT, #83. Divide the square into two right triangles by drawing the diagonal from (2, 7) to (2, 1). Remember that the area of each triangle is half its base times its height. Treat the diagonal as the base of a triangle. Its length is the distance from (2, 7) to (2, 1). Since the x-coordinates are the same, that distance is simply the difference between the y-coordinates, 7 − 1, or 6. The diagonal bisects the square, so the height of the triangle is half the distance from (–1, 4) to (5, 4). We already know that a diagonal of this square is 6, so half the distance is 3. Therefore, the base and height of either triangle are 6 and 3, so the area of each triangle is $\frac{6 \times 3}{2}$, or 9 square units. The square is made up of two such triangles and so has twice the area, or 18 square units.

Alternatively, you could use the Distance Formula to find the length of one side and square that side to find the area.

56. K

Graphing Trigonometric Functions

Key Math Concepts for the ACT, #100. Compared to the graph of $y = \cos\theta$, the graph of $y = 2\cos\theta$ would have twice the amplitude and the same period, choice K. Here you are doubling y, which represents the vertical coordinates, but the θ coordinates stay the same. The amplitude of a trigonometric equation refers to how high or low the curve moves from the horizontal axis. The period refers to the distance required to complete a single wave along the horizontal axis.

57. C

Translating from English into Algebra

Key Math Concepts for the ACT, #65. To solve this problem with algebra, you need to translate each phrase into mathematics. Translated, the problem is $3(x + 15) = 4x - 65$. Solve for x to get 110. Alternatively, you could backsolve starting with the middle value:

$$3(110 + 15) = 4(110) - 65$$
$$3(125) = 440 - 65$$
$$75 = 75$$

Since the two sides are equal, choice C is correct.

58. H

Setting Up a Ratio

Key Math Concepts for the ACT, #36. You're given the formula for the volume of a cylinder in the equation so you can find the volume of both cylinders described. That turns this into a ratio problem where you're comparing the volumes of both cylinders. Pick numbers to make this question more concrete, and plug them into this volume formula. Let's say the smaller cylinder has a height of 1 and a radius of 1 (diameter of 2), for a volume of $\pi(1)^2 \times 1 = \pi$. The larger cylinder would then have a height of 3 and a radius of 2 (diameter of 4), for a volume of $\pi(2)^2 \times 3 = 12\pi$. Thus, it would take 12 fillings of the smaller cylinder to fill the larger cylinder.

59. D

Special Right Triangles

Key Math Concepts for the ACT, #85. Draw a picture of the triangle, and carefully apply your knowledge of the ratio of the lengths of the sides of a 30°-60°-90° triangle ($x : x\sqrt{3} : 2x$). So if the longer leg has a length of 12, the shorter leg has a length of $\frac{12}{\sqrt{3}} = \frac{12\sqrt{3}}{\sqrt{3} \times \sqrt{3}} = \frac{12\sqrt{3}}{3} = 4\sqrt{3}$. Thus, the hypotenuse is twice this, or $8\sqrt{3}$. So the perimeter is the sum of the three sides, or $4\sqrt{3} + 12 + 8\sqrt{3} = 12\sqrt{3} + 12$.

60. J

Average Formula

Key Math Concepts for the ACT, # 41. Remember the average formula on this one. The average formula states, Average $= \frac{\text{Sum of the terms}}{\text{Number of the terms}}$. So to find the total average, find the total sum and divide it by the total number of terms. If a team averages x points in n games, then it scored nx points in n games. In the final game of the season, it scored y points. So the total sum of points for the season is $nx + y$, and the total number of games is $n + 1$. So the team's average score for the entire season is $\frac{nx + y}{n + 1}$, choice J.

Reading Test

Reading questions can be divided into four basic types: Detail questions, Inference questions, Big Picture questions, and Vocabulary-in-Context questions. As you review the answers and explanations, note which types you tend to answer correctly or incorrectly, and tailor your studying to focus on areas where you need improvement.

PASSAGE I

1. C
Detail

The answer can be found in lines 31–36: "The real evils, indeed, of Emma's situation were the power of having rather too much her own way, and a disposition to think a little too well of herself; these were the disadvantages which threatened alloy to her many enjoyments."

2. G
Detail

Isabella's name is given in line 73.

3. B
Detail

The answer can be found in lines 20–21: "Between them it was more the intimacy of sisters."

4. F
Vocabulary-in-Context

As it is used in the sentence, *disposition* means "tendency" or "inclination." It would not make sense for Emma to have choice G, control; choice H, placement; or J, transfer "to think a little too well of herself" (lines 33–34).

5. D
Detail

The answer can be found in lines 62–69: "She recalled her past kindness—the kindness, the affection of sixteen years—how she had taught her and…how she had devoted all her powers to attach and amuse her in health—and how she had nursed her through the various illnesses of childhood."

6. H
Inference

Miss Taylor will continue to be a part of Emma's life, but they will not be as close because Miss Taylor no longer lives with Emma and because Miss Taylor will be primarily concerned with her husband's, not Emma's, well-being.

7. C
Inference

Emma is self-centered, as evidenced by her description of her relationship with Miss Taylor. Among Miss Taylor's admirable qualities, Emma includes the fact that Miss Taylor was "interested in her, in every pleasure, every scheme of hers—one to whom she could speak every thought as it arose, and who had such an affection for her as could never find fault" (lines 78–84). Emma is also clearly headstrong. She is described as "having rather too much her own way" (lines 32–33).

8. G
Big Picture

Emma's description of her friendship with Miss Taylor suggests that Emma most highly values devotion in her friends.

9. B
Detail

The description of Mr. Weston is in lines 53–56: "The marriage had every promise of happiness for her friend. Mr. Weston was a man of unexceptionable character, easy fortune, suitable age, and pleasant manners." None of the other choices match this description.

10. H
Inference

The answer to the question is in lines 28–31: "Emma doing just what she liked, highly esteeming Miss Taylor's judgment, but directed chiefly by her own."

PASSAGE II

11. B
Detail

The passage presents the three main systems of memory and states that these systems are widely accepted—so eliminate choice A—but gives alternate theories about the way long-term memories are formed and possible flaws in the process. Although the passage mentions two early ideas about memory that were too simplistic, choices C and D, this is not the main focus of the passage.

12. H
Inference

Described in paragraph 3, semantic memory holds facts and general knowledge, like the multiplication tables, choice H. Ballet steps, choice F, and riding a bicycle, choice J, would be in procedural memory; a childhood memory, choice G, would be in episodic.

13. B
Inference

All the information you need is in paragraph 3. Memories of one's personal life would be held in episodic memory; therefore, the man's episodic memory was affected. Eliminate choices C and D. Long-term memories are "never lost," but they may become inaccessible; therefore, the author

would most likely agree that the man's episodic memories had become inaccessible to him.

14. F
Big Picture

While memory was once viewed as relatively simple and automatic with memories being held exactly as they were originally received, it is now believed that many factors alter the way memories are formed and retrieved (lines 69–79). Choices G and J contradict this. Choice H is too extreme.

15. C
Inference

In the last paragraph, the author states that assumptions and inferences can affect memory. A person might assume that if the ball hits a window, the window will break. Interference, choice A, is when one unrelated memory alters another. The memory described in the question is not inaccessible, choice B, but wrong. And most of the memory was still correct, not false, choice D.

16. J
Detail

This Detail question requires very careful reading. Refresh your memory by looking at *episodic* in paragraph 3. It's in long-term memory and involves personal events closely identified with a time and place. Choices F, G, and H fit that idea closely. If you're unsure, look at the description of working (short-term) memory in paragraph 2. You'll see that it includes those things briefly remembered and then lost forever—like the face of a stranger passed on the street.

17. B
Inference

Paragraph 2 describes this change in terminology. The term *short-term memory* did not accurately describe all the functions of this category of memory. *Working memory* is more accurate since, although these memories degrade quickly—eliminating choice A—these memories can also be used and manipulated as described in the second paragraph. Choice C and D confuse information in other paragraphs.

18. H

Vocabulary-in-Context

Don't panic. All you have to do is look at the line where this term is defined for you. The term doesn't relate to any of the usual meanings of the word *icon*.

19. B

Big Picture

The second sentence in paragraph 3 states, "Memories recorded in long-term memory are never lost…" Although absolute statements are often too extreme to be correct in Reading, when the passage explicitly supports an absolute statement don't be afraid to choose it. You might choose A if you mistook *short-term* and *working* memory for two separate categories. Choice C is contradicted in paragraph 4, and choice D is contradicted at the end of paragraph 2 and again at the start of paragraph 5.

20. H

Detail

Paragraph 2 states that working memories decay rapidly, which means that they are quickly forgotten. Choices F and G relate to sensory memory. Choice J is characteristic of long-term memory.

PASSAGE III

21. B

Inference

In lines 11–13, Julia Margaret Cameron is described as "the first woman to have achieved eminence in photography." The other answer choices contradict information supplied in the passage.

22. F

Detail

The answer to this question can be found in lines 82–83: "Contemporary taste much prefers her portraits…" and in lines 88–89: "today her fame rests upon her portraits…"

23. D

Detail

The dates used in the passage tell you that this is a chronological account; the author begins with Cameron's birth in 1815, tells of her marriage and then her move to England in 1848, points out that she received her first photographic equipment in 1863, describes one of her photographs from 1864, and then concludes the paragraph with her death in 1874.

24. F

Vocabulary-in-Context

The dictionary definition of *cumbersome* is "difficult to handle because of weight or bulk." Choice F most closely fits this definition, and it is the only answer choice that makes sense within the context of the sentence.

25. B

Inference

Lines 55–56 describe how Cameron "devoted herself wholly to this art," which matches choice B. Choice A contradicts information from the passage, which suggests that Cameron led anything but a conventional life. Neither the money that Cameron earned as a photographer nor her religious beliefs are discussed in the passage, making choices C and D incorrect.

26. F
Big Picture

Lines 60–63 say, "she produced a large body of work that stands up as one of the notable artistic achievements of the Victorian period." To say that she is "the greatest photographer who ever lived" goes beyond anything stated or implied in the passage. The third paragraph does not compare her importance as an artist during her lifetime to her importance today. The passage also does not state that she "revolutionized" any photographic methods.

27. C
Detail

The answer to this question can be found in lines 7–10: "photography, being a new medium outside the traditional academic framework, was wide open to women and offered them opportunities that the older fields did not…"

28. G
Detail

These titles refer to allegorical pictures, as described in lines 78–81: "Victorian critics were particularly impressed by her allegorical pictures, many of them based on the poems of her friend and neighbor Tennyson…"

29. D
Detail

The answer to this question can be found in lines 82–84: "Contemporary taste much prefers her portraits and finds her narrative scenes sentimental and sometimes in bad taste."

30. F
Big Picture

The author says that Cameron "achieved eminence" (line 12) in her field, that she "devoted herself wholly to this art" (lines 55–56), and that "no other woman photographer has ever enjoyed such success" (lines 74–75). Only choice F fits these descriptions.

PASSAGE IV

31. C
Detail

For details about the eye, look at paragraph 3. Only the cornea and stenopaic pupil are relevant, eliminating choices A and D. But the cornea, choice B, is helpful underwater, not on land.

32. G
Inference

The eye is covered in paragraph 3. The seal's cornea improves vision in the water (note the comparison to human underwater vision), but distorts light moving through the air. Another adaptation was then needed to *minimize* (line 53) distortion, but that doesn't mean distortion is completely eliminated, so the seal's vision in the air is distorted, choice G.

33. D
Detail

The vibrissae are discussed only in the last paragraph. They sense wave disturbances made by nearby moving fish, so choice D is correct. Choice B, by using the phrase "in the air," distorts information in the passage.

34. F
Detail

This is stated in the second paragraph, where the seal's hearing is discussed.

35. D
Detail

This appears in the first paragraph, which introduces the influences on the seal's adaptations. They include that the seal "does most of its fishing at night," that "noise levels are high," and that these factors are compounded by the seal's "two habitats."

36. H
Detail

Locating each of these claims in the passage, we find that choice H is *suggested* (line 68) and the subject of speculation, rather than stated as fact. All of the others are given in support of claims.

37. A
Inference

We find in the first paragraph that they live along the northern Atlantic and Pacific coasts. Since they live in both the land and water, the coastlines must be accessible. We can infer that the waters are cold rather than warm, eliminating choice D. Choices B and C are too broad.

38. J
Detail

This feature is mentioned at the end of paragraph 2. It shouldn't be confused with echolocation, which is discussed in paragraph 4, but not connected with any particular sensory organ.

39. B
Big Picture

The entire passage is about how the seal's sensory organs have adapted to life on land and in the water, making B the best choice. Generally, we are told about differences, not similarities, between the sensory organs of humans and harbor seals, eliminating choice A. The relative success of human and seal adaptation to their environments isn't discussed, thus eliminating choices C and D.

40. G
Detail

In paragraph 3, we see that human corneas refract light badly in water, and the seal's corneas perform well.

Science Test

Science questions can be divided into three basic types: Figure questions, Patterns questions, and Scientific Reasoning questions. You may also see Basic Theory questions when you review the Conflicting Viewpoints passage. As you review the answers and explanations, note which types you tend to answer correctly or incorrectly and tailor your studying to focus on areas where you need improvement.

PASSAGE I

1. B
Figure

To answer this question, you have to examine the third column of the table, transmittance range. For a material to transmit light at a wavelength of 25 μm, its transmittance range—the range of wavelengths over which the material is transparent—must include 25 μm. Only potassium bromide (0.3–29 μm) and cesium iodide (0.3–70 μm) have transmittance ranges that include 25 μm, so choice B is correct.

2. F
Figure

The material that contradicts this hypothesis is going to have poor chemical resistance but a transmittance range less than 10 μm. Lithium fluoride, choice F, fits the bill: its chemical resistance is poor, and its transmittance range is less than 6 μm wide. Choices G and J are wrong because both flint glass and quartz have excellent chemical resistance. Choice H is out because cesium iodide has a transmittance range nearly 70 μm wide.

3. D
Scientific Reasoning

The correct answer is a pair of materials in which the refractive index of the first material is greater than that of the second. In choices A,

B, and C, the refractive index of the first material is less than that of the second. In choice D, however, flint glass has a refractive index of 1.66 while calcium fluoride's refractive index is only 1.43. That makes choice D the correct answer.

4. J
Scientific Reasoning

The easiest way to answer this question is to use the first couple of materials and test each hypothesis on them. Choices F and G are incorrect because the transmittance range of lithium fluoride is wider than its useful prism range. Comparing the data on lithium fluoride and calcium fluoride rules out choice H because transmittance range does NOT increase as useful prism range decreases. In fact, looking down the rest of the table, you see that transmittance range seems to decrease as useful prism range decreases. Choice J is the only one left, and the data on lithium fluoride and calcium fluoride as well as all the other materials confirms that the transmittance range is always wider than, and includes within it, the useful prism range.

5. B
Figure

According to the footnote to the table, quartz infused with lead oxide is flint glass. Comparison of the properties of pure quartz and flint glass shows that the transmittance range of flint glass is narrower than that of quartz but that its refractive index is greater. This supports choice B.

PASSAGE II

6. H
Scientific Reasoning

Use the results of both experiments to answer this question. The answer choices all involve temperature, concentration, and solvent in different combinations. To determine whether

osmotic pressure is dependent upon a variable, look for a pair of trials in which all conditions except for that variable are identical. In doing so, you see that temperature and concentration affect osmotic pressure, but solvent does not.

7. C
Figure

Find methanol at 0.5 mol/L, which is in Table 2. The text above the table states that all the trials were conducted under the same temperature (298 K). Therefore, simply look across the row that you identified. The osmotic pressure is 12.23, C.

8. G
Scientific Reasoning

To figure out whether or not the sucrose solution will diffuse across the membrane under the conditions described in the question, go back to the definition of osmotic pressure given in the introduction. Once the external pressure reaches the osmotic pressure, osmosis will not occur. In order for osmosis to occur, the external pressure must be less than the osmotic pressure of the solution. The solution in this question is a 0.1 mol/L aqueous sucrose solution at 298 K; those conditions correspond to an osmotic pressure of 2.45 atm. Since the external pressure is 1 atm, which is less than the osmotic pressure, osmosis will occur. From the definition of osmosis in the passage, it is clear that the solution will diffuse from the side of the membrane with a lower concentration of dissolved material, in this case pure water, to the side with a higher concentration, in this case sucrose solution. Choice G is correct.

9. C
Figure

To determine what the scientists investigated in Experiment 1, look at what they varied and what they measured. In Experiment 1, the scientists varied the concentration and the temperature of sucrose solutions, and they measured the osmotic pressure. Therefore, they were investigating the effect of concentration and temperature on osmotic pressure, choice C. Watch out for choice A: it states what was investigated in Experiment 2, not Experiment 1.

10. F
Patterns

The results in Table 2 indicate that osmotic pressure doesn't depend on the solvent, as discussed in the explanation to question 6. So Statement I is a valid conclusion, and choice G can be eliminated. Statement II is false. The results in Table 1 indicate that osmotic pressure is dependent on concentration as well as temperature. So choice H can be ruled out. Now consider Statement III. It is not a valid conclusion because osmotic pressure is the pressure required to prevent osmosis, so osmosis occurs only if the external pressure is less than the osmotic pressure.

11. D
Figure

To answer questions that ask about the design of an experiment, look at what the scientists are trying to measure. You're told that osmotic pressure is the pressure required to prevent osmosis. In order to measure the osmotic pressure of a solution, scientists need to be able to tell when osmosis begins. If you have two clear solutions with sucrose dissolved in one of them, how can you tell when there's any movement of solvent between the two of them? If the sucrose is dyed, the blue solution will become paler when osmosis starts, i.e., when solvent moves across the membrane to create an equilibrium. Therefore, choice D is correct.

PASSAGE III

12. J
Scientific Reasoning

Even if you do not know how many °C are equivalent to room temperature, you can eliminate all of the incorrect answer choices. Choices F, G, and H all reach a boiling point at low temperatures and, therefore, would all be gases at room temperature. Choice J, at 36°C, is the only logical choice.

13. C
Patterns

To answer this question, you have to look for trends in each table and draw conclusions. This can be done by looking at the values in each category and seeing how they vary with respect to each other. If you look at Tables 1 and 2, you can see that there is a direct variation between boiling point and molecular weight: as one increases, the other increases. Therefore, Statement I is correct, Statement II is false, and you can eliminate choices B and D. Now consider Statement III. To investigate the relationship between molecular structure and boiling point, you have to keep the third variable—molecular weight—constant. Look at the data for two compounds with different molecular structures but the same molecular weight: N_2 and CO match that description and their boiling points differ. Therefore, Statement III is correct, and choice C is the correct response.

14. G
Figure

In order to answer this question, you need to establish where C_6H_{14} would fit in Table 1. It is clear from Table 1 that the boiling point increases as the molecular weight increases, so the boiling point of C_6H_{14} will be between the boiling points of molecules with greater and lesser molecular weights. The molecular weight of C_6H_{14} is 86 g/mol, so it will lie between those hydrocarbons with molecular weights of 72 g/mol and 114 g/mol. Therefore, its boiling point will be between 36°C and 126°C. G, with a value of 70°C, is the only choice that lies between these two boiling points.

15. A
Figure

N_2, a non-polar molecule, and CO, a polar molecule, have identical molecular weights and their boiling points differ by only 4°C. SiH_4 (non-polar) and PH_3 (polar) have nearly identical molecular weights as well, but the difference between their boiling points is 27°C—much greater than the difference between the boiling points of N_2 and CO, which have lower molecular weights than SiH_4 and PH_3. The difference between the boiling points of polar and non-polar substances of similar molecular weight increases as molecular weight increases, so choice A is correct.

16. H
Figure

If you refer to Table 2, you'll see that for polar substances, as the molar weight goes from 78 to 162, the boiling point goes from −55°C to 97°C. You know the molar weight has to be somewhere between 78 and 162, so F is clearly out, and G, 80, is too close to 78 to be the answer. You would expect the molar weight to be closer to 78 than 162, since 0 is closer to −55 than 97. Therefore, J, 132, is out, and choice H is the answer.

PASSAGE IV

17. A
Scientific Reasoning

The question refers to Experiment 2 only, so the correct answer will involve sunlight. Table 2 shows that the average length of the leaves

increased from 5.3 cm to 12.4 cm as the amount of sunlight increased from 0 to 3 hours per day. But as the amount of sunlight increased further, leaf size decreased. Therefore, choice D is incorrect. Neither humidity, choice B, nor water, choice C, is relevant to Experiment 2.

18. G
Figure

Table 1 gives leaf widths at 35% and 55% humidity at 1.8 cm and 2.0 cm, respectively. The leaf width at 40% humidity would most likely be between those two figures. Choice G is the only choice within that range.

19. B
Scientific Reasoning

All the answer choices involve humidity and sunlight, which were investigated in Experiments 1 and 2, respectively. In Table 1, leaf length and width were greatest at 75% humidity. In Table 2, they were greatest at three hours per day of sunlight. Combining those two conditions, as in choice B, would probably produce the largest leaves.

20. F
Scientific Reasoning

This question relates to the method of the study. Each experiment begins with a statement that five groups of seedlings were used. Therefore, choice F is correct. The other choices list variables that were manipulated.

21. D
Scientific Reasoning

Choice D is an assumption that underlies the design of all three experiments. If the seedlings were not equally capable of further growth, then changes in leaf size and density could not be reliably attributed to researcher-controlled changes in humidity, sunlight, and temperature. Choice A is wrong because all the seedlings were 2–3 cm tall. The seedlings' abilities to germinate, choice B, or to produce flowers, choice C, were not mentioned in the passage.

22. H
Scientific Reasoning

Each of the three experiments investigated a different factor related to leaf growth. To produce the most useful new data, researchers would probably vary a fourth condition. Soil mineral content would be an appropriate factor to examine. None of the other choices relate directly to the purpose of the experiments as expressed in paragraph 1 of the passage.

PASSAGE V

23. B
Figure

According to the table, decreasing the cross-sectional area of a given wire always increases resistance, so choice B is correct. Choice C is wrong because resistivity, displayed in the second column, is constant for each material and thus cannot be responsible for variations in resistance for any given material. Gauge varies inversely with cross-sectional area, so choice D is incorrect.

24. G
Patterns

Because resistance varies inversely with cross-sectional area A, as discussed in the previous explanation, the correct answer to this question must place A in the denominator. The only choice that does so is choice G.

25. D
Patterns

Compare the choices two at a time. The wires in A and B are made of the same material and have the same cross-sectional area; only their length is different. Doubling the length doubles

the resistance, so choice B would have a higher resistance than choice A. By similar reasoning, choice D would have a higher resistance than choice C. The only difference between choices B and D is the material. Even though the research team didn't test wire with a 0.33 mm² cross-sectional area, Table 1 shows that tungsten wire has higher levels of resistance than aluminum wire across all factors.

26. J
Scientific Reasoning

The larger circle represents 10-gauge wire; its diameter is 2.59 mm. The smaller circle has a diameter of only 1.29 mm, but it represents 16-gauge wire, so Statement I is true, and you can eliminate choices G and H without even checking Statements II or III. To check Statement III, the table shows that the resistance of an iron (Fe) wire is much higher than that of an aluminum (Al) wire with the same length and cross-sectional area. The first sentence of paragraph 1 defined the resistance of a conductor as "the extent to which it opposes the flow of electricity." Since iron has a higher resistance than aluminum, iron must not conduct electricity as well. Therefore, Statement III is true, and choice J is correct.

27. D
Patterns

The data indicates that the resistivity of a material doesn't change when wire length changes. Therefore, the graph of resistivity versus length for tungsten (or any other) wire is a horizontal line.

PASSAGE VI

28. F
Basic Theory

To answer this question, you have to refer to the examples presented by the scientists to find a point of agreement. Both use the example of giraffes to show how scarcity of food and the need to reach higher and higher branches led to the evolution of long necks; thus, they both agree that environment affects evolution.

29. C
Scientific Reasoning

This Principle question requires that you figure out how new evidence affects the two hypotheses. To answer it, all you have to consider are the hypotheses of the two scientists. Scientist 2 believes that characteristics acquired by an individual over a lifetime are passed on to its offspring, a theory that would be supported by this finding.

30. J
Scientific Reasoning

This question requires some reasoning. Scientist 2 states that all of the changes that occur in an individual's life can be passed on to offspring. Since he believes that any characteristic can undergo change, he must also believe that any characteristic can be inherited.

31. B
Basic Theory

You don't need any information other than the hypothesis of Scientist 1 to answer this question. He believes that random mutations continually occur within a species as it propagates and that advantageous mutations, such as long necks on giraffes, help the species adapt to environmental changes, and thus become more prevalent within the species, which is what choice B states.

32. G
Basic Theory

Here, you don't need any information other than the hypotheses of the two scientists. The crux of their disagreement is over how evolution occurs—whether through random mutations or through the inheritance of acquired characteristics.

33. B
Scientific Reasoning

Recall that Scientist 2 states that evolution occurs through the inheritance of acquired characteristics. In order to account for humans possessing nerve endings now that were not present before the discovery of fire, Scientist 2 would have to believe that new nerve endings could be acquired during a single lifetime. Choice B directly contradicts this idea and would therefore refute the hypothesis.

34. F
Scientific Reasoning

Recall that Scientist 1 explains that evolution occurs as a result of random mutation, while Scientist 2 credits the inheritance of acquired characteristics. Choice G can then be eliminated, since it is related to the explanation of the wrong scientist. Choice H would actually refute Scientist 1's hypothesis, and choice J is irrelevant. Only choice F provides a valid explanation for the increase in average height based on the random mutations described by Scientist 1.

PASSAGE VII

35. D
Figure

In Experiment 1, the researchers vary what is fed to the cows by giving them meat from scrapie-free sheep and from scrapie-infected sheep. The cows are later examined for signs of BSE. One common type of wrong answer choice for Experiment questions are choices, such as choice B for this question, that include factors that are outside the parameters of the experiment.

36. F
Figure

In Experiment 2, the researchers vary what is injected into cows' brains. Any answer choice that discusses ingestion as a focus of this experiment is wrong. This eliminates choices G, H, and J. Often, wrong answer choices for Experiment questions, such as choice G for this question, will include the appropriate information from the wrong experiment.

37. B
Scientific Reasoning

By examining the method used in a given experiment, one can determine the assumptions the researchers made in carrying out the experiment and the sources of error. Often, an error enters the experiment because of the assumptions researchers make. In Experiments 1 and 2, the researchers examined the brains of cows a year and a half after the cows were fed scrapie-infected sheep meat or were injected with scrapie-infected sheep brains. If a year and a half is not a sufficient amount of time for BSE to develop, some of the cows that were counted as not infected might have developed BSE if they had been given more time.

38. H
Scientific Reasoning

To answer this question, you need to determine how to test whether BSE can be transmitted via scrapie-infected goats. To test this, one would compare the effects of feeding cows scrapie-free goat meat with the effects of feeding cows scrapie-infected goat meat and compare the effects of injecting cows with scrapie-free goat brains with the effects of injecting them with scrapie-infected goat brains.

39. A
Scientific Reasoning

Remember that control groups are used as standards of comparison. The control group used in Experiment 1 is the group that is fed scrapie-free sheep meat. If the same proportion of Group A developed BSE as that of Group B, then the researchers would not have any evidence to support the hypothesis that the ingestion of scrapie-infected sheep meat causes BSE.

40. G
Scientific Reasoning

Since the proportion of the group of cows that ate scrapie-infected sheep meat and developed BSE was greater than the proportion of the group that were injected with scrapie-infected sheep brains and developed BSE, one can conclude that a cow that eats scrapie-infected sheep meat is more likely to develop BSE than a cow that is injected with scrapie-infected sheep brains. Mere exposure to scrapie-infected sheep, as opposed to ingestion of it, is never studied in either experiment, so conclusion I can be eliminated.

Writing Test

MODEL ESSAY

Below is an example of what a high-scoring essay might look like. Notice the author states her position clearly in the introductory paragraph and supports that position with evidence in the following paragraphs. This essay also uses transitions, some advanced vocabulary, and an effective "hook" to draw in the reader.

When people think about what students should learn in high school, they often focus on "the three Rs": reading, writing, and arithmetic. It's true that in an increasingly competitive global economy, those skills are more important than ever. However, in our society's rush to make sure students are keeping up through required standardized testing and increased computer education, are we forgetting another important aspect of education? Are we forgetting to teach our students how to think creatively and express themselves artistically? I think that requiring all high school students to take music or visual arts classes would benefit our country's students in several ways.

Learning about art and music actually helps students do better in other subjects. People often forget that studying art or music isn't just about putting paint to canvas or lips to trumpet. There is a lot of background information that students learn as well. When students study music they also have to learn a lot of history: who was the composer, where was he or she from, what was happening politically and socially during the time the music was composed, and how does the work compare historically to music by other composers. The same holds true for the visual arts; students can learn a lot from art history, not just about the artist but also about different cultures and time periods. Studies have shown that students who take music classes do better at math, maybe because these classes emphasize dividing up measures of music and counting out times.

With so much focus on standardized test scores and grade point averages, schools today emphasize individual academic performance and overlook the teaching of teamwork skills. Through playing in my high school's band, I have learned that even though it is important for me to practice so that I can play my best (and maybe move up a chair), what really matters is how we sound as a group. My bandmates and I push each other to succeed, and we get together outside of school to practice for big games and competitions. Band is also where I have made most of my friends. Participation in the arts is a great way for students to build social skills and create school spirit. It teaches students to help one another so that going to school isn't just about getting good grades for one's own benefit.

Learning about art or music is also helpful to students because it teaches them how to think creatively. When you take a photograph or paint a portrait you have to look at things in a new way, and you must try to synthesize your perception into a medium that other people can relate to. Between all the pressure to do well academically and all the social pressure teenagers face to fit in, being a teenager can be really stressful. Art and music can allow students to express their feelings in a positive, constructive way. Such classes can give students who aren't good at traditional academic subjects like math or science a chance to shine.

In conclusion, I think requiring all high school students to take music or visual arts classes would help students not only academically but socially and emotionally as well. Studying the arts actually helps students succeed in traditional subject areas, builds their confidence and social skills, and gives them the opportunity to learn to think creatively, all skills that will help them once they reach the workforce.

You can evaluate your essay and the model essay based on the following criteria, covered in chapter 16:

- Does the author answer the question?
- Is the author's position clearly stated?
- Does the body of the essay support and develop the position taken?
- Are there at least three supporting paragraphs?
- Is the relevance of each supporting paragraph clear?
- Does the writer address the other side of the argument?
- Is the essay organized, with a clear introduction, middle, and end?
- Does the author start a new paragraph for each new idea?
- Is each sentence in a paragraph relevant to the point made in that paragraph?
- Are transitions clear?
- Is the essay easy to read? Is it engaging?
- Are sentences varied?
- Is vocabulary used effectively? Is college-level vocabulary used?

Compute Your Score

 Figure out your score in each section. Refer to the answer keys to figure out the number right in each test section. Enter the results below:

RAW SCORES   English: ▢   Reading: ▢

                    Math: ▢   Science: ▢

 Find your Practice Test scores. Find your raw score on each section in the table below. The score on the far left column indicates your estimated scaled score if this were an actual ACT.

SCALED SCORE	RAW SCORES			
	English	**Mathematics**	**Reading**	**Science**
36	75	60	40	40
35	74	60	40	40
34	73	59	39	39
33	72	58	39	39
32	71	57	38	38
31	70	55–56	37	37
30	69	53–54	36	36
29	68	50–52	35	35
28	67	48–49	34	34
27	65–66	45–47	33	33
26	63–64	43–44	32	32
25	61–62	40–42	31	30–31
24	58–60	38–39	30	28–29
23	56–57	35–37	29	26–27
22	53–55	33–34	28	24–25
21	49–52	31–32	27	21–23
20	46–48	28–30	25–26	19–20
19	44–45	26–27	23–24	17–18
18	41–43	23–25	21–22	16
17	39–40	20–22	19–20	15
16	36–38	17–19	17–18	14

SCALED SCORE	RAW SCORES			
	English	**Mathematics**	**Reading**	**Science**
15	34–35	15–16	15–16	13
14	30–33	13–14	13–14	12
13	28–29	11–12	12–13	11
12	25–27	9–10	10–11	10
11	23–24	8	9	9
10	20–22	7	8	8
9	17–19	6	7	7
8	14–16	5	6	6
7	12–13	4	5	5
6	9–11	3	4	4
5	7–8	2	3	3
4	4–6	1	2	2
3	3	1	1	1
2	2	0	0	0
1	1	0	0	0

SCALED SCORES   English: ☐   Reading: ☐

Math: ☐   Science: ☐

3 **Find your estimated composite score.** To calculate your estimated composite score, simply add together your scaled scores on each subsection and divide by four.

COMPOSITE SCORE   ☐

100 Key
Math Concepts

NUMBER PROPERTIES

1. UNDEFINED

On the ACT, *undefined* almost always means **division by zero.** The expression $\frac{a}{bc}$ is undefined if either b or c equals 0.

2. REAL/IMAGINARY

A real number is a number that has a **location on the number line.** On the ACT, imaginary numbers are numbers that involve the square root of a negative number. $\sqrt{-4}$ is an imaginary number.

3. INTEGER/NONINTEGER

Integers are **whole numbers;** they include negative whole numbers and zero.

4. RATIONAL/IRRATIONAL

A **rational number** is a number that can be expressed as a **ratio of two integers. Irrational numbers** are real numbers—they have locations on the number line—they just **can't be expressed precisely as a fraction or decimal.** For the purposes of the ACT, the most important **irrational numbers** are $\sqrt{2}$, $\sqrt{3}$, and π.

5. ADDING/SUBTRACTING SIGNED NUMBERS

To **add a positive and a negative,** first ignore the signs and find the positive difference between the number parts. Then attach the sign of the original number to the larger number part. For example, to add 23 and –34, first we ignore the minus sign and find the positive difference between 23 and 34—that's 11. Then we attach the sign of the number with the larger number part—in this case, it's the minus sign from the –34. So 23 + (–34) = –11.

Make **subtraction** situations simpler by turning them into addition. For example, think of –17 – (–21) as –17 + (+21).

To **add or subtract a string of positives and negatives,** first turn everything into addition. Then combine the positives and negatives so that the string is reduced to the sum of a single positive number and a single negative number.

6. MULTIPLYING/DIVIDING SIGNED NUMBERS

To multiply and/or divide positives and negatives, treat the number parts as usual and **attach a negative sign if there were originally an odd number of negatives.** To multiply –2, –3, and –5, first multiply the number parts: $2 \times 3 \times 5 = 30$. Then go back and note that there were three—an odd number—negatives, so the product is negative: $(-2) \times (-3) \times (-5) = -30$.

7. PEMDAS

When performing multiple operations, remember **PEMDAS,** which means **Parentheses** first, then **Exponents,** then **Multiplication** and **Division** (left to right), then **Addition** and **Subtraction** (left to right).

In the expression $9 - 2 \times (5 - 3)^2 + 6 \div 3$, begin with the parentheses: $(5 - 3) = 2$. Then do the exponent: $2^2 = 4$. Now the expression is: $9 - 2 \times 4 + 6 \div 3$. Next do the multiplication and division to get $9 - 8 + 2$, which equals 3.

8. ABSOLUTE VALUE

Treat absolute value signs a lot like **parentheses.** Do what's inside them first and then take the absolute value of the result. Don't take the absolute value of each piece between the bars before calculating. In order to calculate $|(-12) + 5 - (-4)| - |5 + (-10)|$, first do what's inside the bars to get: $|-3| - |-5|$, which is $3 - 5$, or –2.

9. COUNTING CONSECUTIVE INTEGERS

To count consecutive integers, **subtract the smallest from the largest and add 1.** To count the integers from 13 through 31, subtract: $31 - 13 = 18$. Then add 1: $18 + 1 = 19$.

DIVISIBILITY

10. FACTOR/MULTIPLE

The **factors** of integer n are the positive integers that divide into n with no remainder. The **multiples** of n are the integers that n divides into with no remainder. Six is a factor of 12, and 24 is a multiple of 12. Twelve is both a factor and a multiple of itself.

11. PRIME FACTORIZATION

A **prime number** is a positive integer that has exactly two positive integer factors: 1 and the integer itself. The first eight prime numbers are 2, 3, 5, 7, 11, 13, 17, and 19.

To find the prime factorization of an integer, just keep breaking it up into factors until **all the factors are prime.** To find the prime factorization of 36, for example, you could begin by breaking it into 4×9:

$$36 = 4 \times 9 = 2 \times 2 \times 3 \times 3$$

12. RELATIVE PRIMES

To determine whether two integers are relative primes, break them both down to their prime factorizations. For example: $35 = 5 \times 7$, and $54 = 2 \times 3 \times 3 \times 3$. They have **no prime factors in common,** so 35 and 54 are relative primes.

13. COMMON MULTIPLE

You can always get a common multiple of two numbers by **multiplying** them, but unless the two numbers are relative primes, the product will not be the least common multiple. For example, to find a common multiple for 12 and 15, you could just multiply: $12 \times 15 = 180$.

14. LEAST COMMON MULTIPLE (LCM)

To find the least common multiple, check out the **multiples of the larger number** until you find one that's **also a multiple of the smaller.**

To find the LCM of 12 and 15, begin by taking the multiples of 15: 15 is not divisible by 12; 30 is not; nor is 45. But the next multiple of 15, 60, is divisible by 12, so it's the LCM.

15. GREATEST COMMON FACTOR (GCF)

To find the greatest common factor, break down both numbers into their prime factorizations, and take **all the prime factors they have in common.** $36 = 2 \times 2 \times 3 \times 3$, and $48 = 2 \times 2 \times 2 \times 2 \times 3$. What they have in common is two 2s and one 3, so the GCF is $2 \times 2 \times 3 = 12$.

16. EVEN/ODD

To predict whether a sum, difference, or product will be even or odd, just **take simple numbers like 1 and 2 and see what happens.** There are rules—"odd times even is even," for example—but there's no need to memorize them. What happens with one set of numbers generally happens with all similar sets.

17. MULTIPLES OF 2 AND 4

An integer is divisible by 2 if the **last digit is even.** An integer is divisible by 4 if the **last two digits form a multiple of 4.** The last digit of 562 is 2, which is even, so 562 is a multiple of 2. The last two digits make 62, which is not divisible by 4, so 562 is not a multiple of 4.

18. MULTIPLES OF 3 AND 9

An integer is divisible by 3 if the **sum of its digits is divisible by 3.** An integer is divisible by 9 if the **sum of its digits is divisible by 9.** The sum of the digits in 957 is 21, which is divisible by 3 but not by 9, so 957 is divisible by 3 but not 9.

19. MULTIPLES OF 5 AND 10

An integer is divisible by 5 if the **last digit is 5 or 0.** An integer is divisible by 10 if the **last digit is 0.** The last digit of 665 is 5, so 665 is a multiple of 5 but not a multiple of 10.

20. REMAINDERS

The remainder is the whole number left over after division. 487 is 2 more than 485, which is a multiple of 5, so when 487 is divided by 5, the remainder will be 2.

FRACTIONS AND DECIMALS

21. REDUCING FRACTIONS

To reduce a fraction to lowest terms, **factor out and cancel** all factors the numerator and denominator have in common.

$$\frac{28}{36} = \frac{4 \times 7}{4 \times 9} = \frac{7}{9}$$

22. ADDING/SUBTRACTING FRACTIONS

To add or subtract fractions, first find a **common denominator,** and then add or subtract the numerators.

$$\frac{2}{15} + \frac{3}{10} = \frac{4}{30} + \frac{9}{30} = \frac{4 \times 9}{30} = \frac{13}{30}$$

23. MULTIPLYING FRACTIONS

To multiply fractions, **multiply** the numerators and **multiply** the denominators.

$$\frac{5}{7} \times \frac{3}{4} = \frac{5 \times 3}{7 \times 4} = \frac{15}{28}$$

24. DIVIDING FRACTIONS

To divide fractions, **invert** the second one and **multiply.**

$$\frac{1}{2} \div \frac{3}{5} = \frac{1}{2} \times \frac{5}{3} = \frac{1 \times 5}{2 \times 3} = \frac{5}{6}$$

25. CONVERTING A MIXED NUMBER TO AN IMPROPER FRACTION

To convert a mixed number to an improper fraction, **multiply** the whole number part by the denominator, then **add** the numerator. The result is the new numerator (over the same denominator). To convert $7\frac{1}{3}$, first multiply 7 by 3, then add 1, to get the new numerator of 22. Put that over the same denominator, 3, to get $\frac{22}{3}$.

26. CONVERTING AN IMPROPER FRACTION TO A MIXED NUMBER

To convert an improper fraction to a mixed number, **divide** the denominator into the numerator to get a **whole number quotient with a remainder.** The quotient becomes the whole number part of the mixed number, and the remainder becomes the new numerator— with the same denominator. For example, to convert $\frac{108}{5}$, first divide 5 into 108, which yields 21 with a remainder of 3. Therefore, $\frac{108}{5} = 21\frac{3}{5}$.

27. RECIPROCAL

To find the reciprocal of a fraction, switch the numerator and the denominator. The reciprocal of $\frac{3}{7}$ is $\frac{7}{3}$. The reciprocal of 5 is $\frac{1}{5}$. The product of reciprocals is 1.

28. COMPARING FRACTIONS

One way to compare fractions is to re-express them with a **common denominator.**

$\frac{3}{4} = \frac{21}{28}$ and $\frac{5}{7} = \frac{20}{28}$; $\frac{21}{28}$ is greater than $\frac{20}{28}$, so $\frac{3}{4}$ is greater than $\frac{5}{7}$.

Another way to compare fractions is to convert them both to **decimals.** $\frac{3}{4}$ converts to .75, and $\frac{5}{7}$ converts to approximately .714.

29. CONVERTING FRACTIONS TO DECIMALS

To convert a fraction to a decimal, **divide the bottom into the top.** To convert $\frac{5}{8}$, divide 8 into 5, yielding .625.

30. REPEATING DECIMAL

To find a particular digit in a repeating decimal, note the **number of digits in the cluster that repeats.** If there are two digits in that cluster, then every second digit is the same. If there are three digits in that cluster, then every third digit is the same. And so on. For example, the decimal equivalent of $\frac{1}{27}$ is .037037037... which is best written $.\overline{037}$.

There are three digits in the repeating cluster, so every third digit is the same: 7. To find the 50th digit, look for the multiple of 3 just less than 50—that's 48. The 48th digit is 7, and with the 49th digit the pattern repeats with 0. The 50th digit is 3.

31. IDENTIFYING THE PARTS AND THE WHOLE

The key to solving most fraction and percent story problems is to identify the part and the whole. Usually, you'll find the **part** associated with the verb *is/are* and the **whole** associated with the word *of.* In the sentence, "Half of the boys are blonds," the whole is the boys ("*of* the boys"), and the part is the blonds ("*are* blonds").

PERCENTS

32. PERCENT FORMULA

Whether you need to find the part, the whole, or the percent, use the same formula:

Part = Percent × Whole

Example: What is 12% of 25?
   Setup: Part = .12 × 25

Example: 15 is 3% of what number?
   Setup: 15 = .03 × Whole

Example: 45 is what percent of 9?
   Setup: 45 = Percent × 9

33. PERCENT INCREASE AND DECREASE

To increase a number by a percent, **add the percent to 100%,** convert to a decimal, and multiply. To increase 40 by 25%, add 25% to 100%, convert 125% to 1.25, and multiply by 40. 1.25 × 40 = 50.

34. FINDING THE ORIGINAL WHOLE

To find the **original whole before a percent increase or decrease,** set up an equation. Think of a 15% increase over x as $1.15x$.

Example: After a 5% increase, the population was 59,346. What was the population *before* the increase?

   Setup: $1.05x = 59,346$

35. COMBINED PERCENT INCREASE AND DECREASE

To determine the combined effect of multiple percents' increase and/or decrease, **start with 100 and see what happens.**

Example: A price went up 10% one year, and the new price went up 20% the next year. What was the combined percent increase?

Setup: First year: 100 + (10% of 100) = 110. Second year: 110 + (20% of 110) = 132. That's a combined 32% increase.

RATIOS, PROPORTIONS, AND RATES

36. SETTING UP A RATIO

To find a ratio, put the number associated with the word *of* **on top** and the quantity associated with the word *to* **on the bottom,** and reduce. The ratio of 20 oranges to 12 apples is $\frac{20}{12}$, which reduces to $\frac{5}{3}$.

37. PART-TO-PART AND PART-TO-WHOLE RATIOS

If the parts add up to the whole, a part-to-part ratio can be turned into two part-to-whole ratios by putting **each number in the original ratio over the sum of the numbers.** If the ratio of males to females is 1 to 2, then the males-to-people ratio is $\frac{1}{1+2} = \frac{1}{3}$ and the females-to-people ratio is $\frac{2}{1+2} = \frac{2}{3}$. Or, $\frac{2}{3}$ of all the people are female.

38. SOLVING A PROPORTION

To solve a proportion, **cross multiply:**

$$\frac{x}{5} = \frac{3}{4}$$

$$4x = 5 \times 3$$

$$x = \frac{15}{4} = 3.75$$

39. RATE

To solve a rate problem, **use the units** to keep things straight.

Example: If snow is falling at the rate of one foot every four hours, how many inches of snow will fall in seven hours?

Setup:
$$\frac{1 \text{ foot}}{4 \text{ hours}} = \frac{x \text{ inches}}{7 \text{ hours}}$$

$$\frac{12 \text{ inches}}{4 \text{ hours}} = \frac{x \text{ inches}}{7 \text{ hours}}$$

$$4x = 12 \times 7$$

$$x = 21$$

40. AVERAGE RATE

Average rate is *not* simply the average of the rates.

$$\text{Average } A \text{ per } B = \frac{\text{Total } A}{\text{Total } B}$$

$$\text{Average speed} = \frac{\text{Total distance}}{\text{Total time}}$$

To find the average speed for 120 miles at 40 mph and 120 miles at 60 mph, **don't just average the two speeds.** First figure out the total distance and the total time. The total distance is 120 + 120 = 240 miles. The times are three hours for the first leg and two hours for the second leg, or five hours total. The average speed, then, is $\frac{240}{5} = 48$ miles per hour.

AVERAGES

41. AVERAGE FORMULA

To find the average of a set of numbers, **add them up and divide by the number of numbers.**

$$\text{Average} = \frac{\text{Sum of the terms}}{\text{Number of the terms}}$$

To find the average of the five numbers 12, 15, 23, 40, and 40, first add them: 12 + 15 + 23 + 40 + 40 = 130. Then divide the sum by 5: 130 ÷ 5 = 26.

42. AVERAGE OF EVENLY SPACED NUMBERS

To find the average of evenly spaced numbers, just **average the smallest and the largest.** The average of all the integers from 13 through 77 is the same as the average of 13 and 77: $\frac{13 + 77}{2} = \frac{90}{2} = 45$.

43. USING THE AVERAGE TO FIND THE SUM

$$\text{Sum} = (\text{Average}) \times (\text{Number of terms})$$

If the average of ten numbers is 50, then they add up to 10 × 50, or 500.

44. FINDING THE MISSING NUMBER

To find a missing number when you're given the average, **use the sum.** If the average of four numbers is 7, then the sum of those four numbers is 4 × 7, or 28. Suppose that three of the numbers are 3, 5, and 8. These numbers add up to 16 of that 28, which leaves 12 for the fourth number.

POSSIBILITIES AND PROBABILITY

45. COUNTING THE POSSIBILITIES

The fundamental counting principle: if there are **m ways** one event can happen and **n ways** a second event can happen, then there are **m × n ways** for the two events to happen. For example, with 5 shirts and 7 pairs of pants to choose from, you can put together 5 × 7 = 35 different outfits.

46. PROBABILITY

$$\text{Probability} = \frac{\text{Favorable outcomes}}{\text{Total possible outcomes}}$$

If you have 12 shirts in a drawer and 9 of them are white, the probability of picking a white shirt at random is $\frac{9}{12} = \frac{3}{4}$. This probability can also be expressed as .75 or 75%.

POWERS AND ROOTS

47. MULTIPLYING AND DIVIDING POWERS

To multiply powers with the same base, **add the exponents:** $x^3 \times x^4 = x^{3+4} = x^7$.

To divide powers with the same base, **subtract the exponents:** $y^{13} \div y^8 = y^{13-8} = y^5$

48. RAISING POWERS TO POWERS

To raise a power to an exponent, **multiply the exponents:** $(x^3)^4 = x^{3 \times 4} = x^{12}$

49. SIMPLIFYING SQUARE ROOTS

To simplify a square root, **factor out the perfect squares** under the radical, unsquare them, and put the result in front:

$$\sqrt{12} = \sqrt{4 \times 3} = \sqrt{4} \times \sqrt{3} = 2\sqrt{3}$$

50. ADDING AND SUBTRACTING ROOTS

You can add or subtract radical expressions only if the part under the radicals is the same:

$$2\sqrt{3} + 3\sqrt{3} = 5\sqrt{3}$$

51. MULTIPLYING AND DIVIDING ROOTS

The product of square roots is equal to the square root of the product:

$$\sqrt{3} \times \sqrt{5} = \sqrt{3 \times 5} = \sqrt{15}$$

The quotient of square roots is equal to the **square root of the quotient:**

$$\frac{\sqrt{6}}{\sqrt{3}} = \sqrt{\frac{6}{3}} = \sqrt{2}$$

ALGEBRAIC EXPRESSIONS

52. EVALUATING AN EXPRESSION

To evaluate an algebraic expression, **plug in** the given values for the unknowns and calculate according to PEMDAS. To find the value of $x^2 + 5x - 6$ when $x = -2$, plug in -2 for x:

$$(-2)^2 + 5(-2) - 6 = 4 - 10 - 6 = -12$$

53. ADDING AND SUBTRACTING MONOMIALS

To combine like terms, **keep the variable part unchanged while adding or subtracting the coefficients:** $2a + 3a = (2 + 3)a = 5a$

54. ADDING AND SUBTRACTING POLYNOMIALS

To add or subtract polynomials, **combine like terms:**

$$(3x^2 + 5x - 7) - (x^2 + 12) =$$
$$(3x^2 - x^2) + 5x + (-7 - 12) = 2x^2 + 5x - 19$$

55. MULTIPLYING MONOMIALS

To multiply monomials, **multiply the coefficients and the variables separately:**

$$2a \times 3a = (2 \times 3)(a \times a) = 6a^2$$

56. MULTIPLYING BINOMIALS—FOIL

To multiply binomials, use **FOIL.** To multiply $(x + 3)$ by $(x + 4)$, first multiply the **F**irst terms: $x \times x = x^2$. Next the **O**uter terms: $x \times 4 = 4x$. Then the **I**nner terms: $3 \times x = 3x$. And finally the **L**ast terms: $3 \times 4 = 12$. Then add and combine like terms: $x^2 + 4x + 3x + 12 = x^2 + 7x + 12$.

57. MULTIPLYING OTHER POLYNOMIALS

FOIL works only when you want to multiply two binomials. If you want to multiply polynomials with more than two terms, make sure you **multiply each term in the first polynomial by each term in the second:**

$$(x^2 + 3x + 4)(x + 5) =$$
$$x^2(x + 5) + 3x(x + 5) + 4(x + 5) =$$
$$x^3 + 5x^2 + 3x^2 + 15x + 4x + 20 =$$
$$x^3 + 8x^2 + 19x + 20$$

FACTORING ALGEBRAIC EXPRESSIONS

58. FACTORING OUT A COMMON DIVISOR

A factor common to all terms of a polynomial can be **factored out.** All three terms in the polynomial $3x^3 + 12x^2 - 6x$ contain a factor of $3x$. Pulling out the common factor yields $3x(x^2 + 4x - 2)$.

59. FACTORING THE DIFFERENCE OF SQUARES

One of the test maker's favorite factorables is the **difference of squares.**

$$a^2 - b^2 = (a - b)(a + b)$$

$x^2 - 9$, for example, factors to $(x - 3)(x + 3)$.

60. FACTORING THE SQUARE OF A BINOMIAL

Learn to recognize polynomials that are squares of binomials:

$$a^2 + 2ab + b^2 = (a + b)^2$$
$$a^2 - 2ab + b^2 = (a - b)^2$$

For example, $4x^2 + 12x + 9$ factors to $(2x + 3)^2$, and $n^2 - 10n + 25$ factors to $(n - 5)^2$.

61. FACTORING OTHER POLYNOMIALS— FOIL IN REVERSE

To factor a quadratic expression, **think about what binomials you could use FOIL on to get that quadratic expression.** To factor $x^2 - 5x + 6$, think about what **F**irst terms will produce x^2, what **L**ast terms will produce $+6$, and what **O**uter and **I**nner terms will produce $-5x$. Common sense—and trial and error—lead you to $(x - 2)(x - 3)$.

62. SIMPLIFYING AN ALGEBRAIC FRACTION

Simplifying an algebraic fraction is a lot like simplifying a numerical fraction. The general idea is to **find factors common to the numerator and denominator and cancel them.** Thus, simplifying an algebraic fraction begins with factoring.

To simplify $\dfrac{x^2 - x - 12}{x^2 - 9}$, first factor the numerator and denominator:

$$\frac{x^2 - x - 12}{x^2 - 9} = \frac{(x - 4)(x + 3)}{(x - 3)(x + 3)}$$

Canceling $x + 3$ from the numerator and denominator leaves you with $\dfrac{x - 4}{x - 3}$.

SOLVING EQUATIONS

63. SOLVING A LINEAR EQUATION

To solve an equation, do whatever is necessary to both sides to **isolate the variable.** To solve $5x - 12 = -2x + 9$, first get all the x terms on one side by adding $2x$ to both sides: $7x - 12 = 9$. Then add 12 to both sides: $7x = 21$, then divide both sides by 7 to get: $x = 3$.

64. SOLVING "IN TERMS OF"

To solve an equation for one variable **in terms of** another means to **isolate the one variable on one side of the equation,** leaving an expression containing the other variable on the other side. To solve $3x - 10y = -5x + 6y$ for x in terms of y, isolate x:

$$3x - 10y = -5x + 6y$$
$$3x + 5x = 6y + 10y$$
$$8x = 16y$$
$$x = 2y$$

65. TRANSLATING FROM ENGLISH INTO ALGEBRA

To translate from English into algebra, look for the key words and systematically turn phrases into algebraic expressions and sentences into equations. Be careful about order, especially when subtraction is called for.

Example: The charge for a phone call is r cents for the first 3 minutes and s cents for each minute thereafter. What is the cost, in cents, of a call lasting exactly t minutes? ($t > 3$)

Setup: The charge begins with r, and then something more is added, depending on the length of the call. The amount added is s times the number of minutes past 3 minutes. If the total number of minutes is t, then the number of minutes past 3 is $t - 3$. So the charge is $r + s(t - 3)$.

INTERMEDIATE ALGEBRA

66. SOLVING A QUADRATIC EQUATION

To solve a quadratic equation, put it in the $ax^2 + bx + c = 0$ form, **factor** the left side (if you can), and set each factor equal to 0 separately to get the two solutions. To solve $x^2 + 12 = 7x$, first rewrite it as $x^2 - 7x + 12 = 0$. Then factor the left side:

$$(x - 3)(x - 4) = 0$$
$$x - 3 = 0 \text{ or } x - 4 = 0$$
$$x = 3 \text{ or } 4$$

Sometimes the left side might not be obviously factorable. You can always use the **quadratic formula.** Just plug in the coefficients a, b, and c from $ax^2 + bx + c = 0$ into the formula:

$$\frac{-b \pm \sqrt{b^2 - 4ac}}{2a}$$

To solve $x^2 + 4x + 2 = 0$, plug $a = 1$, $b = 4$, and $c = 2$ into the formula:

$$x = \frac{-4 \pm \sqrt{4^2 - 4 \times 1 \times 2}}{2 \times 1}$$
$$= \frac{-4 \pm \sqrt{8}}{2} = -2 \pm \sqrt{2}$$

67. SOLVING A SYSTEM OF EQUATIONS

You can solve for two variables only if you have two distinct equations. Two forms of the same equation will not be adequate. **Combine the equations in such a way that one of the variables cancels out.** To solve the two equations $4x + 3y = 8$ and $x + y = 3$, multiply both sides of the second equation by -3 to get: $-3x - 3y = -9$. Now add the equations; the $3y$ and the $-3y$ cancel out, leaving $x = -1$. Plug that back into either one of the original equations and you'll find that $y = 4$.

68. SOLVING AN EQUATION THAT INCLUDES ABSOLUTE VALUE SIGNS

To solve an equation that includes absolute value signs, **think about the two different cases.** For example, to solve the equation $|x - 12| = 3$, think of it as two equations:

$$x - 12 = 3 \quad \text{or} \quad x - 12 = -3$$
$$x = 15 \text{ or } 9$$

69. SOLVING AN INEQUALITY

To solve an inequality, do whatever is necessary to both sides to **isolate the variable.** Just remember that when you **multiply or divide both sides by a negative number,** you must **reverse the sign.** To solve $-5x + 7 < -3$, subtract 7 from both sides to get $-5x < -10$. Now divide both sides by –5, remembering to reverse the sign: $x > 2$.

70. GRAPHING INEQUALITIES

To graph a range of values, use a thick, black line over the number line, and at the end(s) of the range, use a **solid circle** if the point *is included* or an **open circle** if the point is *not included.* The figure here shows the graph of $-3 < x \le 5$.

COORDINATE GEOMETRY

71. FINDING THE DISTANCE BETWEEN TWO POINTS

To find the distance between points, **use the Pythagorean theorem or special right triangles.** The difference between the xs is one leg and the difference between the ys is the other leg.

In the figure above, $\overline{PQ}$ is the hypotenuse of a 3-4-5 triangle, so $\overline{PQ} = 5$.

You can also use the **distance formula:**

$$d = \sqrt{(x_2 - x_1)^2 + (y_2 - y_1)^2}$$

To find the distance between $R(3, 6)$ and $S(5, -2)$:

$$d = \sqrt{(5 - 3)^2 + (-2 - 6)^2}$$
$$= \sqrt{(2)^2 + (-8)^2}$$
$$= \sqrt{68} = 2\sqrt{17}$$

72. USING TWO POINTS TO FIND THE SLOPE

In mathematics, the slope of a line is often called m.

$$\text{Slope} = m = \frac{\text{Change in } y}{\text{Change in } x} = \frac{\text{Rise}}{\text{Run}}$$

The slope of the line that contains the points $A(2, 3)$ and $B(0, -1)$ is:

$$\frac{y_2 - y_1}{x_2 - x_1} = \frac{-1 - 3}{0 - 2} = \frac{-4}{-2} = 2$$

73. USING AN EQUATION TO FIND THE SLOPE

To find the slope of a line from an equation, put the equation into the **slope-intercept** form:

$$y = mx + b$$

The slope is m. To find the slope of the equation $3x + 2y = 4$, reexpress it:

$$3x + 2y = 4$$
$$2y = -3x + 4$$
$$y = -\frac{3}{2}x + 2$$

The slope is $-\frac{3}{2}$.

74. USING AN EQUATION TO FIND AN INTERCEPT

To find the y-intercept, you can either put the equation into **$y = mx + b$ (slope-intercept)** form—in which case b is the y-intercept—or you can just plug $x = 0$ into the equation and solve for y. To find the x-intercept, plug $y = 0$ into the equation and solve for x.

75. EQUATION FOR A CIRCLE

The equation for a circle of radius r and centered at (h, k) is:

$$(x - h)^2 + (y - k)^2 = r^2$$

The figure below shows the graph of the equation $(x - 2)^2 + (y + 1)^2 = 25$:

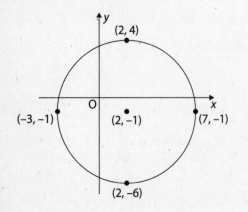

76. EQUATION FOR A PARABOLA

The graph of an equation in the form $y = ax^2 + bx + c$ is a parabola. The figure below shows the graph of seven pairs of numbers that satisfy the equation $y = x^2 - 4x + 3$:

77. EQUATION FOR AN ELLIPSE

The graph of an equation in the form

$$\frac{x^2}{a^2} = \frac{y^2}{b^2} = 1$$

is an ellipse, with $2a$ as the sum of the focal radii and with foci on the x-axis at $(0, -c)$ and $(0, c)$, where $c = \sqrt{a^2 - b^2}$. The following figure shows the graph of $\frac{x^2}{25} + \frac{y^2}{16} = 1$:

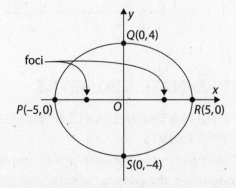

The foci are at $(-3, 0)$ and $(3, 0)$. $\overline{PR}$ is the **major axis,** and $\overline{QS}$ is the **minor axis.** This ellipse is symmetrical about both the x- and y-axes.

LINES AND ANGLES

78. INTERSECTING LINES

When two lines intersect, **adjacent angles are supplementary** and **vertical angles are equal.**

In the figure, the angles marked $a°$ and $b°$ are adjacent and supplementary, so $a + b = 180$. Furthermore, the angles marked $a°$ and $60°$ are vertical and equal, so $a = 60$.

79. PARALLEL LINES AND TRANSVERSALS

A transversal across parallel lines forms **four equal acute angles and four equal obtuse angles.**

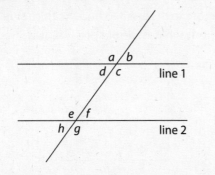

Here, line 1 is parallel to line 2. Angles a, c, e, and g are obtuse, so they are all equal. Angles b, d, f, and h are acute, so they are all equal.

Furthermore, **any of the acute angles is supplementary to any of the obtuse angles.** Angles a and h are supplementary, as are b and e, c and f, and so on.

TRIANGLES—GENERAL

80. INTERIOR ANGLES OF A TRIANGLE

The three angles of any triangle **add up to 180°.**

In the figure above, $x + 50 + 100 = 180$, so $x = 30$.

81. EXTERIOR ANGLES OF A TRIANGLE

An exterior angle of a triangle is equal to the **sum of the remote interior angles.**

In the figure above, the exterior angle labeled $x°$ is equal to the sum of the remote interior angles:

$x = 50 + 100 = 150$

The three exterior angles of any triangle add up to 360°.

In the figure above, $a + b + c = 360$.

82. SIMILAR TRIANGLES

Similar triangles have the same shape: **corresponding angles are equal and corresponding sides are proportional.**

The triangles above are similar because they have the same angles. The 3 corresponds to the 4, and the 6 corresponds to the *s*.

$$\frac{3}{4} = \frac{6}{s}$$
$$3s = 24$$
$$s = 8$$

83. AREA OF A TRIANGLE

Area of Triangle = $\frac{1}{2}$ (Base)(Height)

The height is the perpendicular distance between the side that's chosen as the base and the opposite vertex.

In the triangle above, 4 is the height when the 7 is chosen as the base.

$$Area = \frac{1}{2}bh = \frac{1}{2}(7)(4) = 14$$

RIGHT TRIANGLES

84. PYTHAGOREAN THEOREM

For all right triangles:

$(leg_1)^2 + (leg_2)^2 = (hypotenuse)^2$

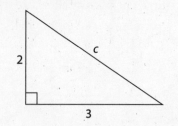

If one leg is 2 and the other leg is 3, then:

$$2^2 + 3^2 = c^2$$
$$c^2 = 4 + 9$$
$$c = \sqrt{13}$$

85. SPECIAL RIGHT TRIANGLES

3-4-5

If a right triangle's leg-to-leg ratio is 3:4 or if the leg-to-hypotenuse ratio is 3:5 or 4:5, then it's a 3-4-5 triangle, and you don't need to use the Pythagorean theorem to find the third side. Just figure out what multiple of 3-4-5 it is.

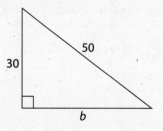

In the right triangle above, one leg is 30 and the hypotenuse is 50. This is 10 times 3-4-5. The other leg is 40.

5-12-13

If a right triangle's leg-to-leg ratio is 5:12 or if the leg-to-hypotenuse ratio is 5:13 or 12:13, then it's a 5-12-13 triangle, and you don't need to use the Pythagorean theorem to find the third side. Just figure out what multiple of 5-12-13 it is.

Here, one leg is 36 and the hypotenuse is 39. This is 3 times 5-12-13. The other leg is 15.

30°-60°-90°

The sides of a 30°-60°-90° triangle are in a ratio of $1:\sqrt{3}:2$. You don't need to use the Pythagorean theorem.

If the hypotenuse is 6, then the shorter leg is half that, or 3; and then the longer leg is equal to the short leg times $\sqrt{3}$, or $3\sqrt{3}$.

45°-45°-90°

The sides of a 45°-45°-90° triangle are in a ratio of $1:1:\sqrt{2}$.

If one leg is 3, then the other leg is also 3, and the hypotenuse is equal to a leg times $\sqrt{2}$, or $3\sqrt{2}$.

OTHER POLYGONS

86. SPECIAL QUADRILATERALS

Rectangle

A rectangle is a **four-sided figure with four right angles.** Opposite sides are equal. Diagonals are equal.

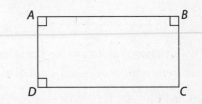

Quadrilateral *ABCD* above is shown to have three right angles. The fourth angle therefore also measures 90°, and *ABCD* is a rectangle. The perimeter of a rectangle is equal to the sum of the lengths of the four sides, which is equivalent to 2(length + width).

Parallelogram

A parallelogram has **two pairs of parallel sides.** Opposite sides are equal. Opposite angles are equal. Consecutive angles add up to 180°.

In the figure above, *s* is the length of the side opposite the 3, so $s = 3$.

Square

A square is a **rectangle with four equal sides.**

If *PQRS* is a square, all sides are the same length as *QR*. The perimeter of a square is equal to four times the length of one side.

Trapezoid

A **trapezoid** is a quadrilateral with one pair of parallel sides and one pair of nonparallel sides.

In the quadrilateral above, sides $\overline{EF}$ and $\overline{GH}$ are parallel, while sides $\overline{EH}$ and $\overline{FG}$ are not parallel. *EFGH* is therefore a trapezoid.

87. AREAS OF SPECIAL QUADRILATERALS

Area of Rectangle = Length × Width

The area of a 7-by-3 rectangle is $7 \times 3 = 21$.

Area of Parallelogram = Base × Height

The area of a parallelogram with a height of 4 and a base of 6 is $4 \times 6 = 24$.

Area of Square = (Side)²

The area of a square with sides of length 5 is $5^2 = 25$.

Area of Trapezoid = $\left(\dfrac{\text{base}_1 - \text{base}_2}{2}\right) \times$ Height

Think of it as the average of the bases (the two parallel sides) times the height (the length of the perpendicular altitude).

In the trapezoid *ABCD* above, you can use side *AD* for the height. The average of the bases is $\dfrac{2 + 14}{2} = 8$, so the area is 5×8, or 40.

88. INTERIOR ANGLES OF A POLYGON

The sum of the measures of the interior angles of a polygon is $(n - 2) \times 180$, where n is the number of sides.

Sum of the Angles = $(n - 2) \times 180$ degrees

The eight angles of an octagon, for example, add up to (8 − 2) × 180 = 1,080.

To find **one angle of a regular polygon,** divide the sum of the angles by the number of angles (which is the same as the number of sides). The formula, therefore, is:

Interior Angle = $\dfrac{(n-2) \times 180}{n}$

Angle A of the regular octagon above measures $\dfrac{1,080}{8}$ = 135 degrees.

CIRCLES

89. CIRCUMFERENCE OF A CIRCLE

Circumference of a Circle = $2\pi r$

Here, the radius is 3, and so the circumference is $2\pi(3) = 6\pi$.

90. LENGTH OF AN ARC

An **arc** is a piece of the circumference. If n is the measure of the arc's central angle, then the formula is:

Length of an Arc = $\dfrac{n}{360}(2\pi r)$

In the figure above, the radius is 5 and the measure of the central angle is 72°. The arc length is $\dfrac{72}{360}$, or $\dfrac{1}{5}$ of the circumference:

$$\left(\dfrac{72}{360}\right)2\pi(5) = \left(\dfrac{1}{5}\right)10\pi = 2\pi$$

91. AREA OF A CIRCLE

Area of a Circle = πr^2

The area of the circle above is $\pi(4)^2 = 16\pi$.

92. AREA OF A SECTOR

A **sector** is a piece of the area of a circle. If n is the measure of the sector's central angle, then the formula is:

Area of a Sector = $\dfrac{n}{360}(\pi r^2)$

In the figure above, the radius is 6 and the measure of the sector's central angle is 30°. The sector has $\dfrac{30}{360}$, or $\dfrac{1}{12}$ of the area of the circle:

$$\left(\dfrac{30}{360}\right)(\pi)(6^2) = \left(\dfrac{1}{12}\right)(36\pi) = 3\pi$$

SOLIDS

93. SURFACE AREA OF A RECTANGULAR SOLID

The surface of a rectangular solid consists of three pairs of identical faces. To find the surface area, find the area of each face and add them up. If the length is l, the width is w, and the height is h, the formula is:

Surface Area = $2lw + 2wh + 2lh$

The surface area of the box above is:

$2 \times 7 \times 3 + 2 \times 3 \times 4 + 2 \times 7 \times 4 =$
$42 + 24 + 56 = 122$

94. VOLUME OF A RECTANGULAR SOLID

Volume of a Rectangular Solid = lwh

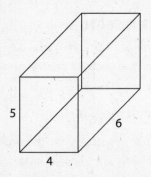

The volume of a 4-by-5-by-6 box is:

$4 \times 5 \times 6 = 120$

A cube is a rectangular solid with length, width, and height all equal. The volume formula if e is the length of an edge of the cube is:

Volume of a Cube = e^3

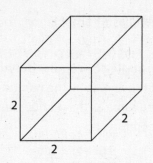

The volume of the cube above is $2^3 = 8$.

95. VOLUME OF OTHER SOLIDS

Volume of a Cylinder = $\pi r^2 h$

The volume of a cylinder where $r = 2$ and $h = 5$ is $\pi(2^2)(5) = 20\pi$.

Volume of a Cone = $\frac{1}{3}\pi r^2 h$

The volume of a cone where $r = 3$ and $h = 6$ is:

$\text{Volume} = \frac{1}{3}\pi(3^2)(6) = 18$

Volume of a Sphere = $\frac{4}{3}\pi r^3$

If the radius of a sphere is 3, then:

$\text{Volume} = \frac{4}{3}\pi(3^3) = 36\pi$

TRIGONOMETRY

96. SINE, COSINE, AND TANGENT OF ACUTE ANGLES

To find the sine, cosine, or tangent of an acute angle, use SOHCAHTOA, which is an abbreviation for the following definitions:

$$Sine = \frac{Opposite}{Hypotenuse}$$

$$Cosine = \frac{Adjacent}{Hypotenuse}$$

$$Tangent = \frac{Opposite}{Adjacent}$$

In the figure above:

$$\sin A = \frac{8}{17}$$

$$\cos A = \frac{15}{17}$$

$$\tan A = \frac{8}{15}$$

97. COTANGENT, SECANT, AND COSECANT OF ACUTE ANGLES

Think of the cotangent, secant, and cosecant as the reciprocals of the SOHCAHTOA functions:

$$Cotangent = \frac{1}{Tangent} = \frac{Adjacent}{Opposite}$$

$$Secant = \frac{1}{Cosine} = \frac{Hypotenuse}{Adjacent}$$

$$Cosecant = \frac{1}{Sine} = \frac{Hypotenuse}{Opposite}$$

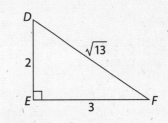

In the preceeding figure:

$$\cot D = \frac{2}{3}$$

$$\sec D = \frac{\sqrt{13}}{2}$$

$$\csc D = \frac{\sqrt{13}}{3}$$

98. TRIGONOMETRIC FUNCTIONS OF OTHER ANGLES

To find a trigonometric function of an angle greater than 90°, sketch a circle of radius 1 centered at the origin of the coordinate grid. Start from the point (1, 0) and rotate the appropriate number of degrees counterclockwise.

In the "unit circle" setup above, the basic trigonometric functions are defined in terms of the coordinates a and b:

$$\sin \theta = b$$
$$\cos \theta = a$$
$$\tan \theta = \frac{b}{a}$$

Example: sin 210° = ?

Setup: Sketch a 210° angle in the coordinate plane:

Because the triangle shown in the figure above is a 30°-60°-90° right triangle, we can determine that the coordinates of point P are $-\frac{\sqrt{3}}{2}, -\frac{1}{2}$. The sine is therefore $-\frac{1}{2}$.

99. SIMPLIFYING TRIGONOMETRIC EXPRESSIONS

To simplify trigonometric expressions, use the inverse function definitions along with the fundamental trigonometric identity:

$$\sin^2 x + \cos^2 x = 1$$

Example: $\dfrac{\sin^2 \theta + \cos^2 \theta}{\cos \theta} = ?$

Setup: The numerator equals 1, so:

$$\frac{\sin^2 \theta + \cos^2 \theta}{\cos \theta} = \frac{1}{\cos \theta} = \sec \theta$$

100. GRAPHING TRIGONOMETRIC FUNCTIONS

To graph trigonometric functions, use the x-axis for the angle and the y-axis for the value of the trigonometric function. Use special angles—0°, 30°, 45°, 60°, 90°, 120°, 135°, 150°, 180°, etc.—to plot key points.

The figure above shows a portion of the graph of $y = \sin x$.